GAY SYDNEY

GARRY WOTHERSPOON, a former academic at the University of Sydney and a former NSW History Fellow, is a leading historian of many aspects of Sydney life. His books include *Sydney's Transport: Studies in Urban History*, *Being Different: Nine Gay Men Remember*, and *City of the Plain: History of a Gay Sub-culture*. His *The Sydney Mechanics' School of Arts: A History* was published in 2013 to commemorate its 180th anniversary, and was shortlisted for the NSW Premier's History Awards. He was awarded Australia's Centenary of Federation medal for his work as an academic, researcher, and human rights activist.

GAY SYDNEY

A HISTORY

GARRY WOTHERSPOON

NEWSOUTH

A NewSouth book

Published by
NewSouth Publishing
University of New South Wales Press Ltd
University of New South Wales
Sydney NSW 2052
AUSTRALIA
newsouthpublishing.com

© Garry Wotherspoon 2016
First published 2016

10 9 8 7 6 5 4 3 2 1

National Library of Australia
Cataloguing-in-Publication entry
Creator: Wotherspoon, Garry – author.
Title: Gay sydney: A history/Garry Wotherspoon.
ISBN: 9781742234830 (paperback)
        9781742247687 (ePDF)
        9781742242316 (ebook)
Notes: Includes index.
Subjects: Gay men—New South Wales—Sydney—History.
Gay men—New South Wales—Sydney—Social conditions.
Gay men—New South Wales—Sydney—Social life and customs.
Gay men—Legal status, laws etc.—New South Wales.
Dewey Number: 306.766209941

Design Josephine Pajor-Markus
Cover design Vivien Valk
Cover images iStock.com

UNSW
AUSTRALIA

CONTENTS

PREFACE   vii

ABBREVIATIONS   xi

CHAPTER 1 'I THOUGHT MEN LIKE THAT SHOT THEMSELVES'   1

Sexuality in a parochial provincial city

CHAPTER 2 ... BUT THEY DIDN'T   37

'Camp' life in Sydney before World War II

CHAPTER 3 AN END TO UNKNOWING   70

The impact of war and the Kinsey Report

CHAPTER 4 THE GREATEST MENACE FACING AUSTRALIA   101

Sydney's homosexual worlds and the Cold War

CHAPTER 5 THE PERSONAL BECOMES THE POLITICAL   140

Social change, the camp world and the advent of
gay liberation

CHAPTER 6 THE PEARL IN THE OYSTER   178

The opening up of Sydney's gay world

CHAPTER 7 IT WAS THE WORST OF TIMES, NEVER THE BEST OF TIMES   219

HIV/AIDS and Sydney's responses

CHAPTER 8 INTO THE NEW MILLENNIUM   252

And a brighter future loomed

CHAPTER 9 JUST LIKE EVERYBODY ELSE?   286

Sydney's gay world today

NOTES   319

INDEX   351

The Oscar Wilde's [sic] of Sydney ... whose presence is advertised by effeminate style of speech and the adoption of the names of celebrated actresses. A haunt is said to exist in Bourke Street Surry Hills, and that part of College-street from Boomerang-street to Park-street is a parade for them.

Scorpion, Sydney, April 1895

Just as the pearl is the result of disease in the oyster, so homosexuality is the result of dysfunction of the glands of the human body, and like the pearl, the manifestations of homosexuality are not always devoid of beauty.

Robert Storer, *Sex in Modern Life*, Sydney, 1933

Two, four, six, eight, gay is just as good as straight.

Sydney street chant, 1970s

Slowly but unmistakably, gay culture is ending ... For many in the gay world, this is both a triumph and a threat. It is a triumph because it is what we always dreamed of: a world in which being gay is a nonissue among our families, friends, and neighbors. But it is a threat in the way that all loss is a threat.

Andrew Sullivan, 'The End of Gay Culture', *New Republic*,
October 2005

Despite taboos and interdictions, men who desired other men ... sometimes in the most inhospitable environments, have found spaces in which to pursue partners in love and lust.

Robert Aldrich, *Gay Life Stories*, Thames and Hudson, 2012

PREFACE

Parts of this book were first published a quarter of a century ago, as *City of the Plain: History of a Gay Sub-culture*. The world has moved a long way since then.

Things that were simply inconceivable then are now commonplace – same-sex adoptions and fostering, same-sex civil partnerships, openly lesbian or gay people holding public office and being major public figures. *City of the Plain* ended with the AIDS crisis in the late 1980s. *Gay Sydney: A history* takes us up to a time when same-sex marriage is legal in over 20 countries around the world, and on the agenda for Australia.

Both books are about Sydney's men with homosexual desires. The first was written for an academic audience. Its Introduction included long explanations about methodology, sources and their verifications, definitions and similar arcana. Its Conclusion drew the reader's attention to what this new research had unearthed, and what it meant. But all those explanations seem unnecessary now, given what the average reader knows.

It is however worth discussing the use of certain terms.

When the first book was written, the gay world was seen as a subculture, the acknowledged academic term for what was emerging, a subset of a wider society. Now 'subculture' is anachronistic, so here I talk about Sydney's 'gay world' and its 'gay life'.

'Gay' is often used interchangeably with 'homosexual' but the words are not necessarily interchangeable. Gay can have a different meaning, depending on who is using the word and in what context. 'Homosexual' was first used by German psychologists in the late nineteenth century and introduced into English at the beginning of the twentieth, adding to the existing terminology of 'sodomites', 'urnings', 'uranists' and 'inverts'. Some medical manuals also used the term 'homosexualist'. When moralists were talking, they often used the terms 'perverts' or 'degenerates', and these passed into common usage in the media for most of the twentieth century.

The community had different terms for themselves. 'Queens', 'fairies' and 'pansies' might be used lightly, but the most common term in Australia up until the 1970s was 'camp', while the heterosexual world was 'square'.

'Gay lib' brought new terminology, and in Australia 'gay' soon replaced 'camp'. But men who designated themselves as 'gay' were making a definitive statement about their identity and how they saw their sexuality. Moreover, 'gay' was a term favoured by gay people themselves, as opposed to 'homosexual', which was coined and popularised in the context of pathology. Colloquially, gay became a shorthand description to replace homosexual or camp.

The notion of a 'homosexual identity' emerged in the late nineteenth century from the particular cultural conditions of the time. Similarly the specific cultural conditions of the post–World War II period led to the creation of a 'gay identity'. And now we also have a 'queer' identity, for those who feel themselves outside of the societal norms in regards to gender or sexuality, thus avoiding the specificity of being 'gay' or 'lesbian' or 'transgender'.

Another point to make is that many people may commit homosexual acts, but this does not make them 'homosexual', if these acts are not seen as being part of their lifestyle or identity, as, for example, men who indulge in only occasional homosexual acts, now defined simply as 'men-who-have-sex-with-men'. In this context, I have used the term 'homoerotically inclined' where it seemed appropriate.

To avoid repeating long titles continuously, I have taken the liberty of using the standard abbreviations for Australian history – thus SMH for the *Sydney Morning Herald*, NSW for New South Wales, *NSWYB* for *New South Wales Year Books*, *NSWPD* for *New South Wales Parliamentary Debates* and *NSWPP* for *New South Wales Parliamentary Papers*; a list of abbreviations used has been included on page xi. Copies of all the interviews referred to in the text are held in the Mitchell Library. They are located in the Garry Wotherspoon Collection: interviews with gay men, 1980–1988 – Call Number MLOH 448.

Any written history reflects selections and omissions, and this work is no exception. There is much more I could have included, but at a certain point I had to distinguish between the minutiae and what is central to a story. Any such omissions, and any errors, are mine alone. I have endeavoured, wherever possible however, to allow the various actors in this story to speak for themselves: hopefully, their voices will have come through, reflecting the times and their concerns.

A special thanks goes to Victoria Chance, whose firm editorial hand and insightful comments have helped make this a better book.

Finally, there is the issue of perspective. I was a participant in many of the events of the late twentieth century, and bring my own set of political values and attitudes to the readings of the people and happenings I document in this book. This account reflects my participation and an ideological framework. And part of my own story is interwoven throughout this history, as I have lived with the changing city since my childhood, and enjoyed its varied offerings.

While this history is but one person's interpretation of the process, it takes the reader on a journey from a hidden and illegal past to Sydney's gay world of today.

ABBREVIATIONS

ADB *Australian Dictionary of Biography*
CT *Canberra Times*
DM *Daily Mirror*
DT *Daily Telegraph*
MT *Melbourne Truth*
NSWLAVP *NSW Legislative Assembly Votes and Proceedings*
NSW PD *NSW Parliamentary Debates*
NSWPP *NSW Parliamentary Papers*
NSWYB *NSW Year Book*
NT *National Times*
OWN *Oxford Weekender News*
SMH *Sydney Morning Herald*
SS *Sydney Sun*
ST *Sydney Truth*
YBA *Year Book of Australia*

CHAPTER 1

'I THOUGHT MEN LIKE THAT SHOT THEMSELVES'

Sexuality in a parochial provincial city

Imagine a parade of some 15 000 people through the streets of Sydney on a warm summer Saturday night, with tens of thousands more watching. The parade has 52 floats, numerous cars and trucks, sundry other vehicles – and even vaqueros on horseback. From the Town Hall it passes down George Street through the cinema crowds, up Liverpool Street to Oxford Street. Here there are searchlights and spotlights and shops hung with bunting and signs. People are crowded onto balconies and at windows; hundreds more sit on the awnings overhanging the footpaths. There are bands and disco music blares out. The crowds are so dense that all traffic other than the parade grinds to a halt. Yet the parade and the reasons for it are not reported as news by any of the mainstream newspapers or television channels in Sydney. For all the media coverage it receives, it might never have occurred.[1]

The Mardi Gras parade in February 1983 was one of the biggest and most colourful peacetime parades that Sydney had ever seen. A columnist in the Melbourne *Age* later bemoaned the fact that it 'put Melbourne's Moomba parade in the shade'.[2]

Certainly nothing in the immediately preceding Festival of Sydney matched it for colour, glamour and excitement.

A commentator described participants dressed as 'bikies, Darth Vaders, cycle sluts, gladiators, Red Indians, Supremes, Carmen Mirandas, wizards, fairies, ballroom dancers, nuns and altar boys' and others wearing just enough 'to keep them out of the Darlinghurst slammer on indecent exposure charges'.[3] After wending its way through the city and up Oxford Street, the so-called 'glitter strip' that included the majority of Sydney's commercial gay venues, the parade continued along Flinders Street and Anzac Parade to the AMP Pavilion at the Sydney Showground. One of the biggest parties the city had ever seen followed. Thousands of people queued to get in to the Pavilion.

I have a photo of myself and friends from the 1983 parade. In the aftermath of the party we are sitting in the gutter, probably in the lane that runs between the Flinders Hotel and the Beresford Hotel – a major gathering place for stalwarts who, by sunrise, are just coming down from whatever they have taken and are not yet ready to go home to bed. My friends, from Newcastle, are dressed as Batman and Robin; my boyfriend, now looking much the worse for wear, had gone in a skimpy wedding dress and gauzy veil, wearing sandshoes, easier for dancing. I am wearing a black jockstrap, black boots and a black leather mask. In the photo I am wearing my boyfriend's wedding veil. We all look exhausted but happy.

Sydney's Gay Mardi Gras occurred, paradoxically, in a city whose criminal law listed sexual acts between males, or attempts to commit those acts, or any soliciting for those acts, or any procuring for those acts, as crimes.[4] Despite this, a few months earlier Neville Wran's state Labor government had passed an amendment to the 1977 *Anti-Discrimination Act*, making it an offence to discriminate against a person on the grounds of their homosexuality.[5] There was a clear contradiction between criminal law and anti-discrimination law.

Gay culture was flourishing. A local *Gay Guide* from the early 1980s shows a veritable plethora of institutions and services available to the city's gay communities. There were seven newspapers and magazines, several gay political groups (including an Australian Labor Party gay group), many social clubs (either city-wide or locally based), a gay choir, a gay radio collective, eight hotels advertising and providing 'gay accommodation', some 15 venues advertising under 'Bars, hotels and discos', a legal defence fund, gay bikie clubs, a group of gay divers, gay student and teacher groups, sundry gay church groups (including the Sisters of Perpetual Indulgence – 'a cosmic order of gay male nuns'), 20 restaurants and coffee shops advertising as openly gay, and a whole range of services including a safari company, gay electricians, male masseurs, mobile discos, dating services, carpet cleaners, gardeners and 'Hinge and Bracket', the camply named Paddington handymen.[6] All this was openly displayed at a time when homosexual acts between males were illegal.

Those paradoxes, or contradictions – a wall of silence about one of the city's largest subcultures; massive public displays by a group whose activities were still branded criminal; a government outlawing discrimination against homosexuals while maintaining laws that made their sexual life a criminal offence; a flourishing commercial gay scene and a public activist movement – highlighted the ambiguous situation of male homosexuals in New South Wales in the early 1980s.

Sydney has a long association with homosexuality, despite official approbation. As the first Governor, Arthur Phillip, put it:

There are two crimes that would merit death – murder and sodomy. For either of these crimes I would wish to confine the criminal till an opportunity offered of delivering him as a prisoner to the natives of New Zealand, and let them eat him.[7]

Human desires being what they are, these words had little effect. A few decades later, Chief Justice Sir Francis Forbes admitted at an enquiry in London that Sydney 'had been called a Sodom in the papers'. And while one witness claimed that 'the unspeakable vice' was 'only confined to the lower class of convicts ... among gentlemen convicts it would excite abhorrence',[8] the evidence says otherwise. The whole social spectrum was charged and convicted of homosexual acts – ranging from frottage to mutual masturbation to fellatio to anal intercourse – including sailors, public servants, farmers, merchants, various tradesmen, even a 'sea captain'.

Over the following decades there were many trials for homosexual acts. Most of this hidden history of homosexuality only appears in the court records.[9] The men convicted were given sentences that varied with the seriousness of the crime.[10] Some cases received newspaper attention, mostly a few lines here and there, but occasionally a case was so sensational it made the headlines. And with Captain Moonlight, the notorious bushranger, the story has another dimension.

The trial of Andrew George Scott, known as Captain Moonlight for his bushranging exploits, received extensive newspaper coverage, and revealed a different aspect of what was considered an 'unmentionable vice'. When James Nesbit, one of Scott's gang, was shot and badly wounded as the police closed in on them:

> Heedless of the firing, Scott had lifted and carried the injured man into the house, where, as Nesbit lay dying, his leader wept over him like a child, laid his head upon his breast, and kissed him passionately.[11]

Nesbit died. At the trial, Scott became quite agitated any time his name was mentioned, displaying 'intense emotion'. Such overt displays of his feelings about Nesbit, and what it implied about their relationship, were considered scandalous. Sydney-siders followed the trial with rapt attention.

Scott was convicted, and sentenced to death. While in Darlinghurst Gaol, he wrote letters to friends, proclaiming his love for Nesbit; spelling it out in one letter, 'we were one in heart and soul, he died in my arms and I long to join him where there shall be no more parting'.[12]

He also tried to make arrangements for his own burial after his hanging, scheduled for 20 January 1880. He wanted to be buried in the same grave as Nesbit, and their joint tombstone was to tell it all:

> This stone covers the remains of two friends
> James P. N., Born 27/8/1858
> Andrew G. S. Born 8/1/1845
> Separated by death 17/11/1879
> United by death 20/1/1880.[13]

By the end of the nineteenth century, Sydney's population was around 400 000. Most lived within five kilometres of the GPO in Martin Place, and the city clearly had a flourishing homosexual life. One newspaper in the mid-1890s, reported on 'The Oscar Wilde's [sic] of Sydney':

The state of things in London as regards this horrible vice
is also the condition of affairs in Sydney. It is idle for people
to shut their eyes to this fact. It has been planted here by the
English exiles. The men who escaped the Cleveland Street
prosecution found shelter in Australia, and there are many of
them at present in Sydney.[14]

The Cleveland Street prosecution refers to the court case after
the discovery, in 1889, of a male homosexual brothel in Cleveland Street, in London's West End with a number of high profile clients. To avoid exposure and prosecution, several clients,
including some from Britain's aristocracy, fled overseas. The
article went on to assert that:

Many of the leading hotels and billiard saloons are haunted
by these characters, whose presence is advertised by
effeminate style of speech, and the adoption of the names of
celebrated actresses.[15]

In an unlikely twist, Oxford Street figured as a haven for
these 'deviants' even then. Men seeking safe places for homoerotic contact could go to the Turkish Baths in Liverpool
Street near where it met Oxford Street – which even figured in
Havelock Ellis's *Studies in the Psychology of Sex*.[16] There was
also Charles Wigzell's Turkish Baths at 143 Oxford Street,
open to 'men only' on Monday and Thursday afternoons and
all day Tuesday, Wednesday, Friday and Saturday. While it was
more a middle-class establishment, it also allowed for a bit of
cross-class dalliance, by offering 'cheap baths ... for workmen
every evening from 5 to 7 pm at 2s [2 shillings] each'.[17]

The opening of the new department stores on lower Oxford
Street early in the twentieth century provided opportunities

for men with homoerotic desires to find jobs near these attractions. One trade journal noted that working in such places was 'suitable only for effeminates and weaklings', and undoubtedly many 'effeminates' and dandies took the opportunity of seeking work there to meet 'others like themselves'.[18]

There were beats nearby as well. Apart from alluding to night-time activities in the city's parks, one paper noted 'that part of College-street from Boomerang-street to Park-street is a parade for them'. And they even had their favourite local pub: a 'haunt is said to exist in Bourke-street, Surry Hills'.[19]

By the early twentieth century attitudes had not changed, but, as one unusual case indicates, homosexuals were still in evidence. During World War I, a woman complained to the police about a house in Carrington Street, by Wynyard Square. She thought that several young women were being held captive in the house, because she never saw them leave the house during the day; they did, however, leave the house at night, always accompanied by several men, who stayed close to them.

A police investigation followed, initially undercover, then followed by a direct police call, on the pretext of confirming who lived there, which was information required for the upcoming conscription referendum in 1917. The police officer, Sergeant Chuck, asked the woman who came to the door for the names of the men who lived there. These were given, but when he asked for the names of the women who lived there, 'the woman became flustered and refused to supply any'. It was then that:

> Chuck realized with a shock that the 'woman' was possibly
> not a woman at all, but a pervert dressed in woman's
> clothes, yet looking so much the part of the well-groomed
> respectable housewife.[20]

Chuck returned to the police station and told his colleagues what he thought he had encountered:

> His story was received at first with incredulity. A house filled entirely with sexual perverts, who were, in every other respect, living normally and honestly, posed a problem without precedent.[21]

After arrests were made and charges laid, the court case brought forth some interesting information about the men's lifestyle. The six men who lived there were 'three couples'. The 'wife' of the lessee was known as 'Mother Superior', and 'her word was law' in the house. The police were horrified that these men told their stories 'without shame', and talked about their circle of homosexual friends, which included at least one lesbian.[22]

It was a very public face to what was still a criminal milieu.

After the war, the League of Nations came into being. Australia's Prime Minister Billy Hughes joined those assembled at Versailles for the signing of the Peace, and he garnered concessions in certain clauses that were seen to benefit the country. But the period after the end of the war began badly. In Sydney in 1919, the Spanish flu epidemic hit, with disastrous results; almost 40 per cent of Sydney's population had influenza and more than 4000 people died.

The following decade became known as the 'Roaring Twenties', an era often seen as a boom era in Sydney, yet also one of growing unemployment and economic uncertainty. The razor gang wars raged in inner Sydney, as crime bosses battled it out for control of the lucrative sex, drug and illegal gambling industries. And the 'boom' ended in October 1929 with the onset of the Great Depression.

A decade of tumult followed as the Depression deepened.

But in line with becoming 'modern', the Australian Broadcasting Commission was set up in Sydney in 1932, the Sydney Harbour Bridge was opened the same year, and Australia's first 'milk bar' opened in Martin Place in 1933. The New Guard's Captain De Groot, a right-wing militiaman, upstaged the Bridge's opening ceremony when he rode his horse forward and slashed the ribbon about to be cut by Premier Jack Lang. On 25 April 1935 the macabre case of what became known as the 'Shark Arm murder' began to unfold, when a captured shark disgorged part of a man's arm in the Coogee Aquarium swimming pool.

In the period between the great wars, Sydney was a parochial provincial city, an obscure if largish outpost of empire on the opposite side of the globe to those great centres of power that had manipulated the world for centuries. London was six weeks away by steamer, San Francisco two weeks, while few people ventured north to Asia, to those yet unmobilised heirs of the great civilisations there. Aeroplanes that were to reduce our isolation so dramatically were now a reality, but air travel remained the preserve of the wealthy or influential.

Physically the city reflected its Victorian and Edwardian heritage: governments had bequeathed some large ornate public buildings and some fine parks, while the base of the city's private wealth – commerce – was indicated by the numerous banks and their branches scattered around the city, by the crammed warehouses that flanked the Quay or climbed the hillside from Darling Harbour to the York Street ridge, and by the busy commercial houses that handled the trade of this entrepôt. There were lavish 'Department Stores', so up to date in all things – Marcus Clarke's at Railway Square, Mark Foys' Italianate extravaganza at the corner of Hyde Park, or David Jones' simple modern store, overlooking the other end of Hyde Park. In the 1930s came more designs: the streamlined *moderne* – looking like landlocked liners – in the suburbs overlooking the harbour, and some art deco creations, like the now-lost Rural Bank head office in Martin Place.

Life for Sydneysiders – as for most Australians – was not easy in this period, and rapidly deteriorated once the Depression hit. Australia's system of social services, once the envy of workers elsewhere in the industrial world, had fallen far behind developments in Europe. People struggled against inflation and falling real wages as their lives were affected by new technologies. Radio and cinema began to have a major impact – the former as the main disseminator of news, the latter as an increasingly common form of popular entertainment. New electrical appliances began to ease the lot of housewives – if they could afford them.

There were two contrasting developments in Sydney in this period: a spread of suburbia on the outer fringes of the city, as thousands sought space and serenity on their quarter acre blocks; and an increasing concentration of people in inner suburbs close to the central business district, or near the harbour and the eastern suburbs beaches – in fashionable new blocks of 'flats'. Large numbers of Sydney's male homosexual population would eventually concentrate here, and also in the boarding houses of Kings Cross and Darlinghurst.

Sydney in the interwar period was ranked among the 15 largest cities in the world in population but it lacked the internationalism it has today, and which it also had in the closing decades of the nineteenth century. Indeed for anyone used to the sophistication and social life of Europe or America, that sense of being at the centre of things, Sydney was quaintly parochial. Perhaps the last word on the subject should be left to Willie Somerset Maugham, the author, who visited Sydney *en route* to Singapore from Honolulu in 1921. Maugham travelled with his attractive young American lover, Gerald Haxton, whom he had met in France during the war. He found the city both 'surprising and amusing'. Sydney, he thought, was

> the Mecca of the decrepit author. The last one they saw was Robert Louis Stevenson and they still speak of him. When I arrived, with nothing more than a brass band and a steam roller to herald my coming, I was received with the most gratifying enthusiasm.[23]

But it wasn't only in its morphology that Sydney remained solidly Victorian. It was reflected in attitudes and social mores, which were of course in turn partly a reflection of the attitudes and mores of the country as a whole. Many writers have commented on the prevalence in Australia of Victorian attitudes until well into the twentieth century, noting in particular the conservatism, the conformity, the provincialism. As one writer commented, there was a

> rigid obsession with appearances and prohibitions, order and authority ... Middle-class men would be bothering about the propriety of whether or not to take off a coat, to loosen a tie, to smoke a cigarette – a pipe was more respectable – or in public, to risk wearing a soft collar to afternoon tea ...[24]

The twin pillars supporting this crushing conventionality were religion and the law. In all developed societies, the written law largely sets the limits to what can or cannot be done by individuals, although it is a truism that in most societies some laws are flouted, even quite flagrantly. But in such a convention-bound conservative society, the laws were often adhered to, or at least paid lip service, and social pressures to conform provided additional control.

Australian laws still derived in many areas directly from English law. Existing English law became the new colony's law with the Anglo-European invasion of 1788. As one expert on Australia's constitutional law has more poetically put it, as soon as 'the original settlers had reached the colony, their invisible and inescapable cargo of English law fell from their shoulders and attached itself to the soil on which they stood'.[25] English law and legal precedent continued to play an important role in Australian law until late in the twentieth century.[26] So Australian law relating to homosexuality was overwhelmingly influenced by English law.

Occasional amendments to the laws relating to male homosexuality in NSW over the nineteenth and twentieth centuries drew varied public responses. The *Criminal Law Amendment Act 1883* formally removed the death penalty, and the last man to be executed for sodomy in Sydney was possibly Thomas Parry, hanged in 1839. The 1883 Act followed nearly 20 years of discussion and ten formal attempts to amend and consolidate laws relating to sexual activity between males, prompted by an increase in the number of convictions of men for crimes relating to sexual behaviour other than buggery. Then, in 1900, NSW Parliament enacted the *Crimes Act*, consolidating existing legislation. Part III of the Act included the provision that 'Whosoever commits the abominable crime of buggery, or bestiality, with mankind, or with any animal, shall be liable to penal servitude for 14 years.' There was little public comment about these changes to, or consolidations of, existing laws: homosexuality was still not a fit topic for discussion. And amendments in 1924 were seen as an acceptable movement away from the draconian penalties (for many crimes) of previous eras.[27]

The law provided the legal framework within which male homosexuals lived out their 'illegal' lives. And it often dealt harshly with 'camp' people it encountered, who were involved in 'deviant sex'.

Despite the separation of church and state, ecclesiastical influences on the law have been great. The legal constraints on homosexuality were originally taken from ecclesiastical law, and reflected the attitudes of the Christian churches to homosexuality. And for the Christian churches, sex and sexuality have always been a 'problematic' area.

Much of our law, particularly that part which relates to 'morality', is a direct derivative of past church law relating to 'sin'. Thus in the 1920s, divorce law was more focused on the churches' view that 'marriage is an indissoluble union' rather than the realities of the breakdown of a relationship, and the consequent need to solve problems of conflict, loss of a sense of worth and access to children.

Conventional, moralistic, agonisingly respectable: this was the Australian society of the interwar period. Such a society was hardly likely to question itself, to encourage change, or deal with divisive issues in an imaginative, sensible way. The period is laden with examples of this predominantly dull, conformist society failing to confront an increasing array of social problems.

A major example is of course the Depression, when those at the lower end of the social scale bore the brunt of the convulsions of the capitalist system, because this was the conventional economic orthodoxy – an orthodoxy that forced far less in the way of sacrifice onto the politicians, the captains of industry or the wealthy businessmen, who had 'managed' the economy into its current crisis. Indeed, on 11 June 1932, Premier Lang was sacked by Governor Sir Philip Game for 'breaches of the law', relating to the government's unacceptable economic policies, in particular the cancellation of interest payments on government borrowings to overseas bondholders and financiers, which included British banks. But it was obvious even prior to the Depression, from the years immediately after World War I when unemployment was growing, that great changes were to be wrought in Australia's social fabric, at least, if what was happening in Europe, or in Asia – for example China – was any example. Yet the issues that the churches grappled with were often little related to social justice or equality. Morality – or rather immorality, in its many manifestations – was their priority.

A minority of church members were concerned with the impact of the Depression and there were some unexpected perspectives. *The Catholic Worker*, a new publication of the 1930s wrote in its first editorial:

> Communism is NOT our great adversary. The exalted
> position of Public Enemy No. 1 is reserved for Capitalism,
> not because it is a system which is intrinsically more evil
> than Communism – they are both equally false, and equally
> fatal to human personality – but because today it dominates
> the world. Capitalism – that is the enemy! … How is it
> possible for us, as Catholics, to have the slightest sympathy
> for a system which has de-christianised the world by its
> insistence on secular education; which has sacrificed the
> Home on the altar of the Machine; which has deprived the
> ordinary man of property and has destroyed his liberty?[28]

The Catholic Archbishop, Daniel Mannix, gave some support to these views, while in the Anglican Church the 'Red Bishop', EH Burgmann, became active in anti-establishment activities. As for the Protestant churches generally, 'except that congregations were less well dressed and stipends lower' they 'were little affected by the depression'.[29] Overall the churches were more concerned with pursuing their role as guardians of public morality and bestowers of legitimacy.

The Christian churches in Australia have always attempted to impose their vision of the perfect society on the rest of the country, and their wowser elements were to the fore in attempting to restrict various forms of social relaxation. Thus drinking, dancing, theatre, sexuality, gambling, and even reading, have been under repeated attack in Australia. Having succeeded in imposing 6 o'clock closing of hotels over much of Australia during World War I – a time coincidentally when young males, the major group of persons to whom drinking would be a primary form of social recreation, were fighting overseas – the wowser element of the churches took up a range of other 'moral' issues during the 1920s, including dancing. During the 1920s and 1930s, most of the dissenting churches attempted to ban all forms of dancing, which was seen as undermining morality. Reverend HE Wallis, at the Methodist Mission in Fitzroy, Melbourne, pithily stated the position:

> The dance hall is the nursery of the Divorce Court, the training ship of prostitution and a modern ulcer that is threatening morality.[30]

This moral anxiety over dancing reached the heights of absurdity in a debate by the Western Australian Presbyterian Church. When their Assembly voted to ban all dancing in 1926, it caused a momentary panic, as the following extract from their minutes indicates:

> Reverend Thorn: Will this motion stop the Highland Fling being danced in a Church Hall?

(Pause.)

The Moderator: Oh no, the Highland Fling is a pastime.[31]

Intelligence seems to have been sacrificed to sophistry here!

The churches were also in the forefront of the push for book censorship. Between 1927 and 1929, the number of books banned from import into Australia jumped from 120 to about 240. By 1936 the list of prohibited publications had jumped to about 5000 books (which included political publications and 'ephemeral novels').[32] These banned works included such literary masterpieces as Daniel Defoe's *Moll Flanders*, Aldous Huxley's *Brave New World*, Ernest Hemingway's *A Farewell to Arms*, George Orwell's *Down and Out in Paris and London*, James Joyce's *Ulysses*, Erskine Caldwell's *God's Little Acre*, and, of course, DH Lawrence's *Lady Chatterley's Lover*. As Peter Coleman points out:

> encouraged by regular resolutions throughout the country
> from church bodies, women's clubs, social groups,
> ex-servicemen's clubs and parent's organizations [the
> government attempted to proscribe] non-conformist
> writers of any kind, moral or political.[33]

Norman Lindsay, after one of his own novels, *Redheap*, was banned, expressed a not inappropriate sentiment:

> [Australia's] intelligent minority is invertebrate; it lets the
> lowest type of official moron wipe his boots on it. Policemen
> as the arbiters of our culture! Lord, what a country![34]

Other targets abounded. Early in the 1930s Catholic Archbishop Michael Kelly in Sydney 'begged the authorities not to allow mixed bathing at Sydney's beaches'.[35] Catholic bishops railed against women exposing their arms in public,[36] and Anglican bishops condemned the motor car, for encouraging immorality, because young couples saved for a car rather than having children straight away.[37] The churches saw it as their right to try to determine the morality of the whole society, not just those who chose to subscribe to their beliefs. The society was predominantly 'straight-laced, drab, and crushed into a narrowness of vision and stridency of statement'.[38]

Sexuality began to be of major concern to many Australians in the interwar period. What the churches saw simply as an 'immorality' issue – with increasing evidence of masturbation, pre-marital sex, birth control, divorce, abortion and 'effeminacy' in men – was in effect the start of a major reassessment of sex in our society. Australians were not alone – this was a phenomenon in most western societies at the time.

From the late nineteenth century there had been major social concern for the public rather than the private dimension of sexual activity – largely for the reproduction of a healthy 'race'. During the interwar period this changed dramatically. The

> influence of psychology and changing media images of
> sexual desirability were tending towards individualising
> and privatising sex, potentially, at least, affecting all social
> strata.[39]

There was even an emerging 'emphasis on sex as a matter of private pleasure'.[40]

Discussion on the place of sex and sexuality in our society

increased and this, of course, involved the churches and society's moralists. But middle-class professionals from a range of fields: mainly medical, such as gynaecology, midwifery, psychology and psychiatry; as well as academics, predominantly from anthropology and sociology, also became important and influential. Women tended to play an increasing role in these debates about sex too, since it was their bodies which were to bear the brunt of society's changing perceptions.

Robert Storer, a doctor prominent in the sex education debate even argued strongly for a moderation of attitudes to homosexuality. He viewed it as a dysfunction of the glands in the human body, but

> just as the pearl is the result of disease in the oyster … like
> the pearl, the manifestations of homosexuality are not always
> devoid of beauty.[41]

From the 'progressive' perspective, it was generally agreed that greater factual sex education was desirable, and a growing number of sex education manuals began to appear. The net effect of all this activity was the breaking down at last of the general and pervasive silence about sexual matters. Yet in general there was very little discussion of homosexuality – or 'effeminacy' in men, as it was so often perceived – in medical or sex education literature. And this limited discussion did not spill over into a more public discourse. Homosexuality was still largely a taboo topic.

The work of Havelock Ellis, Sigmund Freud, and, later, Alfred Kinsey has been important in determining how the medical profession – and ultimately society – have gradually changed their views on homosexuality. Ellis, a one-time resident of Australia, argued that nothing in nature proved that homosexuality was unnatural, indeed the opposite was the case, and that homosexuality was invariably congenital. Thus both moral censure and legal prohibition were inappropriate responses. His critiques made little short-term impact on public perceptions.

A further step in the direction of a scientific approach to homosexuality came from Freud. Freud's view, published in 1935, was that

> homosexuality is nothing to be ashamed of, no vice, no
> degradation; it cannot be classified as an illness: we consider
> it to be a variation of the sexual function ...[42]

In Freudian theory male homosexuality developed from an 'unsuccessful resolution of the Oedipus complex: a boy became excessively attached to his mother, ultimately identified with her (rather than with his father), and then sought in male sexual objects substitute selves whom he might love as he had been loved by his mother'.[43] Freudian theory may have swung the pendulum of interpretation back to the 'acquired' rather than the 'congenital', but it did so in the supposedly more neutral concepts of psychoanalysis, rather than the overtly moralistic tones of Victorian thinkers, most of whom regarded homosexuality as an acquired perversion.

But doctors were subject to both the limitations of their professional knowledge and the prevailing social values. Alex Comfort, in *The Anxiety-makers*, noted how medical 'knowledge' was often no more than moral judgements cloaked in the disguise of scientific expertise. He elaborates:

> when one reads the sexual and hygienic advice dispensed by
> physicians to the public ... one can only stand amazed that
> the authority of the doctor as counsellor has stood up so

well. Generations have retailed to the patients a great flood
of reproductive misinformation, most of it moralistic in
intention as well as content. Diseases and physical mischiefs
have been invented, and produced in the susceptible by
medical intimidation. All due allowance having been made
for unconscious forces in patient and doctor, one can only
conclude that there are none as unscrupulous as the devout,
and that generations of medical men, in the interest of
promoting right conduct, have given advice which they
should have known by observation to be nonsense, and
which had already been demonstrated to be nonsense when
it was given, to patients who knew in their hearts that it was
nonsense, but were driven by anxiety to accept it.[44]

This is certainly true when one looks at the relationship between
ideas about homosexuality and the medical profession in this era.
What Comfort appears to be getting at in a roundabout fashion
has come to be called the 'social construction of sexuality'.

It took time for these new ideas to permeate through both
the medical profession and society. But in the 1930s, as the psychiatric profession achieved greater professional acceptance in
Australia, their perception of homosexuality as an 'illness' gradually gained greater legitimacy, although it was not acknowledged in the courts until the late 1940s.

What did the wider society in general know of homosexuality in this period? The answer is 'probably very little'. It was
not a topic to be discussed at respectable dinner tables, nor did
it often appear in print until well into the 1930s. There were
some references in theatre, film and books, which are discussed
below. But largely there was a 'wall – or conspiracy – of silence'
about all aspects of homosexuality, except in one important
aspect, namely where its 'criminality' impinged on society.

The word homosexuality was not even in the public lexicon. The English writer Beverley Nichols noted that it wasn't until the furore resulting from Radclyffe Hall's novel, *The Well of Loneliness*, published in London in 1928, that 'homosexual' began to enter general circulation.[45] When newspapers discussed what were obviously homosexual cases in the interwar period in Australia, they often did so in such a euphemistic or oblique way that the meaning wasn't clear even to an intelligent reader. Common terms at the time were 'committing an act of indecency', 'offending against decency' or 'committing an unnatural offence', but since this could cover anything from birth control to abortion, from heterosexual oral-genital sex to homosexual acts – or even bestiality – all precision was lost. The Christian church's description of homosexual acts as *non nominandum inter Christianus* (not to be named among Christians) seems to have been literally true.

When, occasionally, discussion of cases relating to homosexual acts did appear in the press, the different ways they were handled illustrates both how perceptions were changing, and the range of contradictory social attitudes that existed side by side. The scandal surrounding the divorce in 1931 of Lord Beauchamp, former Governor of New South Wales, is a good example.

Beauchamp was 'threatened with divorce and criminal proceedings that would reveal his homosexuality, and resigned all of his appointments except the Lord Wardenship of the Cinque Ports, and went into exile'.[46] Yet the major Sydney newspapers made few allusions to the reason behind his resignations – allusions understood only by those in the know – and failed to mention what was at the heart of the matter.

The news first broke, by cable from London, on Thursday 11 June 1931. The *Sydney Morning Herald* simply noted that,

'Earl Beauchamp has resigned the chairmanship of the National Liberal Club, and is taking a cure at Bad Nanheim (Germany). If it is satisfactory he will retain the Liberal leadership in the House of Lords.'[47] That evening the *Sydney Sun* noted that Countess Beauchamp had filed a petition for divorce.[48] The following morning both the *Herald* and the *Daily Telegraph* noted the Countess's actions.[49] But the same edition of the *Daily Telegraph* carried another item in 'The Talk of Sydney', a regular society gossip column. The writer started out by noting that the 'Cabled news of divorce proceedings instituted in England against the Earl Beauchamp … comes tremendously as a surprise, even as a shock to Sydneysiders'. Beauchamp had recently been in Sydney without his wife, and the columnist had enquired of one of the Earl's friends why Lady Beauchamp wasn't with him. The answer given was that it 'had been arranged that the Earl and his wife should come away together, but she took seriously ill, and Beauchamp travelled solo at her express wish. He's very glum about it.' But the columnist continues in a way that immediately – and intentionally – casts doubt on the veracity of this last statement: 'The noble Earl may have disguised his feelings, but he neither looked, nor acted, as one "very glum about it all". He enjoyed himself immensely … but never publicly, or privately – so far as I can ascertain – did he mention his wife'. The columnist goes on with details of what Lord Beauchamp did while he was here, and noted that some people regarded him 'as "a queer chap"'.[50]

On Monday 15 June the *Sydney Morning Herald* reported that Lord Beauchamp's solicitors had declined to make any statement on the subject.[51] On the following Saturday, *Smith's Weekly*, a magazine given to more salacious reporting, tossed in the following tidbit:

> News that the Countess of Beauchamp has instituted
> divorce proceedings did not surprise the people of Sydney …
> Now it has come about, and will give London Society
> something to talk about openly, though no one will get much
> of a shock when the evidence is published.[52]

While the major tabloids were discreet on the matter, it was obvious that the reasons for the divorce were common knowledge among certain circles. Beauchamp was no stranger to Sydney – and he was certainly not a stranger to places with a homosexual ambience here. As 'The Talk of Sydney' columnist implied, no one was surprised at Beauchamp being without his wife. Indeed earlier that same year, the *Sydney Morning Herald* had republished an article by Beauchamp, from the *Empire Review*, that had given lavish praise to Sydney in general – and to Sydney men in particular. The piece has a barely suppressed homoeroticism. After mentioning in a few words the beauty and posture of Sydney women, Beauchamp went on lyrically:

> The men are splendid athletes, like the old Greek statues.
> Their skins are tanned by sun and wind, and I doubt whether
> anywhere in the world are finer specimens of manhood
> than in Sydney. The life-savers at the bathing beaches are
> wonderful.[53]

But the curtain of silence prevailed, and there was no direct mention of homosexuality. In Beauchamp's case, it *may* have been lack of certainty or fear of libel that determined how the case was presented. Then again it may simply have been discretion and a reverence for the English aristocracy.

No such discretion interfered with reporting homosexual offences related to the 'average man-in-the-street'. The police continued to be attentive to the activities of perverts in the city, and newspapers gave details of the cases. In October 1934, 'Phillip', a playwright from Camperdown aged 21, and 'Donald', a fitter from Enfield, aged 40, were arrested in St Leonards Park. Phillip was giving Donald a 'blow job' when apprehended by the police, and he defended his actions, telling police, 'I can't help being a pervert.' Both pleaded guilty and received a sentence of one year's hard labour.[54] Several points are worth noting about this case; first, both were far from home for their sexual encounter – the Harbour Bridge had only been opened two years earlier; second, Phillip saw himself in the terminology of the day, as a 'pervert'; and, third, the newspaper publicity told men of homosexual inclinations that they might meet others like themselves at St Leonards Park, even if in dangerous circumstances.

Later in the decade, after one case received detailed coverage, newspapers appear to have been more willing to discuss homosexuality less obliquely, if still only in criminal terms. The case, in 1937, involved Sydney Aubrey Maddocks, the NSW Commissioner for Road Transport. It was a curious case whose detailed reporting gives insight into police activities, and some indication of prevailing attitudes.

The facts of the case were that Maddocks was arrested by police at Lane Cove on the night of 1 March 1937 in the company of an 18-year-old who gave his name as Michael John Peterson, the name Maddocks knew him by. Police charged Maddocks on 2 March with indecently assaulting Peterson, and later added another charge, that of attempting an unnatural offence with the younger man. The main police witness was Peterson.[55]

At the committal hearing on 16 March, further details were given, and these received wide reportage. Peterson admitted that his real name was Mikiel Adams, and that he had previously been in trouble with the police. The police admitted that Maddocks had been under surveillance for some time, and confirmed that no charges were to be laid against Adams,[56] even though Maddocks had not forced Adams to go to Lane Cove with him.

More details came out at the trial, two weeks later.[57] Adams, under questioning from Maddocks' counsel, made what should have been damaging admissions: he acknowledged that on 1 March, he had rung Maddocks and made an appointment to meet him that afternoon. The same day he had been brought into Sydney from Liverpool by police, and had gone with them to the lonely spot at Lane Cove where later that night police were to 'find' and arrest Maddocks. The police had then driven Adams back to where he was to meet Maddocks in the city. Indeed, Adams admitted that he had in effect arranged for Maddocks to be caught with him.[58]

There are many possible explanations as to why the police should wish to entrap Maddocks. One writer has noted that Maddocks' appointment, as an outsider, to the lucrative position of Transport Commissioner

> was resented by senior departmental officers, and ensuing
> years were full of behind-the-scenes battles for Maddocks,
> whose closet sexuality had leaked to his enemies, although
> still hidden from friends and family. There were many people
> in responsible positions with an axe to grind ... who would
> relish Maddocks being forced from his position in disgrace.[59]

Maddocks had briefly been Secretary of Police in 1930 and likely had enemies in the force. He had clearly been 'set up' in this case by the police. As Maddocks' counsel pointed out in his summing up, 'This is not a case of a young innocent boy who was found in the arms of a man, but a filthy pervert who was the easiest type for criminals to use to prey on a man in a big position … On the evidence, this boy framed that man.'[60] What counsel did not have to point out was that the 'criminals' in this case were the police, who had used the boy to entrap Maddocks.

It was perhaps because of such overwhelming evidence of police involvement that the judge felt constrained to tell the jury that, 'Adams may be a pervert of the worst type. He may have laid a trap.' But then he added: 'Even if you find he laid a trap, this fact is no defence unless the accused was ignorant of the conditions under which he was found.'[61] In saying this, he made it clear that Maddocks ought to be found guilty. And the jury, undoubtedly offended by Maddocks' sexual interest in Adams, did find him guilty, despite the unexplained police inputs into the case.

A later case from the 1930s is worth noting, because it made no bones about what it was reporting, and even used the word 'homo-sexual'. This was the revelation that came out of Germany about the homosexuality of the sensational tennis star Baron Gottfried von Cramm. He had fallen into disfavour with the Nazis, who were trying to improve their image after the Röhm scandals and the massacre of the 'Night of the Long Knives': von Cramm was simply 'removed' from the German tennis scene. His case was noted in the Australian newspapers and the reasons for his fall from grace were clearly spelt out.[62]

Perceptions of homosexuals and homosexuality also emerged from other sources in the interwar years. Popular theatre tended to deal largely in stereotypes. The theatre world of course was a haven for homosexuals; indeed, at that time, one of the euphemisms for homosexually inclined men was 'theatrical'. And in various theatrical productions, deviant sexualities were portrayed. Vaudeville performer Charles Norman remembers one very successful song in his repertoire:

> Sister is busy learning to shave
> Brother just loves his permanent wave
> It's hard to tell them apart today and say ...
> Girls were girls and boys were boys
> When I was a tot
> Now we don't know who is who or even what's what
> Knickers and trousers, baggy and wide
> Nobody knows who's walking inside
> Those masculine women and feminine men.

And Ted Stanley, the 'lively comedian', had a hit with 'I'm a Queen', which clearly spelt out what it was to be an overtly camp man at that time:

> I'm a Queen, I'm a Queen,
> I create such a scene
> What is it? What is it? the people all cry
> And all the boys whistle ('Pretty Joey')
> As I'm strolling by
> I'm some bird, 'pon my word,
> The biggest dare-devil yet seen
> When they say 'Parley Voo',
> I reply 'Fudge to you'
> I'm A Queen, I'm a Queen.

Although a stereotype, it clearly indicates an awareness that certain men rejected the roles that society expected of them.[63]

Two other forms of popular entertainment – novels and films – also brought homosexuality to the notice of a wider public. Perhaps surprisingly, male homosexual characters were portrayed in a wide range of novels; not surprisingly however, with one notable exception, the characters were either stereotypes or caricatures.

A good example of a 'pop' novel with a major homosexual character was *Highly Inflammable*, published by Angus & Robertson in Sydney in 1936. In this tale of high adventure and intrigue, the hero, a serious young Scot, becomes involved in an attempt to bomb the Russian oil pipelines from the wells at Baku to the port of Batum on the Black Sea, to stop the Russians from dumping oil on the world markets at low prices, and thus disrupt the economy of the West. Our hero is pitted against a villain whose 'hands were plump and white with rouged and painted nails', whose eyes, 'darkly liquid, mournful under the drooping lids … would have been lovely in a woman's face', whose voice was 'soft, like a woman's, with a slight lisp', and about whom 'a waft of some heavy cloying perfume hung'. Our healthy Scottish hero also notes that his enemy is a 'creature outside the pale, a man who smoked scented tobacco'.[64] This effeminate villain also uses a small pearl-handled revolver, and is shown to be a coward when the Scot pulls a knife on him.[65]

The dubious human psychology operating in this novel would have us believe that the 'pansy' villain, who now goes by the name of Kuhn, was once an ace Prussian fighter pilot named Baldur von Plessen, who had been transformed into a coward during World War I by the sight of a knife wielded by a British airman when they were on the ground after their planes had come down. Needless to say, the Scottish hero bests the Prussian officer/Jewish homosexual, and saves the economy of the West.

Such a trite tale need not be taken too seriously, except that it did purvey to its audience a particular vision of a homosexual.

But the treatment of homosexuals does not necessarily change even when we move from 'pop' novels to those of higher aspirations. We still find simple caricatures, and the perception is still rarely favourable. Christina Stead's novels are one example. Stead left Australia in 1928, and her novels in this period were published overseas, but she still had a following here, and her work was fairly well received. Homosexual characters appear only marginally in her novels, and the portrayal is neither favourable nor sympathetic. *Seven Poor Men of Sydney* nicely illustrates this.

Two of the seven main characters have brief contact with homosexuals. Joseph Baguenault, a major character, becomes involved with a somewhat bohemian set living on the fringes of university life and centred on the Workers Educational Association. One night he is introduced to a 'little creature', who is known to have a wonderful collection of records, and who 'begins to chatter in a strained, feminine voice'.[66] This is Dacre Esme Eugene, and Stead puts into his mouth several speeches which allow Joseph (and the reader) to dismiss him as a pretentious poseur. For instance, at our first meeting with Dacre, he chatters away, after 'stamping his foot':

> there's Catherine backstage, looking like La Tosca, with
> roses in her arms; I absolutely promised to bring you back
> those paintings, absolutely Raphaelesque. Watkins said, 'You
> should carry through whatever you start: you'll do something
> magnificent'. God, these women with their primeval force,
> their unregimented talents. God, when I think how giddy
> I am and I take a person like you, a female Caesar would
> positively cross the Rubicon twenty times a day; and I see
> how you hold yourself demurely nun-like in the background,
> or else go round with a purple tragic air, Cassandras

predicting the fall of the human race because they have no children. God, I positively weep. We men are nothing to you girls and you let us impose on you. God, it's terrific; a real Euripidean situation.[67]

This is a caricature of the homosexual as a dizzy effeminate.

Later in the novel, Michael, another major character, is contemplating suicide, and is walking out past Rose Bay towards the Gap. While listening to the sea in the distance, he becomes aware of someone close by:

> A young fellow standing near a street lamp came into its light, while approaching Michael modestly. His small hands were manicured, his fine wrists and delicate neck were blackish as with coal dust, but his hairless face, with oval cheeks, was pink and powdered. His eyes, large and timid, looked appealingly at Michael. Michael brushed rudely past him.[68]

In both cases the homosexual is portrayed as 'unmanly'. All the key images are the femininity of the characters – Dacre's 'feminine' and 'fluty' voice, and the young man who approaches Michael with his fine wrists and delicate neck and his hairless face, with cheeks pink and powdered. In both cases the character whose situation we are involved in is – legitimately, it is implied – disdainful of the homosexuals. Yet the novelist has deliberately created such unflattering portraits. It is probable that Stead would have known homosexuals; most people do. However, she may not have known that any of her own friends were homosexual, and 'created' homosexual characters from images and perceptions: hence the stereotypical nature of the homosexual characters in her novel. These points are made not

simply as carping criticism of one of Australia's leading novelists, but to illustrate that even a writer of Stead's stature used
common misperceptions of homosexuals.

Not all novelists were limited in this way, however. Some,
like Frank Dalby Davison, wanted 'Australians to liberate their
minds from the teachings of the Christian Church and the
assumptions of the law on homosexuality'.[69] Others managed,
by close observation or creative insight, to portray homosexuals
as 'simply human beings'. Probably the most sympathetic picture of a male homosexual in an Australian novel until recently
was in Kenneth Seaforth Mackenzie's *The Young Desire It*. This
novel traces the emotional development and sexual awakening
of a schoolboy, Charles Fox. The only person who really under-
stands Charles, and treats him as a human being, is Penworth,
a junior master at his boarding school. And Penworth, it turns
out, is a homosexual.

For a novel published in Australia in the 1930s, *The Young
Desire It* was very advanced indeed, dealing as it did with a topic
normally taboo – male homosexuality – and including explicit
scenes of sexual intent. For example, quite early in the novel
Penworth's interest in Charles is made overt:

> Penworth quite carelessly put out his hand and gripped
> Charles's leg firmly above the knees. His palm was warm
> but dry; Charles hardly noticed it in his relief at not being
> thought rude. The gentle fingers slid slowly upwards under
> the short trouser leg; they touched Charles like moths, in
> sensitive places, for hardly a second, and then as slowly slid
> down again …

> For a moment the silence was hot and intense. Then
> Penworth stretched his arms up, and pulled his head back,

yawning so that the skin creased down his flat, healthy cheeks. He still looked at Charles, sideways, and raised one eyebrow as though he would have said, 'Well, what fools all of us are'. Charles laughed. He had already forgotten the caressive touch, which had seemed almost as dispassionate as the touch of his own hand upon a sheet of paper.[70]

The novel however does not treat Penworth simply as a pervert, a molester of boys. The narration makes this clear:

> Penworth himself would at that time have had great pain to explain, even to his own questing conscience, what were his objects in so cultivating the boy. He knew he wanted to touch him; he knew he felt some kind of complicated pleasure in observing the changing expressions in Charles's pale face, with its steady green-brown eyes and clear red lips; he was pleased, when one of those happy strenuous private lessons was over, to put his own white hand on the boy's tousled, ruddy crown and notice, without appearing to notice, what a fine flash of happiness and gratitude relieved the face below of its intent frown; but he would not have attempted to explain this pleasure, and he took care that the boy should not be aware of it.[71]

Similarly, Charles's feelings about Penworth are neither revulsion nor a romanticised schoolboy crush. Charles often puzzled over Penworth's attitude to him, and also over his own attitude to Penworth:

> He felt happy every time Penworth showed such spontaneous motions of affection, yet he could not bear to be touched or held by any man; and it was difficult to

perceive in himself anything that warranted such gestures which others did not also possess; unless it was that Penworth himself, from loneliness or some other starvation, was beginning to feel for him the affection of a father or a brother. It was all strange and confusing to him, when he considered it as now, striving to make plain to himself the man's reasons and his own feelings.[72]

For this is also the period of Charles's sexual awakening, and – unfortunately for Penworth – Charles's interest lies in the opposite sex. But this rejection is treated sympathetically, and not melodramatically. Our empathies lie with both Charles and Penworth in this difficult situation.

The novel is advanced in another direction too. It spells out quite plainly that attitudes to things such as homosexuality are socially conditioned, and that they vary over time and between societies. Thus there is really no shame attached to homosexuality, except as it is 'created' by a homophobic society. This is made very plain in a scene between Penworth and Charles: Penworth, having come to terms with the fact that Charles's interests lie in quite another direction, tells Charles that some things are not meant to be, largely because of the social attitudes and conventions of the society in which they find themselves. As he puts it, 'different ages, different conventions. Different moralities.'[73]

While novels might only reach a limited audience, the same is not true for the emerging medium of film. By the early 1930s the new talkies were all the rage, and while the market was saturated with Hollywood productions, Australian movies were also shown. Many of these have become classics, most notably the 'Dad and Dave' series, which included *On our Selection* and *Dad and Dave Come to Town*.

An ambiguity in the portrayal of homosexuals dates from

the earliest movies. The net result largely reflected social attitudes: homosexuals tended to be ignored or treated as stereotypes. Homosexual characters appeared in serious situations
in some early European films, but this was rare.[74] In the USA
homosexual characters were hardly ever treated seriously. They
commonly appeared in drag and cross-dressing, usually in
comedy. As Vito Russo has pointed out in *The Celluloid Closet:
Homosexuality in the Movies*, the only way male homosexuals
could be portrayed in American movies from the 1920s to the
1940s, under the Hays Code, was as the 'harmless sissy'.[75] In
Australia, as *Smith's Weekly* noted in a report on film censorship
during the 1930s, homosexuality or 'sex perversion' was one of
the 'positively forbidden' subjects. The list included

> illegal drug traffic; excessive and lustful kissing; suggestive
> postures and gestures; sex perversion or its inference; white
> slavery; miscegenation; the subject of sex hygiene or venereal
> disease; scenes of actual childbirth; the exposing of children's
> sex organs; obscenity in word, gesture, reference, song or
> joke; the use (unless reverently) of the words God, Lord
> Jesus, Christ, hell, damn; complete nudity; indecent or undue
> exposure; dances which emphasise indecent movements
> or suggest sexual actions; ridicule of any religious faith;
> salacious, indecent or obscene titles.[76]

Actors like Franklin Pangborn, Edward Everett Horton, Erik
Rhodes and Grady Sutton created their sissy roles, bringing to
them delightful ambiguities and innuendoes to overcome similar
restrictions in the USA. No hero was ever an overt homosexual.

Australian audiences saw both overseas and locally produced films, but the vast majority of films were Hollywood
productions, so the predominant image of male homosexuality

they saw was the 'sissy'. In Australian films, homosexual characters were most notable by their absence, with one exception: Ken Hall's *Dad and Dave Come to Town*, produced in 1938. In this minor classic, the plot revolves around a dress shop in Sydney which Dad inherits, and his daughter Jill decides to manage. They are, however, swindled by their manager, who sells their designs to a rival dress shop nearby. When this is discovered the manager is sacked. Entwhistle, a male floor-walker who gets on well with Jill is promoted in his place. Entwhistle is the archetypal 'sissy'. Dad describes him as a 'natural born milker'. No one seeing the movie can be in any doubt as to the type of character that Entwhistle, played by Alec Kellaway, was meant to represent.

Perhaps Hall simply modelled the character of Entwhistle on roles created by Franklin Pangborn, as for example the male dressmaker in *Professional Sweetheart* (1933) or the hat-shop proprietor in *Easy Living* (1937). With Pangborn, the 'harmless sissy' assumes 'heroic' characteristics. As Russo points out, in over a hundred movies through the 1930s alone, 'Pangborn played kaleidoscopic variations on the role and became the archetypal sissy'.[77]

Interestingly, even though Entwhistle is the archetypal sissy, he does end up being something of a hero. His actions eventually lead to the thwarting of the 'baddies' and the triumph of the 'goodies'. Perhaps this is simply another parallel with the American style. Russo notes that

> because they were only symbols for failed masculinity and therefore did not represent the threat of actual homosexuals, most sissies ... were not demeaned, nor were they used in cruel or offensive ways.[78]

This was certainly true of Entwhistle.

The portrayal of homosexuals in Australian literature and films in the interwar period tended largely to reflect the prevailing attitudes and prejudices, that common perception of homosexuals as 'effeminates'. Only a rare piece of creative work, like Mackenzie's novel, could transcend its time and place and make statements for all humankind, using a homosexual man as a sympathetically treated major character. It took a long time before 'the homosexual' could be portrayed as the hero.

To sum up, the city's many homosexuals were largely isolated in the interwar years, accepting society's definition of them, and with no sense that thousands of other people like themselves were out there. To express one's sexuality was to court either persecution or prosecution. Indeed the prevailing social *mentalité* was well expressed in King George V's oft-quoted lines on being told of Lord Beauchamp's homosexuality in 1931: 'I thought men like that shot themselves.'[79]

But the king was wrong, so very wrong. As we shall see, men with homoerotic desires in Sydney found a range of ways to live their lives.

CHAPTER 2

... BUT THEY DIDN'T

'Camp' life in Sydney before World War II

If they didn't shoot themselves, what sort of life did male homosexuals in Sydney lead in the interwar period? Their society enacted and enforced harsh laws against them, while they were variously known as 'camp', 'poofters' or 'poofs', 'queens', 'fairies', 'sissies', or possibly 'girlies' or 'pansies'.[1] In fact, negative attitudes to homosexuality were so strong that a majority saw themselves as outcasts or perverts. It should be remembered that we are probably talking here about some tens of thousands of men.

Fortunately, Sydney, like most major cities around the world – and certainly port cities – both reflected and deviated from the dominant cultural values of the wider society around it. While a majority of Sydneysiders undoubtedly conformed or paid lip-service to conventionality and respectability, large numbers did not. One of the great advantages of sizeable cities, particularly those with a large itinerant population, is that the pressure for social conformity can more easily be ignored, and people have more freedom to live their lives as they choose. Sydney in the 1920s and 1930s had its share of social deviants – its bohemians, writers, drinkers and creative artists – people who found the social conventions of the day an anathema. They had their favoured suburbs, their haunts, their own ways of life lived out under the noses of the respectable and pious. As Kylie Tennant has noted, in the interwar years parts of Sydney were 'driving, humorous and truculent'.[2] Many homosexuals were a part of this community of social deviants, and if they put their homoerotic thoughts into action they were also, at least in a technical sense, part of Sydney's criminal element.

So there are two separate answers to the question of how homosexually inclined men lived in Sydney. First, most lived lives much the same as the heterosexually inclined majority – they lived in the suburbs and held down jobs, they saved for vacations and treats, squabbled with relatives, paid off mortgages, and they formed relationships, which might be transitory or, just as probably, might last for long periods of time. These mundane matters are what most of our lives are about. But also at play was the need to avoid attention which might lead to prosecution or persecution, loss of job, ostracism by friends and relatives – indeed, a denial of access to fundamental rights to which even the humblest member of a just society ought to have access. Their lives were lived precariously, in fear of discovery. One false step could mean exposure and gaol, or the necessity of moving. And to satisfy their sexuality, these homosexuals needed access to a world hidden from their heterosexual counterparts, the world of the beats.

Not everyone chose this path. Some homosexuals lived openly in the world alongside others who rejected society's mores, people who had chosen to be different. Homosexuals who did this were no different from their peers who rejected the conventional life, be they artists or bohemians – creative people or just plain drifters – anyone who decided that they wanted to 'march to the sound of a different drum'. It was overwhelmingly difficult to live this sort of life, however, and still operate within social institutions: to hold down a respectable job, to practise a profession, to live on good terms with relatives and with those who stayed within the bounds of conventional society.

So while it was easier therefore for those on the fringes of conventional society to opt for a more overtly homosexual lifestyle, few did so. In fact, many went to great lengths to hide their homosexuality from society. One subterfuge was to be seen in the company of women. Jack Lindsay recalls the situation of a homosexual musician 'who shared his flat with a languidly good-looking medical student'. Since rumours were going around about his proclivities, he took to dining out often with Anna Brennan, daughter of the poet Christopher Brennan, as a means of refuting the rumours.[3]

But to hide one's homosexuality from the heterosexual world was also to hide it from other homosexuals. And this created problems. When people meet in our society, there was – and often still is – a presumption of heterosexuality. Thus heterosexuals can meet potential partners in places that range from church socials to bridge parties, from workplaces to choral societies – the whole range of work and leisure activities bring heterosexuals into contact with each other. But how could one homosexual know they were meeting another, if both were hiding their sexuality?

There have always been widely held views that homosexuals can tell each other on sight, or have distinguishing mannerisms or features that allow them to identify each other. One NSW politician told the Legislative Council, when a homosexual wishes to attract the attention of another, 'the pervert makes use of gestures and signs which, if used by a person with no such evil designs, might be for any number of innocent purposes'.[4] This is patently absurd, how could a 'camp' tell if someone making a gesture or sign 'which, if used by a person with no such evil designs' was actually someone like himself? One false move would be a disaster.

Another oft-repeated claim, with perhaps more validity, was that homosexuals could tell each other by pieces of clothing that they wore. Thus, at various times, a signet ring on the little finger of the left hand, a green carnation in the lapel, red ties, blue suede shoes – and, more recently, a bunch of keys hanging from a belt or an earring in the right ear – have all been claimed as distinguishing insignia for homosexuals. Jack Lindsay noted a variation on this in the 1920s – one night when he and his brother Ray went out wearing black crepe de Chine ties, they were taunted by some of the local hooligans, who were 'sure that only queens could wear such unorthodox ties'.[5]

However, simply 'being different' in Australia has often drawn opprobrium or attack, and this would be particularly true of the conformist 1920s and 1930s. Robert Helpmann, for example, found himself the recipient of unwanted attentions while in Sydney, for this reason. His biographer describes how he

> indulged his taste for flamboyant clothes and even
> experimented with nail polish. He was as exotic a sybarite as
> the city of Sydney had to display.[6]

On one occasion, Helpmann walked along Bondi Beach with a companion. He was dressed in Oxford bags, a pink shirt and purple tie, with plucked eyebrows and his fingernails painted red. By the time the pair reached the end of the beach a large crowd was following them, in silence, 'like mourners behind a cortege'.[7] Among the crowd was a group of lifesavers:

giants among men, as tanned and muscular as any Tarzan,
and these lifesavers picked him up, carried him into the surf,
and dumped him.[8]

Deviance, even in dress, had its costs.

Still, these questionable assertions – that homosexuals
could recognise each other from a telling piece of clothing for
instance – have to be treated with caution. Even if it could be
true, far more institutionalised arrangements were available.
Indeed, many parts of the dominant heterosexual culture have
been subverted by homosexuals for their own purposes, not
least among them being that most ubiquitous of all things Australian, the pub.

Any meeting place for the homosexually inclined had to
offer the safety of relative inconspicuousness. Thus any venue
must legitimately permit men to interact socially in such numbers that individual activities went unnoticed. Hotel bars nicely
fulfilled these requirements. A series of hotels served as meeting
places for homosexuals in this period, although they were not
exclusively or even predominantly homosexual bars. City hotels
favoured by the homosexually inclined ranged in style from the
swank Australia Hotel to 'blood-houses' like the Belfields.

In the late 1930s, the Australia Hotel, on the corner of
Castlereagh and Rowe streets, was arguably the most elegant hotel Australia had ever seen. A Victorian creation of
the baroque architect, GA Mansfield, the hotel was extended
to Martin Place in the mid-1930s with a modern building of
the most striking art deco design, designed by Emil Sodersten.
It was a mix of glass (mainly black and silver), stainless steel,
marble and Australian woods. The entrance foyer and stairs were
a fantasy of black Carrara marble, black glass with silver etch-
ings, and mirrors. It was the showplace of the city, with several

stylish bars, a banqueting hall and an 'intimate' dining room.

The Long Bar at the back of the hotel, also known as the Sportsman's Bar, was the favourite haunt of homosexuals. It had the advantage of several entrances, one directly and discreetly out to Rowe Street, a small quiet street that ran down beside the Commonwealth Bank Head Office to Pitt Street, and others into the interior of the hotel and thence to either Martin Place or Castlereagh Street. As the name implies, it had one long bar down the centre facing outward on both sides, so one could lean on the counter and have an excellent view of those on the other side. While it attracted people from all different social levels, it was undoubtedly a better class bar, catering for professionals, white-collar workers, and, very often, country visitors. It had a wide reputation in the homosexual world for being a congenial pick-up place; here, 'country types and homosexuals might start out warily eyeing the other off, but as the evening progressed, many boundaries were crossed'.[9]

Several other middle-class hotels in the city, all fairly close to each other, were also well-known homosexual meeting places: the Carlton and Metropolitan Ushers both in Castlereagh Street, and Pfahlerts, in Margaret Street, which looked out over Wynyard Park, a notorious city beat.[10]

At the other end of the social scale were the working-class hotels like the Belfields, on the corner of King and George streets. This was basically a workers' pub, often frequented by navy personnel. As one writer has noted:

> pre-war George Street was known as 'Salt-meat Alley', as all sailors on shore leave used to make all the hotels from the Quay to King Street their riotous rendez-vous, and the area, on Saturdays especially, had a reputation almost equivalent to the Rocks a hundred years ago.[11]

Under NSW liquor laws hotels had to close their public bars at 6 pm, so people went to a range of other venues, either after the hotels closed, or as an alternative. Sydney in the inter-war period had several stylish restaurants which attracted largish homosexual clienteles. Two of the best known were the Shalimar, downstairs in the old T & G Insurance Building, on the corner of Elizabeth and Park streets, and the celebrated Latin Cafe, on the first floor of the old Royal Arcade which ran between Pitt and George streets, where the Hilton now stands.

The Shalimar was a middle-class establishment that sometimes had musicians playing light music. There are many stories of the evenings there becoming rowdy and of flirtings 'across a crowded room'. But it maintained a respectable reputation and same-sex couples dancing was never permitted.[12]

The Latin Cafe, run by Madam Helen Pura, was more cosmopolitan, serving excellent European cuisine. Here the clientele covered the social spectrum, from barristers and judges to bookies and jockeys, from actors to artists, and even their 'rough trade'. Madam Pura referred to her extensive homosexual clientele as 'the people I adore', and her restaurant was a major rendezvous on Friday nights.[13] It appeared in Christina Stead's novel *Seven Poor Men of Sydney* lightly disguised as the 'Roman Cafe'.[14] Visiting celebrities were always appearing there, as they did at the Purple Onion in the 1960s. Lord Beauchamp, the former Governor of New South Wales, was a regular diner at the Latin Cafe on his recurring trips to Sydney. While behaviour in the restaurant itself was fairly discreet, many assignations were arranged in its washrooms.[15]

While these two restaurants were much frequented by respectable society, other restaurants of a more raffish nature attracted a broad range of 'social deviants', homosexuals among them. Two such places from the 1920s were Mockbell's – a place where women never went – and Pelligrini's, both the haunt of artists and members of Sydney's bohemian set. The advantage of Mockbell's was that, as one nervous heterosexual client noted, 'you could stay as long as you liked at the marble-topped tables, at ease in good chairs or on leather upholstered seats, with backs safely to the wall'.[16] Pelligrini's was a 'centre for artists, writers and musicians for many years', and attracted members of the camp world at ease in such a milieu. It was referred to in Louis Stone's novel *Betty Wayside*.[17] Another bohemian haunt with a periphery of homosexuals was Andrew's, a Greek club in Castlereagh Street, which served as a meeting place in the 1930s for a little group of artists, writers and poets.[18]

Not all of Sydney's homosexuals were frequenters of stylish hotels or cafe society and bohemian meeting places. For the rest, there was a range of ordinary venues, all meeting the requirements of innocuousness and inconspicuousness. Several of Sydney's better-known coffee shops were also much frequented by the homosexually inclined; and one in particular is remembered fondly as a place for meeting precocious schoolboys, namely Repin's Coffee Shop in King Street, up from the old Theatre Royal, near the long-gone Berkelouw's Bookshop. Repin's was patronised by workers and actors from the Theatre Royal, and its artistic clientele served as an attraction for a wide range of outsiders.[19]

A more discreet meeting place was Cahill's Coffee Shop in Market Street, opposite David Jones' Market Street store. Far less flamboyant than Repin's, many a homosexual pick-up nevertheless took place here, under the eagle eye of the cashier near the door.[20]

Unfortunately Sydney lacked an area with a clearly homosexual ambience and a range of openly homosexual venues like those found in many European cities at the time. Berlin in the 1920s, for example, has been described as 'the Babylon of the world ... Along the entire Kurfürstendamm powdered and rouged young men sauntered ... and in the dimly-lit bars one might see government officials and men of finance tenderly courting drunken sailors without any shame.'[21] Paris, too, had its share of homosexual and lesbian bars. Sydney, in contrast, suffered from the Anglo-Saxon disease of homophobia, although it did have a series of clubs where the demimonde, the underworld and 'society' might meet. Like similar clubs in London, 'their atmosphere was more illicit and daring than an ordinary nightclub today'.[22]

These clubs, of which there were a few, were in more out-of-the-way places. Most operated only at night. Some, like their counterparts in American cities, had quite a reputation. Black Ada's was quite blatantly a homosexual meeting place, as one patron remembers fondly:

> the place for thrills was a dive in Wentworth Avenue – up a long flight of stairs and into a dimly lit large studio, with a dance floor lined with tables – called 'Black Ada's' – it was officially called 'The Academy School of Dancing' and was run by the largest negro you ever saw, called 'Black Ada'. You knocked at the door down-stairs and if Ada knew you, in you went (with friends you had to vouch for) and if Ada didn't know you – No Go! – you didn't get in! The cost of 'dancing lessons' was 2/6 with supper – and it was brilliant. The place was packed to the hilt, dim lights, a bottle of 'plonk', lots of 'knowall' girls as a front and in the half-light everyone looked beautiful. The dancing was real, body to body, pre-war stuff and you haven't lived unless you've really danced – asking some beaut guy for a dance, clasping him in your arms and cheek to cheek – sex on the dance floor!

About 1.00 am the Vice Squad used to make its routine call, and when Black Ada opened the door and saw them she would press a bell and we'd all scatter for our seats leaving only the blokes dancing with girls. So by the time the Vice Boys got to the top of the stairs it looked like a Sunday School hop, and Ada used to call out in time to the music 'one, two, turn – one, two. Will the couple on the right keep in step!' We all pissed ourselves at the tables trying to look as if we were studying the waltz. It was hilarious – Ada was very strict and no 'funny' business went on, but in the half dark how could she see all – in fact the favourite dance routine was to dance with your hands down the back of your partner's trousers – oh the buttocks of it all![23]

Sometimes it was a performer, rather than a place, that developed a following. Thus people might go to wherever the fairly butch 'lady baritone' Des Tooley – known as 'The Rhythm Girl' – might be playing. One historian of jazz in Australia has noted, the 'ambiguous lyrics' in many of her songs made 'one believe they were getting away with a lot more in the twenties than is commonly thought'.[24]

Churches, too, despite their official attitude of condemnation and persecution of homosexuals, have often provided a haven for elements of the homosexual community. John Boswell, in *Christianity, Social Tolerance and Homosexuality*, has detailed the romantic homosexual attachments that formed in church institutions in the twelfth century, and the homosexual and homoerotic literature that issued from these same institutions.[25] And in Sydney some 800 years later, there have been similarities. Not only did St Mary's Roman Catholic Cathedral stand guard over the Archibald Fountain in Hyde Park and Boomerang Street, for many years two of Sydney's main

homosexual trysting places; not only were clergymen prominent in the numbers of people arrested for homosexual crimes;
but some religious institutions in the city have been discreetly
tolerant of homosexuality.

While this may not have been common knowledge, it was
certainly known to many homosexuals. One historian, David
Hilliard, commenting on the lack of meeting places for homosexual men, has noted that Anglo-Catholicism

> provided a visible network of supportive and protective
> institutions – not only in England, but also scattered
> through the Anglican church in cities of the United States,
> Canada, South Africa and Australia. Within these Anglo-
> Catholic congregations, homosexual men, compelled by
> social hostility to remain invisible and avoid social disgrace,
> could make contact with each other and establish discreet
> friendships across class barriers.[26]

Probably the best known of these in Sydney was Christ Church
St Laurence, in George Street near Central Railway, which has
always had a most Christ-like tolerance of homosexuality. Back
in the 1920s it was known as a place where a homosexual who
wished to remain a Christian could have his god and his sexuality living in peaceful co-existence. Likewise, St James Church at
Hyde Park had a sympathetic clergy and congregation.[27]

The other major religious institution with associations with
homosexuality was the Theosophist Society; at least its leader,
Bishop Leadbeater, seemed to exercise 'tolerance'. Perhaps,
with the imminent second coming of Christ (through Sydney
Harbour's Heads) it was felt that such minor human foibles
hardly deserved attention. Jack Lindsay has noted that he occasionally saw the Bishop 'in doddering patriarchal gravity amble

across Circular Quay with a bevy of pretty acolytes'.[28] But even a bishop was not beyond the reach of the law, and Leadbeater was eventually in trouble because of repeated allegations about his teaching 'certain practices' to young boys in the Theosophist Society.[29]

The theatre in Sydney was another milieu where homosexuals might gather without attracting undue attention. Here they might play a creative role, as actors, directors, producers or designers, or simply be 'hangers on', the friends or lovers of cast members. Perhaps also they provided a relatively high proportion of the audience. In particular the Independent Theatre in North Sydney, founded by Doris Fitton, and the Minerva in Kings Cross, home of the Minerva Theatre Players, are mentioned as havens for homosexuals.[30] But any theatre would have its homosexually inclined circle of regulars, as did many of the city's musical societies.[31]

Homosexuals have been prominent in the Australian art world too, as they have in other countries. But whereas in European 'high culture' styles of artistic behaviour were quite flamboyant – and indeed in France where it was almost all homosexual, individual artists supported each other in that flamboyance – in Anglo-Saxon society the equivalent groups were 'paralysingly discreet about their sexual heresy'.[32] Australia was clearly in the Anglo-Saxon mould.

Some artists of this period, true to legend, did live a fairly bohemian and overt lifestyle, with coteries of friends who would be in no doubt about their sexual preference. Others who lived a life that on the surface might be more sedate, even suburban, also lived lives in which there would be no doubt about their homosexuality, sometimes with unconventional twists. For instance, Elioth Gruner admitted to Norman Lindsay in 1918 that he had been terrified of going into the army because of his attraction towards his own sex.[33] Lindsay's pained response was not particularly helpful: 'Look, I think it's best to dismiss such a thing from your mind.' But by the mid-1920s, Gruner had settled down with his long-time friend Jack Lecky into a form of domesticity in the Sydney beach suburb of Tamarama.[34] The advent of a new emotional focus for Gruner in 1928, in the form of Brian Cannell, did not disturb these arrangements. Lecky continued to live in the house, while 'Cannell eventually stay[ed] with Gruner as secretary-manager for the rest of his life'.[35]

So far we have been looking at the hotels and restaurants, the coffee shops, the churches, the theatre, the 'artistic milieu' that represent the more 'public' face of the homosexual world as it existed prior to World War II. But hidden from public gaze was another world of overt homosexual sexuality, the 'beat'. Here the important aspect was sexual access: usually for fast, impersonal sex, but often also a place to meet other people of similar sexual preference; and if a sexual encounter occurred later as a result, then so much the better! There was, and still is, a range of places that homosexuals frequent to meet others for predominantly sexual purposes.

In many societies the 'males only' bath-house has a reputation for being a place where homosexual liaisons can either take place or be arranged. What was true of ancient Greece and Imperial Rome was no less true of twentieth-century Sydney. By the 1970s there was a range of 'males only' – and exclusively homosexual – bath-houses scattered around the city. They were far less common in the interwar period but two in particular are remembered with much affection: the old Turkish Baths, at the Oxford Street end of Liverpool Street, and Giles Hot-Sea Baths, which opened in 1928 at the northern end of Coogee Beach. While both were homosexual cruising places, they were dissimilar in other ways.

The Turkish Baths had a predominantly heterosexual clientele, but was also frequented by homosexuals. Like the steam rooms or saunas of some of the leagues clubs today, while often nothing overtly sexual would occur, contact was made. But occasionally people, exercising extreme caution, could 'get off' in the showers at the rear, usually with a third party acting as a lookout.[36] More commonly, after making contact, the men would meet outside and arrange to go to a more suitable place. In the interwar period this was not as easy as it is now. Affluence, changing social mores and the advent of the motor car have given far greater access to places for private sexual encounters. In the interwar period, when fewer young males lived away from the family home, when public transport was less available, or when the motor vehicle remained the preserve of the well-off, such liaisons were less easy to arrange. Bushes in parks sometimes served as a place for sexual encounters, when nothing else was available.

Giles Baths, at Coogee, was different. Situated on a headland near the sea, it had both indoor and outdoor areas, and a tidal pool below it, reached by a set of stone stairs. So at Giles there were many more places for actual sexual encounters to occur, even within the premises.[37] Also there was no fence at water level, so patrons could wander off to secluded places among the rocks just north of Coogee towards Gordons Bay. Giles Baths was remembered more than the Turkish Baths for the amount of sexual activity that occurred either on the premises or nearby.

The elements that made these bath-houses desirable meeting places for homosexuals – an exclusively male clientele, privacy, legitimate reasons for being naked or semi-clad – were shared by another famous building constructed during the 1920s, namely the Bondi Beach Bathing Pavilion. The

Pavilion had a central courtyard with rows of dressing cubicles and showers nearby where sexual cruising and sexual encounters occurred. Most reports say encounters were far more dangerous than at Giles, since supervision was far stricter. Attendants would wander along the rows of dressing cubicles, looking at the floor under the closed wooden doors to check how many pairs of feet were in each cubicle. It wasn't difficult to get around this, though, since each cubicle included a wooden bench along the wall; one participant would simply stand, or crouch, on the bench – which also had other advantages.[38]

Places such as Giles Baths and the Bondi Pavilion dressing sheds are commonly referred to as 'beats' in homosexual parlance. Technically, any place for picking up other men constitutes a 'beat': however, the term has generally – although not always – been confined to outdoor areas where meetings and pick-ups took place rather than hotels, restaurants and coffee shops. There was a large number of outdoor beats around Sydney chosen because they fulfilled necessary criteria: they provided a legitimate reason why men could be there, and were places one could easily strike up a conversation with another person – to ask for a light, for example, or for the time. Such were the opening moves in what might or might not become a pick-up, depending on the response from the other party. One man remembers the unusual approach of his friend who 'would put nail polish on two nails' when he went out at night to the beats to pick someone up, 'and when he'd ask a man for a match [someone he thought might be a homosexual] he'd show those two nails to him as he thanked him for the match. In other words he used a display of effeminacy to signal to the man.'[39]

As already noted the Archibald Fountain in Hyde Park, and Boomerang Street, just down the hill towards Woolloomooloo, were both well-known beats. Hyde Park had been a beat in Sydney since the nineteenth century. The Archibald Fountain provided a major new focus, after it was constructed in 1937 – it was in a park, it was a striking piece of architecture and it was floodlit at night. So people had a reason to be there 'legitimately', casually loitering, either by day or night.[40] And its subject matter, including several well-muscled and nude men, added a nice homoerotic ambience to the setting.

Legend has it that Boomerang Street, below St Mary's Cathedral, provided a convenient place for homosexually inclined priests to meet outsiders; though this could simply reflect commonly held mythology. It did, however, operate as a beat during the 1930s, often in tandem, and occasionally alternating, with the Archibald Fountain.[41] In general, virtually any park in the city could legitimately be claimed to have been a beat, as police arrest statistics attest.

Homosexuals, then, have been imaginative in creating other uses for a range of institutions established by the dominant culture, be they hotels, restaurants, cafes, baths or dressing sheds, and parks. This has been necessary, since they were denied the ways in which heterosexuals could meet each other openly. One of the more contentious beats has been the use of those generally ugly but ubiquitous facilities: public toilets. It is contentious not only because of the alleged nuisance problem, and alleged danger to minors, but also because it involves the issue of 'public' – and multiple partner – sex, notions that some find distasteful. Needless to say, for many male homosexuals, public toilets provided a venue for both fast anonymous sex[42] and also – and more than just occasionally – a place to simply meet others of one's own kind. While many people may find the notion utterly repugnant, it should be pointed out that denying legitimate meeting places to a minority forces them to develop their own, often by subverting institutions of the dominant culture. So beats – and public toilet sex – serve useful social functions for homosexuals and, as many interviewees confirm, sex there has a special frisson – and excitement – because of the dangers involved.

The usefulness of public toilets as beats and meeting places was particularly important in the suburbs, where many homosexuals lived hidden away. They may never have been to a 'camp' bar in their lives, relying on a well-known public toilet, either in their own locality or nearby, to provide the only contact point they knew. The toilets in Petersham Park and those in the park at St Leonards were well-known meeting places, but there is little reason to doubt that countless other public toilet beats existed – and still exist – around Sydney.[43]

Here is a description of the inside of a beat in a darkened public toilet at night:

> Figures moved in the shadows. [He] could hear them
> breathing, watching. He stood stock still. Vague shapes
> began to loom around him, timid and inquiring ... He felt
> hands reach out to touch him. It was eerie, like the blind
> identifying an object by touch alone ... A cigarette lighter
> flared its fire for a moment. It was held high. For a second,
> faces were illuminated around him, then darkness. In the
> flush of light it was like a witches' coven. Faces illuminated
> against dank walls ... male heads, eyes staring, like ancient
> cave paintings. Then darkness again. The unity was
> primeval.[44]

Using 'beats' was not free from danger. First there were the police. Even a casual reading of the newspapers in the interwar period shows that a large proportion of arrests for homosexual behaviour were made in areas known to be 'beats'. Police knew that male homosexuals used toilets in this way, and often set out deliberately to entrap them. As one medical doctor – often called as an expert witness to government committees – later admitted, 'in 1935 … two policemen gave sworn evidence that their vice-squad had arrested in the course of two years over a hundred and fifty men for homosexual offences in one single lavatory in Hyde Park, Sydney. One policeman used to act as decoy within, while the other observed all from outside through trellis work six feet from the ground.'[45]

A second danger came from groups of marauding youths, now known as 'poofter-bashers', who often frequented beats and bashed men they suspected of being homosexuals. Only rarely did details of this surface in the newspapers. Mostly homosexuals would not report these assaults to the police, since to do so would be to draw unwanted attention to themselves, including questions about what they were doing at such a place at such a time.[46]

While the vast majority of homosexuals lived out their lives, like their heterosexual counterparts, in the broad range of Sydney's suburbs, suburbs like Darlinghurst and Woolloomooloo, Kings Cross and Potts Point, had far more visible homosexuals than did, say, Strathfield or Maroubra. These inner-city suburbs attracted a higher-than-average proportion of male homosexuals and were safer places to live. They had a high level of rental accommodation, a transient population and a reputation for less than total social conformity.

Cities have long acted as a magnet attracting those who feel alienated in their rural environment. The continuing diversity of cities makes them more tolerant of social deviance than rural communities. Sydney is no exception. Not only has it drawn homosexuals from rural areas and country towns, but also from New Zealand, the South Pacific and from other Australian cities. As the narrator in Jon Rose's novel, *At the Cross*, is told, 'But you'll love Sydney, and Sydney will be mad about you.'[47] The adventure, the excitement, the anonymity, the relative freedom, the possible contacts, have all been perceived as advantages of Sydney to those escaping more restrictive environments. And within the city, an inordinately large proportion of these questing immigrants have been drawn to the inner-city suburbs.

Aside from these freedoms, the housing stock available was an important underlying factor in the attraction of these suburbs. The usual form of non-family accommodation for young males, prior to the growth of flats, was boarding houses. These could range from the strictly supervised suburban boarding house, with 'prayers before meals', to more casually managed institutions, often in the inner-city areas, with a larger transient population. Many old mansions in Darlinghurst, Kings Cross and Woolloomooloo had been turned into boarding houses. Neighbourhood attitudes also affected the style of boarding houses, and the lack of neighbourhood pressure to conform was a feature of inner-city areas.

The landlady's attitude was also important. Not all would be as tolerant as the one Jon Rose met when he moved to Sydney (he lived in Kings Cross), whose only rules were 'You can drag back [bring people home], but no sailors or negroes.'[48] It is hard to imagine this as the prevalent attitude in, say, Sutherland or St Ives.

During this period, large numbers of new flats were constructed in Sydney, mainly in these same inner suburbs of Darlinghurst and Kings Cross, as well as in the beach and harbour suburbs. Potts Point was a classier suburb where boarding houses and flats predominated, and it attracted lots of homosexuals.

It is hard to over-emphasise the importance of this. In Australia the most common domestic unit is the nuclear family, and the most common housing stock the detached bungalow with the nuclear family as owner-occupier. Flats and boarding houses provided one of the few situations that allowed people to escape family and peer group pressure, and live their lives as they wanted.

These inner-city areas which attracted social deviants of all kinds were perhaps neither the prettiest nor the nicest of suburbs. Jack Lindsay has given us good descriptions of both Woolloomooloo and Darlinghurst in the 1920s. Here is Woolloomooloo:

> Squalid terraced streets falling to the docks of work, ragged with children whooping, slitted with the famished eyes of scandal, stocked with old-clothes shops, and echoing in the night hours with policemen pacing two-by-two … Someone crying out on the other side of the bobbined curtain and the aspidistras; a girl with a head of rat-tails listening with wide-open mouth, fingering a medal of the Virgin Mary; an old woman sitting on a doorstep and feeling her toothless gums.[49]

Darlinghurst likewise was 'not a nice suburb', housing 'a large proportion of brothels and what-nots',[50] and, increasingly, a large proportion of flats.

In the 1920s Kings Cross was 'already an odd area of larrikins and flat-dwellers … [but it] had not yet become Little Paris with awninged cafes under plane trees'.[51] This transformation began during the 1930s; by the end of that decade, the Cross was commonly described as the 'Paris of the Southern Hemisphere'.[52] To one visitor, it seemed 'to consist of nothing but plane trees, continental food shops, coffee houses, milk bars, and chemist shops'.[53] Many of the large blocks of flats had porters, so, like Potts Point, it was more stylish than Darlinghurst or Woolloomooloo. It was also increasingly a haven for homosexuals who were part of everyday life there. This is nicely illustrated in Jack Lindsay's story about trying to help his drunken uncle Percy home at the Cross. Percy wanted to keep on drinking, and as Jack

> tried to pull him across the road away from the pubs, the paperboys ... thought I was a homo dragging home a well-screwed client. They surrounded us and tried to rescue Percy.[54]

In Darlinghurst and Woolloomooloo, and to a lesser extent Kings Cross and Potts Point, homosexuals could live more openly than in more conformist suburbs. Here they had their friends, their cliques, their milieu. Jack Lindsay has described how a friend of his, Yvonne, was an

> honorary member of a group of male homos. She liked them because they had refined manners, helped her in making and choosing her clothes, and were so much more understanding than proper men who just wanted one thing out of a poor girl.[55]

Jon Rose's book teems with descriptions of groups or gatherings where the heterosexual and homosexual worlds overlapped, for instance these guests at a party in the Cross: 'She's an up and coming actress'; 'He's the best window dresser in Sydney'; 'She's a lesbian painter'; 'He's a sailor, "square" and "bi"'; and Milly, 'who it appeared was "on" with another girl'.[56]

Despite these more public areas where homosexuals might meet others, and where they might live, for safety reasons an important component of 'camp' life was lived away from the public gaze. Private ways of meeting other people, such as intro-ductions through friends and at parties, were important. Par-ties could range from small gatherings of friends to large-scale gala events. Jon Rose provides some vivid descriptions of 'camp' parties in his autobiographical novel.

Rose is a supposedly fairly innocent boy from Melbourne and, like Christopher Isherwood in the Berlin stories, his own homosexuality is never discussed. He plays the 'I am a camera' role, observing and recording everything, but never indicating his own preferences or involvement. Here are two descriptions of Sydney 'camp' parties, the first a small-scale gathering, the second a larger, more elaborate affair.

Jon and his landlady, Bella, give the first party for their friends. Jon, the narrator, has been trying to talk to a friend on the phone, when some dancers knock it out of his hands onto the floor:

> Ducking a tray of tasties, I knelt on the floor and bellowed into the phone 'Yes, bring Mo, the tomcat and all, but for God's sake bring the records as well, O.K.?' Then I hung up. A woman said 'Isn't the back of your head sexy?' I said I didn't know I'd never seen it and went back to the kitchen.
>
> As I was searching for the real scotch, Bella came in with some glasses saying, 'Gawed, I'm nearly knocked up'.
>
> I gave her a peck on the cheek and said 'How do you think it's going?'
>
> 'Like stink, and so is all the food and drink. There must be at least eighty people, and all the gate-crashers here. Any of the good scotch left?'

I fished around and found it under the sink. We had barely finished a large slug of scotch and a sausage roll, when a woman neither of us knew lurched into the kitchen saying 'I julst walnt tho thay that itchs a marvelloos plarty. My name's Glorila –'. Then she fell flat on her face. At the very moment she fell the phone and the doorbell went. I left Bella looking after Gloria, and as I saw Edna answering the door, I answered the phone.

'Jon, could I bring a friend?' I didn't know who it was but I said yes and hung up. Then I saw that Edna was letting in Ross and Melinda, together with half the cast of Peter Pan. I was about to say hello when the phone went again.

'Milly here love, I'm on my way with, oh … er … just a sec, what did you say your name was? Norman, my fiancé'. There was a clattering hanging-up sound so I hung up too and moved towards Ross.

'Ah dear boy –'.

'Hello Melinda, let me get you a drink –'. Then the doorbell rang. I excused myself and opened it. The caretaker was outside. After an uncertain, but rather militant shuffle on the doorstep he said 'Good evening, sir. I don't like complaining during a party, but one of your guests has made a filthy mess in the foyer –'.[57]

After dealing with the caretaker, Jon goes back in to the party:

It seemed to be going very well, actors talked with clients, gate-crashers murmured compliments to friends. I was standing watching the people laughing and talking, when I spotted a woman I didn't know sitting with Mr. Sunday [the cat] on her lap. I couldn't see what she was doing, so I had a closer look. I discovered that she was busily making him up with her lipstick. He had large red eyebrows and a mouth bigger than Dorothy Lamour's. I hesitated, then decided to say nothing and looked in at the people dancing in the bedroom.[58]

From here on, however, the party 'degenerates':

The doorbell rang again and I answered it.

The caretaker stood hovering on the stairs again. 'Sorry sir, but there's some of your friends in my bed, and I can't get them out.'

Bella appeared, saying 'Oh no? Well I will, you stay up here and have a drink.'

The caretaker headed towards the kitchen with such eagerness that I wondered, as I watched him, if he'd put the people in his bed on purpose …

Back in the main room I found George playing a tiny piano while Beryl sang 'Nobody Loves a Fairy when she's Forty'. I crept towards the kitchen, opened the door and stepped in. As I tripped, and nearly fell flat on my face, Edna's voice said 'Aw sorry luv. Just 'aving a parley with Bill'. The caretaker and Edna were sitting on the floor with bottles of beer and an ashtray full of ice cubes. Ignoring them I fiddled around under the sink for the scotch. It had all gone, so I poured myself a beer and went back into the party. Melinda grabbed me ... and I sat down beside her and we tried to talk.[59]

The party continues all night, and the next day is spent recovering.

While this party has a 'mixed' ambience, the one described below is strictly a homosexual – and very camp – gathering. Our narrator, Jon again, arrives with Cliff and Dennis, some 'camps' that he has just met:

> By this time we were in a room with kegs of beer, wine bottles and an archway, through which I thought I saw Queen Victoria. She was sitting unmoving on a dais above an incredible mixture of people who were dancing and doing 'swing' in the huge room.
>
> As we moved forward, Cliff muttered 'Bow and don't laugh'. We forced our way through the dancers and up to the throne. Cliff went first.
>
> 'Good evening Your Majesty'. Her Majesty's eyes moved just slightly. Dennis followed saying the same, then they both said 'May we present Jon'. As they did a large arm shot out, the arm ended in a big heavily jewelled hand. I realized that I was supposed to kiss it, as I had seen people do on the films. As my lips and my eyes neared the big rings, I got the shock of my life, and only a slight pressure from Cliff stopped me either from fainting, laughing or vomiting. The orb held in the left hand was a cabbage with a jewelled cross stuck in the top. The rubies and other jewels around the neck were made of radishes and small onions. The sceptre kept in the crook of the outstretched arm was a long tropical fruit

called 'donkey's doodle'. But what really stunned me was the 'hair' and the 'crown'. The 'wig' was made out of dozens of plaited, uncooked, tiny sausages, the crown was a pie of some kind, decorated with everything from radishes and spring onions to 'real' false jewels. I stepped down. The old man's face underneath the crown just looked at me, the eyes watching me with detached intent.[60]

By the early hours of the morning the party had really warmed up.

By then anything up to a hundred people were swaying and dancing, crying, making love in dark corners, or just plain saying 'Come to bed with me'. I didn't care who said or did what, I loved the gilded lot. Victoria had vanished from her throne at midnight.

I was dancing with Milly when Cliff came up and said 'Arnold wants to meet you'.

We left the floor and walked across to a fat man with bright eyes and a pink face. He said 'Welcome to Sydney', then held out his hand to take mine. As I shook his hand, I knew the eyes I spoke to, and the hand I shook, were Victoria's. It was his house. He then clapped his hands and shouted above the din, 'Ladies and gentlemen, the buffet is now open'. Instantly, a collection of ladies, girls, real and false, together with equally mixed gentleman-type ladies, and lady-type gentlemen, hit the archway, and went into the other room, which now had mountains of candle-lit food in it.[61]

The party goes on all night, with new guests constantly arriving.

Suddenly

> standing in the archway was an enormous negress. Satin
> shone on her, feathers of many hues swayed or stood on and
> around her head. Silver fox furs dripped from her glittering
> arms, her shoe heels sparkled with stones. She uttered a low
> 'Hello, dears'. Arnold, looking pinker, had moved forward,
> 'Zoe darling', he rasped. She inclined a cheek towards him,
> and murmured something.[62]

Parties were important for introducing newcomers into the
camp social life of Sydney. For Sydney's bohemian set, parties
were *the* social institution of the 1920s. They were not always
as lavish as the one described above, but even the most lavish
paled into insignificance when compared to the Artists' Balls, a
recurring feature of bohemian life in Sydney in this period.

The Artists' Balls, bursting with vitality, with their prom-
ise of dancing, abundant alcohol and the possibilities of sexual
adventure, were part of the chaotic response to the horrors and
privations of World War I. First held in Sydney Town Hall,
the balls took their cue from the Parisian art students' Bal des
Quart'z' Arts, the Chelsea Arts Ball and their Berlin counterparts. They were known for their frenetic behaviour and fantasy
costumes. The 1922 ball was described by the *Sydney Morning
Herald* as

> indisputably the most spectacular dance that has taken place
> in the city.
>
> The decorations were in no sense Puritanical. Jazz was the
> keynote in colouring and general tone. The grotesque figures,
> reaching from the floor to the top of the gallery, were most

arresting, and were painted by different artists …

A vaudeville entertainment was given in the early part of
the evening … [and] the basement was the great attraction
of the evening. It was decorated with hessian, and plastered
with picture film advertisements.

It would be impossible to detail the costumes. Hundreds
of people were in fancy dress, others in dominoes, and
altogether it was both weird and wonderful.[63]

Imaginative costumes were *de rigeur*. Dulcie Deamer, a fixture of Sydney's bohemian life, came to the 1923 ball dressed
as a cavewoman in a wrap-around leopard-skin hide, complete
with a dogtooth necklace. The 1924 theme was 'Back to Childhood', which inspired some outrageous costumes. The Town
Hall was crammed to bursting with plump adults in everything
from skimpy nappies to little girlie frocks and sunbonnets. The
Town Hall pillars were decorated with winking kewpie dolls,
while friezes hanging from the galleries were adorned with Jazz
Age nursery rhymes. It was perhaps the most notorious of the
Artists' Balls; 'it turned, if not into an orgy, then into a veritable
bacchanalia'.[64] Dulcie Deamer later noted:

Dreadful tales relating to the Ladies' and Gents' retiring
rooms were town talk afterwards. Apparently they
were as congested as the rest of the building – and very
indiscriminately.[65]

Aside from such 'disreputable' happenings, alcohol consumption also caused problems, leading to drunken brawls. At the
1922 ball, someone spiked the claret cup with whisky, leading

to what was described as 'shocking, scandalous, and disgraceful' behaviour in the alcoves. Eventually the police began monitoring the event, searching people for grog at the door and refusing entry to 'the riff-raff'. Indeed, the 1925 ball became known as the Policeman's Ball, as 'they appeared to be stationed only paces apart',[66] everywhere throughout the Town Hall.

Under this sort of scrutiny, the balls lost their allure, and by the late 1920s they had become far more tame affairs, held elsewhere, with bans on alcohol and more police on hand. They continued on into the 1930s, but ceased with the outbreak of war.

In their way, the parties after the Mardi Gras parades from the early 1980s mirrored those Artists' Balls from the earlier decades. All those old euphemisms – 'artistic, theatrical, musical' – that once referred to people like us, were certainly on display in the Mardi Gras parties when they became extravaganzas. Many had breathtaking shows, but one particularly remains in my mind.

It was the 1988 party, the tenth anniversary of the first Mardi Gras. The DJs had been keeping the dancers going, sweaty but inexhaustible, fuelled by whatever. At some time well after midnight, the music suddenly seemed to pause, the lights dimmed, and as 'Chain Reaction' started to pound out, a spotlight swung onto the stage at one end of the Royal Hall of Industries. And then, up from behind the stage-wide staircase, came not one Diana Ross, but five of them, in fiery red dresses. And as they came down towards the front of the stage, the cheers and whistles roared out across the crowded dance floor. Then suddenly, another spotlight lit the other end of the hall, and on a similar stage there, another five, similarly attired, appeared. And in perfect sync, the ten of them choreographed and mimed their way through that anthem. The crowd went wild, and maybe there was an encore, but what could possibly follow an act like that?

Well, at 4.30 am, to the sounds of 'Stormy Weather', two huge wind machines and tens of kilos of paper snow transformed the hall into a perfect blizzard. At the end of the night, we staggered out into the nearly dawn of Moore Park, and then back to Oxford Street.

As for other parties, some things are best not expanded on. Why, one year, was a DJ set up in the darkened men's toilet? And why, another year, did so many men come back into the party with hay all over their bedraggled clothes? – the horse stables having been put to good use.

But they are other stories …

Books such as Lindsay's *The Roaring Twenties* and Rose's *At the Cross*, interviews and various biographies help paint a picture, and raise several points about the interwar Artists' Balls. State Parliament debated the 'disgraceful events' that were said to have occurred there, with some politicians being particularly concerned about 'the presence of a notorious type of effeminate male, whose behaviour at times was disgusting'; and newspapers reported on them.[67] Many of these balls had large numbers of homosexually inclined patrons, and it was one of the rare occasions when they were able to flaunt themselves publicly. While the police attitude to these public spectacles was vehemently hostile, particularly to their predominantly homosexual patrons, other people whom the homosexuals knew or met in the inner-city areas generally had a more sympathetic attitude. Admittedly this was where many homosexuals lived and where they were not seen as unusual freaks. They were not an ostracised minority, just another group of people in the precinct.

A final point is the interesting similarities with some of the great drag balls that occurred in European cities in the same period. As Stefan Zweig notes, 'even the Rome of Suetonius had never known such orgies as the balls of Berlin, where hundreds of men costumed as women, and hundreds of women costumed as men danced under the benevolent eyes of the police'.[68] And Paris was also known to have its great drag balls. The major dissimilarity between the situations in Europe and Sydney – apart from the scale of course – was the role of the police. In Sydney police raided the balls rather than tolerated them.

Other gala events on the calendar for socially inclined homosexuals in Sydney included parties in the Blue Mountains, west of Sydney. These were a major form of entertainment, mainly for the well-off. Information on homosexuality – and a camp world – in the Blue Mountains comes from interviews, novels and autobiographies.

Sumner Locke Elliott's novel *Eden's Lost*, partly set in the Blue Mountains in this period, gives some vivid descriptions of life at one of the mountain hotels, but only alludes to homosexuality. The manager, Mr Marcus, is a 'middle-aged fairy',[69] with 'a velvet fuzz in his voice and an arch to his shoulders which gave rise to doubts, yet was not effeminate, not like the wispy boys Angus [the hero of the story] was used to seeing in coffee shops' in the city.[70] Mr Marcus flirts slightly with Angus, who is a friend of the hotel owners. When Angus tells Mr Marcus that he is willing to do anything around the hotel, Mr Marcus's response is predictable: "Anything?" Mr Marcus gleamed faintly and smiled his weary little smile: "Well, I certainly can find a use for you when there are turned backs".'[71] There are also a couple of descriptive passages, commenting on women dancing together, 'oddly sapphic and out of keeping with the spirit of respectability that hung as a pall over everything',[72] but little that gives us any information on a hidden world.

The main source of information about homosexual social life in the mountains comes from interviews. While many interviewees report stories of lavish house parties in the mountains, mainly on long weekends, none have first-hand knowledge, although many knew people involved.[73] Interestingly, several of these second-hand stories tell of a Queen Victoria figure who held parties in the mountains in this period, but with a proper frock, and wig made of steel-wool rather than sausages.

The homosexual world in Sydney in the interwar period was secret, fragmentary and tainted by its illegality. The dominant heterosexual culture set the rules, and there was little questioning, even by the persecuted themselves, of their designation or place in society. Most male homosexuals largely accepted society's stigmatisation, and lived lives haunted by guilt; the majority lived in suburbia and faced the problems of earning a living, conducting relationships or planning for the future, as did their heterosexual counterparts. But the one major difference – their sexuality – meant that they faced a whole series of legal and social sanctions that contorted their lives in fundamental ways. They had to live with society's condemnation that they were perverts – whether predatory or effeminate, or both – who should be dealt with by the full force of the law.

While most homosexuals managed to live out their lives despite these sanctions, an important part of it was under a cloak of secrecy. They met other homosexuals, but only with discretion. Because of their stigma they inhabited a double world: the world of the dominant culture, and their own privatised homosexual world. One feature of this 'double life' was how it gave a 'double purpose' to many institutions of Australian society. Many hotels, restaurants, cafes, parks, bath-houses, dressing pavilions and public toilets had not only their specified 'dominant culture' function, but were also homosexual cruising or pick-up places.

Like the tip of an iceberg, aspects of homosexual life in Sydney in this period were visible, but only on a small scale. Clearly some men had a sense of themselves as different, and took an identity based around their sexual preference. They had words to describe themselves – 'camp' and 'queens'; they had milieux in which they could live fairly openly – as clubs such as Black Ada's and the scenes in Jon Rose's book attest. They had ways of meeting others like themselves, and places to do so. They had their argot, and their territory.

The inner-city suburbs were more congenial places for homosexuals to live, and in a few places they could be reasonably open; but this territory was only held at risk. A general blanket of secrecy surrounded the homosexual world and only occasionally did the wider world became aware of it: either in oblique newspaper references, usually regarding the 'crimes' of homosexuality, or in the exotic flowerings of the Artists' Balls that occurred occasionally, in which the persecuted minority put on its full plumage and thumbed its nose at outraged society. And society of course retaliated, with the full force of the law.

But something was about to occur that would start a process of change, although it was not to be a smooth progression.

CHAPTER 3

AN END TO UNKNOWING

The impact of war and the Kinsey Report

Two events in the 1940s had major effects on the lives of men with homoerotic desire. They were World War II, and the publication of Alfred Kinsey's *Sexual Behavior in the Human Male* in 1948. Both were important, albeit in different ways.

The war acted as a catalyst for dramatic changes in social behaviour, in particular sexual behaviour. It shook Australians out of the Depression; indeed, it can be argued that economic recovery only began when the government started large-scale spending in a war economy. And the 'war in the Pacific' had a much greater impact on Sydney and its institutions than World War I; one net effect was that thousands of men and women were able to witness or experience, for the first time, the realities of homoerotic sexuality and love. This not only gave immediate experiential rewards, it had impacts in the longer term.

If war led to a widening and deepening of homosexual experiences in Australia, the Kinsey Report in 1948 was important in showing just how widespread such practices were in modern society. Works such as Kinsey's paved the way for new theories about 'deviant' sexuality. The 1940s was an important decade in Australia's social history because it started the 'end to unknowing' about homoeroticism and homosexuality in Australia.

Many writers have noted the dramatic effects that war can have on societies, at an individual level and in unforeseen directions. As Arthur Marwick has spelled out, 'we see how often the changes which actually took place are totally at variance with the deliberate intentions of political and other leaders'.[1] This was certainly the case in Australia, particularly as far as the lives of those with homoerotic feelings were concerned.

It has become commonplace to acknowledge the intimate link between war and sexuality. This can be seen in the high incidence of rape in war conditions, the officially 'recognised' brothels to service soldiers in many campaigns, and, most recently, the fairly grudging admissions that homosexuality occurs in the armed forces. One commentator has suggested that the

> atmosphere of emergency and the proximity of violence
> will always promote a relaxing of inhibitions ending in a
> special hedonism and lasciviousness. And of course a deeper
> affection as well.[2]

Under wartime conditions, old-time sexual mores in Australia were often abandoned. Some saw this in a positive light. As a character in Eric Lambert's wartime novel *The Veterans* says, 'War turned people inside out. They were unafraid of taboos, and adventures were everyday things.'[3] But moralists and newspaper columnists condemned the 'new immorality', implying it would lead to imminent social collapse. Indeed by the end of the war and in the early postwar era, conservative church and community leaders were bewailing the state of society.[4] No good, they insinuated, could come from such dramatic changes.

They complained that too many women were throwing themselves at soldiers, and it was true that many women became involved with visiting Allied soldiers – particularly the

Americans.[5] Yet while most of the emphasis was on the hetero-sexual abandonment of traditional morality, wartime conditions also presented many opportunities for the development of same-sex relationships. Love often flowered within the sex-segregated institutions of the military. Paul Fussell, in a major study of love, war and sexuality, has pointed out that often, due to the heightened emotional conditions of war, 'the gender of the beloved will not matter very much'.[6]

In societies less reticent than Anglo-Saxon ones, this tradition has often been noted, and indeed, even seen to have its advantages. Antiquity records the existence in Greece of the Theban Band, 'a regiment of mature soldiers, each paired with a younger homosexual companion, who fought to the death in defence of their country and in honour of their love bond'.[7] Recently even Anglo-Saxon reticence has slipped, and several major imperial or military figures such as Cecil Rhodes and Major General Sir Hector MacDonald, KCB, DSO, known as 'Fighting Mac', have had other sides to their character revealed.[8] English writer JR Ackerley has candidly noted that in the war his 'personal runners and servants were usually chosen for their looks; indeed this tendency in war to have the prettiest soldiers about one was observable in many other officers; whether they took more advantage than I dared ... I do not know'.[9]

Playwright Noel Greig, talking of his work on war and sexuality, argued that the 'armed forces were not all full of virile heterosexuals, and a love affair between two young men was highly likely'. He goes on: 'It is well known, but never admitted, that in armed forces at war, passionate relationships do develop between soldiers.'[10] Of course Australia's Nobel Prize–winning novelist Patrick White met his love and life partner Manoly Lascaris during the war.

Despite this long association of homoerotic relationships or more in war conditions, the official response of the Australian military to homosexuality was largely one of non-recognition. The official history of the Australian Army Medical Services in World War I states that there was 'no evidence pointing to any significant homosexuality in the [Australian Infantry Force] and this is on a par with Australian experience in general'.[11] The denials of homosexuality among the Australian troops in World War II were similar. As former President of the Victorian RSL, Bruce Ruxton, stated, 'I don't remember any queers or poofters. I don't know where all these gays and poofters have come from. I don't remember a single one from World War II.'[12] These statements, however, should not be taken too seriously, reflecting as they do the preconceptions or the prejudices of the speakers. A range of other sources give us clearer glimpses of what was actually occurring.

Despite the hysteria of conservative moralists, there is little evidence to indicate any rapid deterioration of the country's social fabric. Indeed, all evidence points to the contrary: that – despite what a small very visible minority might be doing – prevailing social attitudes to a wide range of things changed very little. Material from the time – newspaper reports, sex manuals, church sermons – as well as modern academic studies, memoirs or oral histories of the wartime years, all indicate a continuity of prewar ideas and perceptions into the 1940s. This was certainly true of most people's attitudes to sex and sexuality, and there is no reason to believe it would be otherwise. As historian David Walker has noted, why should there be any difference when 'those who fought in the Second World War were raised within the narrow boundaries of the (existing) sex education literature'.[13] Indeed a major study of Australian wartime experiences and attitudes, John Barrett's *We Were There*, implies that, for most Australians, attitudes did not alter dramatically over the war years.[14] Certainly there was little change in public attitudes to homosexuality.

On the other hand, Walker does go on to confirm that the war provided a widening of experiences: 'Marital disruption, prostitution, adultery, masturbation and homosexuality were far closer in war than they had been in peace.'[15] Whether this broadening of experiences would radically change attitudes – or loosen moral control – is another matter. But there does appear to have been more reportage on homosexual activity during the war in Sydney. This probably reflected a greater newspaper awareness of the issue, rather than any accurate knowledge of increasing activity. The wartime reports of 'civvy' homosexual activity differed little in attitudes and assumptions to prewar reports. The same uncertainty about what it represented, the same occasional sympathetic or perceptive articles, but also the same desire of some newspapers to bolster sales by sensationalising the issues. It tied in nicely with the perception of Australia at war being 'under threat'.

For example, in 1941 the Melbourne *Truth* revealed the existence of a 'sensational vice ring ... threatening the entire Commonwealth'.[16] In fact a small group was circulating through the mail physical culture magazines profusely illustrated with photos of semi-clad men. These magazines, 'falling somewhere between exercise manuals and erotica',[17] had long served a necessary function of providing men with homoerotic desires with 'a potent if limited source of sexual fantasy'[18] at a time when little homosexually erotic material was generally available. They were also important for men with homoerotic feelings who were either loath, or unable, to acknowledge these feelings. Because the magazines had another purpose – the creation of health and vitality through physical fitness – the photos of men's bodies 'could be looked at, admired, venerated, and even desired, safe in the knowledge that one was only interested in abstracted aesthetics, a concept which was reinforced by the use of terms such as "physical culture".[19] In this case, since the photographs were of the beefcake variety, rather than of the cheesecake variety (the latter were undoubtedly used for similar erotic or sexual purposes, and hung in their thousands in lockers or huts in troop barracks around Australia), the newspapers were able to create the impression of an immense scandal. But Australian society was immune to collapse from the vast weight of erotic material that emerged during the war, especially that condoned in the military barracks. In this case it wasn't even a seven-day wonder – it died in the face of news about far more real threats faced in the war zones.

Newspaper reports of course tell us only of homosexuality as a crime or as a 'freak-show', as articles that appeared over the war period show. Headlines such as 'Boy-Girl Becomes Mother', 'Headmaster on Serious Charge – Love letters to RAAF Lad once his College Pupil', 'Gay Masquerader Takes Last Curtain', 'It's a Boy, Not a Girl – Read Astounding Story on Page 8', 'Glamour "Girls" Didn't Fool U.S. Provost Man', 'Lolly Boys Tell of Alleged "Initiation"', 'Men Dressed as Girls had Painted Nails', 'Strange Death of Man in Women's Clothing', 'Boys Charges Against Man', 'Soldiers Strange Story of Death Fight – Known as Dulcie', all brought homosexuality increasingly into the public eye, by portraying people with homoerotic desire as perverts, freaks or child molesters.[20]

In 1942 police and Military Police raided a party at a Scout Hall in Annandale and arrested five men who appeared in court the next day. Four of them were still in drag, 'with their faces powdered and their hair permed … though it was a shame that nasty beards marred the otherwise glamorous appearance', the *Sunday Telegraph* reported.[21] The youngest of these was an

18-year-old army deserter, which explains the presence of the Military Police. He was also the most stylish dresser, in 'black frock, beaded and low cut, with fox furs. Earrings and a heavy matching silver necklet, gold anklets over sheer silk stockings, and high heel shoes.'[22]

Despite such limited perceptions of homosexuality at the level of public discourse, during the war many people enjoyed a wide range of homoerotic experiences that often bore little resemblance to the images purveyed in newspapers. Many of these homoerotic experiences occurred in the armed forces, often in war zones, and – occasionally – under appalling conditions. One inmate of Changi camp has recorded that 'Homosexuals were about', and another prisoner of war, who worked on the Burma railway, claimed that 'homosexuality was evident in many cases in POW areas'.[23]

It's worth noting in passing, too, that it wasn't only Australian women who found American servicemen attractive. John O'Donnell, for example, an Australian serviceman in New Guinea, remembers his encounters with American servicemen thus:

> In my job I was working closely with the Yanks, and I had
> a pretty good liaison with them. Even though it was out-
> of-bounds, I went to their base often, with a friend to see
> the movies they showed. And often, after showing a Shirley
> Temple movie, or whatever, they'd show some porn, pretty
> poor-quality stuff, but porn, and it got all the guys horny.
> They had an old hut on a hill behind the movie area, and
> nobody ever used it. And my friend and I often went up
> there after the porn, and lots of the negro Yanks were up
> there too, looking for sex. I'd just sort of lay on the bed, and
> go at it, and when I got too hot and bothered, head for the

shower where it would all start again. They used to really love to fuck 'white ass'. I found the negro soldiers nice people usually, they wanted to give you something, grog, food or clothing, which was most prized by the Aussies. I refused, saying I wasn't a prostitute. All I wanted was for them to be friends, and some became good friends.[24]

Gore Vidal, the American writer, has reminisced fondly about the homosexual activity of many Australian servicemen in World War II. But his observation, that the Australian soldiers had a reputation right across the Pacific for rolling over on their stomachs most obediently, ought to be seen as somewhat tongue-in-cheek.[25]

Wartime homoerotic experiences were not, of course, confined to military bases and war zones; and these experiences cannot simply be dismissed as 'situational homosexuality'. Many men who had plenty of previous homosexual experience, and who thought of themselves as 'camp', continued to have homoerotic experiences, even love affairs, during the war. One Australian soldier remembered an affair thus:

It was while I was stationed at St Ives that I had a real 'affair', something that was exciting for both of us. I was at a railway station one day, waiting to go into the city. I was on weekend leave, and I got chatting to this Air Force sergeant who was stationed at Bradfield, he was going back into the city on leave too, he was going to visit his sister. Well, we just clicked, he and I, and soon we were having an affair. We'd spend as much time as we could together, and our favourite thing to do – and we did it lots – was to go to the Jenolan Caves for weekends.

We'd get our leave together, and on Friday afternoons catch
the train to Mount Victoria, where the bus met us to take us
to the Caves House. I remember we'd always sit at the back
of the bus – we must have looked good, him in his Air Force
Uniform and me in my Army khakis – and he'd always get a
hard-on. We'd put our greatcoats over our knees, and have a
good time till we got to the hotel. It was always so much fun.[26]

Since the evidence varies, it is hard to determine the general reaction of Australian soldiers to homosexuality. We have
seen above that discretion was thought necessary when satisfy-
ing homoerotic desires amid a prevailing fear of homosexuality.
There was also quite explicit homophobia, such as that of Bruce
Ruxton. Indeed, a range of novels written about the war period
indicates the generally homophobic attitudes that prevailed.
Lawson Glassop's two war novels, *We Were The Rats* and *The Rats
in New Guinea*, both have incidents concerning homosexuality.
In the former novel, published in 1945, the author describes one
scene where a radio announcer with 'an odiously ingratiating
voice' is giving his program. The men call out, 'turn that pansy
bastard off'.[27] In another scene, two men fight after calling each
other 'pansies'. Afterwards, when they become friends, one gives
his reason for fighting: 'I thought ya was a bit of a queen.'[28] In
The Rats in New Guinea, published some years after the war, the
author gives his version of the average digger's attitudes. The
hero, Reynolds, overhears a soldier taunting a newcomer to the
unit, a radio actor:

Nice suede shoes and big muscles. Perce the Pansy, the
darling of the pooftas' parade at the Cross ... knock, knock,
who's there? Baxter. Baxter who? Backs to the wall, here
comes John Hemilton.[29]

Reynolds becomes quite worried: 'Surely Hemilton was not a queer. That was one thing you feared – having a queer in your section.'[30]

Yet other evidence suggests tolerance of individual homosexuals at a day-to-day level. In Barrett's book on Australian soldiers at war, one contributor gave grudging admiration to 'a queer' who, during an escape from a POW camp in Austria, 'strangled a German guard with the piece of phone cable'.[31] Another contributor, an artillery captain who won the Military Cross, noted that 'we had cases of homosexuals falling in love. In the interests of general happiness we re-arranged some room occupants and eventually got all homos in one block.'[32] This may have been to quell nervousness on the part of the majority – homosexuals after all were supposed to be predatory perverts – but it was a reasonably humane solution, and one that the 'homos' probably didn't object to! Potentially they might not have to leave their hut to find 'others like themselves'; indeed, it is likely that they found the war less sexually austere than their heterosexual counterparts.

Such ambivalent responses to homosexuality in the Australian military are not unexpected: after all, they are probably a fair reflection of general Australian attitudes. It is also possible that after the war many Australian soldiers, whose minds were not closed, were less prejudiced against individual homosexuals, since they had often fought beside them and not found them wanting. As Barrett notes, 'the homosexual, of course, could be as effective a soldier as anyone else'.[33]

For 'drag queens', a group usually perceived as homosexual, the war provided both opportunity and unexpected legitimisation. Paradoxically what was seen as evidence of terrible degeneracy in peacetime was quite acceptable in war service: doing it for 'King and Country' made it okay.

During World War II many of the entertainment troupes that travelled around to lighten the lives of the soldiers had shows which required 'femmes' (a sanitised name for 'drag queens'). In many cases, 'femmes' were people with previous experience in 'throwing on a frock'.[34] Indeed, some were so good in their impersonation they attracted male admirers. Michael Pate's potted history of these entertainment troupes gives one such amusing story:

> The femmes of the show were always a great success with audiences. One night during the show I was standing at our 'stage door' – a flap in the dressing-room tent attached to the rear of the stage – with Hugh, one of our drivers who also functioned as security man (he'd been a drover in the Northern Territory). A slightly drunk, smallish black soldier of the US Army came backstage in the middle of the show, asked Hugh 'Are you hep to the jive?', and proceeded to dance on the grass outside the dressing-room. He then said to Hugh, 'Ah must see that woman!' Hugh told him there were no women around, only men. The black soldier insisted he had seen women dancing on-stage during the show, adding he fancied the 'little one'. (From the description this was Jimmy Ricketts.) The black soldier produced a thick wad of paper money (won at a crap game?) and said to Hugh, 'I'll give you all o' this if Ah can see that woman!' It took some time for Hugh and me to convince him that he had seen only female impersonators on the stage. Our 'girls' were so talented and beautiful-looking they could have fooled anyone!!![35]

Military men had their admirers too.

I remember a book that we had on our bookshelves, *Khaki and Green: with the Australian Army at home and overseas.*

Published in 1943 by the Australian War Memorial, it was a morale booster, for both the 'fighting men of Australia' who contributed to it and for those 'at home'.

It contained stories, verse, paintings and drawings by soldiers themselves, as well as photographs. As a young schoolboy I read some of the stories – some comic, some poignant – but the illustrations particularly drew my attention.

No names were given; the contributors were only identified by a numeric of sorts. Thus the two ruggedly handsome 'Jungle Fighters' in their camouflage with face paint, blending in with the foliage, was painted by B3/59, as was the smooth dark muscular bodies in 'Stretcher bearers, New Guinea'.

Several pen drawings showed naked men in the showers, mostly discreet back views, although one showed two men under a bucket shower, one scrubbing the other's back as they laughed together. That was contributed by NX 15943.

I did wonder about one drawing, of two soldiers in front of a bazaar stall somewhere exotic. One of them was holding up against his body a woman's lacy negligee, while the other, smoking a cigarette, looked a bit quizzical. Now I would presume that they were discussing buying something for the girlfriends back home, but what did I think back then?

But the one that I kept going back to, again and again, was titled 'Concert Party, Milne Bay'. It depicted a group of smiling young soldiers watching as one of the 'showgirls', having taken off her falsies, was peeling off her wig, revealing a very attractive young man, grinning back at them.

The changes being wrought by wartime conditions were evident in Sydney. This was apparent to anyone who had been in Sydney before the war, and who had cause to return there during the war: 'The demands of industry had mobilised juveniles and single women; a variety of retired people had been reabsorbed into the workforce; married women were spending half-days working for charitable organisations, and added to it all was the presence of the American servicemen, white and black.'[36]

Sydneysiders adapted to the wartime conditions as best they could – dealing with blackouts, rent control, coupons for such basics as meat, butter, tea and groceries, and petrol rationing. Home brewing of beer became a 'necessary' pastime for men who remained in the city. Women attempted to raise families, hold down jobs, and deal with the unexpected in a topsy-turvy world.

Under the pressures of war, life in the city not only became more fraught with problems, but also more frenetic. Blackouts at night created an atmosphere of mystery and foreboding. Kylie Tennant, in *Tell Morning This*, describes two characters driving through the darkened city one night:

> Shut shops, shut entry ways, blind alleys, newspaper kiosks, advertisement hoardings slipped into the darkness. The searchlights were working through the clouds like the fingers of a woolclasser through fleece, delicately with knowledge, but the bandaged blind city that once wore a gay mantilla of light had done up its beauties in twists of steel and barricades of brick. Hysterical, corrupt, uneasy over those hornet humming dangers from the north, those silver flies for which the searchlights combed and swung and combed again, the city of Sydney turned on its stone pillows to sleep.[37]

The evidence of war is all-intrusive, even in the sleeping city:

> Docks boiled with activity, the arc lights blazing, cargo swinging into the holds of ships. Loaded lorries bumped

down to the wharves. Trucks squealed through the dark shunting goods yards. All night long the whistling and squealing would deny the pretence of sleep that lay over the city, and not until two, three, four in the morning would there come that deadline of stillness that heralded the paper trucks, the milk and bread of a new day.[38]

In this world of carrying on with the mundane, but being prepared for the unexpected, the continuity and change in Sydney's homosexual camp world mirrored what was occurring in the homosexual subcultures around the world affected by the war.[39] Most of the established venues for the homosexually inclined continued: the Long Bar in the Australia Hotel, the Carlton, Ushers and Pfahlert's (all major city hotels) continued to attract patrons, and wartime trade boosted their clientele enormously. Likewise large numbers of servicemen now frequented the so-called 'salt-meat alley' pubs along George Street (especially the Belfields), which remained major places for picking up other homoerotically inclined men. Restaurants such as the Shalimar and the Latin Cafe were still popular places to go with groups of similarly inclined, or with a 'date' or lover.

Coffee shops burgeoned too. Repins in King Street was still favoured, but during the war, coffee shops in Kings Cross, which became a major focus for soldiers on leave looking for a good time, experienced a heyday. The Californian in Darlinghurst Road and the Arabian were both frequented by a homosexual clientele.[40]

A netherworld of short-lived bars and 'sly-grog' drinkeries also flourished during the war. Black Ada's, perhaps a forerunner, boasted lots of young servicemen. One patron remembers many young soldiers and sailors who 'loved it, and packed in to be groped'.[41] But despite the advantage of having all the 'perverts' in one place under their eyes, the Vice Squad closed Ada's early in the war years, considering it too dangerous and corrupting to the young military personnel who flocked there.[42] After this, a spate of other short-lived clubs followed. Jon Rose describes them in *At the Cross*. There were also nightclubs where drag artistes might appear: Lea Sonia was a major attraction at Maxine in Oxford Street, Woollahra, and the Ziegfeld Club in King Street in the city was the favoured haunt of Harry Foy, another drag artiste.

Not all homosexually inclined men, of course, would want to patronise such places. As before the war, the major homophile churches, Christ Church St Laurence and St James, continued to attract a certain sort of homosexual, for whom the high camp elements of ritual, decor and style were important components of their religion.

And of course the ubiquitous beats flourished. The Turkish Baths in Liverpool Street, Giles Baths at Coogee and the dressing sheds at Bondi Pavilion, like their counterparts in San Francisco, all attracted servicemen among their homoerotically inclined clientele.[43] The back rows of the new movie and newsreel theatres provided a place for erotic encounters in a darkened environment, or even for just meeting others like oneself.[44] Toilets at city railway stations were another common meeting spot. The line from the wartime melody 'I'll be seeing you in all the old familiar places' was quite true for many 'camps'. Hyde Park was still a centrally located meeting place, where many night-time encounters occurred. The nearby Domain was also a much-favoured cruising place at night.

The sexually charged atmosphere of the times meant that 'cruising' other men was no longer confined to the strictly defined territory of the beats: it was now possible even in the city's streets. Several soldiers remember their leave in Sydney as being very cruisy – they picked up other men simply walking from Town Hall down 'salt-meat alley', past the many pubs there, or from Town Hall, up Park Street (which becomes William Street) into the Kings Cross area.[45]

The war added its own frisson, with a few extra twists. For example, after Japan's entry into the war in December 1941, a number of air raid shelters were constructed in Sydney. Many built around the city – in the parks or in the Domain – were put to good use by the homoerotically inclined when there was no air raid alert.[46] The darkened atmosphere, the sealed environment and the ability to restrict entry made them like the fuck bars that appeared 30 or so years later.

One aspect that surfaced into public awareness in this period was the camp world's proclivity for gender inversion. At its most mundane level camp men had a tendency to refer to male friends and other camp men as 'she' or 'her': a friendly spoof of the square world's perspectives, turning things a bit topsy-turvy. (It had no implication that one was either effeminate or would wear women's clothes.)

A more elaborate manifestation, not only among camp men in the more overt world of bars and beats, but also among those who moved in their interlocking friendship networks, was that of endowing oneself – or being given by friends – a woman's first name. The name could be chosen in a variety of ways. Sometimes simply by converting your first name into a close female equivalent: thus John could become 'Jeanette' or 'Janet' (an extra twist if one's surname was Lee). Others might take a more alliterative approach, picking a woman's name that matched the first letter of the man's surname: thus someone with the surname Hutley might become 'Hilda'. Or it could be the first name of a famous person (often an actress) with the same surname, much like, as previously noted, 'Sydney's Oscar

Wildes' did in the late nineteenth century world: someone called Williams, for example, might be known as 'Esther' (after the Hollywood swimming star). Often the names represented clever associations and worked on several levels. One from a later period – 'Flora Numbers' – referred to its owner's penchant for spending a lot of time lying on the floor at 'Numbers', one of Sydney's sleazy 'back rooms'. Another – 'Carmen Sutra', also from a later period – was a clever amalgam of two interests in its bearer's life: his passion for opera and his ethnic background. This penchant of the homosexual world clearly added colour to its traditions.

Some of the habitués of this reasonably open world were well known to police, even by their camp names. When details of such 'peculiarities' appeared in the newspapers, who knows what a confused public thought. It may have been incomprehensible, or seen as further proof of the effeminacy or degeneracy of the homosexually inclined, or noted as a liberation from stereotypes and an instance of subversive humour. Some of the names that surfaced into the public gaze via the newspapers in the 1940s – 'Lana' Turner, 'Rita' Hayworth and 'Vivien' Leigh – were well-known identities in the camp world. Others included 'Balmain Betty' and 'Coogee Clive', whose names came from the suburbs they lived in. One American marine who fell in with Sydney's camp world was so impressed by all this that he called himself 'Toongabbie Tex' while he was here.[47]

It is hard to gauge the impact of the Americans. Sydney did not become an American village like Brisbane, despite hosting a large number of US personnel. Many of the American soldiers were often far more sophisticated than the locals, especially those from the major cities like New York, Chicago or San Francisco who were familiar with homosexual bar life. Many fitted well into Sydney's camp scene, and much information about homosexual life overseas was passed on in this way.

Some found the Americans so alluring that they would go to any lengths to get them. Neville McQuade, a young Sydney-sider, who appeared in court several times for wearing women's clothes – once he even wore them at his trial – was caught 'simpering coyly with several American servicemen'.[48] He had been dancing at the Trocadero in Sydney when confronted by a policeman, and 'admitted he was there to pick up American servicemen'.[49] McQuade got off with a fine, but not all camp men in pursuit of Americans were so lucky, since not all Americans were cool sophisticates able to deal with such unusual situations. The female impersonator Harry Foy, for example, was dancing at the Ziegfeld Club just before Christmas 1942, wearing a mix of women's and men's clothing. He attempted to kiss an American sailor, who punched him to the ground. Foy never regained consciousness, and died the next day.[50]

New words made their appearance. 'Camp' or 'Kamp' were still used to describe the homosexual world, or someone who was homoerotically inclined and did something about it. 'Square' was still used to describe the 'other' – the outside heterosexual world and those who inhabited it.[51] The word 'cat' might be used to describe someone who liked sex with other men,[52] while 'dolly dimples', 'tootsies' or 'tootsie dolls' were terms applied to lesbians.[53] In conversation one could often use initials as short-hand conversation, to avoid being overheard – or understood – by either unsympathetic ears or the subject of the conversation. Thus 'TBH' stood for 'to be had' – someone who could be propositioned and gotten off with. 'NTBH' signalled failure – 'not to be had'. Alcohol played its role in homosexual seduction no less than in heterosexual seduction: 'TBHID' 'to be had in drink', meant someone whose inhibitions might be lowered by a few drinks.[54] In fact the word 'gay' used in its modern sense might

well have made its first appearance in Sydney during the war –
or so some Sydney residents who had contacts with Americans
remember.[55] Certainly American servicemen used the words
'fairy' and 'queer' here in this period.[56]

As before the war, parties and balls were a major social focus
for the more open participants of the homosexual world. Parties
were often spontaneous things, organised in the last frenzied
drinking before the pubs shut at 6 pm. The attraction was, of
course, who one might meet, particularly – as was often the case
– young servicemen looking for action.[57]

The balls continued as a major event in the social calendar.
As in the prewar years, they were still mixed events, with heterosexuals as well as 'camps' attending. But the large numbers of
homosexuals gave the balls their ambience. Jon Rose describes
one from the 1940s. The hero and his companions meet at a
friend's house for drinks before the ball:

> Cliff and Dennis were dressed as Greek soldiers. Also in
> the house were ten other people, including two Carmen
> Mirandas, one of whom was frantically trying to turn herself
> into Dolores del Rio.

Finally, they get to the ball:

> Inside the hall, the heat, the noise, the crush was fantastic.
> It was only midnight, but the ball was well away ... half the
> theatre and radio world seemed to be there ... Milly and
> I counted at least eight Carmen Mirandas, most of whom
> glared at one another ...

The police, fulfilling their role as upholders of moral values,
were liable to disrupt any camp venue and they raided this ball,

A drag queen, Melba, had been singing when the police rushed in:

> Melba, who'd nearly strangled on a high note, stood dead centre of the stage, glaring. The leading cop walked down the middle of the hall saying, as he either walked over people, or knocked them flying, 'Come on down, you poofta'. Melba put her hand on her hip and said 'Just supposing you come up and get me, you big bull'. The copper was furious and started yelling 'I told you to get down off there, you great bastard, I'll bash you black and blue when you do'. Melba wagged her lorgnette saying 'Oh you great big impetuous dream boy, why don't you come up to Momma?' The cop glared and bellowed 'you're no Momma, you'll never even be a Poppa'. Melba flashed back 'Really darling, I know you're upset, but that's no way to speak to a dame –' The copper, still trying to get over bodies, almost shrieked 'Dame! Dame!? You're no dame you, you big pervert'. Melba yelled back 'And you're no gent, and I'll bet you're bloody lousy in bed as well'. And that second a tremendous gale of screams rent the air, as twenty-five show girls, getting dressed backstage, started to get an inkling of what was happening in front.
>
> Before the screams had died down, everything in the hall went mad: cops started grabbing people, pulling off wigs, having a look, then slamming a wig back on, and hauling the wig's occupant towards the main doors. Then everyone yelled at everyone else, and the leading cop kept trying to climb up onto the stage, which was difficult for him, because he first had to climb over the stunned orchestra who sat not knowing whether to play, drop dead on the spot, or bash

him and his helpers with their instruments. Some eight feet up, the stage also seethed with activity. Melba and her little friend let the cops have the lot, everything they could lay their hands on. The head cop and Melba fought it out, he trying to climb up, she bashing him down with her lorgnette. The little pianist threw music, her shoes, her wig, and something that, frightened out of my wits as I was, surprised me when I saw it fly overhead. Coming from nowhere, it was a watermelon. It hit a Betty Grable, knocking her out on the spot. Just then Melba, with a triumphant yell, crowned the cop with a pot of flowers.[58]

As this last piece illustrates, police attention was still a major problem. During the war years, police continued their harassment of homosexuals, often acting as *agents provocateurs* to gain convictions. This surfaced occasionally in evidence and allegations in the courts, and received its most public airing in 1943 with the case of Clarence McNulty, the Editor-in-Chief of the *Daily Telegraph*. Two policemen arrested McNulty in a public toilet in Lang Park, off Grosvenor Street. He denied any guilt, and accused one policeman of acting as a decoy.[59] After a long hearing, he was eventually discharged by the magistrate, who found some aspects of the police case unpalatable. The magistrate denied he was concerned at the amazingly high arrest rate of these two officers – it was about five times the average for similar policemen – but he did mention several aspects of their *modus operandi*. In particular, he was concerned that they didn't follow the usual procedure of both policemen observing the crime and making the arrest, a practice which, he noted, they hadn't followed for a long time. In previous cases the defendants had pleaded guilty so the evidence, given by a single policeman, had never been contested.

While nicely sidestepping any condemnation of the police actions in this specific case, the magistrate did note that as he had 'not been able to accept the evidence of the police witnesses as against the evidence of the defendant, the defendant is entitled to the benefit of any doubt'. He noted in his judgement that 'if the accusations of the defence be true, a serious, indeed an alarming, condition has been revealed which will shock the public conscience'.[60] Since there is no reason to believe that police activities during the war were any less homophobic than they had been during the 1930s, or were to be later during the 1950s, it is quite likely that some police were acting as *agents provocateurs* during the war, with either the explicit or implicit connivance of their superiors.

These were the more visible parts of the camp world in the 1940s. However, the majority of homosexually oriented men probably had little to do with this world. Those not in the armed forces might have continued to live their lives in the suburbs, perhaps believing that there was no one else like them; perhaps knowing a handful of others and living a secretive life; or perhaps even having groups of friends who may have known of their orientation, but without becoming involved in the camp world itself. Some might have made an occasional trip to see the places they had read about or heard about on the grapevine. Some may have had recourse to the camp world's illicit pleasures. But the vast majority probably had very little direct contact with the more public manifestations of camp life, even though the war threw many people's lives out of their old patterns, and contact was more likely.

When the war finally ended, and Australians, including Sydneysiders, attempted to settle down to civilian life again, things did not instantly return to 'normal'. Hangovers from wartime conditions had ongoing effects; some wartime controls were slow to be lifted, rationing remained, and policies of economic and social reconstruction were haltingly implemented.

On the bright side, the first Sydney to Hobart Yacht Race ran in 1945 and economic growth was fairly stable from the end of World War II until the early 1970s. Most Australians enjoyed increasing prosperity with only occasional hiccups – a few minor recessions.[61]

But several major concerns of the immediate postwar period had important repercussions for the homoerotically inclined, creating new threats to their status. Foremost among these was postwar reconstruction, the shift from a war-oriented economy to a peacetime one. Significantly, 'reconstruction' was based on the 'desirable' model of the nuclear family: husband and wife and children living in suburban bliss, usually in a double-fronted fibro or brick cottage or semi.[62] This society, of course, had no place for deviants – social, sexual, political or otherwise. Nowhere in Australia's past had such a homogeneous society ever existed; but this did not stop advocates from invoking a mythical past to legitimise their vision of the future.

A vast array of diverse institutions were involved in creating this new society. They included government departments dealing with manpower planning or economic reconstruction; private enterprise creating capital investment to produce the new consumer durables on which this new society would rise; women's magazines invoking pop psychology to urge the women who had worked during the war to give up their new-found economic freedom and become housewives. The *Women's Weekly*, for instance, pontificated that 'the homemaking instinct is too deeply ingrained in women to be eliminated from their characters in three or four years'.[63] Christian churches used their publications to purvey a vision of the perfect suburban society as the appropriate place for bringing up children, and there were legal moves to dismantle wartime regulations that had given women commensurate economic reward for the jobs they did during the war.[64] It was a massive attempt at social reconstruction.

Anxiety about the supposed moral collapse of society during the war was another major postwar concern, with several interwoven strands. First, fears about the abandonment of traditional morality during the war was most obvious in comments on the changes in sexual mores, particularly the way women had behaved with *foreign* servicemen. These concerns were not unique to Australia,[65] but they were directly expressed here by conservative church and community leaders both during the war and in its immediate aftermath.

Second, there was concern about the expected impact on the community of sexually deprived returning servicemen. Given that sexually transmitted diseases denoted immorality, the levels of venereal diseases in the armed forces prompted strong campaigns in the last year of the war, and immediately afterwards, to have the servicemen 'cleaned up' before they returned to civilian life.[66]

A third strand was based on statistical 'evidence' that suggested Australian society was in danger of moral collapse. Churchmen argued that increases in divorce, 'illegitimate' births, sex crimes, and crimes in general were all indicative of society's deteriorating moral climate.[67] Even the NSW Police Commissioner, in his 1945 report, saw the linkage, noting 'a certain moral looseness ... inseparable from wartime conditions'.[68]

Of course the moral collapse of society was not imminent – indeed even the statistical data is suspect when indexed against population growth – but nevertheless the general climate of opinion was that something had to be done. This tied in with an emerging and perhaps commonly held belief, expressed in a variety of forms, 'that a decade of broken norms would have to be paid for by discipline and constraint'.[69]

The Kinsey Report on male sexuality was released into this environment. It produced nothing like the same hue and cry as it did in the USA where the report's revelations of America's sexual mores was met with disbelief and moral outrage from conservative and church figures. But since Australia was increasingly taking much of its inspiration concerning its own future development from the USA, it did prompt the question, 'How relevant is all this to Australia?' The reviewer of Kinsey's book for the *Medical Journal of Australia* put it like this: 'For us in Australia, the future, presumably, holds changes such as that which came to America in the past years.'[70] The reviewer highlighted in a very understated way the main factual findings of the book, mentioning that 'fifty-six pages are devoted to consideration of data dealing with homosexual outlet',[71] and went on to note several of the more important aspects of this.

First he spelt out a finding that was to be quoted again and again as the years went by in a wide variety of contexts: 'more than a third (37%) of white males in *any* population have had at least some homosexual experience'.[72] Kinsey himself emphasised that this had implications for the legal situation of homosexuals, something that the police ought to bear in mind when enforcing the law. If the law was strictly enforced it could lead to a breakdown in society, with, theoretically, less than two-thirds of the male population trying to maintain the remainder in prison. Such a situation would, of course, be ludicrous, and cast the law into disrepute.

Second, the reviewer noted something that probably should have had a greater impact on the medical profession than it did at the time – something increasingly taken up by homophiles and later seized upon by gay liberationists – namely that 'the opinion that homosexual activity in itself provides evidence of a psychopathic personality is materially challenged' by the incidence and frequency data used in the report.[73] This was a particularly significant point to spell out, since psychotherapists and psychiatrists in Australia were increasingly interventionist in their treatment of homosexuals from about this time. In other words, a major authority had seriously questioned the legitimacy of attempting to 'cure' homosexuals or redirect their sexual preferences, even before such treatments had really begun here. Indeed, the reviewer went further, noting that already 'there is an increasing population of the most skilled psychiatrists who make no attempt to redirect behaviour, but who devote their attention to helping an individual accept himself and to conduct himself in such a manner that he does not come into open conflict with society'.[74]

How far these views affected the medical profession in Australia at the time is unknown, but the publication of the Kinsey Report – and such reviews of it – meant that more factual information about homosexuality was slowly becoming available to both the medical profession and the wider community. Norman Haire, the sexologist, occasionally discussed it on radio and in his regular newspaper column. Also during this period, Freudian ideas – often relating to psychoanalysis – were given an increased airing, not only in the medical literature but even in a range of non-specialist journals, such as the Melbourne-based literary magazine, *Angry Penguins*.[75]

Significantly, particularly as far as the medical profession was concerned, from this time the courts were increasingly told that homosexuality was a form of illness, and this ought to be taken into account in considering sentencing. Courts began to pay increasing attention to this view, often seeking the advice of medical experts. Despite much ambiguity in the medical profession's response, the seeds were sown for a new paradigm of homosexuality, based on the authority of large-scale American empirical research.

At the level of popular discourse, there was surprisingly little immediate general public response to the Kinsey Report. A few newspaper articles chose to report it, usually in sensationalist terms such as the *Truth* headline that boldly proclaimed 'SEX BOOK IS DYNAMITE!'[76] A far more accurate metaphor would have been a time bomb: it was only later, and varyingly, that the implications of the Kinsey Report were seized upon or taken up, and its full impact felt in academic fields such as anthropology, social theory or sociology; medical fields such as psychology or psychiatry; and even at a populist level, in the rallying cries of the sexual revolutionaries of the 1960s or the gay liberationists of the 1970s. The seeds of knowledge planted by the report would eventually come to fruition, leading to a rejection of homosexuality as a moral and criminal issue. But this lay in the future. For now, the Kinsey findings provided one of the few non-negative perceptions of homosexuality entering the public discourse.

As the Kinsey Report drew attention to the possible levels of homosexual activity in the wider community, and to the existence of a hard-core of the male population whose sexual preferences were exclusively same sex, Sydney newspapers were highlighting homosexual activity in and around the city. The papers emphasised that there appeared to be a high level of activity by homosexuals who were, of course, still portrayed as deviates, perverts, freaks or child molesters.

A major source for newspapers was the *Annual Reports* of the NSW Police Commissioner. In the postwar years, sexual offences came to receive special mention in these reports, perhaps reflecting the concern over the supposed moral decline of society: 'Sexual offences of all kinds increased from 434 during 1946 to 489 during 1947, an increase of 55 cases or 12 per cent.'[77] Perhaps it was no coincidence that the focus was even more specific in the year following the release of the Kinsey Report. Highlighting a further increase in that year, the Police Commissioner noted that a 'rather unsavoury feature is that of this increase of 34 cases in respect to sexual offences, 31 is in respect of increases in unnatural sexual crimes'.[78] The same year the Police Commissioner introduced a new section into his *Annual Report*, headed 'Vice Suppression'.

The law courts also provided material for the often hysterical newspaper articles.[79] Court cases on homosexual-related charges received more publicity in this period, though the details, while expressing outrage, were often written in euphemistic terms.[80] For example, in 1946, a 17-year-old youth was given the death sentence for committing 'an abominable offence' with a boy under the age of 14.[81] Other headlines noted that men were behaving indecently with youths, that teachers were indecently assaulting their male pupils, that men were assaulting boys in country towns, or that men – or women – were changing their sex.[82] In mid-1948 the growing number of these incidents coming before the courts, and their greater reportage, led one Sydney newspaper to pronounce that the 'increasing number of sex perverts in Sydney ... is causing grave concern not only to the public at large but also to the judges who are charged with the responsibility of administering justice'.[83]

In addition to this reporting, the newspapers undertook their own investigative activities. Intrigued by police claims, by the evidence surfacing in court cases and more general stories from other connections about the homosexual or 'camp' world, some newspapers tried to infiltrate this milieu. Late in 1949 the Sydney *Truth* was able to pull off a major coup – by bribing one participant – to write a major inside story, complete with photos. Under headlines of 'Why Don't The Police Stop This?', *Truth* described in graphic detail what went on at a camp gathering. It first gave itself credit for bringing this information to the public's attention – 'on several occasions in recent weeks *Truth* has published detailed, eyewitness accounts of the goings-on at nocturnal gatherings of Sydney's only too numerous band of effeminate males' – then detailed a particular 'going-on': men dancing with men, men kissing men, cabaret acts, and the attendance of many of Sydney's better-known drag queens: Vivien Leigh, Victoria Lester, 'The Viscountess', Merle Oberon, Ada 'The Parramatta Girl', and many others. Photos brought home the message: there was Vivien (Wally) Leigh dancing with a sailor friend; two handsome young men were doing a quick-step, and other men were sitting on each other's laps and cuddling. Susanne (Michael) Peters was there after her recent triumph in winning a 'Queen of the Pansies' Beauty Parade, where her legs had been judged by the adjudicator as 'just too, too divine'.[84] It was obviously all a bit too, too much for the intrepid *Truth* reporters, but their efforts had paid off with a major exposé.[85]

Another *Truth* article described the start of a big night out for the 'naice boys', as they had begun to refer to male homosexuals, many of whom were wearing drag:

> Giggles and squeals pierced the night air as they tripped daintily along the platform of North Strathfield railway station. High-stepping little things in 'drag' (women's clothing to the uninitiated) were tenderly escorted by their 'boy' friends as they frolicked their way to the darkened street where their 'hostess' for the night awaited them.

Old world courtesy prevailed as the laddies helped the 'girlies' on to the back of an open lorry [to go to] their latest 'do' – one of those ducky little affairs which are now known as 'parties of the painted pansies'.[86]

This, of course, was merely the continuation of the parties that had been a feature since before the war. But the story showed a growing public awareness of aspects of the camp world, and an increasing police attention to it.

The artistic and creative worlds had their share of other visible parts of this mostly hidden world in Sydney during this period. Geoffrey Dutton observes that anyone 'who remembers the 1940s and 1950s will remember occasions when the artist or writer and their works were equated with the word "poofter"'.[87] And at least one group of artists living in Sydney in this period – the inhabitants of Merioola – did little to hide their sexuality.

Merioola was a stately old Victorian mansion in Edgecliff, and from the mid-1940s its tenants included some of Australia's most promising young artists in many fields: painters Donald Friend, Justin O'Brien and Jocelyn Rickards, designer Loudon Sainthill, sculptor Arthur Fleischmann (somewhat older than the rest), photographer Alec Murray, and critic and publisher Harry Tatlock Miller, to name but a few. Many of these were in the forefront of the avant-garde in Australian art. While not all the inhabitants of the house were homosexuals, this didn't stop the mansion from being commonly known as 'Buggery House'.

The existence of the Merioola ménage illustrates another paradox in this tale. Despite 'the hatred and fear that homosexuality inspired in Sydney in the decades of the middle of the century',[88] parts of Sydney society (particularly those groups which aspired to rub shoulders with the art world) seemed to accept the inhabitants of Merioola and their flagrant disregard

for the law and social mores. One resident, the artist and costume designer, Jocelyn Rickards, recalls:

> we lived a very, very open life there. Alec and I lived together
> there. Harry and Loudon lived together and it was a time
> when neither homosexuality nor two people just living
> together was openly accepted. Our lifestyle was extremely
> radical and yet we were totally socially accepted.[89]

Accepted by some maybe, but not generally by the wider public,
or the guardians of public morality.

By the late 1940s in Sydney, it appeared that the secretive
homosexual world that had existed since well before the war was
growing, as more and more detail surfaced into public awareness. Still much of this world continued to be hidden away:
the large networks of friends in the suburbs and the private
parties they organised. Bars, coffee shops, restaurants and the
beats could be tapped into as necessary, but they remained fairly
discreet.

A heightened public profile no doubt alerted men with
homoerotic desires to the fact that 'out there' were probably
hundreds, even thousands, like themselves, but this was not
an unmitigated benefit. It was almost like setting the stage for
tragedy. A long-hidden minority group designated as deviants,
perverts, corrupters of youth and degenerates, these men did not
'fit in' to the new society widely seen as the way to the future.
And with the advent of the Cold War, they found themselves
cast in the role of scapegoat.

CHAPTER 4

THE GREATEST MENACE FACING AUSTRALIA

Sydney's homosexual worlds and the Cold War

Global developments in the late 1940s had long-term impacts, beginning with the Cold War, the postwar confrontation between the USA and the USSR and their respective allies. Fears of communism and the 'domino theory' dominated western strategic thinking for decades. Australian troops fought against the 'communist menace' in the Korean War from June 1950 until July 1953, and also in the Malayan Emergency from 1950 until 1960.

The Cold War had effects in unexpected areas. Its consequences were felt in the social, political, cultural and economic structures of many western societies. This was certainly true of Australia, where historians and social commentators see the postwar era as a time of repressive and restrictive state activity, particularly against anyone who did not conform to the idealised social and political norms.[1] Increasingly, these people were perceived as a threat to Australia's stability.

But there were other developments and undercurrents as well. In 1956 Sydney's city rail loop was finally completed, when the 'dead ends' at St James and Wynyard were joined via a new station at Circular Quay, whose public toilets provided new facilities for homoerotically inclined men. More broadly, a youth culture with its own language, clothing and music emerged in the 1950s in Sydney, as in much of the western world. Up until this time, the fashion and music preferences of Sydney's youth differed only marginally from those of their parents. But, now formally designated 'teenagers', with the advent of the 'rock and roll' era, new forms of music, new sexual standards, and new 'bodgie' and 'widgie' fashion styles started to appear.

It was also an era of mass migration. Europeans, fodder for developmental schemes like the Snowy Mountains Hydro-Electric Scheme or the burgeoning manufacturing industries in the cities, came in droves. Sydney's population increased from 1.9 million in 1954 to 2.8 million in 1971. Recent arrivals from Greece, Italy and eastern Europe, initially single men, were labelled as 'reffos' or 'wogs' by longer-term residents. Officially they were 'New Australians' and they began to recreate their own 'old world' cultures in 'new world' communities in the 1950s in the inner-city suburbs vacated by the native-born. There were exotic new attractions for men who desired other men.

But undoubtedly the most important factor was the impact of the motor car. In the decades after World War II 'ownership of at least one car, formerly something of a luxury, became a normal part of family life'. The 1971 census revealed that in Sydney, 'half of all dwellings … had one car and one quarter had two or more'.[2]

Given the emerging perspective of social reconstruction, with its focus on a return to a simple, moral (if mythical) past, it could be expected that male homosexuals, a shadowy minority of 'wilful perverts', would be subjected to increased social and state harassment. And the evidence confirms this view, across the country. Police paid increasing attention to those who committed homosexual acts. Some states changed their laws, increasing penalties against homosexual activity, and also, as in NSW, creating new 'crimes' associated with homosexuality. Concurrent with this were moves to isolate homosexuals in the state's prisons; government-funded enquiries to discover the 'causes' of homosexuality (so a 'cure' could be found); and the suggestion in State Parliament that male homosexuals be put into annexes of the state's mental hospitals. All of this occurred within a relatively short period of time. Increasing harassment of individual homosexuals, either in the form of discrimination against them, or in the form of violence – the phenomenon of 'poofter-bashing' – happened at a community level, too.

Yet despite this massive mobilisation of the machinery of the state, the camp world not only survived, but thrived. Many individual homosexuals undoubtedly felt isolated, guilty and alienated, and many lost careers – or lives – when scandal unearthed them, but the networks of friends continued to operate, and probably became more crucial in helping individuals to cope. Despite the police campaigns, many of the known venues – bars, restaurants, coffee shops, beats – continued as before, if more discreetly. New venues opened too.

The public campaign had an unexpected side. The attempts to turn the machinery of the state – and even society itself – against homosexuals led to unprecedented levels of publicity about homosexuals and homosexual activity. Notwithstanding the negative effects on some individuals, this potentially benefited those who suddenly discovered a vast homosexual world, and found that they were not isolated and alone. In this sense, probably one effect of the attention was to help create in Australia for the first time a sense of homosexual identity or a 'camp' identity among a broad spectrum of people.

Paradoxically, too, these attempts to stamp out homosexuality generated unprecedented publicity, not only in newspapers, but in parliaments, in medical journals, in academe, in government enquiries, and within government departments. This meant, for the first time, the development of a serious 'public discourse' about homosexuality. Many old concepts and presumptions came under closer scrutiny than they had previously, and they were soon found to be wanting. The developments of the 1970s – of changing perceptions, in time leading to changes in attitudes and, subsequently, in the law – clearly had their origins in the questioning that began in this earlier period. It is a tale with a moral – but one to make the 'moralisers' turn in their graves.

The desire to 're-construct' a new social order in the immediate postwar period required the physical rebuilding and expansion of Australia's major cities, after years of neglect caused by the stringencies of depression and war. In Sydney, the County of Cumberland Planning Scheme drew up plans for the orderly and attractive development of new suburbs on the city's outskirts, to house this new social order.

What eventuated was perhaps not what was anticipated. As Robin Boyd noted in 1960:

> The recent growth of Sydney is mainly confined to three zones. Out west, the wooden villa, or *Villawood Zone* – to use the name of one of its central districts – sweeps from Liverpool north through Parramatta. It is fairly typical Australian working class development, repeating the dreary, ill-considered housing growth on the outskirts of every Australian town … [reducing] the bush to a desert of terracotta roofs relieved only by electric wires and wooden poles. The same approach extends south into the *Tom Ugly Zone* …

where the Georges River opens into Botany Bay. Here the familiar suburban techniques are more destructive because the houses are slightly more pretentious ... The really depressing parts of Sydney, however, are in the *North Shore Executive Zone* ...[3]

Social life in these suburbs usually revolved around school organisations (such as the Parents and Citizens' groups), churches and their 'ladies auxiliaries', all male clubs such as Rotary, Lions and the Masons, sporting organisations, RSL clubs, and the local pubs. For the young, 'hanging around' the local milk bars was a favourite pastime; by the mid-1950s groups known as 'bodgies' (the boys) and 'widgies' (the girls) emerged, and their fashions and activities caused much anxiety among the older generations.

The city itself also began to undergo massive redevelopment from the 1950s. As one journalist enthused:

New tall city buildings, an overhead railway station at Circular Quay and viaducts and tunnels changing Macquarie Street are highlights in the great projects ahead which will effect new and startling alterations to the city skyline as Sydney, ever-growing, adjusts herself to the increasing tempo of the future.[4]

And life, for the hedonistic Sydneysiders, went on. Visiting columnist Eric Linklater noted how open and healthy Australians looked, compared to Europeans:

Hunter Street was crowded, Pitt Street was stormy with opposing tides of traffic, George Street was a maelstrom of humanity ... I had time to look about me, and the crowds that thwarted me I perceived were strangely young and uncommonly attractive … Girls beyond counting, sunburnt and laughing, in bright frocks that all looked made for a holiday. Young men bare-headed and bold of movement with clear skins and confident loud voices. Older men and women, stout and prosperous, genial with good living. But the majority was young and the smell of salt water mingled with the scent of the young girls in their summer frocks, as though their brown arms and legs, dyed by the sun, were perfumed also by Pacific waves.[5]

Yet conservatives and moralists felt this innocent and optimistic society was in moral decline: the war had torn apart the moral fabric and it had to be mended. Cold War rhetoric built on these concerns, leading to increasing agitation over the future. In the early years of the Cold War, the perception that society was in danger was put quite explicitly, and in 'apocalyptic' terms. For example, in 1951, the leaders of the major Christian churches in Australia, along with various representatives of the British monarchy here, issued a 'Call to the People of Australia', which was read by the chairman of the ABC immediately after the 7 pm news on Remembrance Day (11 November). It stated, in part, that

Australia is in danger. We are in danger from abroad. We are in danger at home. We are in danger from moral and intellectual apathy, from the mortal enemies of mankind which sap the will … The dangers demand of all good Australians community of thought and purpose. They demand a restoration of the moral order from which alone true social order can derive.[6]

The statement linked the danger from outside (the Communist threat) with the danger from inside (moral decay) to emphasise the need to unite behind a common banner (the restoration of moral order) to protect Australia.

Homosexuality received increasing amounts of attention in the postwar years, as newspapers, drawing largely on police sources, created headlines by highlighting aspects of the hidden camp world. From late 1948, newspapers noting 'a police war on this nest of perverts', quoted police sources as showing a sharp increase in homosexuality and 'sex perversion' over Australia. As one would expect, the existence of unsuspectedly large numbers of homosexuals in society's midst caused agitation among some groups, particularly after the 1948 Kinsey Report gave quantitative evidence of its incidence. As the newspapers continued to make more and more of this increase over the years, they generated much public hysteria.[7]

For example, in June 1952, the Sydney *Sun* reported on a court case involving 'eight homosexual men ranging in age from 17 to 35', on charges of offensive behaviour and buggery. Detectives from Sydney's Criminal Investigation Bureau and Military Police had arrested them. In an article headlined 'Predatory Men Worst Blot in City's Growing Vice', the reporter outlined details of the case; the Military Police were involved because three of the men were from the Holsworthy army camp. Others were a post office technician, an apprentice typewriter mechanic, a storeman-packer, two salesmen and a mercer who owned his own business. In his summing up, the judge was said to have stated that

the offences should serve as an awakening that
homosexuality was rife in the city and district to a degree

which he had never dreamed of, and he was sure other people had never heard of.[8]

At the court hearing, a medical expert, called to give evidence in support of one defendant, opined that he had 'a 60-40 percentage of masculinity and femininity in his make-up'. Medical advice for another young defendant was that:

> To overcome his tendencies, it would be necessary to re-educate him. He would have to be taken from the home environment and introduced to manly sports such as could be obtained at clubs like the Police Boys Club.[9]

In his memoir about some of the stranger cases that had come before him, Magistrate Arthur Debenham recalled that, because of the growing number of cases that involved 'sexual perversion', he tried to understand the problem: 'I read authorities on the subject – Norbert East, Madder, Hirschfeld, Kraft-Ebing, Cullere'.[10]

The newspaper articles, fed by the police reports, drew predictable responses from several sections of the wider community. For example, at their annual conference in 1949, the Country Women's Association 'decided to seek heavier penalties for sex crimes'.[11] Likewise, the medical profession offered a range of suggestions including stronger sentences, better psychiatric help, the establishment of a bureau to keep records of all sex offenders, and providing alternative institutions to deal with these sorts of offenders.[12] As the public hysteria about 'sex crimes' – particularly those associated with homosexuals – mounted in New South Wales, so too did pressure on the government to do something. Colin Delaney, the Roman Catholic Superintendent of Police, saw it as 'the greatest social menace' in Australia.[13]

An initial step was taken in 1951 with an amendment of the *Crimes Act*. Sections 79–81 of the NSW *Crimes Act* (prior to November 1951) had stated:

> 79. Whosoever commits the abominable crime of buggery, or bestiality, with mankind, or with any animal, shall be liable to penal servitude for fourteen years.[14]

> 80. Whosoever attempts to commit the said abominable crime, or assaults any person with intent to commit the same, shall be liable to penal servitude for five years.

> 81. Whosoever commits an indecent assault upon a male person of whatever age, with or without the consent of such person, shall be liable to penal servitude for five years.

In the 1951 amendment the clause 'with or without the consent of such person' was inserted after 'with intent to commit the same' in Section 80. This apparently minor amendment went through in an 'omnibus' amendment Bill to the *Crimes Act*, and there was no discussion as to its significance, although it was clearly designed to remove the legal loophole of 'consent'.[15] It also brought it in line with the similar clause in Section 81.

It was probably no coincidence, however, that the change was initiated in the wake of a major English spy scandal with homosexual overtones earlier that year. Two British diplomats, Guy Burgess and Donald Maclean, thought in official circles to be homosexual, had defected to the Soviet Union in March 1951.[16] The American government responded by making 'representations to the British to weed out all known homosexuals from Government service as bad security risks, as was already being done in Washington'.[17] Given the close links between the

Australian and British security establishments,[18] it seems highly probable that a similar campaign would be undertaken here.

English novelist Nancy Mitford nicely satirised the mentality that turned homosexuals into threats to the state. In her novel *The Blessing*, at a top-level dinner party in London, a senior American 'official', Hector Dexter, turns the conversation to what he claims is the frivolous attitude of the British to 'sexual perversion':

> 'Have we adopted a frivolous attitude?' said Hughie. 'The poor old dears are always being run in, you know.'

> 'I think I will put it this way. I think it cannot be generally understood and realised in Britain, as we understand and realise it in the States, that morally and politically these people are lepers. They are sickly, morbose, healthless, chlorotic, unbraced, flagging, peccant, vitiated and contaminated, and when I use the word contaminated I use it very specifically in the political sense. But I think you British have absolutely no conception of the danger in your midst, of the harm these perverts can do to the state of which they are citizens. You seem to regard them as a subject for joking rather than as the object of a deep-seated, far-reaching purge.'

> 'But they're not in politics, Heck – hardly any, at least.'

> 'Not openly, no. That's their cunning. They work behind the scenes.'

> 'If you can call it work.'

'For the cause of Communism. The point I am trying
to make is that they are dangerous because politically
contaminated, a political contamination that can, in every
traceable case, be traced to Moscow.'

'I say, hold on, Heck,' said Hughie. 'All the old queens I
know are terrific old Tories.'

'I am bound to contradict you, Hughie, or rather I am bound
to put forward my argument, and you are going to see that it
is a powerful argument, to persuade you of the exact opposite
of what you have just said and to persuade you that what
you have just said is the exact opposite of the truth as known
to my government. We Americans, you may know, have
certain very very sure and reliable, I would even say infallible,
sources of information. We have our Un-American Activities
Committee sections, we have our FBI agents, we have
countless very very brilliant newspaper men and business
men all over the world ... we have also other sources which
I am not at liberty to disclose to you, even off the record.
And our sources of information inform us that nine out of
every ten, and some say ninety-nine out of every hundred,
of these morally sick persons are not only in the very closest
sympathy but in actual contact with Moscow. And I for one
entirely believe these sources.'[19]

Such a perception appears to have found growing acceptance.
In Britain, as in America, the campaign 'was extended to the
pursuit of all homosexuals, whether they were in Government
employment or not'.[20] The Home Office in England instigated
a new drive against 'male vice', which gathered pace from 1951
to the mid-1950s, under the enthusiastic goading of the Roman

Catholic Home Secretary, Sir David Maxwell Fyfe, the Director of Public Prosecutions, Sir Theobald Mathew, and the Metropolitan Police Commissioner, Sir John Nott-Bowes.[21]

A similar campaign appeared to be under way in NSW. In late 1954, in the wake of yet more homosexual scandals in England – this time involving a peer, Lord Montagu of Beaulieu, and his cousin, Michael Pitt-Rivers; a journalist, Peter Wildeblood; the novelist and playwright Rupert Croft-Cooke; and several Royal Air Force personnel – far more detailed amendments were proposed to the *Crimes Act*. With the police constantly reporting an increasing incidence of homosexual offences, it seemed that a 'homosexual wave' was engulfing the state. Billy Sheahan, the Labor Attorney-General, another Roman Catholic, initially denied in a Parliamentary debate that the proposed legislation was 'inspired by, dictated by or directed by any outside organisation'. But clearly police pressure led to the proposed amendments. In fact, under direct questioning, the Attorney-General finally admitted that Delaney, now Commissioner of Police, had expressed concern about the lack of suitable punishment for homosexual 'crimes'. In Sheahan's own words, 'the Police Commissioner holds the view that remedial legislation is an urgent necessity to combat the evil'.[22]

These legislative changes were wide-ranging in their assault on the civil liberties of men thought to have homoerotic desires. First, a new series of crimes relating to homosexuality were created (Sections 81A and 81B of the *Crimes Act*). Under Section 81B, it would now be a crime if a male was caught 'soliciting' or 'inciting' or 'attempting to solicit or incite' another male to commit, or be a party to, any of the crimes outlined in Sections 79, 81 or 81A of the *Crimes Act*. Since Section 80 already dealt with attempts to commit – or even intent to commit – the crime noted in Section 79 (that of buggery), it seemed the police wanted an 'umbrella' clause to make their task easier.

The new Section 81B was seen as necessary after a 1953 Supreme Court decision concerning Section 4(2)(o)(ii) of the *Vagrancy Act 1902*, which stated that, if a person 'being a male person did in a public place … solicit for an immoral purpose'. Police had been using this provision to arrest males whom they considered were soliciting for a homosexual act. The Supreme Court rejected this use, since its original purpose was clearly related to men acting as pimps for female sex workers, rather than men soliciting for sex with others like themselves.

While the new Section 81B, although poorly worded in view of the existing Section 80, may have been *thought* to be necessary, no such case can be made for the new Section 81A. This related to the committing of, or being party to the commission of, or procuring or attempting to procure for, 'any act of indecency' between males, which was already spelt out in Sections 81 and 81B. The overall effect of the various amendments was to spell out, in far more detail and specificity, possible activities now classed as crimes.[23]

Second, the amendments contained an appalling abuse of civil liberties. A new Section 379A allowed that 'in an indictment of an offence under Section 79, 80 or 81 of this Act *a count may be added for an offence under Section 81A of this Act*' (my emphasis). Likewise a new Section 379B stated: 'In an indictment for an unnatural crime, or an attempt to commit the same, *counts may be added under both Section 379 and Section 379A of this Act*' (my emphasis). Thus it was now possible to add extra charges for one offence.

Third, the penalties for a range of homosexual offences were dramatically increased. For example, while charges under the old Section 4 of the *Vagrancy Act* had a maximum sentence of six months gaol, the new Section 81B – its nominal replacement, as the Attorney-General explained – had a twelve-month prison term attached. These increased penalties also applied under other parts of the legislation.

Fourth, the imposition of these higher penalties meant that many of the offences were now indictable, and were therefore moved to the higher courts, rather than remaining in the jurisdiction of the magistrates' courts. While in theory there ought not to be any specific *legal* disadvantage in this, there were other disadvantages, ranging from financial (extra costs) to social (far greater publicity).

Finally, the legislation contained provisions for the suppression of details of the cases coming before the courts. In introducing this provision, Sheahan argued that 'there has, for the last fifty years at least, been a provision empowering judges [in the divorce jurisdiction] to direct that portions of evidence be not published and it is proposed to insert a similar power in the *Crimes Act* referrable to sex offences'.[24] Sheahan contended that this new provision could only be for the public good – 'details of these offences have been published that are repulsive to many people, particularly parents of adolescent children'. Yet there was much concern about this clause from several different perspectives.

One concern related simply to the loss of rights of the individual being tried (this was seen as increasing the possibility of a miscarriage of justice).[25] Another criticism centred on the fact that 'the publicity accompanying such cases acts as a deterrent to others', and so should not be restricted.[26] A third point, from one lawyer Member of Parliament, was that newspaper publicity often worked 'as a means of finding witnesses who might be able to present another side of the picture'.[27] Much of the more general concern arose from the commonly held view that repressing details would protect the police, particularly at a time when charges were increasingly being levelled against them about the use of police decoys and *agents provocateurs*.

Increasing legal penalties and diminishing civil liberties were not the only official moves against homosexuals. If the major purpose of these legislative changes was to facilitate the segregation of homosexuals from the general population, this was mirrored by actions of the state to segregate homosexuals in any 'captive' population already under their control. This policy is most clearly seen with regard to the prison population in NSW.

Two arguments were offered in support of segregation. One was simply a perception that homosexuals ought to be segregated to stop them 'perverting' other members of the prison population. The other more 'humane' argument reflected at base the desire, considered at the time to be legitimate, to 'treat' homosexuals: to study them with a view to discovering the 'causes' of their condition, and then 'cure' them.

It is difficult to pinpoint when this policy of segregation began. Attorney-General Sheahan admitted in 1955 that 'in the penal system these offenders are segregated so that they may be cured of this disease and malady, which needs corrective medical treatment. One gaol has been set apart for this purpose.'[28] Yet the gaol chosen for this purpose, at Cooma, hardly seemed to reflect humane conditions and did not appear to have been designed to encourage sympathetic treatment. As a Cooma prison chaplain poignantly described it:

> In southern New South Wales there is a town that during the winter is constantly swept by cold winds that are born amongst the snows of the mountains. When it rains, the water seems like drops of melting ice. The rain, pushed by the wind, finds every crack in a building, and every hole in

clothing ... [T]he prison is on the outskirts of the town ... [and] on the top floor those who were known homosexuals had their cells.[29]

While it is hard to know if this policy of segregating homosexuals had been longstanding, it seems more likely to have been relatively recent. Indeed, it could well have been part of a program of 'modernisation' of the prison system that, the *Herald* reported in 1957, had been implemented 'over the past seven or eight years by the Attorney General [Sheahan] and Minister of Justice Mr RR Downing'.[30] One should note, however, that whatever politicians and prison authorities might claim to be doing, isolation and containment seem better descriptions than 'modernisation', with its implications of more humane 'treatment'.

It appears that the argument that homosexuals were isolated for the purposes of study was added much later. In fact it could well have been an afterthought, an attempt by the government to deflect criticism. For example, in the Parliamentary Debates of 1955 over the amendments to the *Crimes Act*, the member for Burwood, Dr Parr, had criticised the government's approach of simply increasing legal constraints and enforcing segregation. He suggested that if homosexuals were to be isolated as the government wanted, it could be an opportunity to do something more positive for them: 'Could they not be examined by a group consisting of a psychiatrist, an educationist, a minister of religion, a psycho-analyst and an endocrinologist?'[31]

Sheahan attempted to take the force out of Parr's arguments by claiming that he and the Minister for Justice already had 'under consideration the appointment of a committee to examine the incidence of homosexuality in NSW and to determine the means that should be taken to effect cures'.[32] Such consideration cannot have been all that far advanced however, for it took over three years before the committee's membership was even announced; and then its composition closely resembled that suggested by Parr.[33]

Known as the Trethowan Committee, this government-instigated study was to look at problems of homosexuality in society as well as in gaols. In addition to state funding, money from the University of Sydney (via the Norman Haire Bequest) was also used.[34] The holder of the Haire Fellowship in 1958 and 1959 was Dr JE Lyttle, and his work included interviews and group sessions with homosexual prisoners at Long Bay Gaol, occasional visits to Cooma Prison for the same purpose, therapy sessions, and a study of ways to help integrate homosexuals back into the community.[35] Much interesting detail, on camp life, and on how homosexual men saw themselves, was accumulated by this study.

It took five years before the committee's work was done. Even before it started, the Wolfenden Committee in Britain had released its report, recommending limited decriminalisation for some private homosexual acts. And although the imminent release of the Trethowan Committee's report was finally announced early in March 1963, it has never seen the light of day. There are suggestions that this was because the committee was split on the issue.[36]

In such an atmosphere, it is little wonder that many homosexuals, particularly those of an artistic bent, chose to flee the country.[37] For many people in the arts, Australia was felt to be a cultural desert – and they left Australia for more congenial atmospheres in Britain or America. For artists such as Donald Friend, Loudon Sainthill, Harry Tatlock Miller, Justin O'Brien and Jeffrey Smart, homophobia added another level of difficulty. William Dobell must have been unusual: he spent many years hiding his homosexuality, despite having friends such as Donald

Friend, and despite living for a while in Kings Cross, haven of many overt homosexuals.[38]

When the government introduced measures to restrict reporting on cases of 'sex crimes', criticism came from newspapers, opposition politicians, lawyers and other members of the public. We have seen concerns about the possible miscarriage of justice and the removal of the deterrent effects of publicity. But the greatest concern was, as the *Sydney Morning Herald* put it, that the measure was aimed at 'reducing the checks on the proper administration of justice' in the state.[39] And a major problem with the administration of justice in NSW was the police themselves.

In any society that experiences rapid social change or is composed of a variety of minority groups, the police play a crucial role, since they often come into direct contact with, and must deal with, dissident or minority groups. In NSW, the police were not only involved in enforcing the law against homosexual acts but, in the immediate postwar period, they were increasingly active in turning public attention unfavourably against homosexuals.

Another aspect of the police relationship with homosexuality concerned police tactics: through the use of *agents provocateurs* to incite men to commit homosexual acts, or committing perjury to ensure convictions (stating that men had done things they hadn't done). Yet under Section 81B of the *Crimes Act*, it was a crime if a male was caught 'soliciting' or 'inciting' or 'attempting to solicit or incite' another male to commit, or be a party to, any of the crimes outlined in Sections 79, 81 or 81A of the *Crimes Act*, namely the homosexual crimes. So a policeman soliciting or inciting a man to have sex with him was clearly breaking the law.

All this had received a public airing in the 1943 McNulty case, and compounded recurring evidence from the 1920s that such activity took place, despite continual denials from the police administration. And what was true of the interwar period, and of the 1940s, was also true of the Cold War era. A broad range of evidence has now emerged to indicate that in order to arrest homosexuals, police were still actively engaged in either inciting or soliciting citizens to commit homosexual acts, or claiming that citizens solicited them for such acts.

In 1954, when arguing for the suppression of details of cases involving 'sex crimes', Sheahan had implied that the detailed reporting of events involved in these cases 'impairs the enforcement of the criminal laws'.[40] What the Attorney-General had in mind here was not clear from his speech, but it was likely he wanted to shield from scrutiny the police *agents provocateurs* and their role in homosexual 'crimes' in this period. Any major revelations about their activities would have shown how often the police themselves were in effect the instigators of the 'sex crimes'.

It is worth noting here two important features associated with the 'soliciting' or 'inciting to commit' aspects of homosexual 'crimes'.

First, unlike most crimes, these crimes involved the police as *participants* – they 'solicited' or 'incited'. Thus they were not in a neutral position – they were not a third party called in to investigate what two (or more) other parties might have done. To use a modern terminology, they were themselves 'agents' in the crime.

Second, these 'crimes' had an important impact on the crime statistics, and could be used as both a statistical measure of police efficiency in the state, and a basis for arguing for extra resources to combat the increasing levels of these crimes. Unlike crimes such as robbery or murder, where the police had to 'solve' the crime to catch the criminal, the crimes relating to 'soliciting' or 'inciting' were no sooner 'committed' than they were solved – simply by arresting the person whom police claimed committed the crime. While one would like to believe that police probity was such that they would not have been tempted to move from being a 'passive' agent to becoming an active agent – an *agent provocateur* – we cannot make this assumption. Indeed, there were a large number of scandals involving police in this period, and even the *Police Association Monthly Newsletter* saw fit to complain that senior police officers were pressuring the subordinates, 'using a form of intimidation to boost the number of arrests'.[41]

It is also relevant to note here how often Sydney police themselves were 'solicited' or 'incited' for homosexual acts in this period, in a diversity of places, ranging from parks, to public toilets, to hotels, to beaches – and at most unusual times.[42] While this might be taken to indicate evidence of policemen themselves 'loitering with intent', it is difficult to uncover the amount of this activity. Many people charged with homosexual offences were unwilling to draw publicity to themselves. Contesting police evidence, and going to higher courts, was guaranteed to do this.

It is understandable why many men charged with homosexual offences chose the course of action that guaranteed minimum publicity. They would often plead guilty, and even if they didn't, rarely contested a guilty verdict. Only occasionally would someone charged by the police with homosexual 'crimes' (in which the police themselves were involved as 'agents') fight back in the courts, with all the attendant publicity. But there were some notable cases – usually involving a public figure – when closer scrutiny from the higher levels of the legal system revealed that police evidence was untrustworthy. Many times the police were found to be more than just passive 'agents'; they were indeed *agents provocateurs*. Two cases illustrate this clearly.

The first case was that of Douglas Annand, a Sydney designer who had won three Sulman Awards for murals. He was arrested by three police officers at Chatswood Park toilet one night in mid-1953, and charged with soliciting one of them for immoral purposes. Despite character evidence from such notables as retired general Sir Leslie Morshead, and Director of the Art Gallery of New South Wales, Hal Missingham, he was convicted, on the evidence of three policemen. Annand not only appealed, but also took out writs against the police. At his appeal not only was his conviction overturned, but the judge chose to comment that the arresting sergeant's evidence was a 'wicked lie ... I disbelieve the whole of his evidence'. Indeed, the judge suggested that the police's supporting evidence was put together 'in collaboration', rather than reflecting any individual policeman's recollections. It was clear in this case, the judge noted, that the police themselves were the real 'agents' in the commission of the crime. The arresting police sergeant was suspended.[43]

The next case related to the visiting Chilean pianist, Claudio Arrau, who was charged in August 1957 with offensive behaviour. It was alleged that he went into and out of a toilet in Lang Park in the city late one night and winked at one of two policemen, who just happened to be waiting inside. This case particularly highlights the ways in which prejudice can affect minorities, and indeed how 'crimes' can be invented. In this case Arrau was found guilty,[44] but on appeal the judge, although he thought the offence *might* be legally proved – since two witnesses (the police) said it had, while only one witness (Arrau) said it hadn't – dismissed the charge without conviction, as he thought it of a 'comparatively trivial nature'.[45]

This case received considerable attention in the press

because Arrau was such a famous international figure. The story broke on the night of his first appearance at Sydney Town Hall where he was, reportedly, given a standing ovation before he had time to seat himself at the piano. Such was a more sympathetic Sydney audience's response to the case.[46]

In several major cases, when the police were found to be liars (and in one case found to be indulging in 'brutality'), public outcry led to their suspension and generated a vast amount of damaging publicity.[47] The spotlight was turned from those who were accused of homosexual crimes to the accusers and their methods.

The closer scrutiny by the higher courts was not, however, the only source of evidence of police still being involved as *agents provocateurs* in homosexual crimes. Even a sociologist working in England at the time, preparing reports on a range of 'social problem areas' for the British Home Office, could note, simply in passing in one of his books, that the decoy system, utilising 'good-looking young CID officers is still used in Sydney, Australia'.[48] Academic research in this area has uncovered more details of this.[49]

My own story really begins at this time. For a teenage boy with homoerotic inclinations, exploring one's emerging sexuality was a fraught and dangerous process. So I soon learned to live an important part of my life below the radar of public awareness. I developed a whole safe façade and became a watcher behind my mask. Always be careful, never reveal too much; it might give you away.

And over the next few years, I soon learned that homosexuals were outsiders trapped in a world of conformity to which we didn't belong. We pretended to be like everybody else, we acted as if we accepted the rules, but secretly we ignored those rules, which didn't apply to the real 'us'.

But we had to exercise caution; even to be thought a homosexual was to invite police attention – and who knew where that might end.

Needless to say, all this activity by the state's instrumentalities failed to stamp out homosexuality, even though it undoubtedly brought much misery, even tragedy, at an individual level. In fact it helped to create a public discourse about homosexuality, and bring out into the open something that had previously been hidden away. This discourse became part of a much wider debate focused on sex that erupted in this period. It may have been caused by such diverse things as the widened sexual experiences of many in the war period; by new ideas about educating a 'rational' society; by the impact of Freudian ideas, particularly after the developments associated with psychiatry during the war; and by the definite though slow changes in public attitudes. It was undoubtedly fuelled by the two Kinsey Reports, on male sexuality in 1948 and female sexuality in 1953, and by a variety of new sex manuals prepared by various groups. It manifested itself, in turn, in the long-running argument about the need for more and better sex education for the young (with the churches battling to retain moral authority over society's sexuality); in the establishment of the 1958 Trethowan Committee of enquiry into homosexuality in NSW; and in the rise to prominence in the medical profession of self-professed experts on human sexual behaviour. Paradoxically, then, in this era, one of the great taboo areas in Judeo-Christian society – human sexuality and its many and varied expressions – came out of the closet, at least partly because of its attempted repression and constraint.

The debate over sex education in Australia was coloured by the desire to create a new postwar society, utilising science and technology. During the early 1950s an increasing number of people began to argue for more open and frank discussions about sex, and for teaching sex education in schools.

While the thrust of the argument for sex education came from progressive educationists, they were not alone. In New South Wales, the Marriage Guidance Council supported their approach, suggesting it would help overcome sexual misinformation, which they believed was undermining many marriages. Reverend WG Coghlan, the Executive Officer of the Council, argued that the lack of sex education had disastrous results: 'In the face of widespread ignorance – or distorted knowledge – of facts, and the destructive consequences of both, the realistic approach surely is to ... improve the content and technique of group talk and discussion.'[50] Clearly Kinsey's works – with their wealth of information on human sexual behaviours – could be most useful.

Over the following decade, support increased for a wider dissemination to the general community of knowledge about sexual behaviour, and in particular through school sex education programs. Both the Father and Son Movement and the Mother and Daughter Movement supported this, and inaugurated public lectures.[51] Perhaps unexpectedly, support came too from the Women's Group of the Liberal Party of NSW, whose secretary wrote that the increasing number of sexual attacks on women and children reflected a failure on the part of parents to discharge their proper responsibilities in educating their children.[52] This echoed another writer, who suggested that it is 'not enough to leave it to parents', since many of them would themselves be ignorant of the facts and have their own misconceptions.[53] Even the idea of having school counsellors who were not teachers was raised.[54]

As could be imagined, most of the churches in Sydney – particularly the traditionally fundamentalist ones – fought strongly against this trend, not wanting their authority over sexuality to be replaced by a more scientific approach. The Rector of St Paul's Anglican Church in Cleveland Street Redfern thundered that it was misguided to think that 'giving public instruction and encouraging open discussion' on sexual matters, would 'rid it of its harmful taboos and so raise it to a more realised and intellectual level'.[55] He was not alone. When the Kinsey Report on female sexuality was released, giving more fuel to those in favour of a more scientific approach to sex education, the response was even more agitated. One letter writer, describing herself as a 'housewife', condemned the report as 'nonsensical'[56] – perhaps because it didn't square with her own experiences. And the big guns of the churches came out. The Reverend Gordon Powell, a fashionable preacher of the time, condemned Kinsey's findings, saying his investigations were only about the 'physical and emotional aspects of sex' and 'the main essential of sex was lost if the spiritual element was removed'.[57] This would undoubtedly have been news to hundreds of thousands of Sydneysiders who enjoyed their sex life, unaware that a major element was (according to Powell) missing. And for the Methodist Church, the Reverend Alan Walker argued that 'every Australian must choose between the Christian and the Kinsey view of life'.[58]

If that were so, then increasing numbers of Australians 'chose' the Kinsey view. This is clear, not only from the spate of letters written to newspapers supporting sex education free from moralising, but also from the sex education manuals that became a standard purchase for many educated middle-class Australian families in this period. Increasingly through the 1950s and 1960s the tone of these manuals changed. Those issued by the churches still surrounded any discussion of sex with misconceptions, with the Catholic Church leading in its lurid imagery and purple prose. Freud would have had a field day with the Reverend John A O'Brien who, in *So, You're in Love* (1964) argued that 'In all the long history of humanity, lust, naked and unrestrained, has never failed to deform friendship and love into an orgy of passion, whose denouement is nausea, remorse, shame, bitterness, suffering, death.'[59] Here, as Rosemary Auchmuty argues, 'one cannot help being a little suspicious of advice upon matters like sex and marriage when it is handed out by experts who have experienced neither'.[60] At a time when there was a growing belief in consulting professionals about one's problems, the medical profession was increasingly being seen as having the relevant experts in the field of sex and sexual behaviour. This changing perception played its part in undercutting the authority of the Catholic Church in matters sexual.

But the Catholic Church was not an isolated case. Homosexuality was unlikely to receive calm treatment in booklets sponsored by any of the churches. Welfare associations, like the Father and Son Movement, were not much better. This organisation, founded in 1927, worked in the field of marriage and family guidance. It issued a series of sex education booklets which received wide distribution – its sales of these booklets in 1969 alone exceeded one and a quarter million. 'The Movement probably did more than any other individual or organisation to distribute sex education information among Australians of the postwar generation.'[61]

Homosexuality was touched on in several of the Movement's booklets. These were a veritable goldmine of misinformation. While masturbation was starting to receive some honest treatment, homosexuality was treated either moralistically or inaccurately. In its booklet *Just Friends*, homosexuality was 'grouped with prostitution and rape as misdirected sex drives which are not only unsatisfying by comparison with the joys of marriage, home and family life, but also have "a most debasing effect on character'".[62] The 1956 edition of another sex education booklet, *Children No Longer*, perhaps trying to come to terms with 'new' ideas from Freud and psychoanalysis, suggested that homosexuals were not born, but made – especially by over-possessive mothers.[63]

While these manuals were important in disseminating a 'popular' perception of homosexuality, DJ West's *Homosexuality* (first published in Britain in 1955 and initially banned in Australia, but available from the early 1960s) was influential in determining how the educated and professional classes came to see homosexuality. West's book sold well in Australia after its release in 1961, with annual sales for the rest of the decade between 1500 and 2000. These dropped to just above 1000 by the early 1970s, and they were falling away after 1972–73, when new gay liberationist literature began to take up the running.[64]

From today's perspective, West's book seems hopelessly muddled. For example, his introduction notes that when considering the 'causes' of homosexuality he was 'Anxious to dispel any exaggerated beliefs in the unique strength of constitutional, hereditary, and endocrine influences, and naturally sympathetic to psychiatric and, in particular, psycho-analytic explanations', but he nevertheless 'readily admits the significance of cultural and sociological factors'.[65] Anything that could possibly be a 'cause' was given some attention. At the time, however, it was an important book, outlining a more sympathetic perception of homosexuality, and breaking the ground for further changes in attitudes, and even for possible attempts to alter the law.

Articles that began to appear in various popular magazines around Australia during the 1950s were also important in this widening debate about homosexuality. Probably the magazine that gave homosexuality most coverage – and incidentally acted as a good barometer of changing public perceptions – was *Time*. In 1950, for example, *Time* ran an article on how the medical perception of homosexuality was changing, under the heading 'The Abnormal'. Similarly, a 1953 article concerning a recent spate of arrests in England – including Sir John Gielgud and Tory peer Baron Montagu of Beaulieu – was headed 'The Unspeakable Crime'. But the articles themselves were not wholly negative. The first mentioned in passing that 'every sexual practice which is condemned in modern Western realisation is, or has been, considered normal somewhere, at some time'.[66] Likewise, the second article quoted one writer as saying, 'If we are agreed ... that chains and the whip were not the proper treatment for lunacy, can we be certain that prison is the proper place for the homosexual?'[67] Views dissenting from the common perception of homosexuality as a wilful perversion were gradually being introduced into public debate.[68]

But the articles in *Time* and its stablemate *Life* in the 1960s introduced something quite new – the perception that homosexuality wasn't just an affliction that affected individuals, and that a whole subculture was built around it, information that must have been quite startling news for the majority of the population. *Life* headed a major 1964 article 'A Secret World Grows Open and Bolder', while the *Time* 'Essay' in the January 1966 issue was on 'The Homosexual in America'.[69]

For the rest of the 1960s, further articles kept the issue of homosexuality in the public arena. A whole range of aspects were aired: whether homosexuality was really abnormal, or whether it was just one of many sexual varieties; the distinctions between sexual practices and gender identity; the rights of the state to interfere with 'private' behaviour; how widespread were homosexual subcultures in western societies; the need to recognise transsexuals and transvestites as distinct groups; the methods of police entrapment of homosexuals; the existence of rings of blackmailers who battened onto homosexuals; and even whether homosexuals were influential in determining a society's tastes.[70]

A measure of how perceptions were changing can be gauged from a very sympathetic article which appeared in *Time* in 1969. It commented on the recent release in the USA of the Hooker Report, and concluded that one of the major implications of the report was 'that society has been grossly unfair to the homosexual'.[71] Indeed a *Time* headline late in 1969 neatly encapsulated the evolving situation: 'The Homosexual: Newly Visible, Newly Understood'.[72]

Other magazines available in Australia through the 1960s similarly began to deal more openly – and sympathetically – with the issue of homosexuality. In a major article in the *Bulletin* in 1965, for example, criminologist Gordon Hawkins suggested that in Australia it 'requires no deep psychological insight to guess that this obsessive concern with masculinity and the hatred and contempt with which homosexuals are often regarded, both derive from difficulties involved in the repression of homosexual feelings which are normally present in all human beings'.[73] This was a fairly radical suggestion to make in a public forum in Australia at the time.

An article in the same magazine the following year, discussing the so-called sexual revolution and the changes it might have brought, was right when it noted that the change 'clearly extends from what may be publicly discussed to how it may be discussed'.[74] Certainly homosexuality was now being discussed in a very different way to how it had been just a decade before. The media played a significant role in this. The range of issues discussed and the general quality of the argument support the view that the quality press could lead, and influence, public opinion, rather than just reflect it. Not all the press, of course; Sydney's afternoon newspapers were never known for letting the facts stand in the way of a lurid story. But there was enough quality reporting to help get new perceptions across to opinion makers. These new views, circulating in the public domain, were important underpinnings for developments later in the 1960s.

Even popular magazines began to canvass the topic for their readers. Early in 1969, *Pol* published Ray Taylor's bitchy and critical review of *Boys in the Band*, a landmark play about a group of contemporary homosexuals at a birthday party in New York. The review drew a riposte from Dennis Altman, who pointed out that most of the problems for homosexuals related to the way in which society treated them.[75] And later the same year, *Cosmopolitan* published an article entitled 'Homosexual Men: How I Kicked the Habit'. This was a somewhat snide article about the problems for women who became too involved emotionally with sympathetic homosexual men; but it spelt out the widespread existence of such men.[76] It also noted that homosexuals were in a wide variety of industries, and did not conform to the usual stereotypes: 'They are also sometimes lawyers, advertising executives, high-powered salesmen, even your friendly neighbourhood grocer. I'm not exaggerating.'[77]

In other more literary forms, homosexuality and homosexuals received increasing attention. Whereas once they might not be considered a fit topic to write about, now they made an increasing appearance in novels and other forms of fiction. Indeed, in some of these, homosexuals were major characters and homosexuality the central theme.

Unfortunately, many of the books written overseas in which homosexuality figured were banned in Australia. Thus Gore Vidal's *The City and the Pillar*, first published in the USA in

1949, and James Baldwin's *Another Country* (1962), were not readily available here until the 1970s.[78] Others managed to slip through. Mary Renault's *The Charioteer*, Rodney Garland's *The Heart in Exile*, Gillian Freeman's *The Leather Boys*, all novels of 'queer' import – to use the British publisher Anthony Blond's phrase[79] – were available in Australia in this period. Even the ubiquitous science fiction genre started to get in on the act. In *Stranger in a Strange Land* (1961), Robert Heinlein, author of numerous sci-fi novels, introduces a discussion of human social habits and mores, including homosexuality. In the book a major character notes that history reveals 'the same sad story: a plan for perfect sharing and perfect love, glorious hopes and high ideals – then persecution and failure'.[80]

One interesting sideline is a group of novels with a homosexual theme set either completely or partly in Australia. In *June in Her Spring* (1952) by Colin MacInnes, who grew up in Australia, part of the plot revolves around a homosexual relationship between two major characters. Stuart Lauder's *Wingers Landfall* (1962) starts out in Sydney and focuses on the unresolved homosexual desires of its main character. Under his *nom de plume* Neville Jackson, Australian writer GM Glaskin, who lived in London safely away from Australia's laws, published his *No End to the Way* in 1965, a novel that charts the unhappy homosexual love affair of two men in Australia.[81]

Despite the Cold War climate, Australian journals of literary aspirations made a few tentative gestures towards presenting faintly homoerotic material. Thus in 1959 Queensland-born poet Don Maynard had two pieces published: a poem, 'Athlete', in the *Bulletin*, and a short story, 'conversations' in *Westerly*.[82] But such gestures were rare. Far more commonly, even in the literary world, homophobia prevailed. It even affected professional criticism. Geoffrey Dutton has argued that 'homophobia

[was] behind the hostile reviews that Douglas Stewart wrote of Patrick White's novels'.[83]

Acquaintance with literature such as this – particularly with books like *The Charioteer, The Leather Boys, Quatrefoil, Another Country, No End to the Way,* and eventually *The City and the Pillar* – helped to promote something that had never been acceptable in Australia: sentimental ideas about romantic homosexual love. That most of these books had unhappy endings for their homosexual characters was not necessarily a problem: it was the expected outcome for any 'forbidden' love affairs even for heterosexuals, as the tales of Antony and Cleopatra, Heloise and Abelard, and Romeo and Juliet attest. At least now male homosexuals could find characters with whose emotions they could identify. Books like these, for those with access to them, were a useful antidote to the outpouring of negative images of homosexuality from tabloid newspapers and populist magazines. Like the Kinsey Report, they provided a small beacon of light in a generally darkened world.

Indeed, it was through much of what I read that I began to come to terms with what was then regarded as a 'sexual perversion', everything from Plato's *Phaedrus* to Walt Whitman's *Leaves of Grass* (1855), and more modern novels such as Roger Peyrefitte's *Special Friendships* (1944) or James Baldwin's *Another Country*.

The main sources for these books were various libraries and a seamy little downstairs bookshop in Rowe Street, in the heart of Sydney's financial district, where one could buy 'semi-erotic' banned literature.

I had first gone there in pursuit of Plato's *Phaedrus*, and the bookseller, confronted with a nervous and cautious young man in his late teens, had been helpful in directing my attention to 'other titles you might be interested in'. Eventually

I bought many books there, most of which would now be considered fairly innocuous literature, but which at the time seemed to burn through the plain brown paper wrappings that enclosed them when I left the shop; novels such as Rodney Garland's *The Heart in Exile*, James Barr's *Quatrefoil* (1950), and Mary Renault's *The Charioteer*.

The books allowed me to see that there were others who were as I was, others who wanted what I wanted. Homosexuality was no longer a nameless evil, but something that had existed since time immemorial, and homosexual love was an emotion – deep and passionate – just like heterosexual love, even if it was not equal in the eyes of the society in which I lived.

In this widening public discourse about homosexuality, it was becoming increasingly common to talk about 'the homosexual'. In Parliament, in the courts, in police reports, in newspapers, in sex manuals, in novels, or in medical literature, this personage – the homosexual – now existed. This reflected a clear change from the prewar period, where it was individuals who were seen to indulge in certain acts or commit various crimes. It was part of the process of the creation of a 'homosexual' identity. And this phenomenon of 'defining' homosexuals into existence was mirrored at the level of the individual, who began to think of himself as a homosexual, and act accordingly.

Two institutions of the camp world – one old, one new – played an important role in helping individuals further this process of self-identification as homosexuals. They were the pre-existing friendship networks, and a range of private clubs that began to appear on the scene.

There were still limited opportunities for publicly meeting other people with homosexual inclinations. Among them was the same range of city hotel bars, varying from the swank to the sleazy. After six o'clock closing was repealed in 1954, and hotels were allowed to stay open until 10 pm, night-life in the CBD presented a host of alternative attractions for men with homo-erotic desires. But even with the end of the 'six o'clock swill', for many men, the focus of a night's social life was not drinking in hotel bars; it was not to everyone's taste or inclination, and it was not possible for adolescents. Similarly, while there were always the beats, many people had difficulty in accepting the ethos of the beat or its ethics. Thus for many, the private networks of friends remained the only way to meet others like themselves.

Many of the major social events of the camp world, particularly the parties and dances, were organised through these friendship networks, or several of them in particular. During the 1950s and into the 1960s they had, of necessity, to be far more subdued and discreet than they had been in the interwar years or even during the war. Some were held in public halls, others were held in private residences, but the organisers had to go to extreme lengths to avoid police detection and attention.

If they were held in public halls they were booked under an innocuous name. And care was needed to sell the tickets that were necessary to cover the costs of the hall and food and enter-tainment – one brought one's own drink. One ploy to stop the police hearing of the dance or party was to sell the tickets just before the event, and usually at a major commercial homosex-ual venue. Thus tickets might be sold – to friends and acquaint-ances only – at the Long Bar of the Australia Hotel, or at the Dugout Bar at the Carlton, or at some other hotel, but only on the actual day of the big event. Another ploy was simply to arrange for everyone to meet at a suburban railway station, and then organise bus or car travel from there, but only for those who were vouched for by someone else in the circle.[84] Under these arrangements, homosexual parties were organised around various

Sydney suburbs, and held in such venues as the Library Hall in Glebe, an RSL hall at Mortlake, the Hollywood Tennis Courts Hall in Concord, the Gaiety Dance Hall (behind a milk bar) in Oxford Street, Darlinghurst, and at a public hall in Coogee (this last rented out via a contact in a weightlifting group).[85]

Sometimes the police or newspaper reporters – the latter chasing exposés[86] – were deliberately fed false information. This led to one memorable occasion when two newspaper reporters, armed with cameras and hoping to expose a group of 'effeminate perverts, flung open the doors of a suburban church hall and rushed in – only to find a local Mothers' League meeting in progress'.[87]

Even arranging for a band to play at these dances was not beyond the ingenuity of the organisers. A favoured band was composed of blind musicians, many of them ex-servicemen. Bookings were arranged through the Blind Society, which was happy to find work for this unusual band, which would – presumably – be none the wiser as to the clientele, or who was dancing with whom.[88]

Once a year came the Artists' Ball, now usually at the Trocadero Ballroom in George Street. This extravaganza continued the tradition of those major events from the prewar years, and attracted enormous amounts of publicity. But the publicity and the ostentatious characters – drag queens arriving in removalist vans, since their gowns and wigs were so elaborate there was no other way to get there; one man whose costume had a live chook tied into a nest on top of his head; a male party-goer who came as a tram conductress, and caught a tram up George Street from Central Railway to the Trocadero, making a little money by collecting fares along the way; ball-goers dressed as Adam and Eve, wearing only fig leaves (and getting arrested for their trouble); and much nudity, casually displayed – were all

135

guaranteed to bring the unwanted attention of police.[89] Eventually the constant police harassment over what they saw as 'public displays of degeneracy' – and gate-crashing by larrikins, intent on a brawl – caused these balls to be abandoned.[90]

The friendship networks were also largely responsible for organising parties in the Blue Mountains, often on the Queen's Birthday weekend, during the 1950s and 1960s. The parties were held either at the home of someone in the network or at one of the many 'nice old places up there that people were only too happy to rent out'.[91] There could be a ball, and sometimes a theatrical performance, at which certain well-known public figures from the theatre or movie world might appear – and even perform.[92]

The other 'institution' that made its first appearance in this period was the private homosexual club, and it came to be important in the camp world. It emerged out of the networks of friends and represented, as it were, friendship institutionalised. The first of these was the Knights of Chameleons, founded in 1962. Its antecedents were in the discreetly named North Shore Ball Committee, an informal group of friends who organised a range of social events. And it was soon followed by others: the Pollynesians in 1964, the Boomerangs in 1967, and the Diggers, the Chelsea Players, Tiffany's, Regals, Sundowners, Karingals and others, over the following years.

The names the groups chose tell us something of the times and their origins. Thus the name 'Chameleons' has connotations of hiding one's true identity, changing one's colours to blend in with the surroundings. The Boomerangs derived their name from Boomerang Street (below St Mary's Cathedral), still a major Sydney beat in the 1960s. The Diggers memorialised a connection between friends going back to the days of World War II, while the Pollynesians were formed by a man whose nickname was 'Polly' and an Aboriginal woman friend.[93] These two invited six other friends to join them, adopt a constitution, form a committee, and get in touch with further friends. And so the network spread, with the club gaining new members. This was the pattern for most of these clubs.

Secrecy was an essential ingredient. Mail to members was sent out in plain envelopes with only a post office box number on the back. The clubs organised parties, dances and picnics. They were, as one member said, the gay equivalent of an RSL club. But they should not be dismissed as just 'social' clubs: they also fulfilled vital 'social' functions. They allowed young men, and women, with homosexual inclinations, to meet others like themselves under circumstances of little or no stress. And they helped look after their own in times of crisis. Those lucky enough to come into contact with such a club could find an extended network of other homosexuals, without going public – and the risks that that might entail.[94]

These clubs, like the friendship networks, clearly played their part in the development of homosexual identity. In both of these, young men and women could look to older men and women and learn appropriate behaviours. One commentator has noted how younger men were often introduced into the networks by older men, 'often referred to as aunties'. These 'aunties' would meet younger men almost anywhere, at work, at their local church, at a chess club or local library, and as their relationships were mostly asexual, they were able to assist them through the rites of passage into the networks.[95]

A final point to make is that only a small minority of the friendship networks became institutionalised into clubs: the vast majority of them continued on, remaining as they were, fluid, discreet, and only occasionally overlapping. But many of the friendship networks did overlap with the membership of the new clubs. And many of the major social events of the period, like the dances at such places as the Dispensary Hall in Parramatta Road, Petersham, in the late 1960s, drew on both clubs and various friendship networks for their patrons.[96]

The friendship networks and the emerging clubs played a major role in the social lives of many male homosexuals in this period, and were two of the many factors helping to account for the development of this new homosexual identity. The way in which doctors, criminologists and politicians now talked of 'the homosexual', and the ways in which newspapers and magazines reported this, put this new conception into the public discourse. Taken together, it meant that vital components for the creation of a homosexual identity were in place. They were soon to be joined by another factor, as an increasing number and type of commercial venues catering for 'the homosexual' emerged in Sydney during the 1960s.[97]

From 1956, television was an important factor that began to impact on the series of social changes taking place in Australia, changes that would transform the country. It began to capture the leisure-time interests of an increasing number of Australians, and also made possible new ideas and new ways of thinking and living, bringing them to the attention of Australians, particularly the young.

Clearly then by the late 1960s things were changing. Increased publicity meant that the wider public, and also those with homoerotic interests themselves, knew far more about homosexuality than ever before. The way in which public discourse developed led to the 'creation' of this new identity, the homosexual. And increasing numbers of men with homoerotic desires began to congregate together, in the friendship networks, within the clubs, and at the commercial venues, and often began to see themselves in this way, as 'homosexual' or 'camp'.

What Michel Foucault notes as having been 'created' in Europe from the late nineteenth century had now become quite evident in parts of Australia – and clearly in Sydney. The 'homosexual' had been designated

> a personage, a past, a case history, and a childhood,
> in addition to being a type of life, a life form, and a
> morphology, with an indiscreet anatomy and possibly
> a mysterious physiology. Nothing that went into his
> total composition was unaffected by his sexuality. It was
> everywhere present in him: at the root of all his actions
> because it was their insidious and indefinitely active
> principle; written immodestly on his face and body
> because it was a secret that always gave itself away. It was
> consubstantial with him, less as a habitual sin than as a
> singular nature.[98]

There was an expanding world relating to 'the homosexual', and parts of it had an increasingly public face. Yet by the end of the 1960s, different ideas had started to emerge, ideas that dramatically altered both the face and style of this camp world: the ideas of gay liberation, and a gay identity.

CHAPTER 5

THE PERSONAL BECOMES THE POLITICAL

Social change, the camp world and the advent of gay liberation

A Cold War mentalité undoubtedly dominated Australia in the immediate postwar years, setting the scene for the persecution of anyone seen as different. But a range of other developments, such as demographic and economic change, sociological developments, ideas arising out of the counter-cultural revolution and the sexual liberation movement, along with a growing dissatisfaction among 'homosexuals' with aspects of their lives, combined to lead the 'camp' world in Australia – and in particular in Sydney – along unexpected paths, to far-reaching changes.

Massive social changes in the period from the early 1960s through to the advent of the Whitlam government in 1972 made the world a *very* different place. The so-called swinging sixties hit Sydney with a vengeance, an era goldenly remembered as 'sex & drugs & rock & roll'. The decade started tragically enough with the kidnap and murder of 11-year-old Graeme Thorne at Bondi in July 1960, a failed extortion attempt. The last tram ran in Sydney in 1961, ushering in an era of growing road congestion on the city's streets, although motorists were cheered by the opening of the additional section to the Cahill Expressway in 1962 and the Warringah Expressway in 1968. The Bogle–Chandler case began to intrigue Sydney when two bodies were found by the Lane Cove River on New Year's Day in 1963. And shockwaves reverberated around the world on 22 November 1963, when American President John F Kennedy was assassinated. The decade also saw the South Sydney 'Rabbitohs' make a glorious comeback to the Rugby League stage. When Neil Armstrong walked on the moon surface on 21 July 1969 and spoke those immortal words, 'one small step for [a] man, one giant leap for mankind', it truly seemed the dawn of a new era.

At a cultural level, thousands of screaming young fans turned out on Sydney's streets during the Beatles tumultuous visit in 1964, while the satirical magazine *OZ*, published from 1963 to 1969, incurred the wrath of the police and respectable Sydneysiders, leading to several obscenity trials. *The Mavis Bramston Show*, on television from 1964 to 1968, brought satire to a gob-smacked Sydney audience. The decade drew to a close with the musical *Hair*, joyfully embracing nudity, homosexuality and obscenities galore. Sydney would never be the same again.

The major social movements, or social changes, seem to dominate the stage. The counter-cultural revolution, the sexual revolution, the advent of second-wave feminism, student power, the anti-censorship battles around 'porno-politics', and the anti-war movement all come to mind. At a more popular level, 'the swinging sixties' had connotations of hedonistic living, alternative lifestyles, greater access to recreational drugs, and, of course, sexual experimentation. Indeed the 1960s can, at one level, be seen as a period of almost continuous turmoil, when one generation turned dramatically against the values of its elders, leading to ongoing agitation on a range of fronts. Demonstrations in the streets of Australia's major cities led to recurring confrontations between police and protesters. Anti–Vietnam War demonstrations in Sydney from the mid-1960s, for instance, saw the burning of draft cards and tens of thousands of people marching through the city's streets. It was a time of increased radicalisation and action in Australia.

The young played a particularly important role. There was massive population growth in Australia, with the total jumping from 8.3 million in 1950 to 10.4 million in 1960 to 12.6 million in 1970, and a higher proportion of the population were young. By the early 1960s, the postwar 'baby boom' was moving into the employable age group or, increasingly, into the tertiary institutions, which had expanded rapidly after a significant growth in university funding from the conservative coalition government in Canberra. By 1966 'the federal share of Australia's educational expenditure was 17 per cent, 6 per cent more than a mere five years before'.[1] Old universities were transformed and new universities and colleges were built to meet an intense demand for educational opportunity.

A radicalisation of academe occurred partly because of the increasing academisation of Australia's radical intelligentsia.[2] Many bright young radicals gained academic positions, mainly in the social sciences, as more and more jobs became available in the expanding university system. Indeed, as Andrew Milner has noted, the university system 'came to provide the radical intelligentsia with a relatively safe base from which to criticise the conservatism of the wider Australian society'.[3]

Many of the 1960s social movements were centred on the universities, but they were not simply student movements. They may have used student newspapers and magazines as their mouthpieces, and the campuses were undoubtedly the single most important centre for much of the organisational activity –

particularly the anti-war movement. But the connections spread out far beyond the universities to those in 'cultural' occupations – teachers and musicians, even priests – and the young generally. The universities played a critical role by providing a distinctly receptive and sympathetic social milieu for the emerging 'new left' and its associated social movements. They were also a site for successful radical political mobilisation and forays into the outside world,[4] drawing most of their activist support from middle-class youth – increasingly affluent, educated and disenchanted with the world of their parents.

These activities have been loosely grouped together as the 'counter-culture'. This was more than just a rebellious youth culture: it was a youth culture with a political purpose. The counter-culture first emerged in the USA, but the same sort of economic and social conditions led to its development in Australia. Similar patterns are evident over all western societies. As Dennis Altman notes:

> the existence of comparatively large numbers of persons
> drawn almost exclusively from the middle class and not yet
> fully integrated into 'the system' through jobs and marriage,
> but at least partially free to question the system, was the
> basic pre-condition for a counter-culture.[5]

But despite these similarities, the counter-culture in each country had its own special concerns, its own distinctive characteristics.

Frank Moorhouse and Craig McGregor have chronicled in fiction and in journalism the many and varied aspects of counter-cultural life in Australia through the 1960s, and particularly in Sydney. In some ways the traditions of Sydney's libertarians and The Push blended in with the counter-culture, although the new youth culture was far more diverse, more bizarre – outrageous even – than those older groups could ever have been. Still there were continuities. McGregor, commenting on these sociological changes, notes that if one wanted to understand 'Australia and the life Australians lead … one must turn to pubs rather than play-readings, sex-roles not symphonies, parties not paintings'.[6] Pubs and parties, something the old libertarians understood, continued as a focus for counter-cultural life. In Moorhouse's stories, parties like the one described below catch the essence of the times.

> The party burned with dancing, political talk, drinking, pot smoking, sexual hunting … Canned Heat and Bob Dylan tried to engage him as he drank beer from a paper cup and talked about his country high school and conditions in Cuba.[7]

I have my own recollections of those times, and this night was not untypical. I went with some friends to a big old two-storey house in New South Head Road, Double Bay. It was fairly decrepit, and supposedly empty, or the hippie inhabitants were moving out soon and were having a farewell party. We had come from the pub, and had taken along our own booze and drugs. As we climbed the steps to the front door – open and waiting for us – we could hear the music pounding out.

There was entertainment, a group called Sylvia and the Synthetics. They had just begun to appear at events around Sydney, a group of usually five or six mainly gay men who cross-dressed and performed outrageous acts – in public. The core were Doris Fish (aka Philip Mills), Danny Aboud and Rod (now Ros) Palmer, with occasional others like Candy Darling and sometimes female friends like Cherry Ripe. There never was a Sylvia though, and the night always started with someone apologising that Sylvia wouldn't be there tonight!

Live sex on stage was *de rigueur*, and the well-endowed Danny was always cheered, and sometimes enticed to offer his charms to those nearby. But this night, the makeshift stage – built out from the lower stairs going to the upper level – collapsed, probably because of the frenetic dancing. So what was new! Since everyone was on drugs, there was little coherence in what happened – but that didn't matter. During the night, about 50 people turned up at the house, and darkened rooms held their own excitements: it was a time when you could get some 'square' guy to try a bit of homosexual adventure, with the line 'How do you know if you haven't tried it?' I did, and he enjoyed it, but I lost him soon after.

I remember I went there with Cameron and John and Gary, but I can't remember who I left with.

Amid this turmoil and questioning of past values, many of the long-dominant institutions of Australian society began to lose their authority. Certainly the churches saw a major decline in their power. One writer has noted a number of things that took their toll:

> affluence, a much better educated laity, a more hedonistically
> self-confident youth, pervasive anti-authoritarianism,
> divisive new theologies, falling clerical recruitment, and
> weakening family cohesiveness.[8]

This was most obviously reflected in declining attendances at churches. The percentage that had attended church in the previous seven days dropped from 30 per cent in 1960 and 1966 to 25 per cent in 1970, to 20 per cent in 1976 and 19 per cent in 1980, according to Morgan Gallup polls. Indifference, rather than hostility, was the root cause.[9]

Other factors may have been important too: the dilemma

faced by many Catholics with the general availability of the birth control pill from the early 1960s, and how this affected their relationship with their church; the impact of Vatican II on social tolerance and sexual morality; the churches' willingness to campaign together for state aid for religious schools, and how this affected their individual identity and authority; and the emergence of divergent and dissenting voices within particular denominations. The Anglican Church could have two almost opposing viewpoints on major social issues, depending on whether they were expressed by the progressive Melbourne Synod or the arch-conservative Sydney one. All these factors played their part in the changed situation of the churches in Australian society from the 1960s into the 1980s. Perhaps the religious voices on Sydney radio over a half century best epitomise the difference: Dr Leslie Rumble from the late 1920s was concerned with sectarianism and dissent from church authority; in the 1980s the Reverend Roger Bush was concerned with how a compassionate church should respond to major social problems.

This diversity and loss of authority within the churches was important for many of the emerging social movements, certainly for the changing perception of homosexuality, because the churches no longer spoke with one voice. Indeed religious figures were often involved in many of these social movements on the side of change. And despite the decline in power of the churches in Australia in this period, religion – and the churches – did maintain their influence as a major pressure group. Michael Hogan observes that while 'most Australians do not care very much about what church leaders say, and ... lead largely secular lives ... there are a number of aspects of Australian life where religion is central', notably, 'the family, the culture of sexual morality ... [and] the limits of social tolerance'.[10] The debate on homosexuality in Australian society impinges on all three areas.

In a period of ferment, there were also major cultural developments within Australia. The country came out of its cultural backwater and a range of activities, previously suspect as 'poofy', became more commonplace. The arts flourished, and homosexual men no longer felt the necessity to go into exile overseas to avoid persecution over their private life.[11]

In Sydney this cultural flourishing manifested itself at both a mainstream and counter-cultural level. The building of the Sydney Opera House began in 1957, and it opened in 1973, while the Yellow House in Macleay Street, Kings Cross, an old terrace taken over by a group of artists, among them Martin Sharp, was a focus for many outside-the-mainstream activities by the early 1970s. The causes of this cultural renaissance have been ascribed by one historian to

> wider education, the European migrant influence, affluence, and, it could be suspected, the psychological impact both of a new sense of Australian involvement in the mainstream of world affairs and a diminishing sense of isolation in the face of revolutionary change in transport and communications.[12]

Social movements and cultural renaissance are but part of the story. Australian society was also in the process of relocating itself in and around its major cities. The postwar flow of migration into Australia had played its part in the unprecedented growth of the cities. It was a time of bustle and expansion, and the physical aspects of the cities changed. Sydney was in the forefront of this development. Robin Boyd noted in 1960, when comparing Sydney with the other capitals, that it had

> the tallest buildings, the brightest lights, the best and closest beaches with the burliest lifesavers, the fiercest colours in the

fastest taxis with the toughest drivers, the patchiest parks
and the busiest traffic. Sydney has the only facilities for night
life worth mentioning, the highest standards in popular
entertainment, the smartest and tawdriest elements of the
Australian pattern.[13]

Sydney clearly still retained its attractiveness to the outsider.
But the boom had its costs. The character of the city changed,
particularly in those areas around the old core, the CBD and
the nearby suburbs.

Until the early postwar years, the CBD had a monopoly
on the retail stores and the major entertainment venues – the
major department stores; live theatres; ballrooms like the Trocadero which hosted some of the major drag balls; and first-run
cinemas including the Prince Edward, the Regent and the State.
But from the early 1960s, with the ever-increasing use of the
motor car, the focus of life began to move to the suburbs. New
'drive-in' shopping centres were built, which provided an alternative to the CBD. Television – and the developers' hammer –
delivered a deathblow to many of the city cinemas. Life became
largely suburbanised.[14]

This was reflected, too, in the inner suburbs. Hugh Stretton,
writing in 1970, bewailed the changes of the ever-expanding
suburbia and the shift in focus from the city proper. In particular, he regretted the end of that 'bohemia' that had existed in the
Kings Cross and Darlinghurst areas:

The more artistic and inventive productions are dispersing
from central Sydney. Already the rents around Kings Cross
make sure that the sale and consumption of urban goods
drive out the distilling. Most of the novels discussed and
pictures sold there are nowadays written and painted in

Sarsaparillan suburbs, or the bush. The little theatres play five miles away, in different directions. The dwindling number of picturesque characters now have an angle, or a pusher … Bohemian life and adventurous taste are already driven over the hill to Paddington, and somewhat monotonised even there by the rents that will soon drive them from 'city' altogether. An ambling hippie culture may settle here and there for short sojourns; but there will be very little hope of any old-style Chelsea or Bloomsbury or Left Bank or Greenwich Village: no central place with cheap land and cheap old buildings on a main skein of good passenger transport and with plenty of cheap beds of its own, where the young and the arts and the ideas can rely on meeting one another.[15]

Behind all these changes – the spread of suburbia, the growing use of the motor vehicle, the increasing activism of middle-class youth, the emergence of new social movements, the deterioration and then regeneration of the old inner-city areas – sweeping economic changes underpinned the transformation of Australia. As one historian has noted, the early 1950s through to the early 1970s were 'kind decades for Australia. The mass of her people enjoyed peace, security and stability on a previously unknown scale.'[16] The economic base for this rested on rapid industrial expansion and the intensive settlement of previously unused land, all facilitated by rapid population increase. Despite some minor hiccups, the 1950s and 1960s were a period when children grew to adulthood and, later, started raising their own families, never having known, at a personal level, the impact of depression.

Social critic Donald Horne pointed out that 'There never had been such material prosperity. People were now living in an age in which a miracle had occurred: there were jobs for everyone.'[17] Low levels of unemployment and record economic growth ensured, statistically at least, growing affluence for the average Australian.[18] Substantial population growth, from both immigration and natural increase, aided this improved material prosperity.

The acceleration of economic expansion became much more marked after the early 1960s, which one historian has suggested 'had much to do with the age-composition of the Australian population'.[19] In contrast to a marked decline in birth-rates associated with both the 1930s Depression and World War II, the return to peace 'was signalled by a "baby boom" which greatly added to the population of dependants in the total population' in the immediate postwar years.[20] But by the 1960s, 'this post-war bulge had moved into the employable age-group'.[21] The Australian population was, statistically, not only increasingly younger, but also increasingly affluent.

This phenomenon of the young and affluent occurred in all western industrial countries as the new youth market of the 'teenager' developed.[22] Their existence in Australia was recognised in various ways. In 1959 for example, the *Australian Women's Weekly* launched a new supplement, *Teenager's Weekly*, aimed at this young and affluent group.[23]

With growing affluence, a greatly increased range of consumer durable goods became available. Many of these – vacuum cleaners, pop-up toasters, refrigerators, radiograms, television sets – were aimed at the average household. But others were of particular importance to young males, particularly homosexual ones.

The most significant was the car. The number of motor cars in Australia jumped from just over 880 000 in 1950 to just under 2.1 million in 1960, and to just under 3.9 million in

1970.[24] Much of this increased car ownership was among the young. The expansion of hire purchase facilities in this period turned what had been a largely middle-class market into a 'true mass market'.[25]

This rapid expansion in car ownership was clearly evident in NSW, where the number of cars jumped from just under 270 000 in 1950 to over 623 000 in 1960, and up to 1.1 million in 1970.[26] As one historian has noted, 'the motor car greatly extended the freedom of movement around the large conurbations, permitting greater use of urban facilities, a less restricted range of employment opportunities, and greater leisure possibilities'.[27]

The motor vehicle certainly permitted many things not previously feasible. One was greater sexual experimentation. Since the 1920s, society's moralisers had been warning about the impact of the motor vehicle. Back in 1935 the Bishop of Bendigo, in an article 'The Car Conquers the Cradle', had criticised young married couples for putting off having children, to enable them to save money to buy a car.[28] Later generations of moralisers complained that cars became in effect 'mobile bedrooms'. The novelist Murray Bail has nicely caught the essence of this teenage sexual experimentation:

> Late at night he drove the Wolseley through the deserted
> streets ... the little car responding well ... while behind
> him on the slippery leather a talkative girl in a humid skirt
> submitted to the hectic experiments of one or sometimes two
> of his mechanically minded friends, their muffled breathing
> and rustlings, snapping of elastic, sending the barometric
> lump in his throat down once again to his trousers.[29]

As Bail notes, it was indeed an age of 'auto' eroticism!

This availability of a 'mobile bedroom' undoubtedly affected the sexual mores of Australia's adolescents, irrespective of whether they were heterosexually or homosexually inclined. But it had a special significance for young male homosexuals in that it gave them a place for sexual experimentation away from both family and their peer group, most of whom were probably heterosexual.[30]

The car also gave greater mobility. This was particularly important to young homosexuals growing up in the dormitory suburbs on Sydney's ever-expanding fringes. It allowed them access to the established camp world in the city, enabled them to join in the friendship networks and clubs in the suburbs, and it permitted them to go to – and experience – the beats that they might hear about.[31]

The motor car began to make its impact on life for the young male homosexual from the 1950s. A decade later, another phenomenon of the increasingly young and affluent postwar society was a dramatic change in domicile. Once again, improving economic conditions permitted changes to a long-established pattern.

Immediately after the war, a large pent-up demand for housing led to a massive expansion in the housing market, mostly in 'the newly sub-divided areas on the outskirts of the cities'.[32] This in turn increased the housing stock available in the old 'slum' suburbs close to the CBD, areas of predominantly terrace housing, from whence the nuclear families had fled to the clean air and cleaner lifestyles of the outer suburbs.

The reasons were clear. The ethos to create the most favourable home environment for the raising of a family increasingly became associated with the outer suburbs; with its cleaner air, and – by implication – better environment. As money was diverted to provide the necessary infrastructure for this – roads and electricity, water supply and sewerage, telephones and transport – the inner cities were neglected, and rental accommodation became relatively cheap there. Immigrants often found resting places in these old inner-city suburbs, which in itself may have hastened the flight of Anglo-Australian families, who moved away from what were increasingly seen as 'wog' suburbs.

But migrants were not the only group to find the inner city an appropriate place to live.[33] In Sydney, the inner-city areas, particularly around Darlinghurst and Kings Cross, had long been havens for those who lived outside the mainstream. Next door was Paddington, and the population mix of this and other close inner-city suburbs changed dramatically during the 1960s. The process of gentrification was starting. As Peter Spearritt notes, it was

> precisely those areas considered to be 'slum suburbs' such as Paddington, Balmain and Glebe, which witnessed a striking process of embourgeoisement since the sixties. Between the 1966 and 1971 census the percentage of professional and upper white collar workers in the Sydney workforce rose by only one half of one per cent. But in the area covered by the Paddington postcode it rose a remarkable seven per cent, fourteen times the metropolitan average, while Balmain and Glebe saw increases of six and five per cent respectively.[34]

There was a high homosexual component in this, too, as was recognised in the satirical magazine *OZ* which lampooned the trendy homosexual gentrifier in a 1964 pen portrait. A smart 'queen', after telling us where he shops and what he does, goes on:

> and I have an absolutely MAD little terrace house in Paddington ... it's just too too DIVINE ... it was really

nothing when I got it … and so cheap too … and *Vouge* [sic]
are going to do a colour feature on it and I'm just too thrilled
for words.[35]

This homosexual component of gentrification was not unique
to Sydney. It occurred in other Australian cities with nineteenth
century housing stock close to the CBD, and in cities around
the world, particularly in the USA.[36]

And while some middle-class homosexuals were undoubtedly buying and renovating in the inner-city areas, this was but
one of several patterns that were emerging. The census figures
also indicate the increasing incidence of young males leaving
the family home to set up places of residence of their own, prior
to – or independent of – marriage.

It had long been the tradition in Australia that young males
would live at home until marriage – as it has been put, they
would only abandon the mother-servant when they acquired
the wife-servant. Economic necessity cemented this social tradition in place as much as anything else. But the pattern changed
with the increasing affluence from the late 1950s, the creation
of the teenager, and the coming of new economic and social
freedoms for the young. Once again, the census figures indicate
that this was initially a middle-class phenomenon rather than a
working-class one, but it did change over time.

This trend, of young people moving away from home, gathered pace from the early 1960s. Away from parental control,
young people could experience greater economic, social and
sexual freedom. Male homosexuals living in Sydney in this
period, with access to a motor vehicle or living away from home,
had an expanding camp world to explore.

First, the old haunts: the coffee shops and restaurants in
the city proper that attracted a larger-than-usual homosexual

clientele. Several of the Cahills and Repins coffee shops, particularly those in Market and King streets, were still prominent. Restaurants like the Shalimar and Madam Pura's Latin Cafe also continued their long association with camp patrons.

Second, other places in the city were occasional homosexual venues, such as the Music Academy in Rowe Street, behind the Commonwealth Bank. This building housed several music studios, one-room affairs where violin or piano lessons were given during the week. But they also served as the location for occasional parties – usually on Saturday nights. The admission price was 5 shillings, and several adjoining studios were used, one of which might have little or no lighting, to encourage 'romance'.[37] Likewise, Saturday night camp parties were held at the Burlakov's Ballet School, on the first floor of an old building near Circular Quay.[38]

The major attraction remained the bars of the old city hotels, which – although their days were numbered – still drew their homosexual clienteles. The Australia, Ushers and the Carlton were still the favoured meeting places of the respectable middle-class camp. One man who grew to adulthood in this period recalls that, from the early 1950s:

> Sydney's three gayest bars mid-week were the Carlton,
> Ushers, and the Long Bar of the Australia – close together
> in Castlereagh Street between Martin Place and King Street.
> Between 5 and 6 o'clock each week night, but especially on
> Wednesdays and Fridays, these bars swarmed with what was
> unquestionably Sydney's most smartly dressed collection
> of young men. Formality was the keynote. Fashion decreed
> well-cut, single breasted suits, mostly in charcoal grey
> with narrow silk ties, and olive green or grey Trilby hats
> predominated. More audacious dressers occasionally affected

pink or even mauve shirts. Open-neck shirts were unthought of![39]

Other hotels in the city which attracted a homosexual clientele were much the same as before: the 'salt-meat alley' hotels in George Street – the Belfields, the Tatler and the Town Hall. The patrons were largely working-class, or those who fancied a bit of 'rough trade', and – of course – the police. One patron remembers the 'men in Akubras' who stood at the bar of the Belfields trying to look inconspicuous as they watched who was doing what with whom.[40]

For those discovering the 'camp' world, it sometimes required courage to go into one of these hotels. Here's how the protagonist in one novel set in 1960s Australia described his feelings:

> So, in you go, then! Open the door and keep yourself slow, and don't look around too much until you get to the bar at the end of the room. Try to look nonchalant, as though you're just dropping in for a casual drink after a cocktail party or something, and don't want the night to burn out so quickly. Try and find someone you know well enough to talk with, but someone that won't get you tied up into something you don't want and won't try to tie himself up with whatever you do want.[41]

Most pubs with a camp clientele would try to be discreet, and not draw too much attention to themselves. This following description could be of any number of camp bars in Sydney in the 1960s.

The three counters of the rectangular bar are all crowded, sometimes two and three deep. Some that can't fit in pose carefully in small clusters in the middle of the large high-ceilinged old fashioned room. Lots of tired mirrors in gilt frames, ornate pillars and paint peeling off like sun-burn. Rows and rows of bottles, mostly fancy liqueurs that rarely get opened from one year to another. Beer and cigarette ads and some dried flowers stuffed in a vase. Toy dogs or dolls that the barmaids get as gifts from some of the more gushing types, and keep for mascots on their tills. All a bit tatty, and not entirely clean. The kind of pub the gays always seem to pick out and make their own, the world over. A bit tizzy, but not too flash to keep out the rough trade, like sailors and that.[42]

However, from the late 1950s – and certainly by the early 1960s – the focus of the camp world began to shift away from these CBD hotels. There were several reasons for this. An increasing amount of police surveillance and harassment associated with the Cold War was no doubt off-putting in itself; and in this atmosphere, many licensees, afraid of drawing unwanted police attention to their hotels, often tried to discourage their homo-sexual clientele. But probably just as important were changes in the state's liquor laws.

In 1954 NSW amended its laws to allow for 10 pm clos-ing of hotels, instead of 6 pm. This had a fairly immediate and direct effect on the drinking habits of Sydney males. No longer were the major city hotels crammed between 5 pm and 6 pm; increasing numbers of people now went home to have dinner first and go out afterwards. People did not necessarily want to come back into the CBD and camp men soon found a range of other venues opening in other places.[43]

Kings Cross had long had its bohemian reputation, and during the war years it had experienced a boom, with night-clubs and sly grog shops proliferating. This prior reputation, and the fact that it was a major night-life area, probably accounts for the opening of a range of venues catering for homosexuals from the 1950s. Indeed through the 1950s and 1960s Kings Cross increasingly became the focal point for the commercial venues of the camp world, and its long-held homosexual ambience became more apparent. The Rex Hotel in Macleay Street was a place to meet other camp men, even by the early 1950s.[44] And at the top of William Street the 'Hasty Tasty', an all-night hamburger joint, was a favourite camp pick-up haunt. When the new Chevron Hotel in Macleay Street opened in the early 1960s, its downstairs bar, 'The Quarter Deck', soon became another favoured drinking place for camps, not least because of the large number of young sailors among the patrons.[45] In the argot of the day, it was a great place to get a 'seafood cock-tail'. In the early 1960s the Annexe opened late at night. You entered through the Kings Cross Theatrette once it had fin-ished its nightly screenings. There was a jukebox, coffee and soft drinks were served, and same-sex dancing was an attraction. It had only a brief life, but it was a major added attraction in the Kings Cross area.[46]

But something new also developed in Kings Cross at this time: namely, the drag show clubs. What this sudden flower-ing of drag shows represented is open to conjecture, but given the common conceptions of homosexuals at the time, being 'effeminate' was one way for men with homoerotic desires to express their different gender identity. Suprisingly, these venues emerged publicly at a time of continuing police har-assment of camps and their world; in contrast, the other major development of the time – the private homosexual clubs –

were also expanding dramatically, but behind a veil of secrecy.

There had been drag artistes and drag shows previously,[47] but these paled into insignificance with the developments of the 1960s. The Stork Club, out near Tom Ugly's Bridge over the Georges River, had a drag show. It had, apparently, associations back to the Kiwis, a famous drag entertainment troupe from World War II and just after. Rose Jackson, one of Sydney's better-known drag artistes, remembers driving out to Sylvania Waters to sing at the club with various bands. But the club suffered constant harassment from the Vice Squad and exposés in the newspapers.[48] From 1961 onwards, however, a series of clubs opened, mainly in Sydney's inner suburbs, which had more public success, with one of them, Les Girls, operating for decades. The shows were much more lavish, and the number of performers grew quite rapidly. Kings Cross was the locus of most of these ventures.

The first to open, in late 1961, was the Jewel Box, in Darlinghurst Road, Kings Cross. Les Girls in Roslyn Street, less than 100 metres away, followed soon after.[49] Both proved to be popular, and attracted a large camp clientele. A typical show could have half a dozen performers, with individual numbers and some ensemble work. Most artistes mimed popular songs, although some used their own voices. This was the general pattern that emerged in other new venues too: the Purple Onion in Anzac Parade, Kensington, in mid-1962, and Kandy's 'Garden of Eden' Koffee House in Enmore Road, Newtown, early in 1963. Kandy's mother, Mrs Johnson, sat at the entrance to this latter venue, and collected the takings.[50]

This rapid growth in the number of drag shows in Sydney was noted at the time. OZ magazine suggested disparagingly that, in the 'upsurge of camp venues around Sydney' there was 'little satire, wit, or anything else; the sole entertainment is in the fact that the performers are men in drag'.[51] While this may have been true of most of these, *OZ* may, however, have been taking its debunking role too seriously. Katharine Brisbane, the theatre critic, certainly saw some drag shows in a different light. Writing in *Pol* later that decade, she said, 'The Purple Onion is one of my favourite theatrical haunts – a place where anything is possible and nothing is what it seems ... As it is just now it is exactly right.'[52] Brisbane added that what the Purple Onion offered was 'a piece of rare and authentic burlesque; shrewd, witty, obscene, and always up-to-date; and in no other atmosphere could it possibly work so well'.[53] While the 'entertainment' aspect might draw heterosexuals to these venues, the added attraction for those with homoerotic inclinations was that others like themselves would be there too, both as performers and audience.

Hotels outside the CBD or Kings Cross also developed as new camp venues: the Montgomery Hotel, just over Pyrmont Bridge in Union Street, was known as a place to pick up rough trade – particularly sailors; the Sussex Hotel, at the corner of Sussex and Liverpool streets near Darling Harbour, became a place with an increasingly camp clientele, particularly lesbians.[54] The Macquarie Hotel, in Wentworth Avenue, was briefly a camp pub.[55] How long these hotels had attracted their camp clientele is hard to determine, but they certainly became popularly known. The proliferation of newspaper reporting, and the generally high public profile now being given to things 'camp' or homosexual, meant that it was far easier to find them.

Their clientele could be quite varied. If a pub developed a reputation as 'camp', not only would obvious homosexuals come, but also secretive ones, and often those about to take the plunge. One novelist, describing the clientele of an inner-city pub with a homosexual reputation, noted that some of [the] so-called squares like to take a look or two, and maybe size up something for later on. All kinds of visiting firemen – bankers, commercial travellers, visiting MP's, Government wallahs, a farmer or two, professional sportsmen … casual adventurers. Or week-end dabblers. Sometimes only once a month, once a year. And bisexuals. There's no end to the variety of types in the game.[56]

During the late 1960s Oxford Street started to develop commercial venues catering for a camp clientele. Several factors made Oxford Street attractive. It was close to Kings Cross and the existing night-life there, but the Cross, once it became the locale for American soldiers on R & R leave from the war in Vietnam, became a fairly unpleasant place. Drugs and prostitution and drunken soldiers were not an attractive atmosphere for Sydney's camps. Also rents were far cheaper in Oxford Street than in the Cross, because there was plenty of unused building stock available there.

There were other attractions too. The old Turkish Baths at the bottom of Liverpool Street continued to have a homosexual clientele. Further, Sydney had long had a series of wine bars, which over the years had become the 'province of the derelict, selling sweet sherry as the cheapest alcohol available'.[57] But in the early 1960s, several entrepreneurs began to buy up the licences of the old 'plonk shops' and turn them into smart bars. They couldn't sell beer or spirits, but they had less restrictive licensing arrangements, being able to stay open until midnight. There were several in Oxford Street, and one of them, French's Tavern, provided a venue for many emerging bands, such as Midnight Oil, Cold Chisel and the Reels. Another, Martin's Bar, became extremely fashionable. Some developed a strong homosexual clientele, while two – Enzo's, in Oxford Street,

Paddington, and Chez Ivy, in Oxford Street, Bondi Junction – became exclusively camp.[58]

Chez Ivy attracted a very diverse crowd:

> Behind the bar there are the same drag queens, the same green lights muting into scarlet and then into mauve as the coloured disc spins in front of the spotlight ... Around the corners of the room are little swingers, Bondi's early teen sun set. In the centre of the room are a few scattered camps, girls and boys not quite at ease, offended by the heterosexuality of the side tables ... Near us is a group of queens: six footers, very big boys indeed with high heels emphasising their ludicrous disproportion, heavily made up, big boned and big muscled.[59]

Enzo's and Chez Ivy were two of my favourite places. Enzo's, opposite the Paddington Town Hall, was quite an elegant place. A new wine bar, it was the epitome of smart, its décor put together by one of Sydney's better-known interior designers, a melange of red, green and white and a scattering of Roman busts – in keeping with the Italian theme – and piped opera arias, but not too loud. It had a pleasant back courtyard, loggia style with a grapevine-covered portico.

It was a great place to meet up for an after-work drink, before going on to dinner or something more adventurous.

Chez Ivy was further out, in Bondi Junction. Tuesday nights were my favourite nights there, although I can't remember why. Perhaps it was because Barbara would perform one of her signature numbers then, after the jukebox was turned off, usually to loud protests if 'Lola', that camp hymn by the Kinks, was playing.

On Tuesdays Barbara usually gave us Cher's 'Half-Breed'.

And standing on the dance floor, wearing a *faux* Red Indian squaw outfit, her naked perfect half-orb silicone boobs proudly on display, and with lots of hand movements, she mimed her way through the song. As the number wound down, the audience would shower her with coins, in appreciation of her guts in giving such a performance, which was otherwise completely lacking in talent.

On Saturday nights her favoured tune was Dionne Warwick's 'Promises, Promises', and often she nearly fell off the tiny stage/dance floor, as she spun around and around to the closing bars of the song. But it was all just part of the fun.

Chez Ivy was a good place to pick up guys, many of them cute surfie boys, who would not be seen anywhere near the more obvious gay area in lower Oxford Street.

Sydney's first exclusively gay steam bath opened on Oxford Street close to Chez Ivy early in 1968. This was the Bondi Junction Steam Baths, or Viking Sauna.

Oxford Street as a focus for camp entertainment was reinforced early in 1969 when Ivy's Birdcage, a major venue for drag shows, opened at Taylor Square. When it burned out later that year, a new late-night bar opened in Oxford Street, closer to the CBD. This was Capriccio's, a nightclub with a theatre restaurant licence – and thus able to serve drinks till 3 am.[60] Like the Birdcage, it had drag shows, many of them opulent extravaganzas that became legendary in Sydney's gay history. As one habitué remembers, 'there has never been a venue along Oxford Street which has staged anything like those shows'.[61]

I can recall the excitement of going into Caps, as we called it. The show space was up two flights of stairs, and at the top the door opened into a large room. In front, as one entered, was a bar which sold extremely expensive drinks, and often sitting there, perched on her stool, was Lesley, a senior librarian at the

State Library, whom I knew from my frequent research visits there. We would nod to each other, and I would wander off to get a table near to where the floor show would be.

Because of the licensing laws, Caps, as a theatre restaurant, was nominally obliged to serve food to its patrons, but what was on offer was not at all enticing; spaghetti Bolognese or a barely recognisable piece of chicken resting on a doleful looking piece of lettuce with a slice or two of tomato. But no one went there for the food; it was the magic of entering another world, a place of drag extravaganzas, where we were transported to a land of make-believe.

On the Darlinghurst ridge, at the Maccabean Hall in Darlinghurst Road, overlooking the beat at Green Park, the Aquarius Club operated on Friday nights. It was only a few minutes walk from Oxford Street. *Nation* journalist John Edwards described the Aquarius Club:

> Here, long tables are striped like vertebrae down the sides of the dance-hall. On them are scattered plates of sandwiches and bottles of booze gleaming as the revolving globe studded with mirrors suspended from the ceiling reflects in glittering patterns the changing colours of the spotlight. Bottle after bottle of Cinzano. Around the tables hundreds of camp people; talking, laughing, caressing; or wetly kissing, hands pushing through the other's hair, fingers stroking thighs, male with male, beard to beard, shaven lip to shaven lip. All quite ordinary after a few minutes.
>
> Most are young working class camps, dressed in ordinary clothes: slacks, shirts, some ties. Even short hair. They have routine undemanding jobs like telephonists, clerks, shop assistants, and low incomes. Some are stupid and some are

intelligent, but all are totally dominated by the fact that they are camp in a way that camps with complex and absorbing interests are not. They have a highly developed exclusively camp culture, on the solidarity of which places like this nightclub are able to prosper.[62]

And of course the friendship networks and emerging homosexual clubs also played an important role in providing a rewarding social life for camps. Visitors to Sydney who were 'in the club' were taken in and shown around; as Robin Maugham noted, when he travelled to Australia in the 1960s researching his Victorian novel, *The Link*, he was 'most warmly welcomed everywhere'.[63] Like his uncle, Somerset Maugham, who had visited Sydney four decades earlier, he brought his boyfriend with him.

Even with the emergence of the idea of 'the homosexual' as a specific sort of person, not all men with homoerotic desires saw themselves as 'homosexuals', or considered getting involved in the camp world. Large numbers of homosexually inclined men still chose to marry, either because they felt obliged to, or in the belief that their desires would go away once they married. Other homosexually inclined men might continue to live out their lives avoiding any contact with the camp world, because they feared contact might lead to exposure. If they needed to find satisfaction for their sexual desires, there were still the beats. In the city the Domain remained a popular cruising ground,[64] as did Hyde Park around the Archibald Fountain, and Boomerang Street below St Mary's Cathedral.[65] The toilets at the railway stations; certain swimming pools like Giles at Coogee or even the Domain Baths; parks like Fitzroy Gardens at Kings Cross, or Green Park in Darlinghurst;[66] all continued to be used by people who had either little opportunity of meeting others in another way, or who preferred encounters in these circumstances. And out in the suburbs, there was usually a local beat where men might go to, occasionally or often.[67]

Aspects of this generally hidden world sometimes entered into public knowledge, usually through the newspapers, or sometimes through fiction. In Kylie Tennant's *Tell Morning This*, published in 1967, the Archibald Fountain is acknowledged as a homosexual 'beat'. One particular scene in the novel opens at a public meeting where a fracas occurs, caused by 'a number of young men with little feathers in their hats'.[68] The heroine, Nonnie, confronts their leaders, and finds that there is a misunderstanding: the young men thought that the meeting was to have the Archibald Fountain pulled down, and they were there to show their opposition. Afterwards Nonnie talks with her companion, Dr Cranitz:

'You saw those young men?' Nonnie asked. 'They thought we were trying to get the Archibald Fountain removed. So extraordinary!'

'Homosexuals,' Dr. Cranitz said blandly.

'But why should they worry about the fountain? I admit it's a beautiful thing, and I wouldn't like to see it removed myself …'

'It is their meeting place.'

'Surely not! How do you know?'

'My dear lady,' Dr. Cranitz said resignedly, 'it is so. I assure you.'

'He looked quite a nice young man', Nonnie said
doubtfully ...[69]

These were the formal and informal 'institutions' of the camp
world for men with homosexual desires in Sydney by the late
1960s. Many of these men were undoubtedly aware of the
increasing public debate about homosexuality and probably
identified themselves as 'homosexuals'. Some started to question the way in which homosexuality had become defined. This
questioning of something that had been taken as a given for so
long, mirrored the awareness of young people at the time of the
emerging new ideas and social movements, and of the changes
taking place in the political culture. Many of them – homosexual and heterosexual alike – would soon be actively involved in
contesting old values and creating new social movements. As
one commentator observed:

> one of the crucial changes of this period was the emergence
> of a new style of radical politics, one that supplemented the
> traditional leftist discourse based on class divisions with an
> awareness of new dimensions of oppression and potential
> mobilisation about new themes.[70]

Growing opposition to the Vietnam War was one marker
of change. It cut across party lines, and, with a growing number
of major public figures speaking out against it, gradually
gave legitimacy to dissent. Similarly the anti-nuclear, anti-
censorship, and pro-environmental movements pushed politics
in new directions, cutting across the old – mainly class – divisions of our society. As with the anti–Vietnam War activities,
dissent spread in all directions, even among establishment figures. Writer Frank Moorhouse has called these heady times

'Days of Wine and Rage', a neat encapsulation of both the essence and the surface texture of what went on.[71] Australia's emerging new social movements fitted in with patterns developing over the rest of the world.

The feminist movement brought sexual politics into the public arena, and it gave a catch-cry – 'the personal is political' – that exemplified a new perception of politics. Altman notes that in America 'the emergence of the contemporary feminist movement is often linked to the civil rights movement, and later the counter-culture and anti-war movements' but 'in Australia the dynamics were somewhat different'.[72] Still, by the late 1960s a new feminist movement had emerged, and it was soon followed by something unprecedented for Australia – a gay rights movement.

Australia had no prior history of gay activism. In Britain, for example, there had been a longish history of moves for law reform, going back to the early decades of the twentieth century, to Havelock Ellis and the World League for Sexual Reform. The Homosexual Law Reform Society was founded in the late 1950s, and was, as Jeffrey Weeks notes, 'a classical middle-class single-issue pressure group of a type which flourished in the 1960s'.[73] It was established when it became obvious that the government was disinclined to respond to the 1957 Wolfenden Report, which had recommended the partial decriminalisation of male homosexual activity. The publicity generated in Australia by the Wolfenden Report, and the debate about the need for law reform – which escalated over the next ten years – also helped in changing public perceptions here.[74]

Similarly, America had a history of activism towards altering the place of the homosexual in society. In particular, networks of returned service women and men in major US cities formed nuclei from which activist organisations, like The Mattachine

Society, One Inc and the Daughters of Bilitis, emerged.[75] The so-called Stonewall Riots of 1969 in New York – when patrons of the Stonewall Inn fought back against police harassment over three nights, in ever-escalating confrontations – ought to be seen more as a symbolic moment for gay activism in the USA, rather than its historical beginnings.

While no similar gay activist movements appeared in Australia, at the end of the 1960s a homophile group emerged in Canberra pushing for homosexual law reform, and law reform sub-committees were also established within the Humanist Societies of New South Wales and Victoria. Clearly any attempt to change the status of homosexuals involved altering the laws that institutionalised their criminal status. In England this had finally been achieved in 1967, ten years after the recommendations of the Wolfenden Report. An attack on the legal framework was also on the agenda of the homophile and gay movements that were developing in America.[76]

In New South Wales the need for law reform was evident. A range of experts – academics, criminologists, civil libertarian lawyers, members of the medical profession – all argued that homosexuality no longer deserved a criminal status, and that law reform was overdue. But the law-makers themselves, both in their own attitudes and in their perception that they should not act before public demand dictated, were not convinced.

The likelihood that the initiative for law reform would come from politicians was clearly slim. The quality of debate in State Parliament, when the issue of homosexuality came up, engendered little confidence in the ability of politicians to deal in a progressive manner – or even sensibly – with the issue. Indeed one Parliamentarian had, in a debate during the mid-1950s about the apparent rise of homosexual activity in western societies, suggested that Germany had become like a 'Mohammedan state': 'one of the reasons of course is that in countries which by reason of their religious beliefs are non-alcoholic the people go to other extremes'.[77] How this explained what might be occurring in West Germany – or even in NSW for that matter – is hard to see, but it does indicate that there were major hurdles of ignorance and idiocy to be overcome.

That politicians were loath to alter the law, despite expert opinion, was even more evident in 1963 with their suppression of the report of the Trethowan Committee. The committee had no brief concerning law reform, but was established in 1958 to look at homosexuality in prisons and society generally, concentrating on 'causes' and 'cures'. The 'professionals' on the committee were not convinced that homosexuality itself was the problem, but rather society's attitudes to it. The government decided this view was unacceptable and refused to release the report.[78]

Despite this government inertia, experts continued to push the issue. Criminologist Gordon Hawkins publicly argued for law reform, even while acknowledging the chances were slim.[79] Academic Henry Mayer, in his regular 'Speaking Freely' column in the *Australian*, took the position that law reform was justified.[80] But public opinion polls showed little public support for law reform. Even in 1968, despite the clearly changed 'educated' perceptions about homosexuality, the majority of Australians appeared reluctant to alter the status quo. A survey by two academics that year, on attitudes to abortion, prostitution and homosexuality, found only 27 per cent agreed with the statement 'Abortions should not be legal or allowed under any circumstances', and 46 per cent agreed with the statement that prostitution should not be legalised under any circumstances. But 64 per cent did not agree with the statement 'It should no longer be an offence for consenting males to engage in homosexual acts in private'. Twenty-two per cent agreed, 12 per cent were not sure, and 2 per cent did not answer.[81]

The survey found that levels of education 'had a strong influence on the way in which the question was answered'. For example, 48 per cent of those with tertiary education thought male homosexual activity should no longer be illegal, compared with 23 per cent of those with secondary level education and only 9 per cent of those who did not go beyond primary school. It also noted that 'a move to reform … would meet with strong opposition from churches and many other powerful institutions in society'. The survey report went on to speculate on whether a 'courageous government' which attempted to legalise abortion, prostitution or homosexuality 'would alienate a large voting section of the electorate and thus perhaps commit political sui-cide'. The writers' contention was that it would not, since 'there would not be a solid block of voters united by their bitterness towards the three liberal laws'.[82] But the politicians were not convinced, and were content to allow the status quo to remain.

Despite this, there were gradual changes in public discus-sions about homosexuality. And the emergence of the 'homo-sexual', as both a specific identity and a group, meant there was now a visible class of people whose rights as individuals could be argued for. This 'creation' of a new minority was important in giving a more legitimate basis upon which to argue for homosex-ual rights, and therefore law reform. And from this group, some activists took up the running from a gay liberation perspective.

The initial push for law reform, which picked up momen-tum in the second half of the 1960s, did not come from homo-sexuals themselves, but from several Christian churches. This reflected the changes within these institutions, in turn reflect-ing the impact of the major social movements of the 1960s. In October 1966, for example, the Methodist Church decided to look into the problem of homosexuality, after the Reverend Ted Noffs, of the Wayside Chapel at Kings Cross, claimed that homosexuals were afraid to come forward for 'treatment' because of the law.[83] Likewise, early in 1967 the Presbyterian Church announced it was also setting up a committee to examine the issue of homosexuality in society.[84] And this committee, when it reported, recommended that the law be changed.[85] The potential this had for changing the minds of church-goers and politicians alike was strengthened when the General Assembly of the Presbyterian Church in NSW agreed that homosexual behaviour between consenting adults in private ought to be decriminalised.[86]

The moral authority of the churches, still strong in Australia at this time, ensured these views would receive attention. And over the next few years, churches, or individual churchmen, continued to speak out strongly in favour of law reform. In August 1967 the Anglican Church in Western Australia set up a committee to consider its attitude to homosexuality.[87] This was occurring while a Bill to reform the law was finally going through the English Parliament; this was passed in July 1967, which increased the pressure in Australia. That same year, Bill Hayden, a prominent member of the ALP, and later Governor-General of Australia, also spoke out in support of the idea of homosexual law reform.[88] And early in 1969 the Humanist Society of NSW announced that it supported the idea.

Two specific incidents in the late 1960s probably triggered the actual formation of organisations that aimed to do something concrete. The first was the publicity surrounding the following incident on a Canberra beat:

In 1968 a 19-year-old Canberra boy was stabbed whilst doing a local beat. And though the man who committed the assault was arrested and sentenced to one year's gaol, his victim was also prosecuted and convicted of indecent assault.[89]

Another case which sparked major public debate, and was followed soon after by the establishment of Australia's first homosexual law reform group, also occurred in Canberra, early in 1969. A policeman came across a car parked in secluded bushland on the outskirts of Canberra. Two men in the car were, as a newspaper reported, 'engaging in homosexual practices'. They were arrested, charged, and in the ensuing court case one of the men was sentenced to six months prison for 'indecent assault',[90] even though in court it was agreed on all sides that there was no physical 'assault' in the commonly understood sense of that word. Whatever had happened had been consensual. But the law clearly stated that what had occurred was to be considered an assault. And so, as one commentator noted, 'a good citizen was sent to prison'.[91]

Why this case should have triggered such an overt response is not clear: such situations had been occurring in Australia for years, even decades. But the issue generated almost daily debate in the columns of the *Canberra Times* and led to the setting up of the ACT Homosexual Law Reform Society.[92] It was at an apposite time, since the new draft Criminal Code for the Australian Territories was before Federal Parliament, but there were no provisions for reforming the law as regards homosexuality.

All the arguments for and against came out in the debate conducted in the *Canberra Times*. Ultimately, of course, the issue revolved around morality and the law. Should the law enforce moralities? As several writers pointed out, the law no longer penalised adultery or fornication; and masturbation was also outside the law. Why should homosexuality remain a criminal act in the Australian Territories, when it was increasingly no longer a crime in most western countries? As academic and *Canberra Times* columnist Don Aitkin noted, setting the issue in civil libertarian terms, it is

> one of the contradictions of our society that while we insist
> on every man's right to conduct his own farm or factory in
> his own way, to belong to the church of his preference or
> none at all, or to speak his mind on politics or not as he
> wishes, we still assert that others should decide what kinds
> of books he can read, what films he can see, and what kinds
> of sexual behaviour he will be allowed.[93]

But he also pointed out a more practical reason for law reform: if 'you ban anything that 600,000 Australians are likely to want to do, you are going to have a hefty law-enforcement problem'.[94]

This Canberra case, and the effect it had on setting up a homosexual law reform group, received wide media coverage, not only in the ACT but also around Australia. It clearly signalled a major development: the beginning of organised resistance to official views and practices regarding homosexuality.[95] In this favourable atmosphere, a gay rights movement quickly developed in Australia.

The first group appeared in Melbourne as a branch of the Daughters of Bilitis, a major US lesbian organisation, in January 1970, calling itself the Australian Lesbian Movement. But the group which had the greatest impact on the place of homosexuals in Australian society, and on the lives of homosexuals themselves, was established in Sydney in July 1970. This was the Campaign Against Moral Persecution Inc. (CAMP Inc.), the first 'political' homosexual organisation in Australia, established with the expressed intention of bringing about social change. It held its first public meeting in February 1971.[96]

A political group built around sexual orientation was something new for Australia. While sexual politics came to Australia with women's liberation, the politics of sexual preference was far more specialised. The aims of the new group reflected the change that it represented.[97] It would take up law reform as an issue, continuing the work already set in motion by the Humanist Society of Victoria, various churches, the civil libertarians, and the Homosexual Law Reform Society of the ACT; and it would act as a support group for lesbians and homosexual men, thereby continuing a function fulfilled less formally by those long-lasting friendship networks, and more formally by the clubs that had developed in the 1960s. What was new was its aim to *publicly* confront aspects of society's treatment of homosexuals. In particular, it was concerned with attitudes to homosexuals and homosexuality, including those of some of society's most powerful institutions, that were based on misconceptions, prejudice and fear.

CAMP Inc. aimed to challenge the commonly held perception of homosexuals as 'sick or criminal or sinful'. It contested the medical profession's definitions of homosexuality that allowed for barbarisms such as psycho-surgery and aversion therapy to be used against homosexuals in a so-called civilised society. It hoped to convince the wider community that homosexuals were basically just like everybody else – except that they preferred bed-partners of the same gender. And it wanted lesbians and homosexual men to be open about their sexual preference, to family, to friends, to neighbours, and to the outside world. This was a dramatic change, given that homosexuality had so long been deliberately hidden away, not only because of social attitudes, medical perceptions and church definitions, but also because male homosexual activity was still illegal.

In effect CAMP Inc. planned a complete restructuring of the place of the homosexual in modern society. And it planned to do all this openly and publicly. One writer has suggested that this emphasis on 'coming out' – on being open about one's sexual preferences to all and sundry – as one of the primary aims of CAMP Inc., qualified it as a 'political organisation'.[98] And while the organisation was not in the old mould of political groups, based as they were largely on class interests, it clearly had a political agenda which would put it in the public arena.

While today we would see this organisation as a 'gay' political group – it was open about being based on sexual orientation, it was up-front in dealing with the public, it was activist and aimed to change society – the choice of the name CAMP was deliberate. Two of its founders, Chris Poll and John Ware, insisted that the Australian homosexual movement arose in a specifically Australian context, and did not want to be seen as slavishly imitating American trends.[99] They had no objection to the term 'gay', but the word had no particular Australian connotations, whereas 'camp' had long associations with the Australian homosexual worlds – hence the clever acronym.

While Poll and Ware might argue that this movement arose out of a specific situation in Australia, there are several levels at which it should be seen more broadly. First, its aims were far more than just law reform. It was trying to change social relationships, therefore, whether it understood it or not, it was more than just a reformist movement.

Second, arising partly from this, it clearly reflected emerging liberationist ideas about the restructuring of society. While a major source of these new ideas was undoubtedly the New Left, a whole range of other 'isms' had their intellectual inputs too. Many early members of the group had a background in academe, and in the various social movements of the 1960s.

Third, it represented the advent of politics developed around a gay identity, politics committed to questioning – and changing – the system.

Finally, the founding of CAMP Inc. represented more than just a development in Australia. It was one part of a worldwide trend that saw the emergence of similar gay groups, committed to similar programs of social change, in places as diverse as San Francisco, New York, Paris, London, Vancouver, Ottawa, Toronto, Montreal – and Sydney: indeed, 'within two years from the Stonewall Rebellion, gay liberation groups emerged in every major city and campus in the United States, Canada, Australia, and Western Europe'.[100] Thus by 1970 gay liberation had come to Australia, and neither Australia – nor its homosexual or camp worlds – would ever be the same again.

CHAPTER 6

THE PEARL IN THE OYSTER

The opening up of Sydney's gay world

Only occasionally in history can an oppressed minority group pinpoint a moment when the tide begins to turn for them. For lesbians and homosexual men in Australia, the formation of CAMP Inc. in 1970 was such a moment.

CAMP Inc. was a forerunner of and an example for other groupings of homosexuals aiming to do something about their situation, both in Sydney and around Australia. No less significantly, it changed the way the homosexual was defined in our society. Previously it was the major institutions of society that had largely ordained how homosexuality was perceived, and it was portrayed negatively by the law, the churches and the medical profession, and only gradually and grudgingly had attitudes begun improving in the media. From this point onwards, however, new gay groups increasingly took the initiative. The way in which lesbians and gay men are defined in Australia today has largely developed from the more positive perceptions portrayed by their subcultures from the early 1970s. The changes faced strong opposition, and the process was excruciatingly slow, but it had started.

Change was in the air. The ALP under Gough Whitlam took power in December 1972, after 23 years of conservative federal government. Despite periods of inflation and rising unemployment, an oil crisis and concern over Japanese investment in Australia, the 1970s were generally good years for Sydney. Major redevelopment projects were undertaken in the city, and by 1981 the population was 3.2 million.

Protest marchers on the streets of Australian cities – debunked in the previous decade as just long-haired students and the 'ratbag fringe' – now included such personages as Nobel Prize winner Patrick White. And there was still much to protest about, even after Whitlam pulled the troops out of Vietnam in January 1973. The power of youthful outrage was seen continuously over the decade, expressing a growing awareness of environmental concerns, in anti-nuclear protests, and a public hostility to big business and the authority of various government bodies. Marchers on city streets called out 'stop police attacks on gays, women and blacks'.

The Queen opened the Sydney Opera House on 20 October 1973, and the same year the city's historic Rocks area was saved from demolition by unionists under 'Green Bans', some of the first environmental activism in Sydney. The process of 'gentrification', begun in the 1960s, continued as young professionals turned dingy terrace houses, once regarded as slums, into smart inner-urban residences in many of Sydney's older suburbs.

On 11 November 1975, the Governor-General Sir John Kerr sacked the Whitlam government. The following month, the Coalition won a clear majority in the election, and Malcolm Fraser became Prime Minister, staying for the next seven and a quarter years. On 13 February 1978, a bomb exploded outside the Hilton Hotel in George Street where the first Commonwealth Heads of Government Regional Meeting (CHOGRM) was taking place. The blast killed two garbagemen and a police officer, with several others injured.

The worlds of Sydney's homosexuals were affected by several new developments. A new force had appeared, as active and vocal groups developed a high public profile by directly confronting several major institutions in our society. Their highly political activity was not always welcomed by parts of Sydney's camp community, those who had learned to live, albeit uneasily, with the status quo. The expansion and geographical relocation of venues catering for much of Sydney's old homosexual and camp worlds – the bars and coffee shops, steam baths, restaurants and bookshops – provided a backdrop to these changes. In addition, new elements – such as gay welfare, social, political and religious groups – emerged. It was a period of dramatic change.

CAMP Inc.'s importance can be inferred from both its rapid growth and also how quickly it was emulated. After a year, its membership was up to about 1500, and by the end of 1971 similar organisations had been established in all state capitals. In some cities there were actually several groups. In Sydney, for example, there were bodies on campuses at Sydney University and UNSW, both known as CAMPus CAMP.[1]

A generous and anonymous supporter had donated the use of a large two-storey freestanding Victorian mansion, set in its own grounds, at 393 Darling Street, Balmain, for CAMP (NSW), the state branch of CAMP Inc. It was used for office work and meetings, and quite often for parties, usually on Saturday nights.

It was next door to the Balmain Fire Station, and on occasion the firemen, intrigued by their new neighbours, stood on boxes and peered over the back fence. They were never hostile, just amazed.

Legend has it that one night, one of them jumped over and found a kindred spirit for some fun in the bushes down the back of the yard.

If the new groups hoped to put an alternative point of view across to the public, they soon realised that the mainstream media was not a helpful vehicle. There was some publicity when CAMP Inc. was established, some of it sympathetic, but, given its past performance, the mainstream media was unlikely to provide adequate or appropriate coverage of the issues to be canvassed, or the point of view from which they could be seen.[2] Prevailing attitudes were of course, part of the problem. As Dennis Altman pointed out at the time, media reporting of homosexuality or gay liberation reflected a predictable range of attitudes, which he characterised as

> the Victorian, which holds it best not to mention the subject;
> the Conservative, which sees homosexuality as undesirable
> and condemns it as making for the weakening of moral fibre;
> [and] the Liberal, which sees homosexuals as victims of their
> parents if not of society in general.[3]

Sydney's major newspaper, the *Sydney Morning Herald*, was clearly 'Victorian' in its approach. As activist Lex Watson noted, when

> the Wolfenden Committee was set up in England in 1954,
> and even though it was officially called 'The Committee
> on Homosexual Offences and Prostitution', that was too
> much for the *Herald*. It always talked of an inquiry into
> prostitution and 'perversion'. For eight years after the gay
> political movement started in Sydney, the *Herald* preferred
> not to mention it or anything to do with homosexuals.[4]

Other Sydney newspapers tended towards the 'conservative', although the *Australian*, then in a 'liberal' phase, gave the best newspaper coverage to the emerging gay movement in Sydney.

Consequently CAMP Inc. decided to put out its own magazine, *CAMP INK*.[5] The first edition came out in November 1970, and Sydney's homosexuals now had access to a magazine that provided their own news and relevant information. The following year *Gay Times*, a free bar paper, appeared, and six months later, Sydney – and Australia – had its first commercial gay magazine, *William and John*. In 1972 the first *Sydney Gay Liberation Newsletter* appeared. Thus within less than two years a 'gay' press had emerged.

This flurry of activity – the rapid expansion of groups, the increasing number of people willing to identify publicly as lesbian or homosexual and the emergence of new publications seeking to serve this community and project its views to the wider world – was mostly confined to Sydney. John Ware found when he visited Melbourne, to talk to people involved in setting up a similar organisation in Victoria, that 'no one was allowed to state to the media that they were openly gay … Melbourne was very, very different to Sydney'.[6] In the other state capitals, too, there was a general reluctance to be as open as the Sydney group. Perhaps this encouraged young homosexuals more sympathetic to a radical approach to migrate to Sydney from other states. Many certainly did, to Sydney's benefit.

But the flurry of activity was not without its strains. As one would expect of any political movement based solely on sexual preference, it included people of diverse political views. The political inclinations of many activists were progressive or 'liberal', but with a few undoubtedly located more at the conservative end of the spectrum. Some, influenced by the new liberationist ideas, were often unhappy with CAMP Inc. They disliked the structure of the organisation, and particularly the tactics adopted in dealing publicly with various issues. The different philosophical perspectives of those committed to a radical liberationist approach is epitomised by one of their early actions: they formed a separate 'consciousness-raising' group within CAMP (NSW) and by early 1972 its members had hived off to form Sydney Gay Liberation. Over the next year, 'gay liberation fronts' were established – or replaced the CAMPus CAMP groups – at the University of Sydney and UNSW in Sydney, and also at the Australian National University, Melbourne University and Newcastle University.

This issue has been explained, perhaps over-simplistically, as a disagreement between those who wished to operate under the constraints of accepted political discourse and those who preferred to try less conventional political tactics. The former were labelled as reformist, while the latter were seen as radical and revolutionary.[7] While personal animosities and ambitions played their part, it might be more appropriate to interpret what was happening as a 'maturing' of a political process, in which different groups separated to pursue their own agenda, developing strategies that matched their ideologies.

We can see this if we look at a related development. At a time of turmoil and change in the women's movement, many lesbians started to take ideas of separatism more seriously. Whereas there had been close cooperation between lesbians and gay men in the early days of CAMP Inc., it soon became clear that the two groups faced different constraints and needed to pursue different agendas for their objectives. The result – which could be seen as an advantage – was that a range of politicised groups all pursued the general aim of improving the lot of lesbians and gay men in Sydney, and by implication, in Australian society, each choosing their own specific tactics.

Through all this activity, a new gay identity emerged. Despite similar aspects – the centrality of same-sex preference for instance – this new identity was distinct from the old homo-sexual or camp identities.

The first difference of this new identity was an absolute belief in the validity of one's sexual orientation, and the out-right rejection of homosexuality as an illness, a crime or a sin. This validation of homosexuality came from a range of intel-lectually acceptable sources. These included the Freudian belief in the biological bisexuality of all, taken up as a belief in 'pol-ymorphous perversity' by writers such as Herbert Marcuse; the liberationist ideas, which argued that society repressed and labelled as deviant any forms of sexuality that it saw as a threat to its own stability; or new ideas about the social construction of knowledge in general, and of gender in particular.

Second, a gay identity meant being open about one's homo-sexuality. This was a dramatic change from previous forms of homosexual identity, which had tended to remain hidden. One ought to 'come out', to face family, friends, neighbours, co-workers – the whole outside world – with the fact of one's homosexuality.[8]

Part of the reason for this public face was to demystify homosexuality at both a personal and societal level. Previous definitions had labelled the homosexual as a pervert, a child molester, a shadowy figure doing unspeakable things. Acknowl-edging the reality that a homosexual was someone's son, brother, neighbour, fellow worker – someone known, and liked – ought to help change those perceptions at a personal level. And as more and more homosexuals came out, whether average citizens or famous names, the previous group image of homosexuals as a small minority of misfits and maladjusted should also fall away.

Third, there was an emphasis on collective endeavour. Partly this was practical: fully accepting one's homosexuality openly in a society which was still basically hostile to homosexuality

– as the continuing illegality of male homosexual acts attested
– could be extremely difficult if attempted alone. Therefore
gays should be supportive of others who, like themselves, were
trying to pursue these new precepts. But the idea of collective
endeavour also owed something to the ideology of the counter-
cultural revolution, a turning away from traditional institutionalised forms, whether social, cultural or political. As Barry
Adam notes: "'New left' ideals called for broad-based, egalitar-
ian, participatory democracy, eschewing bureaucracy and leadership for fear the voices of the masses would rapidly disappear
through institutionalisation."[9] Again, gay identity represented
new aspects of thought and activity related to the emerging
social movements of the time.

But another paradox in this tale is that the idea of a 'gay
identity' is inherently problematic. The thrust of the gay liberation argument was that the creation of sexual categories was
arbitrary, and in the past this had been to the detriment of those
designated as homosexuals. So it is ironic that the creation of
another arbitrary sexual category/identity – gay – provided a
new ideological rallying cry and the base on which to build a
political movement.

The divergences that occurred in Sydney's homosexual
world at this time – in ideas of identity, in the creation of new
groups, in appropriate policies to pursue and tactics to be used –
undoubtedly created antagonisms, but did not necessarily imply
a breakdown in interaction within the activist element. Various
groups were willing and able to combine from time to time on
a range of activities seen as crucial. For example, both CAMP
(NSW) and the various gay liberation elements in Sydney
combined for a demonstration outside Liberal Party headquarters in Ash Street in October 1971, in support of the Federal
Attorney-General, Tom Hughes. Jim Cameron, a right-wing

Christian fundamentalist had challenged Hughes, who had publicly supported limited homosexual law reform, for pre-selection.[10] Whether the noisy demonstration – which received scarcely any mainstream media attention – helped the panel inside reach its decision will never be known, but Hughes won the preselection by a wide margin.[11]

Similarly, various Sydney groups combined to sponsor a Sexual Liberation Forum at Sydney University in October 1971, with writer Dennis Altman as principal speaker, and another forum the following January, this time with Germaine Greer, Gillian Leahy and Altman as speakers. In July 1972 the groups supported and participated together in a march through the streets of Sydney to mark the fifth anniversary of homosexual law reform in England.[12]

These public appearances were, in effect, mass 'comings out'. But 'coming out' was also an individual decision, done solo, hopefully with attendant publicity. Thus John Ware, Chris Poll and Michael Cass, all involved in the formation of CAMP Inc., were interviewed for a major article in the *Weekend Australian* in September 1970.[13] A few days later, Ware appeared on the ABC-TV program *This Day Tonight*, discussing his homosexuality and the organisation.[14] Dr Ian Black, an academic and member of CAMP (NSW), was interviewed by Anne Deveson on Radio 2GB 'Newsmakers' program in March 1971.

Well-known public figures who came out were likely to attract publicity, which contributed to the aim to get a better public airing for homosexuality. Thus when Dennis Altman discussed his homosexuality on Australian television in July 1972, after the launch of his book *Homosexual: Oppression and Liberation* in Sydney – it had been released in the USA the previous September – there was a flurry of publicity. Critics claimed that the decision of the *Sydney Morning Herald* not to review the book was a form of censorship.[15] At the time, major battles were still being fought over the rights of Australians to read what they wished. A series of well-publicised court cases – over *OZ* magazine in the late 1960s, and student newspapers *Tharunka*, *Thor* and *Thorunka* in 1970 and 1971 – epitomised the wowser push to restrict reading materials, and the responses from groups such as the Council of Civil Liberties, by individual writers, and by the supporters of a 'free' press.

While most who 'came out' were the new young activists, occasionally someone from another milieu would too. It was quite a different thing for Richard Brennan, film producer and member of The Push – Sydney's libertarian fringe – to come out publicly in print in 1975.[16] Brennan's image – 'Mitchum and Marlboroughish' as Richard Neville described him – and his milieu, made his 'coming out' significant, and indicated that the new ideas, and new openness, had an impact far beyond the narrow confines of the gay activist world.[17] Though somewhat later, Patrick White's discussion of his homosexuality in his autobiography represented a major coup from a liberationist perspective – a public declaration of his sexuality by a major Australian figure.[18] Such 'comings out' played a significant part in altering stereotypical perceptions of homosexuals.

But the cost of publicly 'coming out' could be high. The secretary of CAMP (NSW), Peter Bonsall-Boone, appeared on the ABC-TV program *Chequerboard* in October 1972, with his lover and a lesbian couple. Bonsall-Boone was also secretary of St Clement's Anglican Church in the Sydney suburb of Mosman, and the program treated his situation as both a homosexual and practising Christian sympathetically. His fellow parishioners were less charitable, having him dismissed from his church post. It was not his homosexuality they objected to, since this had been known within the church for some time, but his public and proud admission of it.[19] Various Sydney gay groups combined to hold a demonstration outside the Mosman church early in November 1972, and this received wide media coverage.[20]

The Christian churches were not the only major Sydney institutions to attract the unwanted attentions of gay activists in those early days. The activities of parts of the medical profession, in particular psychotherapists and psychiatrists who practised aversion therapy, received more attention than any other issue in the early volumes of *CAMP INK*.[21] A strong dislike for it and what it represented were important planks in the platforms of both CAMP and the gay liberationists.

Gay liberationists accepted the validity of their sexual orientation, rejecting the view that heterosexuality was the *one* 'normal' orientation. It is little wonder then that aversion therapy – the use of techniques to force people to conform to social norms – was condemned, and its underlying principles and practitioners received so much vocal opposition.

The main practitioner of aversion therapy was Dr Neil McConaghy, an academic at UNSW. So, in line with the new ideals of confronting institutions that oppressed homosexuals, the gay liberation group at UNSW decided in August 1972 to hold a demonstration against the use of aversion therapy. The demonstration used street theatre techniques, and began 'with a dramatisation of electric shock therapy administered by "The Man from McConaghy", who was finally vanquished by the "Good Gay Lib Fairy"'.[22] The demonstration was later repeated outside the university library, 'and the students were told about the use of aversion therapy, the implication of the university in its practice, and the negative way homosexuality was treated in courses'.[23] A year later, the gay liberation groups 'zapped' a psychiatry conference at Prince Henry Hospital, publicly confronting McConaghy about his work.[24]

Activities like these gave Sydney homosexuals a heightened profile in the early 1970s. Reviewing the year 1972 for the *Bulletin*, journalist Marion MacDonald commented on how far 'sexual liberation' had come in Sydney that year. She noted, among other things, the marching of gay power groups with other demonstrators through the streets of Sydney; the launch of a major book about homosexuality; 'a swell of public indignation when a Sydney church sacked its secretary'; the growth of CAMP Inc.; an openly gay candidate standing for a seat in Federal Parliament; and, finally, that homosexuals were now talked about under their real names 'in clean family newspapers'.[25]

The year was indeed a watershed, and not just for Sydney homosexuals. A new Labor government had taken power in Canberra – the first for nearly a quarter of a century – and its initial flurry of activity, and broad program of social reform, heralded a period of dramatic change. The country seemed set to once again become an innovator, a nation in the vanguard of change.

The federal government began funding major programs to upgrade the cities, and money flowed rapidly to the states. Spending on roads, education and sewerage ensured that growth focused on urban areas. The major cities, certainly Sydney, reflected this new burst of activity with a surge of development. Patrick White's novel *The Eye of the Storm* catches something of the frenetic pace of life in the city, even while describing the mundane:

> The life of Sydney was streaming past and around, you could
> sense as well as hear, pouring out of factories and offices:
> by this hour men in bars … had begun inflating their self-
> importance with beer; ambulances were hurtling towards
> disasters in crumpled steel and glass confetti …[26]

The developments MacDonald noted clearly reflected the

magnitude of the changes beginning to take place. But they did not occur in a vacuum: perceptions of sexuality in general were changing, as well as homosexuality in particular. Movies and television, accessible to a mass audience, played a critical role in helping to reshape opinions. While they reflected general attitudes to homosexuality, they also brought new perceptions of homosexuals to a wider audience.

Movies, as noted earlier, had historically dealt poorly with homosexual characters, rarely portraying them, and then usually only as stereotyped effeminates. Australian movies were no exception. With the emergence of 'adult' – often explicitly sexual – themes in films from the 1950s, new images of homosexuals began to appear, though until the 1970s they were rarely positive. Instead new stereotypes were added to the mix: the sad, pathetic, maladjusted homosexual; the ineffectual victim; the deviant, habitué of a demimonde; and the evil corrupter.[27] If, as one modern writer argues, films are 'socially produced systems for signifying and organising reality',[28] then the 'reality' of homosexuality in films over this period was clearly false. No recognition was ever given to the fact that most homosexuals were fully functional human beings.

Nevertheless from the 1960s an increasing number of films depicted homosexuality. Most films released in Australia in this period came from Britain or America. Homosexual characters were generally treated more sympathetically in British films, as for example, in *Victim*, *The L-Shaped Room* (1962), *A Taste of Honey* (1961) and *The Killing of Sister George* (1968). In American films the homosexual world was seen as a sad, destructive world and stereotypes abounded: *Advise and Consent* (1962), *Reflections in a Golden Eye* (1967), *The Sergeant* and *The Detective* (both 1968), continued Hollywood's negative portrayals. All these films were shown in Sydney cinemas.

This 'explosion' of films about homosexuality culminated in 1970 with the release of *Boys in the Band* which, while it still had stereotypes, also portrayed some attractive and functional homosexual men. This represented a significant change. The film reached a wider audience than the play, which had been successfully produced in Sydney in 1968. From this time, there was a constant stream of films dealing with homosexual themes. Some, like the mainstream *Sunday Bloody Sunday* (1971), had an impact simply because they showed two men kissing each other passionately on the lips, something that audiences – even homosexual men – would never have seen before. Others made by openly gay directors and writers portrayed sympathetic and positive perceptions of aspects of homosexual life. For example *A Very Natural Thing* (1973), *Word is Out* and *The Consequence* (both 1977), *Nighthawks* and *The Deputy* (both 1978) and two locally made films, *Squeeze*, by Richard Turner – shot in New Zealand in 1979 and released in Sydney in February 1981 – and the locally made *The Clinic* (1982), all appeared in Sydney cinemas over the following years. As Vito Russo suggests, these films were important since they showed affection as part of male homosexual love.[29] Previously it had simply been seen as something occurring from the waist down.

A far wider impact came from television, in spite of its less *explicit* depiction of homosexual imagery and practices. As critic David Lyle noted, the 'protection from "offensive" material that dominated American film and TV didn't overwhelm' British and Australian programs in this period.[30] Thus, in explaining why a show whose main character was homosexual flopped in America, despite having a popular star – Tony Randall – in the lead, Lyle continues: the 'American public found it difficult to laugh with a homosexual portrayed on television. The surprise is not that the show failed, but that it ever made it to air in the first place.'[31]

Australian television 'grew up' in the late 1960s, and began to portray 'adult' material factually and openly. Perhaps it was influenced by the success of the British series, *Till Death Us Do Part* (1965–75), which dealt with a range of previously taboo subjects – racism, alcoholism, sex and death – and yet managed to 'attract viewers rather than causing them to switch off in disgust'.[32] Also in the '60s, *The Mavis Bramston Show* pushed the limits even further, with satirical treatment of many of Australia's sacred cows. Its ratings zoomed.[33]

But the show that probably did more than any other single thing to make homosexuality acceptable to Sydneysiders was *Number 96*. This long-running and immensely popular locally made 'soapie' was first broadcast in 1972. One character, Don Finlayson, was the sort of young man all mums and dads would want their daughters to marry – an outcome the daughters would probably have been quite happy with. Only after his character had been developed as a nice guy and he had found a place in the hearts of viewers, was it revealed that he was homosexual. And no holds were barred as to what went on in Don's life. As scriptwriter David Sale noted, during the series

> everything that could ever happen to a homosexual happened to Don. He fell in and out of love, he had relationships, long relationships, he even went off the rails and has a series of one-night stands when he was very low, he was blackmailed, he had his job ... with a law firm [threatened] because someone who wanted this promotion found out he was homosexual and was going to use this to tell the boss. That happened and the boss said it doesn't matter ...[34]

Having such an openly homosexual character did not hurt the ratings. The show was immensely popular: it ran for six years and

at its peak it was seen five nights a week in prime time. And as
Sale noted – a point confirmed by many – the series seemed to do
a great deal to make homosexuality acceptable as a talking point,
which had not previously been the case.[35] It also spawned imita-
tors, including *The Box,* which also had homosexual characters.

After that, homosexuality generally had fairer treatment
on television. While many gays objected to what they saw as
'negative' stereotype portrayals, in such shows as *Are You Being
Served?* (1972–85), others like *The Naked Civil Servant* (1975),
Brideshead Revisted (1981), and many documentaries – such
as those on AIDS, the Sisters of Perpetual Indulgence, homosexual parents, the rights of lesbian mothers, being a teenager
and gay, for example – gave a more complete picture of what
life was like for homosexuals living in our society. In general,
during the 1970s, television projected more-positive images of
homosexuals to its audiences. Whether these images were powerful enough to counteract other negative projections is open to
conjecture.

Sydney's theatres likewise had some effect from the 1960s in
projecting different images of homosexuals to society. Certainly
Mart Crowley's *The Boys in the Band* at Sydney's Playbox Theatre, and John Herbert's *Fortune and Men's Eyes* at the Ensemble in Kirribilli, both in 1968, and *Hair,* opening at the Metro
in Kings Cross the following year, portrayed very different
images of homosexuals. The Chief Secretary of NSW in 1969,
Eric Willis, was appalled that *Hair* 'loudly promoted almost
every vice from blasphemy and drug-taking to homosexuality
and draft dodging'.[36] From then on, Sydney saw Simon Gray's
Butley as well as local plays, Peter Kenna's *A Hard God,* Steve
J Spears' *The Elocution of Benjamin Franklin* and dozens more.
From 1970 onwards, good theatre reflected newer perceptions
of homosexuality, rather than falling back onto stereotypes.[37]

That perceptions *were* changing was indicated by a series of public opinion polls. In 1968, 64 per cent of those interviewed had been opposed to equal treatment in law for homosexuals, but by 1974 this proportion had dropped to 39 per cent.[38] It continued to fall over the 1970s, to 33 per cent in 1977 and 29 per cent in 1978.[39] The 'baby boomers' were making their opinions felt.

A further change in the mid-1970s showed increasing public acceptance. *Nation Review,* an independent and often iconoclastic weekly newspaper, found space for homosexuals to make contact, and also had a gay voice. Its 'D-Notices' – a form of Personal Ads – allowed homosexuals to advertise, in a similar manner to heterosexuals, for a variety of purposes. Such blatant advertising often drew the wrath of the moral guardians of the community. But Martin Smith's regular 'Gayzette' column, which gave a gay point of view on many issues, most often drew wrath, ironically, from the radical and left-wing gay activists, who had little time for his conservative perspective.

This increasing acceptance was mirrored, in its way, by an increasing public profile for Sydney's homosexual and gay worlds that took various forms. A proliferation of special interest groups served their needs; such things as counselling services; religious groups like the Metropolitan Community Church, Chutzpah – a Jewish gay social group, the Sisters of Perpetual Indulgence – an order of gay male nuns, and Acceptance – a Catholic gay group; a Homosexual Law Reform Group; gay groups within several of the mainstream political parties – the Communist Party of Australia Gay Collective, and the ALP Gay Group; a Gay Union of Tertiary Staff from Sydney's universities; a Gay Task Force – working for changes in society, its institutions and structures; a gay theatre company; gay groups for youth; a gay 'mysticism' group; various gay radio programs on community radio; and a range of other 'welfare' or service groups. Some of these had emerged earlier in the 1970s, and many had simply expanded. Other specialised groups had emerged in Sydney by the early 1980s too.[40] A series of national homosexual conferences from 1975 through to the mid-1980s allowed for various groups and individuals to come together to discuss issues of mutual concern, and plan strategies for mutual benefit.

Another major manifestation of the higher public profile of the homosexual worlds was the growth in the number and variety of commercial venues from the early 1970s. Sydney had a small number of such venues, scattered in and around the city in 1970. But then came a veritable flood.

The CBD area declined in its importance as a meeting place. The property boom and redevelopment of much of the city from the 1960s led to the demolition of some hotels with gay bars – the Australia, Ushers and Pfahlert's – although new hotel hours from the mid-1950s had already seen these bars decline in importance. The Carlton lingered on awhile, but eventually it lost its homosexual clientele, except perhaps for those out-of-towners who might turn up, recalling its past reputation. Even the Belfields was eventually sold – it became a chocolate shop.

A major new development in the CBD, though, was the opening of two gay steam baths. First was King Steam in the early 1970s, which over the years had four different locations, three of them in or near King Street – hence its name – and the last in Oxford Street.[41] Later came the Roman Baths, in The Block in Pitt Street, which lasted until the mid-1980s. Their convenient locations ensured they were well patronised.

The CBD also had several places which were gay only on specific nights of the week. One was Stranded, a downstairs disco in the newly renovated Strand Arcade, in what had previously been an elegant upmarket corset salon. It had retained the old fittings from its previous days – striped flocked wallpaper, heavy gilt mirrors, replica Empire chairs, and chandeliers. This made for a marvellously incongruous setting for the 1981 Sydney 'Mr Leather' Contest finals, in which dozens of leather-clad gay men strutted on a catwalk, while hundreds of members of Sydney's gay communities yelled their admiration and encouragement.

Another venue for regular gay nights, Isadora's in Day Street on the fringes of the CBD, held a cabaret-style party on Friday and Saturday nights. Nearby in Kent Street, the 'Roos was a meeting place for one of Sydney's early gay bikie clubs. And down near Central Station, Kandy's Krystal Pistol, opposite Her Majesty's Theatre was a short-lived nightclub in the early 1970s. By late 1974 it had become Capers; by 1975 it was gone. Later, a gay steam bath – Barefoot Boy – had a brief existence on the same site.

Kings Cross also experienced change in its gay venues. Les Girls continued on but the Annexe and the Jewel Box closed down. New meeting places appeared: coffee shops like the Adonis, just down the street from the Wayside Chapel; the Black Cat in Victoria Street; and Doddy's, also in Victoria Street, but they tended to have a fairly short life, as did Feathers, a club in Bayswater Road. Other new bars with a slightly longer life were the Barrell Inn in Challis Avenue, opening in 1972 on the site of the old Vadims Cafe, and Castello's, initially in Rockwell Crescent, and later in Kellett Street. It was eventually transformed into Tricks. In the late 1970s part of it also became the Bunkhouse, a gay steam bath, but because it attracted male 'prostitutes' it soon fell into disfavour and closed. Stallions, a gay steam bath in Darlinghurst Road, opened in 1978 and lasted for just over a year.

Tina's at the top of William Street was another late night bar that had a brief life from late 1979. A different sort of venue was the Brutus, a private club (members got a key to the door): it opened in Bayswater Road early in the 1970s, but eventually closed a few years later, when its proprietor was involved in a shooting scandal in the nearby beat at Rushcutters Bay Park.

But increasingly from the early 1970s, Oxford Street became the focus for gay venues. After establishing its initial attraction in the late 1960s, it became the logical place for new gay venues to locate, particularly when further changes to Kings Cross made this latter area less attractive for the gay world. After the Vietnam War ended, the Cross was mostly packed with suburban voyeurs, come to look at the weirdos. As Sasha Soldatow notes, in *Private – Do Not Open*:

> Darlinghurst Road, the heart of the Cross, [was] packed out on Saturday night. Full of men bemoaning their fate, prostitutes on heroin and fifty-year old lust-driven women. Everyone else is just looking. At the spruikers lying about live sex acts on stage, hoods in ice-cream parlours, coffee shops with windows facing the street, fast-food joints, illegal watch-sellers, drunk buskers and fortune-tellers.[42]

Due to its growing reputation as a gay area, Oxford Street began to attract more new venues, which in turn added to its reputation and encouraged even more venues. In the early 1980s, the stretch between Hyde Park and the Paddington Town Hall became known as the 'Glitter Strip' or 'The Golden Mile', and the surrounding area was 'The Ghetto', an acknowledgment of the high concentration of gay men there and places catering for them. For nearly two decades this area was the focus of Sydney's gay world. Similar things occurred in various American cities, with the Castro in San Francisco, New York's Chelsea and West

Hollywood in Los Angeles, becoming the foci for gay life in those cities.

Ivy's Birdcage and Capriccio's, the first gay clubs, had opened in Oxford Street in the late 1960s and a flood of new clubs and bars followed. Patches, with its dance floor lit from underneath, was first, in April 1976,[43] followed by Flo's Palace, The Tropicana – which became the Midnight Shift – the Ox, Pete's Bar, Palms – later Scooters, then Palms again, Syd's – in Crown Street just off Oxford Street, Buck's, Saddle-tramps – in the Exchange Hotel, Querelle, Club 45, The Handlebar, The Old Bank, and Four AM. Ruby Red's, a lesbian bar, opened nearby in Crown Street; it later became Headquarters, a gay fuck bar. Many of these bars were short-lived; some, like Capriccio's, which was burnt out in 1982, lasted longer. A mere handful survived for more than a few years.

Early in the 1970s, '253', a new steam bath opened at 253 Oxford Street with a party that became legend. A stylish place, its 'tongue-in-cheek' sign out front advised clients that it had an 'Entrance at Rear'. Its most famous feature was a large, low glass-topped coffee table in the lounge area: looking down through the glass you could see directly through to the spa pool below with its cavorting naked patrons.

Most of the gay press in this period had offices in and around Oxford Street. It was also the locus of a new form of bar that appeared in Sydney in the 1970s: the back room or fuck bar. Signal, the first of these, opened in Oxford Square in 1977, it later moved to Crown Lane in nearby East Sydney, between Oxford Street and William Street. Another, Club 80, originally at 80 William Street, near Kings Cross, eventually moved to The Ghetto area, reopening in Little Oxford Street, near Taylor Square, and later relocating in Oxford Street, several hundred metres east of Taylor Square. It closed after being raided by police in 1983.

Writer Gary Dunne, in *If Blood Should Stain the Lino*, has given us a description of the interior of a fuck bar:

A large room, blue neon lights and bare wooden floor. Scattered around the edges, like wall-flowers at a deb ball, about twenty entrants in a Marlon Brando look-alike competition. Mostly clad in leather jackets and tight jeans, a conspicuous lack of helmets. On one wall, a solitary poster, Marlon himself, similarly clad, astride a motor bike. No furniture. More cool and bored than aggressive looking, each copy was leaning or slouched against the wall. In one of a number of variations on a basic butch pose … Behind us, a makeshift bar. Behind it, a blackboard. 'Orange Juice 40c. Amyl Nitrite $1'. In chalk.[44]

The group who have come to the fuck bar go upstairs to where the action is:

Pitch black. Noises. Whispers and groans. Davis stood in the doorway and lit a cigarette. Lines on his face, shadowed by matchlight. And a fresco against the opposite wall. Erotic confusion. Legs, arms, bodies, all intertwined. Moving. On the floor, dust and clothing. Two faces looked over. And in a split second, the match was out. Darkness … Through several rooms, all pitch black and smelling of amyl and leather. Couples, groups, and wandering singles.[45]

They wander into the last room, and see 'two holes in a galvanised iron roof that sloped to meet the floor on one side. A dusty moonlit attic'; looking out, they see 'Sydney, a familiar maze of colours and lights. Washed in sea-breeze and moonlight.'[46]

The language changed too. Reflecting American influences,

'camp' became 'gay', in both the gay world and in general public discourse. 'Square' – the heterosexual world or those that inhabited it – became 'straight'. Fashion changes interacted with the gay world to create new meanings in language. The phrases 'what a lovely lunch', 'that's a packed lunch' or 'wouldn't you just love to eat that lunch', take on new dimensions when it is known that 'lunch' refers to the bulge in a man's pants in the genital region. Fashion changes – from the loose baggy trousers of the 1950s to hip-hugging jeans – created a new focus for attention, and discussion.

The new language appeared increasingly in books on or by gay men; and new bookshops opened in Oxford Street, selling gay books and magazines. There were also 'sex shops' with erotica and sex aids for sale, and – usually – a back room for sexual encounters. One of these, Numbers, had a maze of corridors and cubicles. Another, Toolshed, had a large rear room with gay porn videos showing, its prevalent furniture earned it the soubriquet 'Club Beanbag'. And there were restaurants and coffee shops – like the Green Park Diner – that attracted a large gay clientele, perhaps because they advertised extensively in the gay press.

This incredible concentration of activity within a relatively short space of time, in a discrete geographic area, all occurred in a city where male homosexual activity was still illegal. It helped to create a sense of gay identity; there was now a definite area where the new gay man could feel at home, in territory that was clearly stamped in his image. But behind the scenes, as the new 'macho' gay man made his appearance, the old 'camp' world continued on. Rose Jackson, the drag artiste, recalls that in Kinsela's Funeral Chapel in Taylor Square, the caretaker still 'had big parties in the funeral parlour and we'd keep the booze in the cool room'.[47]

The 'gay ghetto' was not confined to Oxford Street; gay venues began to appear in the nearby suburbs. To the north, new gay venues emerged in East Sydney and Darlinghurst, an area that had long had its homosexual inhabitants. The Lord Roberts Hotel at the corner of Riley and Stanley streets had briefly gone 'camp' in the late 1960s and its proprietor, Kandy, had put on drag shows in the back bar, the 'Volga Room'. Nearby in Crown Street, Jools, a swank new gay nightclub to rival Capriccio's, opened in the 1970s.

The Ghetto also began to expand in a southerly direction, into Surry Hills. This was associated with another phenomenon of the times – the 'gayification of the inner-city pubs', as one journalist put it.[48] He went on to note that several old hotels around Oxford Street had been taken over by new management and redecorated, to attract a new clientele, gay men:

> The area's accessibility to the Oxford Street 'Golden Mile'
> of gay commercial life makes the choice obvious. The five
> hotels are the Beresford, the Cricketer's Arms and the
> Flinders in Surry Hills, and the Albury and the Unicorn in
> Paddington.[49]

The Unicorn and the Albury were both on the 'Golden Mile', and had 'gone gay' in 1978 and 1980 respectively. The Cricketer's Arms had started the process in 1973, and the Beresford and Flinders followed, along with the Oxford in 1982, and the Exchange, which already had one gay bar, several years later, both on the 'Golden Mile'.

The same thing happened in other suburbs with a high proportion of gay men. Thus Balmain's Town Hall Hotel went gay, as did the Newtown Hotel and Cecchini's, both in King Street, Newtown.

The pattern did not always succeed; an attempt to make Redfern's Court House Hotel a gay pub failed in 1982, probably because not enough gay men lived in the area at the time. An earlier failure, in the 1970s, was the Rocky Horror Cafe, a wine bar in Redfern Street, Redfern, which tried to develop a gay clientele. Yet the Britannia, nearby in Cleveland Street, Chippendale, had some success.

Alongside these new gay pubs was Karen's Kastle, in Cleveland Street, Redfern, a short-lived attempt in the 1970s to get a gay cabaret going. In the 1980s, plans to take over a failing football club on the corner of Cleveland and Morehead streets in Redfern, and turn it into a gay disco, met with strong local resident opposition. A major lesbian bar did appear in the area in the 1970s – and lasted until well into the 1980s – on the site of the Buck's Steakhouse restaurant, it became known variously as the Playground, Rubyfruits and The Jungle. The Trolley Car Bar, in King Street, Chippendale, enjoyed a brief life from 1968, as did Champers in Newtown. Once increasing numbers of gay men moved into Surry Hills, Redfern and Newtown – the so-called 'Pink Triangle' – the chances for the commercial success of venues catering to them improved immensely.

There were further changes out east along Oxford Street. Chez Ivy in Bondi Junction finally closed. The Bondi Junction Steam Baths became the Pits early in 1980, but soon closed (and became the first office for the Sydney Swans). Enzo's became the Traffic Lights around 1980, and lost its gay clientele. Just up the street, at Paddington's Imperial Hotel, one bar – the Apollo Room – became a gay bar. And across the street, during the 1970s and 1980s, the Paddington Town Hall was the scene of many gay dances, fund-raising events, community meetings and homosexual conferences.

Even suburban Randwick had its touches of gay ambience. Ken's Baths – a gay steam bath – opened in Belmore Road, Randwick, in late 1971, just around the corner from a major beat in Alison Park. In 1972 it moved to Anzac Parade, Kensington, in the building where the Purple Onion had been.

Here's how I remember my first visit to a steam bath, namely Ken's, when it was still in Randwick.

It was up some rickety stairs, a dimly lit place of meandering corridors, alcoves and rooms with semi-naked figures moving through the gloom, or waiting, enticingly, in the doorways ... A steam room seemed filled with characters from a Fellini movie. In one room I came upon an orgy – bodies entwined and doing things that even the *Kama Sutra* might not have believed possible. I was immediately attracted and aroused and, after watching for a while, I joined in.

Fantasy Island, another major drag venue, opened in Alison Road, Randwick, in 1982 and enjoyed a brief life. And in Kensington, the wine bar with the long-winded name, 'The Decline and Fall of Western Civilization As We Know It', was known as an 'occasional' gay bar, largely associated with students from the nearby University of New South Wales Gay Society. North of the harbour, Yolanta's wine bar in Manly enjoyed a short heyday in the late 1970s.

The existence of this gay world in its many and varied manifestations from the early 1970s made Sydney a magnet for homosexual and gay men. It also represented a high level of commercial entrepreneurship aiming at the gay dollar. It showed that money could be made from catering to this emerging gay market and that there was a gay community, premised on the existence of a large number of people with a gay identity. Apart from the factors already mentioned, several new features were important in helping to create and maintain this sense of identity.

Gay characters began to appear more regularly in Australian fiction, in both mainstream books and specifically gay novels and short stories. These characters were often based on the lifestyles of those who had either been involved in the various social movements of the 1960s and 1970s – including the gay liberation movement – or who now lived in the inner-city areas around the ghetto. Frank Moorhouse on the one hand, and Gary Dunne, Sasha Soldatow and Ian MacNeill on the other, spring to mind.

Moorhouse, a member of Sydney's libertarian fringe The Push in the 1960s, was a mainstream writer who introduced homosexual characters to the Australian reading public early on. In some works – as in *The Americans, Baby* (1972) – the situation of homosexuals is central. Others have homosexual characters, or – less often – describe parts of the gay world.

Moorhouse has been criticised for his treatment of homosexuals. One criticism was that many of his homosexual characters display confusing and anti-social trends, but then the same is often true of his heterosexual characters too. In other words, the traits are not portrayed as intrinsic to homosexuals, and the criticism can be easily dismissed. Other criticisms deserve more attention. One is that his views on the formation of sexual identity are within a traditional psychodynamic framework; thus accepting one's sexuality is an individual, privatised process, devoid of any reference to the wider political and social context. Here, one writer has suggested that Moorhouse works out his ideas within the old libertarian, individualistic, framework[50] – the product of his times – a period which predates the full development of ideas about such a subculture and the social construction of a gay identity.

But it is his *The Everlasting Secret Family* that has been a particular focus of criticism, because its themes are seen to reiterate stereotypical views of homosexuals as child molesters, seducers of the young, and as evil and perverted. It's a criticism, of course, that reflects a 'politically correct' approach to writing, that writers should not write characters that reflect badly on an oppressed social group or minority. But it is a knee-jerk reaction, a product of its times, and if taken to its logical extreme, would sanitise all creative writing. Perhaps the novel should be seen as simply an expression of Moorhouse's own psyche, or relating more to his novelistic fantasies; it need not be seen as reflecting on the city's gay life and the proclivities of the majority of its denizens.

The other writers mentioned, writing from their own experiences, present a different view of the city's gay life. Both Ian MacNeill and Gary Dunne have given us portraits of days and nights in The Ghetto. Here's a description of one aspect of Oxford Street night-life from Ian MacNeill:

> I sit in the bar of the Albury watching. Outside it is cold and blustery, inside …
>
> Snake-eyes in the 501s is eyeing me off.
>
> I like him, he looks as though he has a big cock. Anyway, he's a big man. Got to have something.
>
> His eyes bore into me. If I smile I know I'll spoil everything for him. He heads towards the toilets, giving me a look.
>
> I'm almost tempted – to see what he's got. Then I think about the escape and how bad I'll feel whenever I'll see him again. And I will see him again. And I will, I will.[51]

Another novelist, Simon Payne, gives an insight into the lifestyles of homoerotically inclined men in the 1980s, including this description of a beat inside a public toilet during the day:

> Inside the place was surprisingly crowded. An elderly man
> occupied one of the cubicles. Two younger guys lent against
> the wall, waiting. One wore a dark business suit devoid of
> style. A double flash of white shirt shone, exposed either side
> of his dark tie … The other seemed to be in a tracksuit. In
> the far corner a further two figures were engrossed in fairly
> advanced foreplay …[52]

Novels and short stories such as these, which present gay characters realistically in all their diversity and complexity, gave a
range of role models for other gay men, helping to foster new
styles of gay identity.

The development of a gay press also promoted this sense of
gay identity, and thus a gay 'community', in several ways. First,
it was implicit in the way it directed attention to the city's gay
life and the increasing number of men now participating in it.
More importantly, several parts of the gay press explicitly aimed
at fostering the idea of a gay identity and community. Finally,
the growth of a gay press was in itself a manifestation of the
higher public profile of the gay world.

CAMP INK, the first gay magazine to appear, was soon followed by others. By 1972, as noted, there was a gay movement
magazine, a commercial magazine and a bar paper. Other publications from various liberationist groups soon appeared. And
in 1973 there was a 'minor explosion' of commercial gay publications which went in two different directions.[53]

First came the expansion into what is called 'material
aimed at sexual gratification' – erotica. Previously, physical culture magazines had been the major source of imagery for sexual
fantasy, and these were now supplemented by new magazines

openly addressing themselves to gay men.[54] *Australia's Golden Boys* appeared around 1972. One connoisseur assesses it as 'quite good'; at least it had original material. Others of far lesser quality also serviced an existing need.

Sydney's commercial gay newspaper market also expanded in 1973. Titles such as *Apollo, Gayzette, Stallion, Butch, Gay* and *Little Butch* all made brief appearances but only *Gay*, which shifted to a more glossy 'porn' format, survived into the 1990s. The others disappeared, generally unlamented, into oblivion. Distribution was limited, largely restricted to sex shops and a few newsagents in The Ghetto area, so the circulation was never large.

Australia's first monthly gay magazine, *Campaign*, appeared in 1975. Financed by the owners of some Sydney gay bars, it enjoyed considerable commercial success. It was the first gay magazine to have wide distribution through local newsagents, so it was accessible to those outside Sydney, people who otherwise had little contact with the urban gay world. For many years it played an important role in keeping suburban (and rural) gays in touch with news and information. It had a fairly ambivalent attitude to gay politics, and often played little part in the major political debates of the gay community during the latter half of the 1970s. But it could not stay uninvolved in the debates about political activities in 1978, after the Mardi Gras fracas when there were major confrontations between police and gays in the streets of Sydney. These events received enormous coverage in the mainstream media as well.

Soon afterwards, perhaps significantly, a rash of new papers appeared: *Cruiser, Sydney Advocate, Playguy* and *Libertine*. These were followed, in ensuing years, by the *Star* (later the *Star Observer*, the *Sydney Star Observer*, then *Star Observer* again), the *Oxford Weekender News, 9PM* and the *Sydney Fart* – this last a spoof of the *Star* and its preoccupation with the new macho image for gay men. These papers were mostly distributed in the gay pubs around Oxford Street, and several survived for some years. The Melbourne-based *Gay Community News*, later becoming *OutRage*, was also available in Sydney from the late 1970s.

Gay Information, a more *intellectual* magazine, appeared early in 1980. Its credo was 'information *and* ideas as a catalyst for thought and a stimulus for action', and it aimed to present serious and well-researched articles on a variety of social, literary and political subjects. It was well written and not at all ponderous, a problem of many journals aiming to analyse fringe group situations. Finally throughout the 1970s and 1980s, there were

> innumerable small-circulation newsletters and in-house
> magazines produced by dozens of special interest gay groups,
> from the political to the religious and including everything
> in between.[55]

Sydney's gay press fulfilled several important functions. First, it ensured that 'anything, no matter how obscure, that is in any way involved with anyone or anything homosexual will eventually be reprinted'.[56] In this it was probably similar to the newspapers and publications serving various ethnic communities that gave out information specifically of interest to its particular readership.

Second, it allowed a gay view of events to be presented. This was a significant purpose behind the creation of *CAMP INK* and the other community-based newspapers. The gay press served as the major purveyor of a wide variety of gay perspectives.

Finally, the gay press played its role in the development of identity and community, not only by catering for the varied interests of homosexual men, but also, and quite explicitly at times, by trying to create a sense of a gay identity. Thus, for example, the *Sydney Star*, from its first issue in 1979, often printed notices 'Think Gay, Buy Gay'. Its editorials directly addressed the issues of identifying as gay, helping to engender a sense of gay identity, and – by implication – community. *Campaign*, in its early issues, often took a similar approach; one article in late 1981 was even entitled 'What "identity" offers you'.

I inhabited various worlds in those days: respectable academe by day during the week, with teaching and research; and then demos and discussions and conferences by day at weekends; and parties and dope any night. They were halcyon days when we thought we could remake the world, make it a better place.

But I was also part of two other worlds from the early 1970s: the commercial gay scene and the political activist world (but avoiding consciousness-raising groups). On the one hand there were the bars, back rooms and saunas, and on the other Gay Lib, CAMP and running off posters.

The idiosyncrasies of these different worlds, some antipathetic to each other, never ceased to amaze me. I, for one, appreciated the differences between all of those worlds that I inhabited, and enjoyed what each of them had to offer me.

Clearly there was a high-profile gay life in Sydney by the late 1970s, although it still catered for only a small minority of Sydney's male homosexual population. The majority of Sydney's homoerotically inclined men would still rarely – if ever – come into contact with this world. Most still led secretive lives in the suburbs, choosing to hide their difference. A large majority probably lived in regular close relationships, seeing a special 'friend' on a continuing basis, or perhaps cohabiting. There were, as the euphemisms go, many 'pairs of bachelor schoolteachers sharing accommodation', or 'best friends who have been together since schooldays', or 'cousins who have moved interstate together', living in Sydney's suburbs.[57]

Did all those homosexuals living out in the suburbs, and the high-profile and visible gay world of the inner city, really constitute something that could be called a 'gay community'?

This issue agitated the hearts and minds of gay activists and intellectuals alike. Increasing numbers of men frequented the bars in and around Oxford Street: the term 'clone' graphically depicting these men as a distinguishable 'type'; there was a burgeoning commercial scene; there were activists pursuing a range of issues, most notably the need for law reform. There was a wide variety of gay pressure groups serving everything from the Christian god to mammon. It was the very visible face of the new homosexuality – but did it constitute a separate 'community'? Had the concept of 'gay' moved from an individual statement to a social category?

And if there was a gay community, then who would speak for it? Would it be the activists, or would it be the commercial venue owners? Clearly the way in which the communities' concerns would be addressed would be very different, depending on the speaker. From an historical perspective, there is little doubt that a gay community had emerged and existed; and like other communities, it had its internal divisions, its conflicts, and – even – its moments of agreement.

The concern over whether a community existed was not just navel-gazing by a small clique; it had wider relevance. The ideas of 'community' and 'communities' were increasingly relevant in Australia from the late 1970s. As historian Stuart Macintyre noted, one of the trends in Australian politics in the early 1980s was the growing acceptance that society was composed of various communities. Multiculturalism was an early expression of this idea. In respect of Aborigines and women, Macintyre notes that the 'State has in both cases accepted that the claimants constitute a distinct group with special needs and entitlements

– and the creation of advisory bodies was a formal acknowledgment of the fact.'[58] There was, however, a general reluctance to grant similar status to homosexuals in Australia, despite the obvious need for such responses. Some states, including NSW, still designated them as criminals, few had given them the full protection of anti-discrimination legislation, and they were targeted by the ignorant and prejudiced. Yet the overt growth of gay life in Sydney demonstrated a 'gay community', and, at the public level, an apparent acceptance of homosexuals. Homosexuals were taxpayers and voters, with legitimate expectations that governments would respond to their concerns.

State acceptance of the legitimacy of lesbian and gay claims was far more advanced in many northern European countries than in Anglo-Saxon ones like Australia. Yet developments in a number of countries have often been similar, due to the same underlying economic, political and social processes. What occurred in Sydney – new ideas about acceptable sexual practices; changing images of homosexuality on film and TV and in print; the growing activism of lesbians and gay men; the burgeoning of a gay commercial scene and gay groups, with the concomitant emergence of the new gay identity and ideas of a gay community – occurred in other Australian cities, albeit on a smaller scale, and much more so in major cities around the western world. These developments depended on a whole range of social factors, not least society's attitude to sexuality and its status as a public or private matter.

The reluctance in Australia is perhaps best epitomised in the separate ideas of 'tolerance' and 'acceptance'. While public opinion polls indicated an increasing opposition to maintaining the criminal status of homosexuals – reflecting greater 'tolerance' – it could be a different matter when voting such people into public office, perhaps a better indicator of real 'acceptance'.

So through the 1970s and into the 1980s the gay community began to involve itself more directly in electoral politics, with openly gay candidates standing for election to public office, and attempts to influence the mainstream political parties, as a pressure group, or by wielding a gay vote. Most of this activity was in Sydney; it can perhaps be seen as an oblique indicator of changing levels of 'acceptance'.

As noted earlier in this chapter, journalist Marion MacDonald had mentioned that an openly gay candidate had stood for a seat in the federal elections of 1972. This was David Widdup, who stood against the Prime Minister, Billy McMahon, with the catchy campaign slogan 'I've got my eye on Billy's seat'.[59] Widdup had no chance of winning the seat; his purpose was simply to generate publicity for the gay movement in its early days. Similar aims were behind several other nominations by gay candidates for seats at state elections during the 1970s. Martin Smith stood for the seat of Waverley in November 1972; Graeme Donkin, a gay Christian activist, stood for the seat of Bligh in May 1976, while in July 1978, journalist Peter Blazey stood against the ex-Premier, Eric Willis, for the seat of Earlwood. None of these candidates expected to win the seats, but they gained considerable publicity for gay issues, particularly the need for law reform.

The issue of homosexual law reform was a major cause by the late 1970s. An attack on the legal framework that clearly designated the gay community as second-class citizens focused on something all homosexuals could relate to. It gave activists, habitués of the gay commercial scene, or those living secretly in the suburbs, a common bond. It was clearly in line with existing ideas about civil liberties and self-determination for minorities. The campaign was waged, on and off, with varying degrees of intensity, for 15 years, in its own way helping to further create

212

gay identity and ideas of a gay community. It received increasing support from a broad range of public institutions, and, eventually public opinion polls showed only a small minority in the wider community opposed to it.[60]

While several candidates had stood as independents, a major breakthrough occurred in 1982, when Max Pearce, an activist for the gay movement, gained ALP preselection for a forthcoming federal election. The seat was the blue-ribbon Liberal electorate of Wentworth, so he had little chance of winning. But, significantly, one of the mainstream parties had selected an openly gay candidate for the first time.

While success at the ballot box eluded these attempts at parliamentary seats, gay candidates began to contest local government elections from 1980 with more rewarding results. Max Pearce had been preselected as an ALP candidate for his ward in the City of Sydney elections in April that year, although his low position on the ballot paper meant he was not elected. At the 1984 City of Sydney elections, however, three openly gay candidates were elected to the City Council, Bill Hunt and Brian McGahen as independents, and Craig Johnston for the ALP. McGahen's election was particularly significant, since he was not a member of any group (Hunt was a member of the South Sydney Resident Action Group). His campaign had largely been conducted through the gay media, and his election was more clearly a direct 'gay vote'. With other gay aldermen and sympathetic supporters, these three were able to implement policies designed to help change community attitudes at a local level, and ensure that Council services did not discriminate against gay people.

The power of the gay vote was most clearly demonstrated in the late 1980s. At the state election in March 1988, independent Clover Moore won the seat of Bligh, an inner-city seat covering Surry Hills, Darlinghurst, Kings Cross and Paddington – areas with a traditionally high concentration of homosexuals – over the sitting Liberal member, Michael Yabsley. A large state-wide swing to the conservative parties saw the Labor Party lose government, but the trend in Bligh was in the opposite direction. Yabsley had a poor profile with the gay community, and a strong campaign in the gay press urged voters to support Moore. As the *Bulletin* ruefully noted after the election, 'Gay Power' had hung Yabsley.[61]

So by the late 1980s, Sydney's inner-city gay community had flexed its collective political muscle. This was not a new phenomenon – it had been flexing its muscles from the early 1970s, in a range of campaigns. Probably the hardest fought was that to obtain law reform, finally achieved in 1984. It also fought a long and difficult campaign against the Catholic Church, which contested the gay community's right to appear before the Royal Commission on Human Relationships in 1975.[62] It had fought against police harassment, and their raids on a gay bar, Club 80, in 1983.[63] And it continued to fight to get positive and sympathetic material about homosexuality introduced into the state's schools, and in a range of other campaigns to gain equality for homosexuals, for lesbians and gay men, in the wider society.

Things had changed dramatically for Sydney's gay world and its increasing number of communities. Wider social attitudes to homosexuals had altered, even though there were still groups contesting the legitimacy of homosexuals in Australian society. Right-wing groups, conservative politicians and Christian fundamentalists saw lesbians and gay men, like ethnic and other minorities, as a threat to their vision of what Australian society ought to be like, based on some mythical past or an idealised concept.

By the early 1980s, Sydney's gay world existed openly for all who cared to sample it. There was increasing inter-action between lesbians and gay men; many of the acrimonious debates of the 1970s were now history. Politicians were aware of the gay vote, and capitalists wooed the gay dollar. Most, but not all, homoerotically inclined men welcomed the changes. Some hankered for their own mythical past, when the excitement of being in a demimonde made their world seem brighter, more glamorous – or that is how they remembered it. Others feared that homosexuals had lost their sense of solidarity, their sense of cohesion in adversity, their awareness that the fight was not yet over. They pointed to the changing nature of Sydney's Gay Mardi Gras as indicative of the changes they disliked.

The first Mardi Gras parade through Sydney, in June 1978, had ended in confrontations with police, extreme levels of vio-lence, and pitched battles in the streets of Kings Cross, to which the parade had wended its way via College and William streets, after police tried to disband it in Hyde Park. The *Australian*, under the heading 'How a carnival turned into a vicious brawl', reported it as follows:

> Saturday was International Homosexual Solidarity day – a
> day when gays would celebrate, get together and have a good
> time.
>
> At 10.30 pm Australia's first homosexual Mardi Gras was
> in full swing, with about 1000 people singing and dancing
> down Sydney's Oxford Street, caught up in the excitement
> of a jubilant crowd.
>
> One hour later, the mardi gras had become a two-hour spree
> of screaming, bashing and arrests.

In one incident, police took off their identification numbers and waded into a crowd of homosexuals.

By early yesterday, police had made 53 arrests, several demonstrators and two police had been taken to hospital and Kings Cross was back to normal …[64]

My own night ended somewhat differently, however.

There were so many demonstrations in those days, and this one had started out like any other. How were we to know that it would become 'history'?

We started the day with a march through Sydney, and then later in the afternoon there was a public meeting at Paddington Town Hall.

That night, we gathered at about 10 pm at Taylor Square, and later set off down Oxford Street, with the usual chants, 'two, four, six, eight, gay is just as good as straight' and 'out of the bars, and into the streets'. And people did come out of the bars to watch the parade, and some even joined in. The crowd had swelled somewhat by the time we were outside Patches nightclub.

But I missed some of the more violent scuffles that took place later on in the evening, dropping out of the parade at the bottom of Oxford Street where it joined College Street. I went with some friends back to the Exchange Hotel.

The Exchange was a funky place, with three very different bars. The front bar was Saddle-tramps, out back was the Lamp-shade Bar, while downstairs was another bar, with flashing strobe lights and disco music; to get to it you had to go through the men's toilet.

The Saddle-tramps Bar had a strange décor, with cow skulls and stuffed animals on the wall near the entrance, and saddles on the stools, but it was always a fun venue; Maggie Burns was the DJ there.

We left the parade because it was a cold night – it was well into winter – and we preferred to be in a nice warm bar, rather than standing around in Hyde Park listening to the usual diatribe from the back of a truck that the treatment of homosexuals was a disease of late capitalist society, and would eventually disappear in the bracing air of post-revolutionary socialism.

Having read about the treatment of homosexuals in Stalin's Russia and Castro's Cuba, I didn't buy that argument at all. But some of the activists were really socialists at heart, and incidentally homosexual, so overthrowing capitalism was the main game. If one could add an argument – however flawed – about how happy homosexuals would be under socialism, so be it.

The circumstances of the first parade make it unsurprising that those in the immediately following years were always conducted in a situation of some tension; it was an overt political statement by the marchers. Only in 1981, when the parade was staged in its current summer setting of February, did it become more of a party, a mass celebration by the gay community of its identity and achievements, a trend that continued over the next few years.

The changing nature of Mardi Gras became an issue in the gay community. Some gay men argued that, from being a major show of gay solidarity, a march demonstrating a commitment to an identity and lifestyle – a major political statement – it had become simply a festival, a parade of dressed-up queens through the streets of Sydney – a cultural event open to all and sundry. Others argued that this simply reflected a different sort of political statement, a statement appropriate for the 1980s. Perhaps it still served its function of creating a sense of gay identity for thousands of the homosexually inclined who may never otherwise have come to Oxford Street and The Ghetto, who may never have been willing to make a political stance on the various issues, but who did identify with the sentiments behind the parade, and so came out to see it, and even – perhaps – participate in it.

Ironically, Sydney's Gay Mardi Gras has now become one of the city's major public events. From February 1982 the parade through the city's streets was followed by a party, much in the style of those major parties long associated with Sydney's camp past: the so-called 'Drag and Drain' parties of the 1930s and 1940s, and the 'Artists Balls' of the 1950s and early 1960s. This undoubtedly added to the aura of the Mardi Gras. Thousands attended these parties, which were noted for their imaginative costumes and dazzling spectacles. Documentaries were made about the Mardi Gras parade, thousands of overseas tourists came to participate or watch, heterosexuals flocked in from the suburbs in their tens of thousands to see it, and the mainstream media began to cover the event.

By the early years of the 1980s, the Mardi Gras parade was seen by Sydney's gay communities and their world as a symbol of things to come: of being more than merely tolerated, and well on the way, hopefully, to being accepted on their own terms.

But it was not to be so, just yet.

CHAPTER 7

IT WAS THE WORST OF TIMES, NEVER THE BEST OF TIMES

HIV/AIDS and Sydney's responses

The 1980s were a tumultuous decade for Australians. The banks were deregulated, and an ensuing period of financial excesses reached such a scale that the 1990 recession – the 'recession we had to have', as Treasurer Paul Keating put it – was inevitable. The period became known as the 'me decade' – a reference to the prevailing climate of economic greed and conspicuous consumption. Typical were Christopher Skase and Alan Bond, flamboyant entrepreneurs whose massively over-geared business empires were built on interlocking companies with mountains of debt inadequately secured against problematic assets. Both empires crashed spectacularly. After being charged with fraud, Skase fled to Spain to avoid prosecution, while Bond served several gaol sentences. Yet in the public imagination, Bond remains the man who won the America's Cup for Australia.

Wider issues also gripped people's attention. In the early 1980s, the Franklin River campaign helped to gather support for the growing conservation movement in Australia. Decades of deforestation had led to major land erosion and salinity, and initiatives like mass tree-plantings and Clean Up Australia Day were set up to address these pressing issues. In October 1985, the Commonwealth government granted land rights over Uluru, or Ayers Rock, returning it to its traditional owners, under the condition that it would be leased back to the National Parks and Wildlife Service for 99 years.

Major social changes were also under way. By the 1980s, migrants from all over the world had settled in Australia. Immigration rates peaked in 1988, when 254 000 people arrived in the country, and not just from Europe. The old policy of 'assimilation', which had stipulated that migrants should abandon their cultures and languages and 'blend in' to the existing population, had been firmly supplanted by multiculturalism, particularly in Sydney, home to many of the new arrivals. Sydneysiders worried about high air pollution levels in the city, and, as usual, complained about the city's transport.

In November 1982 the first case of HIV/AIDS was diagnosed in Sydney, heralding the onset of an epidemic that terrified the country.

Something utterly unexpected, HIV/AIDS had the potential to destroy the gains made by Sydney's gay communities in the previous years, and once again make Sydney's gay men a group of outcasts, a danger to the wider society. The impact that HIV/AIDS had on the city's gay community and Australia generally, both initially and in the long term, was an object lesson in how ephemeral 'progress' can be. It was a moment of despair, but it became a lesson in hope.

It wasn't as though Sydneysiders hadn't survived many epidemics and pandemics in the past. In 1789, smallpox wiped out a large proportion of the local Indigenous population; there was a measles epidemic in 1867; the scarlet fever epidemic in the 1870s; another smallpox epidemic of 1881–82; the so-called

Asiatic Flu Pandemic of 1890–91; the plague in 1900; and the Spanish flu epidemic of 1918–19. All of these affected thousands of people, and some had high death rates.[1] But from the 1920s, a range of medical developments, such as the appearance of sulphanomide (in the 1930s) and penicillin treatments (in the 1940s), with inoculations and vaccinations (such as the Salk vaccine for polio in the 1950s) on top of existing strict quarantine regulations, led to a belief that medical science had at last got 'disease' under control. Since World War II, new generations grew up in Australia secure in the belief that epidemics were a thing of the past; they themselves would not have to face something that had been almost commonplace in their grandparents' generation.

But then along came HIV/AIDS. While we now know that HIV/AIDS is an infection contractible by anyone, irrespective of age, gender, ethnicity or sexuality, its initial 'appearance' was among gay men, both in the USA and here in Australia.[2] No one knew what it was, how it was transmitted or how to deal with it.

When news first broke in the world press, attention was focused on the gay communities in America. In Australia, this meant that the immediate press attention would turn to Sydney's gay world, the largest collection of gay men in Australia. And, of course, this is where the first cases were diagnosed.[3] The unknown nature of the disease, its apparent deadliness, and its association with a minority only recently 'discovered' and only gradually being accepted by the population at large, meant that responses were unlikely to be favourable.

Sympathetic they certainly were not. As journalist Evan Whitton noted some years later – in an article tellingly entitled 'AIDS: The Media, Paranoia, and the Wrath of God' – the 'high level of AIDS-induced paranoia may be ascribed to a number of factors: ignorance; fear, not of what has happened but of what might happen; medical scare-mongering; media reportage; and political over-reaction'.[4] He might well have added – as his title certainly spelt out – the deliberate fanning of prejudices by homophobes, with Christian fundamentalists at the forefront.

Whitton noted that there had been two peaks in the Australian paranoia level, the first in November 1984 and the one current at the time he was writing, in August 1985, which he dated from the previous month. The disease had first been reported in December 1981, and from then 'until May 1983 most of the stories were speculation about the nature and course of the disease'.[5] Parts of the gay press had been reporting on it early on. For example, in 1982 Dr Simon Quest wrote about the unusually large number of cases of Kaposi's sarcoma – a form of cancer usually found in elderly Mediterranean men – appearing among Europe's and America's gay communities.[6]

Homophobic hysteria appears to have started in May 1983 when the Sydney *Daily Mirror* ran the headline 'AIDS: The Killer Disease that's expected to sweep Australia'.[7] Fred Nile, a Christian fundamentalist member of the NSW Parliament, demanded that homosexuals be proscribed from entering or leaving the country, and that all gay venues be closed. The NSW Health Minister, Laurie Brereton, rejected the suggestion. His response that Nile's suggestions made him 'feel ashamed' found favour among the gay community; it was rare that leading politicians spoke out in their support.

Nile was a known homophobe who had long conducted campaigns against homosexuals. But homophobia surfaced elsewhere, even in professions from which one could have expected better. For example, the *Medical Journal of Australia* in June 1983 tried what it later claimed was a 'satirical approach': its cover showed a skull and an X-ray, and carried the headlines 'The black plague of the eighties … perhaps we've reached a situation like this to show us what we've known all along – depravity kills!' 'Depravity'? If this was satire, it back-fired – people took the message quite literally, condemning what were called 'gay lifestyles'.

Similarly, homophobia was fanned in academic and intel-lectual circles. Early in 1987 an article in the Sydney-based right-wing journal *Quadrant* took as its starting point Dennis Altman's book on AIDS in America.[8] The article was in effect a Christian fundamentalist interpretation of AIDS. It attacked the view that homosexuals were a legitimate minority in Aus-tralian society, or that AIDS was a public health issue rather than a morality one. In a giveaway line the author, Andrew Lansdown – after copious quotes about the types of sexual activity some homosexuals might have engaged in – declaimed 'Stop the decadence to stop the deaths'.[9]

The same month, Lachlan Chipman, a professor at Wol-longong University, just south of Sydney, asked in his regular column in the *Illawarra Mercury*, 'Did homosexual activists deliberately poison Australia's blood supply?'[10] The article itself, however, was more concerned with details of sexual activi-ties it implied were typical of homosexual lifestyles. Professor Chipman presented no evidence (a quality which would surely have seen him fail in any university course!), but nevertheless he concluded that 'it is the irresponsibility of male homosexuals where the historical blame lies'.[11]

But Nile and Lansdown and Chipman were only some among many. Some years later, former Treasury Secretary John Stone complained about any money being spent on AIDS edu-cation programs. While condemning those 'people who have … deliberately chosen to run the grave medical risks that go with an actively homosexual lifestyle', he dismissed these education programs, since 'they also work towards breaking down those very "taboos" which are our chief protection against a wider incidence of AIDS among Australians'.[12]

In works like these, AIDS was depicted as the Christian god's response to homosexual behaviour, linking non-reproductive sexual acts with divine punishment. But since the incidence of AIDS among lesbians, the other major homosexual group in our society, is extremely low, then one can only presume that the Christian god must have been either swayed by recent feminist arguments – and so showed favoured treatment to women – or had found himself confronting a more powerful deity who was protecting these women – perhaps some earth mother figure!

Homophobia found its expression in more than just words. There were constant reports in the mainstream media and the gay press about increasing discrimination against homosexuals in general by individuals and businesses,[13] and even government departments.[14] AIDS often seemed to be a factor in an increase in poofter-bashing as well. In the background – and partly feeding on it – was the sensationalising media. As one writer despairingly noted, the quality of reporting on AIDS did not 'give a great deal of confidence in the Australian print media and its responsibility on this issue'.[15] In this, the writer was echoing the views of journalists like Evan Whitton, health ministers around Australia, and responsible community leaders.

And then death notices began to appear in the gay papers.

In the face of an uncomprehending wider Australian public, initial government inaction, and a hostile tabloid press, something had to be done. The first responses came from within Sydney's gay community. A variety of reactions to different aspects of the epidemic emerged, to both the medical issues and the social responses.

First, a wide range of support services was established within the gay community, to deal with various issues arising from the disease. This included special counselling services; 'carers' to help people with AIDS and AIDS-related infections; fund-raising benefits in commercial venues; and eventually the creation of collectives to buy bulk quantities of appropriate drugs and medications cheaply, as they became available. Indeed a whole range of support networks were developed in Sydney's gay world. Of particular note was the formation of the AIDS Action Committee in mid-1983; the following year it changed its name to the AIDS Council of NSW (ACON), which was incorporated in 1985. ACON provided coordination for the gay communities' responses to AIDS. It later widened its purview to deal with those affected in the wider Australian public as well.

Three other major groups were set up within the gay community in 1985: Ankali, to train volunteers to provide emotional and social support to people living with HIV/AIDS; the Community Support Network (CSN), to care for affected people in their homes, because the official community care organisations wouldn't, because of their fears about the transmission of the illness; and the Bobby Goldsmith Foundation, to provide direct financial assistance, financial counselling, and housing and employment support to people living with HIV in NSW. Bobby Goldsmith was one of the first Australians to die from an AIDS-related illness in 1984, when he was just 38 years old.[16]

These wide-ranging responses meant that no other group with the infection was so well served; wider Australian support services were later built on some of these groups.[17]

The increase in homophobia was a major concern. ACON tried to establish better education programs (about AIDS as a medical and social problem), to get a greater police response to stop poofter-bashing, and it also helped individual gays with cases before the state's Anti-Discrimination Board.

As the magnitude of the epidemic emerged, other effects were felt within Sydney's gay community. In those early days, the treatment of those who contracted the disease was affected by the fear it generated. Gays may have experienced a distancing by their neighbours, and found that even their friends might treat them cautiously. In hospitals, people with HIV/AIDS might find their food left outside the door to their rooms by fearful staff. And the number of death notices, a constant feature in the weekly gay papers, kept increasing.

All this certainly affected how people with the infection saw their own prospects. Many people with HIV did what those with death looming sometimes do: they sold up everything and prepared to enjoy what was left of their life. They were not the only casualties either. As journalist Adele Horin noted in 1988, 'the victims of AIDS are not just the ones who die, but the lovers left behind'. This comment was in response to news that a man whose lover had died had been excluded from family grief counselling, perhaps by an inexperienced grief counsellor. As Horin added, it was to be hoped that the counsellor would in time learn about same-sex partners.[18]

By the late 1980s, with a rising death rate, many gay men found that increasing numbers of their friends and acquaintances were dying. People in the community were being forced to face the facts of grieving over the deaths of friends or lovers, way too soon, in a society where not long before, they would not have been permitted any public expressions of grief.

The AIDS epidemic seemed indiscriminate in who it took. After the first few years, the load of those dying in Ward 17 South at St Vincent's Hospital became too great, so in 1986 a new ward was opened at Little Bay's Prince Henry Hospital. Prince Henry had an isolation ward, first set up in the 1881–82 smallpox outbreak, and used from time to time during Sydney's subsequent epidemics.

It was always a soul-searing trip, going out there to see friends who were dying. To see people who once had been lively laughing attractive men, now lying there, living skeletons, looking like those photos of people liberated from the Nazi concentration camps at the end of the war.

Their eyes told it all, the anguish and the horror of what they were experiencing as they waited to die. And who could not but think 'there, but for the grace of whatever, go I'; nothing that they had done I hadn't done, but the finger of death had beckoned them and not me.

Some years later, as the death toll rolled on, 1 December was declared World AIDS Day. In Sydney, as elsewhere in the western world, it was marked by an annual candlelight vigil, as a way of remembering those who have been lost to the epidemic. It used to start in Green Park, and solemnly wend its way down Oxford Street, in the centre of which were a line of brown paper bags filled with sand, a candle stuck in each, lighting our way to Hyde Park. There, not far from the Archibald Fountain, during an emotional ceremony, the names of those who had died were read out. All around, one could hear the sounds of people weeping. It was a distressing time.

One impact of AIDS – that television brought into the homes of millions of Sydneysiders – was to give a heightened public profile to such expressions of strongly felt emotions by gay men, usually in a situation (the death of a loved one) with which many Sydneysiders could empathise.

The growing magnitude of the disease soon made it plain to the gay community that, on its own, it simply did not have the resources to deal effectively with HIV/AIDS. Like other affected groups, it turned increasingly to governments to gain access to major financial support. At the same time, as governments became aware of the magnitude of the public health problem they were facing, they turned increasingly to the gay community, both for more information about aspects of gay lifestyles that might affect the spread of the disease, and also to utilise – and build on – their established support networks.

The problem became more urgent as the infection spread into the wider Australian community, with disastrous social ramifications. In July 1985, a newly diagnosed three-year-old girl was banned from attending her local preschool at Gosford, after fearful parents there threatened to withdraw their own children if the girl was not removed. Without either a vaccine or cure, a national education program on how to respond to HIV/AIDS became a key priority, as part of an integrated prevention strategy.

The national education programs were based on 'rationality and reason', by respecting the importance of evidence, both from medical research and from the perspective of the experiences of those with HIV/AIDS. Probably the most notorious was the 'Grim Reaper' campaign, in which the figure of death, scythe in one hand, bowls a ball down the lane at a bowling alley, knocking over all the skittles – a group of average Australians standing there, waiting for death to strike. It drew divergent responses, hysterically opposed to vehemently supportive, but no one could say they didn't know about AIDS after that campaign. But what exactly DID they learn? Was there enough factual material available to structure any individual's response? Or was it simply overkill?

The 'Grim Reaper' campaign was undoubtedly controversial, and tensions over it developed in the gay community. There were several stances taken on this, as well as over the wider question of 'getting into bed with governments'. One group argued that gays were a legitimate community in Australian society, and should receive recognition from governments and other public authorities – as had been granted women and Aboriginal People from the 1970s. Thus gays had both a legitimate claim on governments for spending to deal with the AIDS problem among homosexual men, and they were also the best group to look after those men – particularly in a society that had shown such reluctant tolerance of homosexuals in the past and which was now, in the face of AIDS, displaying increasing homophobic tendencies.

Against this perception were those who argued that AIDS was a public health problem – it concerned more than just the gay community – and so it should be dealt with at that level. There were two separate lines of argument here. The first one was that it was a more efficient use of resources to have existing networks and services available to all (and greater funding would allow the gay community to provide better facilities for its own AIDS sufferers). The second argued that by deliberately 'de-homosexualising' the disease, the gay community was likely to break down homophobia and get better responses, both from governments and the wider Australian community.[19] This latter argument drew the criticism from some activists that it was a 'backhand' way of trying to gain legitimacy for gays, something that ought to be acknowledged and granted anyway. These contesting positions were the source of much tension in various gay community-based bodies, such as ACON, and there was heated debate in the gay press. Often old friendships were broken.[20]

Hedonism is a word that has frequently been associated with gay lifestyles in Sydney although this is a trait that could more fairly be attributed to Sydneysiders in general. In any event, government bodies felt they required more information about aspects of the 'hedonistic gay lifestyle' that might facilitate the spread of the disease, to be better able to deal with AIDS; this particularly related to sexual habits. So AIDS also led to various programs being established to look at social (as well as medical) aspects of the lives of homosexual men in Sydney.

One such project was the Social Aspects of the Prevention of AIDS (SAPA), undertaken jointly by ACON and the School of Behavioural Sciences at Sydney's Macquarie University. This two-year-long project brought to light interesting detail, not only about gay lifestyles and sexual practices, but also on gay identity. The study indicated that Sydney actually had 'a variety of "gay communities", and that Oxford Street, while the most public (and publicised) of these, was not the only one to promote a strong sense of identity'.[21] Far more detailed sociological information about the gay subculture, much of it of interest to the academic world – including ideas of identity and community – came from this research.

Homophobes, such as Nile and Chipman, claimed that gay men could not change their sexual practices, and similar views were widely reported. For example, in a major article in the *Australian* in 1985, a doctor – who asked not to be named – said that 'medical history showed that it was extremely difficult to fundamentally change people's sexual habits'.[22] If so, Sydney's gay community made medical history, for the SAPA report noted that, in response to various education campaigns, homosexual men did indeed alter their sexual practices. And, as the report stated, 'the move towards safe sex is particularly marked amongst those who continue to have casual sex, who do use recreational drugs, and who have multiple sexual relationships',[23] that is, the people the campaigns had been designed to target.

An indirect measure of this success comes from sexually

transmitted infections data, which indicated that 'the widespread changes in sexual behaviour made by gay men in response to HIV were sufficient to curtail the epidemics of gonorrhoea and syphilis – their incidence dropping to almost zero levels amongst gay men in the late 1980s'.[24] The various 'safe sex' education programs paid off.

Such projects and the publishing of their results served not only to increase Sydney's gay community's – or communities' – knowledge about themselves, they also gave a heightened profile on homosexuality to the wider society, at a pertinent time for multicultural Australia in the late twentieth century.

But still the death rates continued to climb, and the number of death notices appearing in the gay papers continued to grow. Death notices mentioning AIDS even began to appear in the mainstream press, particularly with well-known people, as with Sydney Symphony Orchestra conductor Stuart Challender, who died in December 1991.[25] To misquote Charles Dickens, it was the worst of times, never the best of times.

AIDS, of course, had a clear political dimension that did not need spelling out. It dealt with a range of issues that were always contentious in Australian society, neatly summarised as 'homosexuality, prostitution, sex education in schools, what goes on in prisons, sexual behaviour generally, gay rights, occupational health, discrimination, the safety of the blood bank, problems in health care delivery systems, patients' rights, antibody testing, intravenous drug use, confidentiality, the use and availability of condoms and many more'.[26] Governments and politicians had to deal with the homosexual communities on a range of these issues. This had two major repercussions.

First, it led to a reversal of the stance of the gay movement which, since the 1960s, aimed to reduce the amount of state interaction with homosexuals. During the late 1970s there was some variation in this, when the state could be a potentially useful ally – as for anti-discrimination legislation, and for funding various projects. It changed even further with AIDS, when gays found that they should – and could – deal with government bodies.

Not only did gays alter their attitudes to governments, but governments, both to provide the services and to bring about behavioural modification, had to come into closer contact with homosexuals. AIDS 'forced governments to recognise gay organisations which they had previously ignored, and has meant the strengthening of such organisations, often with the use of state resources'.[27] This of course had wider implications. From a situation where the gay movement had been actively hostile to government instrumentalities, there now emerged partnerships with a wide range of government authorities.

Sydney's gay community was lucky with certain individual health ministers at the time, who clearly influenced how the epidemic was dealt with. In particular Neal Blewett at the federal level, and Laurie Brereton and Peter Anderson in NSW, played pivotal roles at a crucial time when the disease was breaking in Australia, and they valued the input of the gay community on this public health problem. The commonsense and sympathetic approach of these ministers was an immense advantage to Australian society in facing up to the problems associated with AIDS. Often with their encouragement, some openly gay men were co-opted into state and federal bureaucracies to deal with aspects of the disease in various areas. And many of these men had an impact there – if only to dispel myths about stereotypes.

The long battle for law reform, which had been going on since the late 1970s, was making steady progress prior to the outbreak of AIDS. Early in 1980, Lex Watson and fellow activist Craig Johnston helped set up the Gay Rights Lobby, to lobby for decriminalisation of male homosexual acts. In November they wrote to Premier Wran calling for the repeal of anti-homosexual laws, but the response was lukewarm. The Lobby's first public meeting was held in February 1981. Johnston was elected President and Watson was Convenor, and they gave the 'highest priority' to homosexual law reform.[28] This marked the start of a concerted campaign for both law reform and a Bill to incorporate homosexuality under the terms of the *Anti-Discrimination Act*. As Lex Watson told Jason Bartlett:

> The Gay Rights Lobby, when Craig Johnston and I decided to form it at the end of 1980, was intended to be a single aim, short term organisation.
>
> There was a renewed interest in some quarters in homosexual law reform, the repeal of the sections of the Crimes Act that criminalised all male/male sexual acts, and the State Government of Neville Wran gave us an unintended opportunity which we seized.[29]

The unintended opportunity was amendments to the *Anti-Discrimination Act*. The campaign for law reform stepped up the pace over the next few years, with protests and lobbying. But this involved working with Parliamentarians who introduced various law reform bills, and did not always get the support of other activists.

The first attempt was an amendment to the *Crimes (Sexual Assault) Amendment Act 1981*, put by George Petersen in April 1981. This would have legalised consenting acts between adults, and had growing support in public opinion polls. It was supported by progressive elements within the ALP, including the Attorney-General Frank Walker. However, the amendment was defeated by the Catholic-dominated majority right faction of NSW Labor even before the Act's introduction. It could not even be debated in the Legislative Assembly, as the Speaker, Laurie Kelly, ruled it 'out of order'. Under threat of expulsion from the party, Petersen did not appeal Kelly's ruling.[30]

Later that year, in November, Petersen introduced a Private Members Bill, to decriminalise male homosexual acts, and include an equal age of consent. But once again the opponents of law reform triumphed, and after its first reading, the Bill was adjourned. When the Bill came to a second reading, the Liberal–Country opposition voted as a bloc against it, and over half of the Labor side, given a conscience vote, joined them, to defeat it 67 votes to 28.[31]

The Gay Rights Lobby and other members of the gay communities kept up the pressure. The next attempt was the Unsworth Bill, introduced into State Parliament in February 1982. Since it was clear that the issue of homosexual law reform would not go away, there were attempts to sidetrack the campaign, by introducing Bills that failed to completely decriminalise male homosexual acts, usually with different ages of consent to heterosexuals – as was the case with the Unsworth Bill. Whether to support or oppose these Bills split the Lobby and the community, and there was a vigorous campaign against the Unsworth Bill. It was eventually defeated in the Legislative Assembly by five votes.[32]

The pressure continued, with more public demonstrations. The campaign was given additional impetus following repeated police raids on gay venues during 1983. On 6 September that year, protesters – drawing inspiration from the Aborigines Tent Embassy outside Parliament House in Canberra – set up a caravan as the Gay Embassy outside Premier Wran's home in Woollahra. It was designed to embarrass him and draw public attention to the issue. And in case he didn't get the message from the various banners on display, the protesters delivered a letter to him explaining that:

> The central aim of the Gay Rights Embassy that is parked in Wallis Street is to put across our concern over the NSW anti-gay laws and their enforcement in three police raids this year.[33]

So it came about that, in 1984, Premier Neville Wran, introduced, as a Private Member's Bill, the *Crimes (Amendment) Act 1984*, to decriminalise male homosexual acts in NSW. The Bill was seconded by the leader of the Liberal Party, Nick Greiner, and after heated debate, was passed on 22 May and assented to on 8 June 1984. However, the age of consent remained at 18, rather than 16 as for heterosexual and lesbian couples. It took another 19 years before the NSW Government equalised the age of consent to 16 under a further *Crimes Amendment Act* in May 2003. NSW was the last state to reform its unequal age of consent law.

This renewed activism soon diverted its attention to the AIDS epidemic that was sweeping the state, leading to a major resurgence of political activity to fight to protect the interests of both gays and people with HIV. And this in turn bridged the gap between the gay movement – the activist element – and the wider gay community. The battle for law reform was waged in this context.

Two important groups – People Living With AIDS (PLWA – as it was then) and ACT-UP – were set up in those early years from this growing communality. Faster access to medications, more research on the side effects of the available medications, better treatment for people with HIV, and relevant education programs aimed at the wider Australian community were all on the agenda of those initial activist groups.[34] And action was necessary; drug availability was of prime concern. In 1986 the US Food and Drug Administration (FDA) had approved the first antiviral drug zidovudine (ZDV; or azidothymidine – AZT) for use in preventing HIV replication. After 1991, several other drugs were added to the anti-HIV arsenal, including a new class of anti-HIV drugs – the non-nucleoside analog reverse transcriptase inhibitors. The class of antiviral drugs known as protease inhibitors were the next to be developed. These were distinctly different from the reverse transcriptase inhibitors because they did not seek to prevent infection of a host cell, but rather to prevent an already infected cell from producing more copies of HIV.

Despite this gradual proliferation of drug options, the standard antiviral therapy for HIV-infected persons between 1986 and 1995 mostly remained 'monotherapy', treatment with a single drug. Such drugs appeared to be partly efficacious, although there was a great variation in effectiveness among individuals, and many experienced severe adverse side effects.

During this period, there were significant advances in the understanding of how HIV functions in the body. Whereas it was once believed that individuals went into a latency period of ten years or more after their initial infection with HIV, it now came to be understood that huge amounts of viral replication continued throughout the entire period of infection, even when an individual was not exhibiting any symptoms of illness. Thus, the onset of symptoms of AIDS was not the result of a sudden resurgence of a latent virus, but rather a slow war of attrition as the host immune system was whittled away by HIV.

This meant that monotherapy was of limited usefulness, because HIV could quickly develop resistance to any one medication. In the February 1996 Mardi Gras parade, the AIDS entry was a 50-metre long, spot-lit red ribbon, carried by those affected by the virus; it spoke volumes, a sad remembrance of things past. But within a few months, a new future was to emerge and the whole HIV/AIDS scenario changed.

One of the most challenging aspects of the epidemic had been the sheer intractability of the virus. At the Vancouver AIDS conference in July 1996, news about a new combination therapy 'went round like wildfire':

> In the annals of AIDS, 1996 will always be the 'protease moment' – the year that the advent of effective treatment for HIV was announced, framed in a new but soon to be very familiar terminology: protease inhibitors in combination therapy.[35]

The benefits of the new combination therapy drugs soon became apparent – suddenly people seemingly on their deathbeds became 'alive' again; they now had an appetite and ate; they put on weight and became stronger, they were able to re-establish their lives in the community – and they even had a sex drive again! The focus shifted from dying from AIDS to living with HIV, although it wasn't clear at that point how dramatically the death rates in Australia would start falling. They fell, even as people continued to die.

Ironically, one of the effects of AIDS was an improvement in the level of sexual knowledge, not only in the wider community, but even in schools. Sex education programs were particularly significant here. *Time* magazine, noting that 'condoms and sex [are] discussed openly on television like recipes on a cooking show', made the following perceptive summation: 'What liberals in large parts of the Western world have advocated in vain for decades, the fear of AIDS has achieved in a couple of years.'[36] This certainly happened in Sydney schools, and the gay community played its part in devising the school education kits.

Social commentators also noted some other paradoxical effects of AIDS. One suggested that although it was unfortunate that AIDS occurred in a period of growing social conservatism in most western societies (and thus had the effect of increasing stigma against homosexuals and homosexuality), 'it has also meant a much greater recognition of a homosexual community and a homosexual movement' by the larger society.[37] And while homophobia became more visible, and AIDS initially gave ammunition to the enemies of the gay communities, in the long run it continued that process of giving a heightened public profile to both homosexuals and homosexuality, and to Sydney's gay worlds. This helped to further break down a major barrier – the lack of knowledge that so easily leads to misunderstandings.

But the ability to control the spread of HIV saw a drop-off in concern about HIV, both among those likely to contract it, and even among those with it. And complacency had its costs; fluctuating infection rates developed, which led to the need for new education programs aimed at younger Australians (the Grim Reaper came back as the 'Glam Reaper', a creature of the first decade of the twenty-first century). The public health response has meant that nowadays any doctor with a high number of gay patients is up to date with the latest information, and there are medications immediately available for those who need them. And so perhaps HIV no longer has the centrality in the lives of people with HIV – or of the gay community – that it once did. People are just getting on with their lives.

The end of the 'death sentence' for people with HIV was only achieved by many actions, from communities, governments, educators and activists alike. But now that HIV is largely a chronic illness, is it still a rallying point for the gay communities? Has the need for a separate HIV identity started to wane?

AIDS had an enormous impact on Sydney's gay communities, not only about dealing with deaths, sorrow and grieving, but also with the growth of a whole new range of community-based networks, the resurgence of political activism, and the increasing involvement of gay men with a range of government bodies. All these played a part in developing a sense of a community, of which they, as gay men, were a part.

Partly because of AIDS and the subsequent research that had been carried out on 'the gay lifestyle', other aspects of the gay world began to receive initially polite attention in the media and public discourse, and coverage in the broadsheets gradually changed. No longer was AIDS the sole focus for any news on homosexuality. A range of articles dealt with such things as tapping the gay dollar ('capitalism works in mysterious ways'), the impact of gays on electoral politics, and gay social life around Sydney; with very little effort, you could also read explicit information about gay sex life. Even the *Sydney Morning Herald*, which had once published the names and addresses of men convicted of 'homosexual' crimes – of sex between consenting adults in private – began to treat gays as just another facet of Sydney's diverse lifestyles and cultures.

So in the end AIDS continued the process of making aspects of homosexuality better known in Australia and altering attitudes in the wider community, in turn facilitating the process of legitimation for the gay community, something that previously had seemed unlikely.[38]

The commercial gay scene experienced some impact from the epidemic. Many of the sex-on-premises venues had an initial drop in numbers, but clients returned with the development of safe-sex education programs. Some of the bath-houses closed, although it is unclear how much this was to do with AIDS, since these venues have always had a high turnover rate in the Sydney commercial gay scene. But bars continued to do well, as did the remaining bath-houses and sex shops. And new commercial gay establishments continued to open, although the centrality of Oxford Street was no longer critical. As often as not, new bars appeared in suburbs such as Newtown, where an increasing number of gay men were making their homes.

Oxford Street remained the site of the most iconic of Sydney's gay events, the annual Mardi Gras parade. One historian has suggested that the 1988 Bicentennial, a defining event of the decade, was the starting date for the 'event-led economy' of NSW. And Mardi Gras was a major feature of this economy.[39] In 1991 the Australian Graduate School of Management prepared a report for Mardi Gras, which showed that it brought in nearly $40 million to the Sydney and NSW economy, and had a greater economic impact than any other 'hallmark' event.[40]

In its early years, under the creative artistic direction of Peter Tully and with collaboration from David McDiarmid, Mardi Gras combined satire with politics and spectacle. But it gradually lost its bite. Its spectacle, with such gems as Brent Beadle's Miss New Zealand, Ron Muncaster's fantasy extravaganzas, one guy by himself carrying a sign saying 'I've got something to tell you, Mum', and Brenton Heath-Kerr's zany gingham creations, attracted tourists. And in the float that led the 1988 parade, 200 years after the British invasion of Australia began, gay Aboriginal actor Malcolm Cole, dressed as Captain Cook, was standing with two 'black' men beside him in the prow of a rowing boat that was being pulled along by a group of white men. But many in Sydney's gay communities became increasingly ambiguous about Mardi Gras, complaining about a growing blandness. Satire, as with Fred Nile's head on a plate à la

John the Baptist, or Imelda Marcos and her hundreds of shoes, was on the wane.

Mardi Gras has always attracted criticism. In its early days, most came from homophobes like Fred Nile. Criticism continued during the early AIDS years until the mid-1990s. The 1985 parade was almost cancelled after the head of Australia's AIDS Task Force, perhaps bowing to public pressures, appealed to 'the gays to be responsible enough to cancel the Mardi Gras activities'.[41] But the crowds continued to swell, from 200 000 in 1989 to over 500 000 in 1993. Large numbers of interstate and international travellers started flying in for the event, generating an estimated $38 million for the NSW economy.[42]

In 1994, Mardi Gras Festival adopted the theme, 'We are Family', in a nod to the International Year of the Family, and the ABC, the national broadcaster, telecast the parade for the first time. It provoked a massive outcry from conservative elements, but it gave the ABC its best-ever Sunday night ratings. Then, in 1997, Channel Ten became the first commercial broadcaster to cover the event. They also broadcast the 2001 parade, with its theme of gay and lesbian parenting.

Within the LGBTQI (Lesbian, Gay, Bisexual, Transgender, Queer or Questioning and Intersex) communities, most of the criticism focused on the fact that the parade had lost its satirical and political bite. Some claimed that the reason for this loss was to accommodate the 'standards' of its corporate sponsors, who were – and still are – increasingly necessary for the economic viability of the whole Mardi Gras Festival. One trenchant critic was Craig Johnston, an activist from the early days of gay lib, who disliked the changing nature of Mardi Gras and argued against its role in garnering support from corporate sponsors and seeking what he called a 'political dividend' from governments, because of its economic impact.[43]

There is always a float or two in the Mardi Gras Parade remembering HIV/AIDS, and there are other ways that the epidemic left an enduring mark on Sydney. Perhaps reflecting one of those earlier euphemisms about homosexuals being 'artistic', gay communities came up with a variety of creative responses to commemorate those who had died in the pandemic. One was *Love and Death*, an anthology of poetry and prose on the theme of HIV/AIDs and death, published in 1987.[44]

Another was *Holding the Man*, a memoir by the writer and actor Timothy Conigrave, published in February 1995, a few months after his death. It told the story of Tim's life and of his relationship with his lover of 15 years, John Caleo; the pair met in the mid-1970s while at school.[45] It was adapted into a play by Tommy Murphy in 2006, and had successful runs in most Australian capital cities and, internationally, including London's West End. Like Tony Kushner's *Angels in America: A Gay Fantasia on National Themes*, which won a Pulitzer Prize for Drama in 1993 and Tony Awards for Best Play in 1993 and 1994, it will become a classic of the theatre of HIV/AIDS. A film version directed by Neil Armfield was presented as the Closing Night film at the 62nd Sydney Film Festival in 2015.

Another unusual – and symbolic – method of commemorating those who died of HIV-related illness was the Quilt.

The concept of a commemorative quilt originated in San Francisco in June 1987, when a small group gathered to document the lives of those they feared that history would neglect. Their goal was to create a memorial for those who had died of AIDS, and to thereby help people understand the devastating impact of the disease.[46]

The Australian AIDS Memorial Quilt was launched in 1988, with a mere 35 panels. Each unique panel is a memorial made by friends, families and lovers, and often includes mementoes like clothing, favourite objects and photographs. Some panels memorialise groups of people rather than individuals. There are now 122 quilt blocks, each with around eight panels, commemorating the approximately 2,700 Australians who have died of AIDS-related illnesses.[47] The quilts are held offsite by Sydney's Powerhouse Museum. There are 37 quilt projects worldwide.

One important new development for Sydney's gay world occurred in the city's academe in the 1980s. Sydney University had long been associated with gay activism, from the early days of CAMPus Camp and Sydney University Gay Liberation to the various conferences and events held there. A group of gay academics had formed GUTS, the Gay Union of Tertiary Staff, in the late 1970s, and the Merewether Building, the location of the Departments of Government, Political Economy and Economic History, was home to gay academic activism, with staff like Dennis Altman, Lex Watson, Sue Wills, Craig Johnston, Kate Harrison, Ernie Chaples, Steve Tomsen, Antony Green and Robert Aldrich, among others.[48]

These staff members were the centre of much of the gay political movement, and led developments in courses and research. In mid-1988, the Australian Gay History Project was started; this comprised an ongoing series of seminars, allowing researchers to give papers and get critical feedback. Topics covered were from the disciplines of history, sociology, geography, literature, art, biography and language, among other areas. Part of the reason for the seminar series was an acknowledgment that any culture needs its history, to establish its legitimacy and to let the wider world know about it. Certainly this underlay its publishing program, when the best of these papers were gathered together in the *Gay Perspectives* series, published every two years, commencing late in 1991.

The success of these seminars – and the publications, the first of which ran into a second print run within weeks – encouraged staff at the university to pursue a then-radical idea for an Australian university – to set up a centre for research on LGBTQI issues. And so, in 1994, the Governor-General of Australia, Bill Hayden, launched the Australian Centre for Lesbian and Gay Research. It was one of only three in the world, along with the University of Amsterdam and the City University of New York.

The Sydney Centre's 'credo' was 'Interdisciplinary research and resources in gay and lesbian issues'. Apart from continuing the *Gay Perspectives* series, it also worked to ensure that research into gays and lesbians made it into mainstream academic publications. The Centre invited noted overseas academics to become Fellows and address staff and students at the university. It promoted conferences, worked towards documenting Australia's gay and lesbian past, as well as publishing on a wide range of topics, including some leading research on homelessness and workplace discrimination faced by lesbians and gay men.

Other positive developments in those decades include the Lesbian and Gay Anti-Violence Project, another pivotal moment in the development of the Gay and Lesbian Rights Lobby (GLRL) which led to the establishment of a Gay and Lesbian Liaison Officer in the Attorney-General's Department.[49] It followed a spate of savage bashings – and killings – of gay men in Sydney. This had been going on since the late 1970s, although many details only surfaced much later.[50]

In 1993 the GLRL faced another battle over a new law. As its former convenor Stevie Clayton remembers:

Clover Moore's homosexual anti-vilification bill was our first major challenge in 1993.

There was a major community campaign facilitated by the GLRL in support of the bill. It included several rallies with thousands of people outside parliament house, petitions, letter writing, faxing, and direct lobbying.

Memorably Fred Nile tried to stop the bill by filibustering in his pyjamas and a wheelchair but the bill ultimately passed in the small hours of the morning.[51]

And then, a decade later:

In 2003, when no major party would fully support age of consent legislation, the Lobby with its allies and supporters undertook the painstaking job of winning a conscience vote by persuading enough members of Parliament in both houses to get it through, one vote at a time, member by member.[52]

The early years of the 1990s were fraught with continuing uncertainty in Australia and in Sydney. Economic downturns in both Australia and Japan threatened to have detrimental effects for Sydneysiders, given the city's emerging role as a financial centre for the South Asian region. But there were successes too. A range of issues started to find resolution in this decade.

One major achievement was on relationship rights – something many of us take for granted today. Barrister Kathy Sant, a former GLRL convenor, recalls the struggle:

Relationship rights were achieved in NSW in 1999 – at a time when same-sex relationship recognition was almost non-existent globally and no Australians enjoyed the sorts of comprehensive rights achieved here – with the support of

245

not only the fairly right-wing Carr Government but also the Liberals and National Party.[53]

The importance of relationship rights had come to the forefront somewhat earlier. In a landmark custody case in 1983, Justice Baker of the Family Court said that the question of whether gays produce gays was the first matter to be considered when a homosexual parent sought custody or access. Clearly the answer was in the negative, and in that case, custody of the two children of the marriage, boys aged nine and 13 respectively, was awarded to their homosexual father.[54]

And then, in the mid-1990s, disaster struck.

On 13 May 1994, after many accusations about, and growing evidence of, police corruption in NSW, the Coalition state government of John Fahey set up the Royal Commission into the NSW Police Service. It authorised Justice James Wood 'to investigate the existence and extent of systemic and entrenched corruption in the NSW Police Service'.[55] The Commission went about its work uncovering plenty of evidence of massive police corruption, up to very high levels in the force.

In December 1994, allegations were made that members of the NSW police were protecting paedophiles, and the scope of the Commission was expanded. Its terms of reference now included investigation of the activities of organised paedophile networks in New South Wales, the suitability of care arrangements for at-risk minors; and the effectiveness of police guidelines for the investigation of sex offences against minors.[56]

It was unfortunate that two state Labor Parliamentarians, Deirdre Grusovin in the Legislative Assembly, and Franca Arena in the Legislative Council, seemed to have an obsession with paedophilia. Both were apparently convinced that male children were turned into homosexuals by being sexually abused;

they refused to acknowledge that men might be born homoerotically inclined. To equate paedophilia only with homosexuality is clearly homophobic, since the evidence from the behavioural sciences even then showed that the vast majority of child sexual abuse was, and still is, carried out by adult males on female children, and that the greatest incidence was from persons known to the victim, most often a relative or mother's latest boyfriend.

The political background to the widened terms of reference came from an ongoing sensationalist controversy generated by Grusovin's claims that a 'circle' of homosexual paedophiles in 'high places' in Sydney had police protection.[57] Grusovin had become the ALP member for the electorate of Heffron, in Sydney's east, after it was vacated by her brother Laurie Brereton, a right-wing power-broker, who had transferred to Federal Parliament.

Matters escalated even further in 1996 at a Labor Caucus meeting. The ALP was now in government, having won the 1995 election, and Arena and Grusovin tried to widen the Royal Commission's focus again, 'to convert the Royal Commission into a prosecutorial authority on paedophilia'.[58]

Then on 17 September 1997 Arena made a speech in the Legislative Council, alleging, in effect, a conspiracy between leading public figures, including Premier Bob Carr, then Leader of the State Opposition Peter Collins, and even Commissioner Justice Wood, to suppress findings against 'people in high places'.[59] All the people so accused vehemently denied her assertions. Premier Carr rejected them 'with contempt' and Peter Collins with 'distaste'.[60]

Most troubling was the definition of paedophilia that the Commission seemed to be using; Paddy Bergin, Counsel Assisting, when asked how to define 'paedophiles or pederasts', replied 'people who commit sexual assaults on boys under the age of 18 and girls under the age of 16'.[61] Those were simply the ages of consent in NSW at the time, and ignored the World Health Organization's scientific definition of paedophilia as 'sexual activity with a pre-pubescent child generally aged 13 or younger', which was similar to the definition of the Australian Institute of Criminology.

But the damage was done. Such was the growing concern within Sydney's gay community about what had degenerated into a witch-hunt with the obvious bias of the Commission's approach, that in 1996 Commission Watch was set up to monitor the Commission and respond to its doings and sayings. Indeed, as an academic at the Southern Cross University School of Law and Justice pointed out, 'Child sexual abuse within the family does not receive much attention in the Royal Commission's Report. Of the many case studies which appear in the report, only three dealt with familial sexual abuse.'[62] Concerns were also raised that, because of the publicity generated, the police felt free to pursue cases against men who had previously had consensual relationships with other men over the age of 16.

In 1996, even Sydney University's prestigious Australian Centre for Lesbian and Gay Research was 'investigated'. Its possible crime: a sociologist from the University of Newcastle had given a paper at the Centre's monthly seminar series, on 'Intergenerational Sex: The Ethical Issues'. His paper, one of the 82 that the Centre had auspiced over the years, looked at some of the issues raised by sex between teenage boys and adult males, and had nothing to do with paedophilia. But someone had reported that the Centre was permitting – even encouraging – discussions about paedophilia. The Commission's somewhat unsophisticated approach was nicely illustrated when its investigator queried who gave 'approval' for such a topic to be discussed at a seminar at an Australian university. It had to be

pointed out to him that academics were recognised as authorities in their chosen fields, and had the authority to conduct
research appropriate for their work, and that such research
could feed back into policy making.[63]

According to Jennifer Wilson, a Commission Watch
spokesperson, at least nine men committed suicide after being
charged over allegations made against them, many by suspect
witnesses who had axes to grind: 'It is not surprising that these
men felt suicidal after their experience in the Commission and
the ensuing treatment at the hands of the NSW Police.'[64] One
of these was Justice David Yeldham, who after Arena's accusations against him in Parliament were made public, committed
suicide in November 1996. He was one of 12 people enmeshed
in the Wood Royal Commission who finally took their own
lives.[65]

When the Commission finally published its findings, it
cleared both Yeldham and Frank Arkell, a former mayor of
Wollongong, whom Arena had also named in Parliament, of
any wrongdoing. It found that Arena's claims of a high-level
cover-up of paedophilic activity were 'false in all respects'.

The concern in the NSW Parliament, about the false
accusations that had led to those deaths and so many ruined
reputations, led the Legislative Council to authorise a special Commission of Inquiry. It consisted of a retired judge of
the Supreme Court of the Northern Territory, Mr JA Nader,
QC, and was set up to inquire into the circumstances of
Mrs Arena's allegations. She, however, declined to give evidence. Nader's inquiry found that there was no evidence to support any of her allegations, and dismissed them accordingly.[66]

All those ruined reputations and suicides were just collat-
eral damage. The repercussions of that witch-hunt lingered on
for many years in both Sydney and the wider world.

The decade ended on what appeared to be a better note for Sydney's LGBTQI communities; in November 1997, it was announced that Sydney had won the right to put on the 2002 Gay Games.

Euphoria in Sydney greeted the decision which was announced at a presentation ceremony in Denver, Colorado. Sydney had beaten Dallas, Long Beach, Montreal and Toronto. It was Sydney's third attempt to win the games, which began in San Francisco in 1982.[67]

Once again, economic factors seemed to play a great part of general acceptance. The managing director of Tourism Council Australia, Bruce Baird, said the games had the potential to bring to Australia up to 40 000 visitors and predicted they would inject between $100 and $160 million into the NSW economy. Many of the events, including the opening ceremony, would be held in the new facilities at Sydney Olympic Park. More than 10 000 people were expected to participate in 30 official sports, six demonstration sports, artistic events, lectures on gender and sexuality in sport, and a giant dance party.[68]

As expected, there were the critics. Chief among them, of course, was Fred Nile of the Christian Democratic Party, who dubbed the event the 'Sad Games' and said overseas athletes should be tested for HIV/AIDS before being granted visas. He went on to say that 'The Carr Government is to be condemned that in the middle of a paedophile scare they actively promoted the Sydney bid and gave thousands of taxpayer dollars to help finance the bid. Sydney has enough social and moral problems without thousands of homosexuals descending on the city.'[69] The NSW National Party Leader, Ian Armstrong, dismissed the games as a minority event for which the government should not provide any funding. The state government had given a grant of $75 000 to assist the bid.

Sydney's gay male community certainly looked forward with great anticipation to that influx of muscular athletes, and the joys they might bring with them.

My own life was much more settled by then. I had a partner, and lived a much more sedate life, although we did venture out more than just occasionally.

After my father died, my partner and I would often take my mother out to lunch. Enzo's was no longer Enzo's, having become Traffic Lights, still a wine bar, and then Landmark, a restaurant. But it retained the old charm, with its pleasant outdoor courtyard, so we often went there with her.

I knew Graham and Richard, the two guys who ran the place, and I had arranged with them that, if Mum ever arrived there before us, they would give her a pot of tea to make her feel at home.

It must have been one of the first times we were there, and Mum was settled in at a table out in the courtyard, with her pot of tea. As my partner and I sat down, she looked around and pointed to what she said were 'all those abandoned men sitting there alone'. Around the courtyard there were several guys sitting by themselves at their tables, obviously waiting for their dates to arrive.

We explained to Mum that it would all soon be much more lively.

CHAPTER 8

INTO THE NEW MILLENNIUM

And a brighter future loomed

From the late twentieth century, property interests grew more powerful with Sydney's rise as a financial capital in the Asia–Pacific area. Vast new building projects created ongoing change in the metropolis, and a range of urban manufacturing industries gradually disappeared. Sydney found economic strength partly in its commerce and financial services functions, and tourism was now a major earner for the city. In 2000 Sydney hosted the Olympic Games and the trains ran on time, to everyone's relief. The global financial crisis of 2008–09 led to job losses in various sectors, from retailing to finance, and there was an increased 'casualisation' of the city's workforce.

As in the decades after the 1850s gold rushes, the ethnic diversity of Sydney's population began to increase – 32 per cent of its population was born overseas and well over half had at least one parent born overseas. Cultural complexity and widespread tolerance has been marketed as one of Sydney's strengths, but a dark underbelly emerged with confrontations between police and Indigenous teenagers, many of them unemployed, in the 2004 Redfern riots sparked by the death of 17-year-old Thomas Hickey;[1] and the racially motivated Cronulla riots in December 2005, after text messages that incited 'Aussies' to take action against 'Lebs and wogs', led to violent clashes at Cronulla Beach and surrounding suburbs.[2]

On a more positive note, the future looked bright for LGBTQI people at the start of the twenty-first century. Such luminaries as social theorist Richard Florida and demographer Gary Gates extolled the contribution of gays as 'creative classes' in the new global cities,[3] of which Sydney was clearly one. Much had changed in the decades since that first march in Sydney in 1978, and this escalated the process of 'gay liberation' in Australia.

A highlight for gay Sydney was the Gay Games, held in November 2002 although the euphoria that erupted when Sydney won the right to host the Games back in 1997 had diminished by the early years of the new century, when the complexity of organising the event became clear.

The Games had originally been called the 'Gay Olympics', founded by former Olympian Dr Tom Waddell in San Francisco in 1982. However, a lawsuit filed less than three weeks before the first opening ceremony forced the name change to 'Gay Games'. Its goals, as stated by Waddell, were to promote the spirit of inclusion and participation, as well as to promote the pursuit of personal growth in a sporting event.

Many events mirrored those of the Olympics, among them swimming, cycling, sailing, the triathalon, track and field events including the marathon, and power lifting. Others, such as ballroom dancing, bodybuilding, billiards, flag football or even golf, were unlikely to be considered as Olympian by the average sports fan. But they certainly added a 'high camp' element to the global competition. Context is everything.

Sydney, famed for its New Year's Eve fireworks displays, loves a spectacle. Indeed, one historian has noted that commentators have dubbed it the 'City of Spectacle',[4] and the opening ceremony of the Sydney Gay Games lived up to this reputation. As the *Sydney Morning Herald* review gushed:

> It is hard to avoid using the words 'colourful' and 'spectacular' to describe such a large-scale event, but they only partly express the celebratory atmosphere and mood of the Gay Games Opening Ceremony.
>
> The sight of thousands of participants – representing 77 countries from Antarctica to Zimbabwe – spilling into the stadium to the strains of the Southern Stars and the Village People was remarkable. As their numbers grew and filled the stadium seats the effect was uplifting.[5]

How could it not be a night to remember? The night showcased celebrities such as Justice Michael Kirby, Deborah Cheetham, Jimmy Somerville, Paul Capsis and kd lang, while Judi Connelli channelled the old Purple Onion with her do-or-die versions of 'This is My Life' and 'I Am What I Am'. The ceremony also included a showgirl-and-fireworks finale, and a nod to the musical *South Pacific*, with the *de rigueur* volcanic eruption. When Peretta Anggerek belted out both 'Bali Hai' and Puccini's 'Un bel Di', all ends of the musical spectrum were covered.

As the *Herald* journo concluded, 'The evening was, in a word, fabulous'.[6]

After that, it was down to the competition. The week-long event used many venues from the 2000 Games, and organisers had made special efforts to involve the Asia–Pacific region. In addition to the competing athletes, there were 1100 'cultural participants' from more than 70 countries.[7]

But running the event demanded both personnel and money, and the Games ate money. When it was over, its records went to the Mitchell Library, and a biographical note in the library's catalogue sums things up:

> Sydney 2002 Gay Games Ltd was the host organisation for the Gay Games and Cultural Festival. The Company had a contract with the Federation of Gay Games. It had a board of 12 directors, approx. 60 full-time staff and approx. 300 volunteers. At the conclusion of the Games, the company abruptly dissolved – offices were abandoned, creditors moved in and the Website disappeared from the Internet.[8]

The Sydney 2002 Gay Games lost US$1.1 million, compared with Amsterdam losing US$1.8 million in 1998. One analyst spelt out the lesson: 'organisers overspent on non-sports events that showcased everything from poetry to activism. They also overestimated the number of sponsors they could get.'[9]

If the Gay Games helped to raise the city's profile as a 'City of Spectacle', it did little to diminish public homophobia. Earlier that year, Justice Michael Kirby had been the subject of two very public attacks. The first was from Senator Bill Heffernan, commonly referred to as Prime Minister John Howard's 'bovver boy',[10] doing the public head-kicking that the Prime Minister himself couldn't be seen to indulge in.

In the Senate on 12 March 2002, Heffernan made a long speech, in which he accused a High Court judge of using Commonwealth cars to procure young men for sex.[11] Heffernan, then Cabinet Secretary to the Prime Minister, had been spreading the accusation among colleagues and media since at least mid-1999 without gaining much traction. It was perhaps no coincidence that this speech came less than a year after Kirby's public 'outing' of himself, when he named his male partner in his annual *Who's Who in Australia* entry.[12]

In his speech, Heffernan alleged that there was a High Court judge who was 'not fit and proper to sit in judgment of people charged with sex offences against children'. He only named Michael Kirby in the final two words of the speech, which alleged that a judge had 'indiscreetly, improperly and illegally used Comcar' and 'trawled for rough trade at the Darlinghurst Wall'.[13]

These allegations caused a furore on the High Court Bench; if they were true, Kirby would have to resign for the court to retain its integrity.[14] Kirby prepared a statement refuting the allegations, giving it to the High Court registrar to distribute in Parliament House. The statement read:

> Senator Heffernan's homophobic accusations against me in the Senate are false and absurd. If he has such accusations, he should approach the proper authorities, not slander a fellow citizen in Parliament. In so far as he attempts to interfere in the performance of my duties as a judge I reject the attempt utterly.[15]

In late 2000, Heffernan had apparently met in secret with Wayne Patterson, who had been Prime Minister Howard's driver. Patterson gave him some documents, supposedly driver's records that purported to show that Kirby had used cars to pick up and return a 'young male companion'. Heffernan described these documents to the Senate as concrete evidence of Kirby's 'inappropriateness' to sit on the country's highest court.[16]

The legal profession, and people who knew Kirby personally, condemned Heffernan's attack. The Senate ruled that Heffernan had breached standing orders by making a personal attack on a judicial officer under Parliamentary Privilege. But the Howard government rallied behind Heffernan, with

Howard himself repeating and extending the allegations in the House of Representatives.[17]

If the evidence were true, the issue could only be resolved by some type of inquiry into Kirby's fitness for office.

And unfortunately for Heffernan, the documents turned out to be false. Almost a year earlier he had asked the Department of Finance and Administration if some of the records were fakes, and had been told it was 'not possible to comment' on their authenticity. But Heffernan went ahead anyway. Eventually, Comcar management said that the 'records' supplied by Heffernan to the Senate had been 'examined by several long-serving Comcar administration staff who came to the unanimous conclusion that they were bogus', a fact that Patterson later confirmed; the records were just 'mock-ups'.[18]

There was a media frenzy, and behind the scenes there was much to-ing and fro-ing, especially in the High Court, with two judges arguing that 'if faked evidence was involved, this must be seen as an attack on the whole court'; and of course, the evidence *was* faked.[19]

Heffernan was forced to resign as Cabinet Secretary, but otherwise suffered no major consequences. As ABC reporter Linda Mottram noted later:

> Beyond his resignation as Cabinet Secretary and from the children overboard inquiry, his position in the Senate looks secure.[20]

Senator Heffernan was still a member of the Coalition government as of late 2015.

Coming as it did so soon after the 'children overboard' affair, in which a senior Cabinet minister, in the lead-up to a federal election, falsely alleged that asylum-seekers were throwing their children overboard in a ploy to secure rescue and passage to Australia, the political reputations of the government and Prime Minister assuredly suffered. Kirby was seen as the victim of unseemly prejudice and homophobia.

But the following month, Kirby was publicly attacked again. This time it was from within the Anglican Church.

The Reverend Richard Lane, the rector of St Stephen's Church in Bellevue Hill, denounced Justice Kirby for calling himself a Christian Anglican while living in an openly gay relationship. He warned Kirby that, as a 'messenger, watchman and steward of the Lord in the Anglican Church of Australia', he faced God's judgement. In language that could hardly be called moderate, Lane said that for Kirby to call himself a Christian Anglican was a 'perversion of truth' and to continue to do so without changing his lifestyle would brand him, like Herod, a 'coward, a liar, a deceiver' and a 'lawless one'.[21]

Kirby complained to the Anglican Archbishop of Sydney, Peter Jensen, about the tone of such a letter, but Jensen, who also asserts that 'homosexual practices' are sinful, gave him no satisfaction.

Why did Michael Kirby attract such public attacks? His public persona and high public office made him, as an open homosexual, an obvious target. He was also a supporter of 'progressive' causes that were against the politics and values of his attackers. In some, prejudice lived on.

A few years later, the Australian Centre for Lesbian and Gay Research (ACLGR) at Sydney University closed. This was not, however, because of any lack of interest or perceived failure, but because attitudes to dissident sexualities had changed, both in academe and also in the wider Australian community. The change was noticeable in many areas, with alterations to laws, and increasing support in mainstream society for same-sex adoption and fostering, and same-sex marriage. The Centre, over its productive ten years, had played an important role in bringing LGBTQI research into the 'respectable' academic domain; by the middle of the first decade of the twenty-first century, LGBTQI research was well established in all of Australia's secular universities. In these universities, it was now possible to research and publish on topics once considered taboo. The necessity for such a Centre had gone.

Sydney University had long been involved in activism associated with the various 'social movements'. In the early 1970s, Dennis Altman was a member of the University's Department of Government and Public Administration when he published *Homosexual: Liberation and Oppression*. His department was located in the Merewether Building, the home of the Faculty of Economics. Other lesbian and gay members of the Faculty were closely involved in radical political activism.[22] Lex Watson was a tutor there when he was involved in the moves for law reform and the decriminalisation of consensual sex between adult males, achieved in 1984. Indeed, a recent history has noted that, 'for a number of years the Merewether Building was "gay and lesbian central"'.[23]

Other relevant aspects of political activism at Sydney University include setting up Women's Studies courses in the 1970s, which later developed into the Department of Gender Studies and Cultural Studies. Similarly, the Faculty of Law made major contributions to the advancement of LGBTQI issues, including the publication of the *Australasian Gay and Lesbian Law Journal*. The university's Students' Representative Council now has a LGBTQI liaison officer, and *Honi Soit*, the student newspaper, publishes a gay-themed issue once a year. And the gay rainbow flag was flown over the university's clock-tower during the 2015 Mardi Gras.

Activism is not unique to Sydney University. Other universities in the city have academics teaching, researching and publishing on LGBTQI issues: Gail Mason, Robert Aldrich, Jenni Millbank, Steve Tomsen, Robert Reynolds, Shirleene Robinson, Kane Race, Elspeth Probyn, Scott McKinnon and Andrew Gorman-Murray, to name a few, are academics who have all worked in these areas. Indeed, the story of how gay studies have moved from the margins to the mainstream in academe has played its part in changing attitudes in important Australian institutions. The links between activism and academia, and the range of issues studied in the 'ivory towers' – gay history, homophobic violence, health issues (including AIDS), contributions to 'culture' (literature, music, cinema, art), law, politics and 'queer theory', is revealing. Today, reflecting current intellectual developments, gender, including gay and lesbian subjects, now pervades most of the arts, social sciences and cognate departments in the way that class pervaded academic interests over much of the twentieth century.

The demise of the Centre did not see an end to interest in the city's history of diverse sexualities; the Pride History Group has taken over some of the initiatives of the ACLGR, publishing booklets on the city's lesbian and gay history, and organising conferences like the Australian Homosexual Histories Conference at the University of Technology Sydney in November 2014. Along with the Sisters of Perpetual Indulgence, they also organise History Walks, which take visitors and those interested on a tour of Sydney's gay past.

In Sydney's gay calendar, the Sydney Gay and Lesbian Mardi Gras remains a marquee event. It still involves the city's LGBTQI communities, and continues to attract overseas and interstate visitors, although not in the same numbers as a decade ago. At one point it claimed that its Festival 'was one of the three wonders of Sydney, along with the Opera House and the Harbour Bridge'.[24]

It certainly brings major financial benefit to the city and the Australian economy, as visitors spend on shopping, dining out and accommodation, generating more than $30 million of direct economic benefit each year, with the added benefit of being an international showcase of the city's diversity.[25] Politicians with 'progressive' credentials now send messages of support that are published in the program. It has become so 'mainstream' that banks, the police, the defence forces, the State Emergency Services, political parties, and even a dental care company, all have contingents in the parade, joining such 'old faithfuls' as Lord Mayor Clover Moore, former President of the NSW Legislative Council Meredith Burgmann, Amnesty International, ACON, the Greens, the Asian Marching Boys, the Harbour City Bears, Positive Life NSW, and the ever-adored Dykes on Bikes. In 2015, even a group of students from Macquarie Grammar School marched in the parade, a night for them to remember.

But its economic viability is not guaranteed. Mardi Gras claimed that 'it came as a huge surprise to many when the Sydney Gay and Lesbian Mardi Gras went into receivership in March 2002',[26] leaving debts of half a million dollars, 'a gay community divided, and the rest of the world mildly surprised'.[27] As the *Irish Times* dryly observed, 'right now the Mardi Gras is looking like a rather tired drag queen limping to the finishing line of the parade'.[28]

But for many members of Sydney's gay communities, it was no surprise at all. By then Mardi Gras, with its associated Festival, had become an extravaganza requiring far too much funding simply to take place. The Festival included art exhibitions, plays, fun runs, bushwalks, the popular Fair Day at Victoria Park, receptions at Parliament House, cabaret, burlesque, salsa classes and self-defence workshops, all of which bore no relationship to its origins.

A new organisation, New Mardi Gras, was formed to take over the running of the events associated with Mardi Gras. It was a salutary lesson in what was achievable, and although the Festival and parade continued on, the former was dramatically diminished, being nowhere near as ambitious as previously.

Then, in 2011 the Board of Mardi Gras decided to change the name to the Sydney Mardi Gras; it was announced amid great hoopla with a reception at Paddington Town Hall. The result was outrage from within the city's LGBTQI communities, and the Board hurriedly attempted to minimise the damage, by organising formal 'community consultations' to gather feedback on the name change. It wasn't only debated in the gay press; even the *Sydney Morning Herald* entered the fray, with an article 'Should Mardi Gras remain "Gay & Lesbian"?'[29] There was fairly sensationalised media coverage, and the question was put, why was Mardi Gras 'going straight'?

The Board's justification was that in order for Mardi Gras to be for everyone, it needed to be about everyone. As one speaker put it, the name was changed 'to better welcome those of a younger generation less bound by traditional sexuality "labels"'.[30] Opponents suggested the real reasoning behind the name change was to gain a wider world audience for the iconic event; 'de-gaying' the name and positioning it like the Rio Carnival or the Munich Beer Festival might reverse the trend of diminishing overseas numbers and garner increased corporate sponsorship.

The arguments within the communities became quite heated. As one participant in the original 1978 demonstration argued:

the parades have become controlled spectator sports, harnessing unpaid community creativity and labour to profit mainstream tourism and retailers, to advertise corporate sponsors, to showcase government services and politicians. Whether gay, lesbian or queer is in the name doesn't matter as much as the slow but lethal mainstreaming and sanitising of Mardi Gras' irreverent sensuality and politics. The parade and festival are on track to become as glamorous, edgy, witty and exciting as Melbourne's Moomba.[31]

At one of the many community gatherings, Mardi Gras Board CEO Michael Rolik stated that 'We don't think we've made a mistake with the name change. But I think we could've done a better job in the process.'[32] However, in the face of the communities' ongoing opposition to such a 'travesty',[33] the Mardi Gras Board had to respond. Its bland statement that it 'would change its name back to Sydney Gay and Lesbian Mardi Gras to provide a link to our past' gave no indication of the furore that had gone on. But it reverted to its original iconic name, and history was saved.

As for the parade itself, those heady days when half a million people might turn out on a Saturday night to see it are long gone, although it still has a global significance. In 2006 it was named 'one of the world's top ten costume parades' by Condé Nast and also 'the best gay event in the world' by PlanetOut, a LGBTQI tourist website. Its local significance can be seen in the complaints that made headlines for months when it was announced that the 2011 Mardi Gras parade and party would be held on separate dates, a week apart. This had never before occurred, and it was seen as no coincidence that an Atlantis Cruise ship packed with gay tourists would arrive in the week after the parade. Was this change made to accommodate a sponsorship deal with Atlantis Cruises? Mardi Gras management denied this, saying it was due to a 'booking oversight'. The fact that it created such a furore shows its ongoing importance, even though today's Mardi Gras bears little resemblance to that event of 1978 from which it originated, and which it is supposed to commemorate.

While Mardi Gras has lost any particular political purpose, it does bring in thousands of tourists each year. It is now just tourist bait; a delicious but sad irony that a commemoration of a radical political demonstration has become the ongoing marker of Sydney as a 'city of spectacle' on the world stage.

While the NSW Police Force has participated in the Mardi Gras parade since 1996, the police and the Mardi Gras can still have issues.[34] In 2013, a widely circulated video captured graphic and frightening images of police aggressively arresting a young man at Mardi Gras. The court ruled that in this case – and in one other incident that night – the police used excessive force. There were also allegations of illegal body and cavity searches performed on those attending the party that followed the parade. Such incidents are jarring, not only because they point out that some parts of the police force may not be 'gay-friendly', but also because they remind us of a not-so-distant past when LGBTQI people in Australia were openly harassed and persecuted by police.[35] And of course they hark back to the events of that original Mardi Gras that started at Taylor Square and wended its way down Oxford Street and then up to Kings Cross, and into Sydney's history.

Oxford Street has been specifically known in the public imagination as *the* gay precinct, going back to its early commercial developments in the late 1960s, when a few clubs and bars opened there.[36] But the world is changing. While Oxford Street is still the site of the Mardi Gras parade, it may be losing its title as 'gay central'. A headline in an online magazine early in 2007 said it all: 'Whither gay Sydney: the decline of Oxford Street as gay space.'[37]

Why Oxford Street is no longer the vibrant, dynamic, erotic gay space it once was has vexed the gay community for years. As one observer noted:

> In the '80s and '90s, the street's role as a gay political, cultural and leisure precinct grew. Homosexuals from suburban and country areas migrated there, escaping the intolerance of home and finding a supportive, exciting community in which to come out. The AIDS crisis consolidated the gay community there.
>
> The area was not so much a ghetto, but a self-made enclave offering flamboyant lifestyles and safety in numbers. The hegemony of heterosexuality found elsewhere in the city had been visibly transgressed with active difference. Gay culture emerged, expressed through leisure, fashion, nightlife and sex.[38]

But it is a slow death. People have commented on the decline of Oxford Street since the early years after the onset of AIDS. Was it due to HIV/AIDS? Despite an initial falling-off in attendances at many of the sex-on-premises venues, the bars remained open and business flourished. So other reasons were suggested, such as changing lifestyles, demographics and even real estate costs, especially when rentals began to escalate on the 'gay golden mile'.

By the early 1990s, the decline was being investigated. In his 1993 study, Town Planner, Andrew Leese referred to Oxford Street as the 'focal point' of the spatial distribution of 'gay subcultures' in Sydney. Its drawcards were safety in numbers, community employment, social events, an argot and a synergy with the gay political movement. And visibility. But Leese also noted an increase in the number of 'straight' or mixed institutions on the strip, leading to 'concerns about the decline of the "gay heart".[39] Already the 'straight' world was moving in on Oxford Street.

In July 1998, the activist Craig Johnston asked in the *Sydney Star Observer*: 'How gay is my Oxford Street?'[40] He looked back at the early glory days of gay Oxford Street, describing a weekend night in 1982:

> lines of men merge with other lines, become streams, waves at the pedestrian crossings, meandering and rushing and then dispersing to [Club] Eighty, the Barracks, Capriccio's, Palms, Eighty Five, Flo's, Patches, or down the valley to Signal.
>
> Men with checked shirts, short hair, mustaches, leather jackets, muscles waiting to be pumped, a uniform that advertised gayness (not just homosexuality, a lifestyle). Clones of each other because they were constructing a community.[41]

He noted that some things were still there, nearly 20 years later:

> The Balkan, Piggotts 24 hours newsstand, the Taxi Club, the TAB, sex-on-premises venues, the grotesquery of Gilligan's island. The homeless people. The Wall (but not a beat as it was in the 70s).[42]

The change was partly due to ongoing gentrification, a process that gays had a role in worldwide. As discussed earlier, in Sydney it started in Paddington in the 1960s and 1970s.[43] Indeed, for more than 30 years, most big cities in the western world have had a district either explicitly or implicitly understood to be the place to go if you were gay.[44] West Village and Chelsea in New York City, the Castro in San Francisco, Washington's Dupont Circle or Boston's South End; the Marais in Paris; Old Compton Street and Soho in London, or Canal Street in Manchester; and, of course, Oxford Street in Sydney. But over time, as gays and lesbians won legal rights and greater social acceptance, there was less need to live in or near a ghetto. Other people began to move into these gentrified areas, which now had such attractive features as a 'teeming blend of cafes, street markets, bistros, and small galleries, a new type of "street level culture"'.[45]

So gays were being displaced, as they had once displaced the original inhabitants of what were usually working-class areas. It was happening in and around Oxford Street, and recent research in the USA shows similar trends there. An article, 'The Geography of Same-Sex Couples', showed that many US cities now have same-sex households recorded in the census figures, and many of these are now in suburban areas.[46]

In Sydney this process of dispersal has occurred, and, with greater acceptance, 'gay life' has spread, most obviously into the inner west, to Newtown, Erskineville and Enmore, and to Chippendale, Darlington, Waterloo, Alexandria and Zetland, even perhaps to Stanmore and Summer Hill. All these suburbs have seen increases in their gay and lesbian populations, and these changes in demographics have impacted on local lifestyles. Gay and lesbian households now blend into these neighbourhoods, sitting alongside the young heterosexual families and older residents.

Newtown is probably the centre of this shift to the inner west, and its King Street is where this is most obvious. As cultural geographer Andrew Gorman-Murray has noted, 'In academic terms, I look at Oxford Street as "gay", and King Street as "queer".'[47] He sees Newtown's main streets and their surrounds as more gay-friendly than specifically gay. The change is most notable in what might be called the 'street presence':

> On Oxford Street a lot of the venues seem to cater to white, middle-class men of a certain body type. Of course there are exceptions. But it seems to be very specific, and what some researchers call 'homonormative'.[48]

Prue Foreman, the Newtown South main street coordinator for Marrickville Council, says the inner west is particularly attractive to Richard Florida's 'creative class'. Florida noted in 2002 that cities with more people employed in creative occupations were more vibrant, more attractive. Foreman suggests that the Marrickville Local Government Area has one of the highest concentrations of people working in cultural fields in Australia, and a lot of the people working in these fields are gay and lesbian.[49]

Newtown's shopping district appears to be going from strength to strength. Occupancy rates are high, particularly from the Seymour Centre to Newtown train station, and retail trade is brisk, particularly on weekends. By contrast, commentators and Surry Hills businesses talk about the flagging fortunes of Oxford Street. But its decline is not simply about the exodus of its gay population; it is also connected to economics and finance, and the changing nature of retailing.

The glory days of the 'gay golden mile', as Oxford Street was known from the late 1980s, led to rapidly increasing rents.

However, in 2003, the Sydney property market stagnated, slowing retail growth. The following year the revamped, expanded Westfield in Bondi Junction opened, sending much of Oxford Street retailing into a tailspin. Then in 2008 came the global financial crisis, swiftly followed by the arrival of the next Westfield, in Pitt Street in the CBD. Oxford Street retailers were book-ended by two mega-malls.

So the slump is largely blamed on two mega-malls and unreasonably high rental rates, and the fact that owners can take advantage of negative gearing, described by one critic as the 'last bastion of middle-class tax breaks'. An empty shop is no calamity when the landlord can pick up a tax break along the way. The situation hasn't been helped by the arrival of online retailing. So in recent years, an ongoing retail and restaurant exodus from Oxford Street has left it with empty shopfronts. Prominent 'For Lease' signs, darkened windows and dog-eared posters characterise parts of what used to be a vibrant street.[50]

Another problem is that Oxford Street is controlled by three councils, and an overarching lack of consistency in planning is the result. A colourful and disparate group of landlords and stakeholders overseeing its many hundreds of buildings has done little to help rescue the street. Perhaps Oxford Street has fallen victim to its once-celebrated diversity. The Mardi Gras parade through the heart of the old gay ghetto is one of the few times that Oxford Street harks back to the glory days as 'gay central'.

For me, the end of Oxford Street as a gay precinct was a poignant personal loss. It had always been familiar territory for me, going way back.

As a child growing up in Maroubra, I remember 'going to town', as we called it then, with my mother and brother and sister. When my mother went shopping in the CBD, past Hyde

Park to David Jones or Farmers or Beard Watsons, she always wore a hat and gloves. But for shopping on Oxford Street, at Buckinghams or Brasch's or Edward Arnold or Winn's Department stores, it seemed only gloves were necessary.

And I felt great anticipation for the Oxford Street trip, for it also meant that I would have my favourite lunch, which was a meat pie with mashed potato, peas, gravy and tomato sauce, at the cafeteria at the back of Winn's store in lower Oxford Street.

Later, I frequented Martin's Bar, and even later, Caps and Ivy's Birdcage, and then all the other bars and clubs and sex-on-premises venues along the 'golden mile'. It was a setting that I was at ease with, almost at home in.

A sense of community still exists, despite geographic dispersal, although its nature has clearly changed. Political activism has faded now that many of its political objectives have been achieved, and a new generation lead the gay and lesbian communities. In the new more accepting world, tactics are different. Gone are the heady days of street marches and demonstrations, protests that led to pitched battles in the streets, followed by arrests. That was then. Today, advocacy and pressure groups speak for the gay and lesbian communities.

Sydney's LGBTQI communities now have multiple voices: there are openly gay members of State and Federal Parliaments and on local councils; the mainstream broadsheet press are supportive, and there are institutions like ACON, the Gay and Lesbian Business Association, Gay and Lesbian Tourism Australia, and the various community churches, among others. For HIV-positive people, both Positive Life and The Institute of Many, the latter a peer-run social umbrella for HIV-positive people, operate online. All these groups have their areas of expertise and their voices heard.[51] Older community-based organisations continue to exist and new ones emerge. Many local councils also have a designated officer responsible for LGBTQI issues.

One indicative transformation has been that of ACON. Developing out of the AIDS Action Committee which was set up in 1983 to deal with the onset of the AIDS crisis, its programs changed gradually, from mainly caring for people as they became sick, helping them to die with dignity while supporting family and friends, to a more holistic approach as medical advances meant a change in emphasis to 'living with HIV'.[52] It also became more widely involved in becoming a health promotion agency for the LGBTQI communities. By 2010, it was Australia's largest community-based LGBT health and HIV/AIDS organisation. Its evolution reflected changes that were occurring in the health and wellbeing needs of the state's LGBTQI communities.[53]

Last, but certainly not least, the internet has reduced the need for gay services and entertainment to be physically close together, and this has helped radically transform the way gay men meet and conduct their lives.

Sydney then has what can be called a 'non-contiguous gay community' whose sense of community is maintained in different ways. One of these is through the gay media.

From the early 1970s, the various gay media played an important role in keeping the emerging communities informed about matters that would be of import to them, and also helped to foster a sense of gay identity, and thus worked to create a gay 'community'.[54]

During the AIDS era, the gay press played a most important role in counteracting some of the more hysterical responses from the tabloid media.[55] In this situation, the need for a gay media, able to deal sympathetically with the new infection, was absolutely critical.

But the experiences of the gay media in Sydney have often been fraught.

The trend towards privatisation, a feature of the business world and stock markets in the 1980s and 1990s, was mirrored in the gay and lesbian media. Much of Sydney's previously 'community-owned' or 'community-focused' print media underwent rapid ownership changes.

Greg Fisher, a Sydney property developer, who owned the Beresford and Beauchamp hotels in Sydney, was brought in as an investor by Melbourne's chronically cash-strapped Bluestone Media in April 1999. Soon after, he took over the company, thus acquiring Melbourne's *OutRage* and *Melbourne Star Observer*. In November he bought out *BrotherSister*, and also acquired Sydney's *Capital Q*. Adding titles from other states, he created Satellite Media, a gay and lesbian media investment group, and then announced plans for a 'pink' float. This occurred on the Sydney Stock Exchange in November 1999, and prominent Sydney lesbian identity Kerryn Phelps was appointed chairman of the Satellite Group. But Fisher's attempt to build up an Australia-wide LGBTQI media empire ended in disaster: it collapsed spectacularly in 2000, and Fisher was convicted on six counts of fraud and for the importation of cocaine, and sent to gaol.[56] As a result, the money raised and the fortunes lost severely damaged the reputation of the Australian gay and lesbian communities as places to invest and do business. The collapse also took down much of Australia's gay and lesbian media.

Some publications reappeared over time, under different names, often restarted by former employees. There was continuity with the Sydney Gay & Lesbian Community Publishing Limited's *Star Observer*, originally started in 1979. A major new player has been Evolution Media, which currently operates a series of gay and lesbian periodicals around Australia. These include *SX* in Sydney, *Melbourne Community Voice*, *Queensland Pride*, *SX National*, *AX National* and *Fellow Traveller*. Evolution also publish *DNA*, a monthly glossy 'sex, fashion, and lifestyle' magazine launched in Australia in 2000 and now available in bookstores throughout Canada, the US and Europe.

Today, while print still flourishes, the fastest growing area is electronic media. All the major print media have electronic versions, and there are purely web-based publications such as *samesame.com* and *Pinkboard,* in addition to online gay dating services and gay sex-contact websites.

As Dennis Altman noted, 'One of the most important developments in the emergence of both gay culture and gay community has been the growth of a gay press; not surprisingly, gay movements often saw as one of their first priorities the creation of a gay magazine or paper.'[57] And indeed the gay press facilitated the spread of ideas that empowered a successful social movement in Australia, one that has born its fruit.

A healthy society needs a free and independent media. Media monopolies are always a thoroughly bad thing, and minorities' voices may struggle to be heard. So while names such as *Gay Community News, Labrys, Green Park Observer, Queensland Pride, Lesbian News, Gay Changes, Cruiser, Sydney Advocate, Gay Rays, OutRage, Playguy, Canary, Libertine, 9PM, Melbourne Star Observer, Sydney Fart, Oxford Weekender News, Lesbiana, Bliss, Now, West Side Observer, Village Voice, Gay Information, Harbour City Times* and *Wicked Women* have all had their 'fifteen minutes of fame' and disappeared, Australia's LGBTQI communities have been well-served by their media over the last four decades, in helping them become an integral and accepted part of Australian society.[58]

Another good indicator of a flourishing community is its

'social scene'. And Sydney's scene has a vibrancy, with many and varied activities for the community members to be involved in, if so inclined.

As gay men grow older, and leave behind that 'trim, taut, terrific' body image, their lifestyles can diverge quite dramatically from that of their heterosexual counterparts. To the average Australian, describing someone as 'middle-aged, fat and hairy' does not necessarily compute with 'sexy'. But in the gay world, this transformation has been achieved; the 'gay sensibility' has given it a makeover – with 'the Bear'.

Bears are typically chubby, hairy and – usually – bearded gay men, who have created a new social category for themselves. The first Australian club, *Ozbears Australia*, started in Sydney in 1990, but only lasted a few years. In August 1995, a group met at the Stronghold Bar, a leather den in Surry Hills, and started a new club, the *Harbour City Bears*.[59] Over the years, various venues around the 'gay ghetto' have been their home: the Barracks, the Beresford Hotel, the Flinders Hotel, the Oxford Hotel, the Lord Roberts Hotel in East Sydney, and the Oxford again. They have an active social calendar and legendary parties – such as Underbear, Advance Australia Fur, Chunky, Wet Fur, and Bear Essentials. A major player in the Sydney social scene, they are a congenial home for many gay men, especially those no longer interested in the young 'twinkies' or the 'muscle marys' who cluster in the surrounding gyms. As one satisfied participant has noted:

> By creating the Bear, something any bloke could be, gay men made it possible for generations to grow old gracefully while acting completely disgracefully. Only gay men could devise a pension plan based on one's appearance.[60]

Their weekly Tuesday nights at the gay sauna Kingsteam on Oxford Street were affectionately referred to as 'Gorillas in the Mist'.[61] And as the growth in the number of 'cubs' also indicates, there are younger gay men who also find the bear image congenial and sexy; after all, Bears are just 'blokes who like blokes'.[62]

Another major fixture in Sydney's gay scene, in a country known to be football mad, is the city's own 'rugger buggers', the Sydney Convicts Rugby Union Club. Formed in 2004, their primary aim is 'the enjoyment of rugby in a prejudice free environment'.[63] Along the way to achieving this goal, the Convicts have broken down barriers and challenged stereotypes, not just on the rugby field but also in the wider community. They compete in the Sydney Suburban Rugby Union championship, and also in the worldwide gay rugby tournament, the Bingham Cup. The Bingham Cup was founded in 2002 to highlight the problem of homophobia in sport.[64] It is named after Mark Bingham, a former UC Berkeley football star, who died helping to bring down United Airlines Flight 93 before hijackers could fly the plane into the Capitol Building in Washington DC. It crashed into a vacant field in Pennsylvania, killing all those on board.[65] Bingham's mother, Alice Hoagland, explained how he had used his rugby skills to help foil the hijackers. As she said, 'He and about three other guys decided that they weren't going to put up with being hijacked ... They weren't able to save their own lives that day, but they did manage to save a good many people on the ground.'[66]

The Sydney Convicts hosted the 2014 Bingham Cup in Sydney. As the then Prime Minister Julia Gillard said at the time:

Australia is a sports-loving nation which also has an abiding commitment to diversity and mutual respect.

In recent years, Sydney has hosted the gay games, the Olympics and the Rugby World Cup with a remarkable spirit of openness and celebration.

I know that Bingham Cup participants would receive the same warm and generous welcome.[67]

Once again, the event was seen as being of 'direct economic benefit' to the city, bringing in over $4 million.[68]

The Sydney Rangers, Australia's first gay men's soccer club, has, since 2009, competed for the Justin Fashanu Cup, which forms part of the annual Pride Football Australia tournament. The Justin Fashanu Cup remembers and celebrates the life of the first gay man to publicly come out in professional soccer, in 1990.[69]

And what would the Sydney scene be without drag.

The 1995 movie *The Adventures of Priscilla, Queen of the Desert* brought the high profile enjoyed by drag queens in Sydney to world attention, but the city has a long tradition of cross-dressing going back into the nineteenth century, for entertainment or for personal satisfaction.[70] And while there continues to be drag queens who embody the traditional Carmen/Carlotta style of drag, others continue to embrace satire, as seen in some of their names, such as Carmen Geddit, Maude Boat, Minnie Cooper, Sandy Toggs, Victoria Bitter, Kitty Glitter, Kirsten Damned, Tess Tickle and Farren Heit.[71]

Cross-dressing in public no longer causes fear and consternation among the citizens of Sydney. Drag lost its bite when troupes like Les Girls, once considered risqué in Kings Cross, began to appear at suburban Leagues clubs. The popular live television show *The Footy Show* wouldn't be half as much fun if it didn't feature drag more than occasionally, although those footballers could take a few lessons in fashion.

Another major event in the Sydney LGBTQI social calendar is Fair Day, one of the biggest and most colourful events of the Mardi Gras Festival, which now kick-starts the Festival in Victoria Park. Once an event largely for the gay and lesbian communities and their friends, it is now part of the broader Sydney social calendar, with many locals and families also coming for a 'day out'. Estimates of between 70 000 and 80 000 people attend. Its marketing appeals to all:

> From pooches to Pad Thai and dodgems to drag, Fair Day
> is a smorgasbord of fun for all ages and tastes. Both a picnic
> and a party, you'll find gourmet food, rides for the kids,
> market stalls, comedy, dance and live music on the main
> stage. And for our four-legged friends, the world famous
> DoggyWood dog show.[72]

There are other features of Sydney's gay social scene worth mentioning too. There are still saunas, although far fewer than a decade ago; one tired old sauna in Oxford Street, Kingsteam, reopened recently as the Sydney Sauna, but its over-glamorous interior means that it has lost most of its sleazy appeal. And there are still sex-on-premises venues scattered around, and the club scene continues for intrepid party-goers, with day clubs like Daywash (at where else, but Chinese Laundry) and Extra Dirty. Increasingly, these have become mixed events, with gays and straights among the clients. More recently, changes in the state's drinking laws, to deal with alcohol-fuelled violence largely in Kings Cross, also affected parts of lower Oxford Street, and many of the big club parties ended.

Another Sydney institution is Bingay, or gay bingo, 'which means there's classic disco tunes, weird rules and penalties, outrageous antics, hilarious repartee, deliciously lewd bingo calls, and prizes that range from the silly and camp to great theatre tickets and restaurant vouchers'.[73]

Also on any social calendar are two commemorations, the Candlelight Memorial Rally and the Sydney Pride Festival.

The Candlelight Memorial Rally is Sydney's remembrance event for people lost to HIV/AIDS, and it takes place every year. It used to be held on World AIDS Day, 1 December, and was preceded by a solemn procession of people carrying candles, down Oxford Street from Green Park to Hyde Park, and the names of those lost to the infection were read out during the ceremony there. It is now held in May, to coincide with International Candlelight Memorial Day.[74]

The Sydney Pride Festival in late June commemorates both those who led the way in the so-called Stonewall Riots in New York in June 1969, and those who marched in the first Sydney Mardi Gras in 1978. The festival now features art exhibitions, cinema, trivia nights, debates, sports and fund-raising activities, and club events across Sydney.[75]

One disturbing aspect of Sydney life that surfaced in the early twenty-first century related to violence against gay men, and it surfaced in an unusual way.

There has always been some level of 'poofter-bashing' in Sydney, but it was rarely reported as such, and even more rarely made it into the mainstream press.[76] But in December 1988, a young American, Scott Johnson, was found dead at the foot of the cliffs at Bluefish Point near Manly. The coroner's verdict, based on the evidence that the police provided, was suicide.

Scott Johnson's brother Steve, a resident of Boston, could not believe that his brother would have committed suicide.

Scott had just completed his PhD and was going to be working at the Australian National University. He had planned to visit his brother in the US soon, to see his newly born niece. They were close.

Much later when Steve read an article by investigative journalist Dan Glick about the death of child beauty queen JonBenet Ramsey, he thought Dan might be able to help find the truth about his brother. So Steve sent Dan to Sydney to see what he could uncover. Dan began examining the case in 2007 and travelled to Sydney many times over the following years, to interview potential witnesses and chase up leads that the Johnson family believed police had failed to investigate. Dan uncovered much new evidence, including court records showing that gangs of men had committed dozens of violent assaults on gay men across Sydney around the time Scott died.[77]

The inquest into Scott's death was reopened in mid-2012, predominantly because of this new evidence. The inquest heard that there were up to ten more deaths at Sydney beaches involving gay men in the years around Scott's death. At the new inquest, Coroner Carmel Forbes changed the suicide verdict to an open verdict, and ordered cold case detectives to immediately re-examine the case.

But warning bells should have rung much earlier. Detective-Sergeant Stephen Page had become aware of a whole series of violent assaults on, and the deaths of, gay men at Sydney's eastern suburbs beats when he was stationed at Paddington police station in the late 1980s.[78] Page began an investigation, and found evidence of hate-filled gangs of teenagers – boys *and* girls – who, as a pack, bashed, robbed and murdered men at known gay beats in Marks Park at Bondi, and in Alexandria and Randwick. Known as Operation Taradale, Page's investigations and findings led to an inquest into some of these

Bondi deaths. In March 2005 Coroner Jacqueline Milledge, while handing down her findings, praised Page for his work, describing it as a shining example of how police investigations should be conducted, and recommended Page for official police commendation.

Page also uncovered a whole range of information about gay murders at beats that had long been known to the police, but never acted on, at a time when gangs of marauding youths hunted gay men for 'sport'.

According to Page, an internal NSW police report, written as far back as 1991, found evidence that 'two gay men may have been murdered in Sydney in 1989'. Their deaths had simply been written off as an accident and a missing person. The report also identified and named witnesses and suspects, including one person who 'admitted being involved in approximately 70 to 100 gang assault and robberies on homosexual men'. The same man had actually confessed to throwing a gay man off the cliff at Bondi, and then taking the victim's car keys and searching his brown car, before throwing the keys into the ocean.

This person should have become an instant suspect in what a coroner decided – but confirmed only a decade later – was the murder of Wollongong newsreader Ross Warren, who had disappeared in mid-1989. His body was never found, but his car keys were recovered from a rock ledge at Bondi, and his brown car was found parked near Bondi after he disappeared.

Then there was John Russell, whose body was found lying beneath a Bondi cliff in November 1989. Police initially claimed that he had died accidentally, despite having a clump of someone else's hair clutched in his hand. The 1991 report acknowledged, '[This] death and the circumstances surrounding his demise are disturbing to say the least'. Indeed, commenting on police ineptitude, Coroner Milledge said that the investigation of Mr Russell's death was 'inadequate and naive', and it was 'disgraceful' that vital forensic material – that tuft of hair – had been lost. At the time, police had simply closed these cases.

And no one was ever convicted for either of these killings.

The material that Page uncovered was used in the reopened Scott Johnson case. On 11 February 2013, the ABC's *Australian Story*'s 'On The Precipice' focused on the death of Scott Johnson, although the program also touched on a number of other deaths at beats in Sydney in the late 1980s and early 1990s. After the program aired, there was an incredible outpouring of public support via Twitter, email and Facebook, and it brought forth a whole range of new information, including even more evidence of these gay hate murders. It made clear the level of homophobia that had existed in Sydney for decades, and of the many deaths on the beats that occurred around Sydney from the 1980s, and possibly even earlier.

At a coronial hearing in April 2015, Coroner Michael Barnes confirmed that an open verdict be recorded and, in the light of new evidence, ordered that there be a third inquest into Scott Johnson's death.

Attitudes in the police force are clearly an issue in this matter. Detective Chief Inspector Pamela Young, the police officer in charge of re-investigating the Scott Johnson case, went on the ABC's *Lateline* program a few nights after the hearing, and was dismissive of the level of homophobia that existed at that time, suggesting that there *might* be only one incidence of homophobia by a police officer at Manly involved in the Scott Johnson case. Her comments led Coroner Barnes to ask that she be removed from investigating the case; as he pointed out, in doing what she did, she had 'engaged in a departure from the usual standards of conduct'.[79]

The publicity generated by the latest inquest, and DCI Young's comments, led to developments within the gay community. At the behest of ACON's CEO, Nicolas Parkhill, a meeting of community stakeholders was convened to discuss these issues and develop a plan of action. That meeting took place on Wednesday 29 April 2015. There, it was decided to compile a register of those who have probably died or been 'disappeared' [or been assaulted] in the series of gay hate crimes that occurred in Sydney over this period – and possibly even earlier, from the 1970s. Such a register would be useful for countering any claims that there was no epidemic of gay hate crimes committed in Sydney from the early 1980s, and would be useful for any future inquests into any such deaths.

Homophobia does not just exist in individuals or in institutions like the police force. Philip Leung's unusual legal case highlights what might be seen as institutionalised homophobia. He is the first person in NSW legal history to stand trial three times over the same death, since Louisa the 'Botany Murderess' Collins, the last woman to be hanged in the state, in 1889.[80]

Leung's story begins the morning of Easter Saturday in 2007, when neighbours found him cradling the head of his lover, Mario Guzzetti, at the bottom of the stairs in their Alexandria terrace. By the time paramedics arrived, Guzzetti had stopped breathing. Leung told police that his lover had fallen down the stairs, but nearby was a juicer which had bloodstains on it.

Leung was charged with murder. In the first trial, in 2009, prosecutors alleged that Leung struck his lover with the juicer following a fight, and that he had also applied pressure to Guzzetti's neck.[81] The evidence against him included what he said when he called for an ambulance: 'I had a fight with my friend … now my friend is dead.'[82]

However, before Leung could give evidence, Justice

Stephen Rothman delivered a 'directed not guilty' verdict, ruling the prosecution did not have enough evidence: was it not possible that Guzzetti had been carrying the juicer when he fell, and that is how the blood got on it?[83]

Next, the Crown used NSW's controversial double jeopardy laws, introduced in 2006, to have the verdict quashed in the Court of Criminal Appeal, and the matter was sent back for retrial. This time, the Crown brought a manslaughter charge against Leung, but in an unexpected twist, in April 2011 Justice Michael Adams directed a second jury to return a not guilty verdict. Leung thus became the first person in Australian legal history to be twice acquitted by a judge's directed verdict.[84]

The Crown appealed the decision, and in March 2012, the Court of Criminal Appeal ruled another trial ought to take place, again for manslaughter. But this did not occur until 2013. In the meantime Leung had to surrender his passport and start bail, reporting weekly to Newtown police station. By this stage, and due to what seemed to be ongoing persecution, Leung was being treated by a psychiatrist and was taking anti-depressants. He said it felt like he was stuck in an endless cycle.[85]

At the third trial, this time before a jury, Leung was found guilty of manslaughter, and sentenced to a minimum four and a half years in gaol.

During his closing address, Justice Price highlighted the 'unique' nature of the three-trial case and the 'fluctuating outcomes' – namely the two acquittals and two successful DPP appeals – which had clearly had an 'adverse psychological effect' on Leung.[86] And as he was led away, Leung yelled out, 'This is wrong.'[87]

Leung's experience with Corrective Services NSW is also revealing. He had been shifted between Silverwater, Parklea, Cessnock, Bathurst and Muswellbrook prison facilities, encountering repeated 'homophobic' violence and abuse along the way:

> I was attacked in a laundry at Parklea and had three ribs broken. In Cessnock, I was targeted and needed stitches above my left eye. I refused to argue … I tried to avoid trouble. But always, I was bullied.[88]

An appeal by Leung's supporters was in process, and his conviction was sensationally thrown out by the NSW Court of Criminal Appeal. In their decision, Justice Elizabeth Fullerton and Justice Christine Adamson ruled the evidence before the court was insufficient to convict Mr Leung 'beyond reasonable doubt'. Specifically, they could find no evidence that the juicer was used in any offence. Neither did the evidence 'go so far as to exclude a fall'.[89]

At that point, Leung was still facing two and a half years behind bars. Just days before Christmas 2014, he heard the news from his solicitor, and was released from prison on Monday 22 December. He scrambled to make the last train out of Muswellbrook, at 7.30 pm – so that he did not have to spend a further night in prison – and arrived at Sydney's Central Station at 12.30 am on Tuesday 23 December, 'dazed', jaded, but joyous.

> I wandered streets, sat in bus stops … I just wanted to be by myself, feel freedom, smell the air … deal with emotions.

Commenting on what he called the Crown's 'relentless pursuit' of Mr Leung, his solicitor asked, 'How much pain and suffering should one man have to be put through?'[90]

The Leung case raises some worrying questions about

possible homophobia in various institutions of the state's so-called justice system. Was this a case of justice being pursued, or was it really a case of a gay – and Asian – man being pursued because he was gay – and Asian; a case of homophobic prejudice?

It is a reminder that the price of our freedoms is eternal vigilance.

But there seems to be a different mind-set today, in so many ways.

Many young people now have no awareness that in the late 1960s, in many places around the world, there was a belief that 'revolution' was both a necessity and a possibility, that the world could be remade a better place, and that what happened in Paris in 1968 and the Stonewall Riots in New York in 1969 were part of this process of disillusionment and response. It was seen as not just speculation, rather a matter of timing. In those days, the young wanted to change the world.

While we are all the products of our era's zeitgeist and our upbringing, conditioned by the values and education of our times, we are not its prisoners. The world moves on, and 'the right order of things' continues to change.

Perhaps today, the younger generation has no past from which to flee; they live in a world of freedoms, and presume they are unassailable, while we older men, who remember – with anger, rage or sadness – the world we grew up in and fought to change, know that nothing need be permanent.

And so the Leung case stands as a warning.

CHAPTER 9

JUST LIKE EVERYBODY ELSE?

Sydney's gay world today

Things seem to have changed for the better, but in the second decade of the twenty-first century, how far have they come?

Decriminalisation of male homosexual acts has occurred in all states and territories, so our emotional and sexual lives are on a par with our heterosexual friends and families. Between 2007 and 2010, the federal Labor government amended over 70 pieces of legislation to remove ongoing discrimination, so that gay and lesbian couples are treated like heterosexual couples for purposes of welfare and taxation. But while NSW passed anti-discrimination laws to protect the LGBTQI community decades ago, the federal government has not yet done so.

Attitudes to 'dissident sexualities' have changed radically. Today a number of public figures are open about their sexuality, and it is not an issue: SBS TV anchor Anton Enus, journalists David Marr and Benjamin Law, Qantas CEO Alan Joyce, former David Jones CEO Paul Zahra, Human Rights Commissioner Tim Wilson, comedian Josh Thomas, Olympians Ian Thorpe and Matthew Mitcham, actress Magda Szubanski, federal Senator Penny Wong, Sydney City Councillors Robyn

Kemmis and Christine Forster, are all examples of this change. The NSW Parliament has gay members in both houses including Liberals Shayne Mallard, Don Harwin and Bruce Notley-Smith, the ALP's Penny Sharpe, Mark Pearson of the Animal Justice Party, and independent Alex Greenwich. Sharpe, Greenwich and Notley-Smith are members of the NSW Parliamentary LGBTI Cross-Party Working Group, which includes the Green's Jenny Leong and the National Party's Trevor Khan, a group that has had some success in moving same-sex issues forward at the state level.

There is now widespread social acceptance of same-sex relationships. The state government launched the NSW Relationships Register in 2010; the City of Sydney had set up its own Relationships Declaration Program in July 2004. Aside from a registered civil relationship, lesbians and gays in NSW can foster and adopt children, be out at most workplaces, and kiss and cuddle in public in certain parts of the city without being assaulted. At some 'progressive' schools, kids can take their same-sex partners to their end-of-year school parties. Perhaps most significantly, when a major public figure dies, their same-sex partner can now be openly acknowledged in the bereaved party at their funeral.

Early in 2014, the *Crimes Amendment (Provocation) Bill 2014* passed through NSW Parliament, signalling the end of the so-called 'gay panic' defence laws. The Bill effectively removed the legal foundation of the common-law defence of provocation, known as the Homosexual Advance Defence, in cases involving a non-violent sexual advance. In the past, people successfully claimed they were 'provoked' by someone's alleged sexual advances in order to reduce a murder conviction to manslaughter, and receive a lesser sentence. According to the NSW GLR Lobby, this had occurred a number of times exclusively in cases involving a non-violent sexual advance by a male towards another male. The Lobby welcomed the amendment, calling it the end of the 'most homophobic legal defence on the statute books' in the state.

There have been significant improvements since CAMP Inc. was formed over four decades ago, and one is happy for the generations growing up now and into the future. Their lives, and the way they find love, will be very different from their predecessors.

Once upon a time, centuries ago, to find love was restricted to the local village or community. Then urbanisation came along; in the cities and towns, the circle widened with opportunities to meet others from just a block away or from afar, as people travelled for work or pleasure. And then came air travel, and many marriages were literally 'made in heaven', as tens of thousands flew around the globe. Today, many marriages are still made in heaven, but now via the ether, as satellites bounce literally billions of romantic notes back and forth around the world.

The new technologies have had a major impact on how gay men meet others for friendship, love or sex. Internet dating has been a major growth area. In the gay world, web addresses like Gaydar, Manhunt, Silver Daddies, Squirt.org, Jack'd, Grindr, GROWLr, Daddyhunt, Hornet, u4Bear, PlanetRomeo, BBRT [Bareback Real Time] and Recon, among many others, all ply a busy trade. At any point in time, thousands of gay men will be online, so you can interact with persons from anywhere, from Glebe to Gdansk, from Woollahra to Wyoming, from Perth to Phnom Penh – and everywhere in between. The net has 'de-materialised' gay life away from a particular neighbourhood; in Sydney's case, away from Oxford Street

Feminism, Indigenous rights, environmentalism, the anti-war campaigns and the gay rights movement precipitated social revolutions in Australia in the second half of the twentieth century. Much of this occurred within a context of multiculturalism, then a new idea for Australia. In this view, Australia was a society made up of many cultures, all of which should be treated with respect. While multiculturalism was conceived in relation to people from different ethnic and racial backgrounds, it also proved an effective way of recognising other minority cultures, including the LGBTQI communities.

Australia has made a relative success of multiculturalism, and it has enabled the LGBTQI communities to be seen as legitimate parts of Australian society. The multicultural idea still has its enemies, but despite the Howard years and the condemnation by conservative commentators, it has worked well. Neverthless, racism and prejudice are still obvious in parts of Australia, and even within the LGBTQI communities. Unfortunately, there is no guarantee that the persecution and harassment of one minority will necessarily lead them to be sensitive about the plight of other minorities. And in the gay community, this is still the case. Indeed, the whole of Oxford Street's social milieu could seem a brittle, forbidding place for young men of other ethnicities, and the bars – then as now – can be alienating places for them.

The recent events involving the Islamic State, and the barbarities and atrocities it commits, has given rise to a backlash against Muslims in Australia. A national survey has found that one in four Australians holds a negative attitude towards Muslims.[1] The *Social Cohesion Report*, published by Monash University and the Scanlon Foundation, measured public attitudes on issues like immigration and multiculturalism. It found that people were five times more likely to hold negative attitudes towards Muslims than towards any other religious group. And this has translated into some discrimination against gay

Muslims within the gay communities. Yet at the same time, Club Arak, an Arab-flavoured dance party for 'queers of all colours', is popular on the Sydney scene. It began in Sydney in 2002, and has become somewhat of an institution in Sydney's LGBTQI nightlife, being open to everyone – Arab-Australians and their admirers, their friends, and their family.[2]

Indeed the major problems for gays and lesbians from Arab and Muslim backgrounds come from within their families and their communities. After the 2003 report *You Shouldn't Have to Hide to Be Safe*[3] revealed disturbing patterns of violence within Arab and Muslim families, ACON decided to investigate the issue. The idea was to work with organisations and individuals in the Arab communities – both Muslim and Christian – to examine the impact of homophobia within their families.

The project took seven years, and the report, *We're Family Too*, launched in State Parliament in 2012, detailed the effects of homophobia in Arabic-speaking communities in New South Wales. It was such a sensitive project that no one who took part was named: not the priests and imams consulted by the steering committee, nor the gay men and women – many recruited through Club Arak – who spoke of the violence and threats of violence they had experienced within their families and their communities, because of their sexuality.[4]

Ghassan Kassisieh, a lawyer brought in to write the report, highlighted the problem:

> In Arab cultural understandings, it is selfish, it is turning
> your back on your family to come out and move out ... It is
> risking the family's happiness and the family's honour and
> the family's reputation in the community for the sake of your
> own desires. So that's a tension there: as Australians we value
> autonomy, but the Arab family values collectiveness.[5]

But just as gay life in Australia has been transformed by the internet, so men from Arab and Muslim backgrounds with homoerotic desires have been able to meet online both for sex and to talk about the difficulties of their lives.

While the new electronic world offers greater opportunities to meet, prejudices continue to exist. Benjamin Law detailed this in 'Kiss me, I'm Asian', an article in the *Good Weekend*, when discussing meeting people on Grindr, the gay sex/dating website:

> Naturally, Grindr users all look for different things: hairy/
> smooth, slim/athletic. Many also state what they're avoiding.
> 'No femmes', say some. 'No fat, no old', say others. 'No
> Asians.' That last one – 'No Asians' – comes up a lot.[6]

This wasn't new. Before Grindr, personal advertisements in the *Sydney Star*, for example, often specified, 'no Asians' need apply. Poor media representation of Asian men is partly the cause. How many Asian male sex symbols are there in western media? When screenwriter and director Tony Ayres, a Chinese-Australian, 'came out', he encountered in Oxford Street a world that was not only body-conscious but profoundly racist.[7] This might be another reason why Oxford Street is no longer seen as a 'safe harbour' for many young men coming to terms with their sexuality.

There have been efforts to change this. The Midnight Shift ran successful Gay Asian Nights for many years.[8] For over two years in the mid-1990s, Chinese poet Bing Yu, newly arrived in Australia, wrote a weekly Chinese language column in *Capital Q Weekly*, guiding young Asians into the arcane and often unfriendly world of Sydney's gay life. This was the first time a column not written in English appeared in an Australian gay newspaper, reflecting an outreach by the gay mainstream to minority groups within their communities. For his work, Bing was awarded an Australian Federation of AIDS Organisations Media Award, 'in recognition of outstanding contribution to media coverage of HIV/AIDS in Australia'.

Young gay men from Asia not only experience discrimination and stereotyping, they also face cultural issues, with family and community pressures. ACON runs the Gay Asian Men's Project, which provides support services to improve and maintain the health and wellbeing of gay Asian men in NSW, in order to deal with these issues. Its Asian Tea Room evenings are a congenial meeting place for Asian gay men to meet. Recent topics discussed here have included 'Migrating to Sydney – What's In, What's Out'; 'Gay King/Gay Queen: being gay in Thailand'; 'Oppression Olympics'; 'That's not racist, you're just too sensitive'; 'Happy Moon Festival'; and 'Exploring Asian consciousness and AIDS 2014'.

Project Officer Min Fuh Teh says that as Sydney's Asian and LGBTQI communities become more integrated in the city's social and cultural fabric, Asian LGBTQI people face a range of unique issues:

> Being a minority within a minority is a significant experience
> for many Asian GLBT people and something with which
> many often struggle. In some Asian communities, it can
> be hard to address something as taboo as the issue of sex
> – especially gay sex – but not talking about it encourages a
> sense of disempowerment, and that can lead to all kinds of
> issues in terms of sexual health.[9]

Particularly encouraging has been the launch of ACON's *A-Men* magazine which, using images and text, breaks down the stereotypical views that people might have of Asian gay men, as alien, effeminate and manipulative. The Long Yang Club aims to provide a friendly and supportive environment for gay Asians and their friends, chiefly through a program of social events and other activities. It is part of a global network.[10]

The dilemma of a dissident sexuality in certain cultures may never be resolved satisfactorily for either family or children, particularly when homosexuality is seen as neither inherent nor appropriate behaviour in the culture. This can be true for gay men of Indigenous backgrounds – the original Australians – who are commonly told homosexuality is against their 'traditions'. Boxer Anthony Mundine expressed this view on Facebook in late 2013, after he saw an episode of the TV series *Redfern Now*:

> Watching redfern now & they promoting homosexuality! (Like it's ok in our culture) that ain't in our culture & our ancestors would have there [sic] head for it![11]

Mundine's comments gave room for other Indigenous people to express their homophobic beliefs. As activist Steven Lindsay Ross so succinctly put it:

> Of course, there will be narrow-minded people in our communities, too. We may dislike the Fred Niles, George Pells or Tony Abbotts of mainstream culture, but we are not surprised that those voices exist in a liberal democracy. There are narrow-minded indigenous people. There are also indigenous fundamentalists, climate-change deniers, racists and misogynists.[12]

This prejudice has been exploited too. In the early 1990s, the Reverend Fred Nile's Call to Australia Party led annual 'Cleansing Marches' down Oxford Street, and one Indigenous activist noted that it was often largely Aboriginal people, brought in from rural New South Wales, sitting on the back of their trucks.[13]

But the Mundine outburst did lead to a more open discussion within the Indigenous world of what it meant to be an Aboriginal with a 'dissident' sexuality. As one commentator has noted, it also encouraged support and advocacy for black LGBTQI peoples in local and broader representations.

It is not only their sexuality that can make life fraught for gay men of Indigenous backgrounds, but their 'ethnicity' as well. As one gay Indigenous man notes:

> When you're Aboriginal, you're always reminded of your difference – from the sideways glance of a shop assistant to the excitable look of school children when you're delivering a Welcome to Country. When you're Aboriginal and gay, there are layers of difference and this can be challenging for some people.[14]

A study conducted by the National Centre in HIV Social Research at Macquarie University, which made copious use of interviews, reported that 'the racism in the Sydney gay community was an issue with most of the Aboriginal interviewees'.[15]

Racism exists in Australia, as it does in any ethnically and culturally diverse country. As Australia's Human Rights Commission notes:

> Culturally and linguistically diverse communities in Australia are themselves diverse, each community and generation having quite different experiences of migration

and settlement. As a result, their experiences of racism vary considerably, and have also varied over time.

The Commission found that 'visible' ethnic and religious minorities such as Arabs, Muslims, Africans, Jews, Palestinians and Turkish people were more likely to be regularly subjected to racism. And the report went on to note that Indigenous Australians certainly experienced racism; 'we know this is a fact. Our own complaints at the Australian Human Rights Commission tell us that, and it is also identified in research.'[16]

Australia's efforts to combat racism are open to criticism. As a report from the Human Rights and Equal Opportunity Commission noted:

> Australia does not perform well on the basis of objective
> criteria for international human rights accountability – we
> have not responded to the views of several committees
> in relation to individual communications; we do not
> have universal ratification of individual communication
> mechanisms; and we submit reports significantly late and do
> not meet our core obligations under international treaties in
> a timely manner.[17]

ACON developed the ACON Aboriginal project, to face up to racism within Sydney's gay communities. It aims at improving the health and wellbeing of Aboriginal and Torres Strait Islander people who are gay, lesbian, bisexual, transgender/sistergirl, HIV positive, engaged in sex work, or who inject drugs. The project adopts a holistic approach to health, recognising the importance of emotional, spiritual, social and mental wellbeing, and provides information, skills, resources and social networks.

A disturbing example of reverse racism with some tragic consequences came in the early days of the HIV epidemic. An Indigenous man noted at the time, 'AIDS is seen as a gay white disease and I really think a lot of people see themselves as immune to it.'[18] This had disastrous results for Indigenous men who had an active sex life, but never saw the need for testing.

As to whether racism is a bigger problem within the gay community than the broader community, there is perhaps no clear answer. The issue of sexual stereotyping comes into play here, and enters the fraught area of the politics of desire and desirability.[19] Combating racism is an ongoing, never-ending endeavour, and one can only hope that education programs and activities such as Wear it Purple Day, which aims to foster greater acceptance of diversity in Australia, can help the process. We need to develop strategies that focus on individuals. The greatest difficulty is how to get the messages across.

As far as racism in the LGBTQI communities goes, the National Centre in HIV Social Research report made this perceptive comment:

> There is considerable irony here in the fact that it was the civil rights and the black power movements in the United States in the 1960s that served as inspirational models for early gay activists, yet it is gay men and women of colour today that are relegated to the boundary of gay community.[20]

Another area of concern relates to refugees and sexuality. Since 1992, Australia has formally recognised that sexual minorities of a particular country can be a 'particular social group' for the purposes of seeking asylum under the Refugee Convention 1951 and the 1967 Protocol. However, actions speak louder than words. In practice, refugees who come here claiming asylum on sexuality grounds face great difficulties, and once again, cultural differences can create problems.

What sort of questions can the Refugee Review Tribunal (RRT) ask to verify that someone is fleeing persecution, and in some countries, death, because of their sexuality, when they are from a country where gay life as we know it does not exist? As Amnesty International Australia's Senthorun Raj puts it:

> What do Madonna, Oscar Wilde, Greco-Roman wrestling, clubbing at Stonewall and an active sexual life have in common?

> Not much really, other than that refugee decision-makers use these cultural tropes to determine whether a refugee is 'genuinely' gay and subject to a well-founded fear of persecution.[21]

With an increasing number of asylum claims based on sexual orientation or gender identity being processed in Australia, decision-makers have a challenging obligation to ensure that claims are treated with the appropriate cultural sensitivity.[22] And, of course, it raises the whole question of 'identity'.

Australia's unlawful and increasingly punitive treatment of asylum seekers has been condemned on the world stage many times. A statement prepared by the Human Rights Law Centre, and delivered to the UN's Human Rights Council in Geneva, the world's peak human rights body, late in 2014, spelt it out:

> Australia is sending gay asylum seekers to a country that criminalises homosexuality, exposing them to serious risks of harm and breaching international law. Australia's cruel policies are made crueller by their inflexible application.[23]

The statement called on the Human Rights Council and member states to condemn Australia for ignoring its international human rights obligations, and to remind it that countries need to share, not shift, responsibility for refugee protection. The statement noted the particular danger posed to LGBTQI asylum seekers by Australia's offshore processing policies. A report by *Guardian Australia* confirmed that Manus Island detention centre was hell on earth for gay asylum seekers, reporting one asylum seeker who said he was raped twice in detention in the preceding four months, but was told he would be gaoled for being a homosexual if he went to the police.[24]

In mid-2015, Zeid Ra'ad Al Hussein, the United Nations High Commissioner for Human Rights, condemned Australia over its asylum seeker policies, describing its approach as 'hostile and contemptuous'. He went on to say that:

> Such policies should not be considered a model by any country. Given that most of today's Australians themselves descend from migrants – and given that the country maintains sizeable regular programs for migration and resettlement – I am bewildered by the hostility and contempt for these women, men and children that is so widespread among the country's politicians.[25]

Even the *New York Times* felt compelled to comment. On 3 September 2015, an editorial headlined 'Australia's Brutal Treatment of Migrants' noted:

> Prime Minister Tony Abbott has overseen a ruthlessly effective effort to stop boats packed with migrants, many of them refugees, from reaching Australia's shores. His policies have been inhumane, of dubious legality and strikingly

at odds with the country's tradition of welcoming people fleeing persecution and war.

Since 2013, Australia has deployed its navy to turn back boats with migrants, including asylum seekers, before they could get close to its shores. Military personnel force vessels carrying people from Iraq, Afghanistan, Sudan, Eritrea and other conflict-roiled nations toward Indonesia, where most of the journeys begin.[26]

Legislation passed late in 2014, which triggered the Human Rights Law Centre's statement to the UN's Human Rights Council, will deny protection to asylum seekers if they can instead be sent back home and asked to take 'reasonable steps' to 'modify' their behaviour unless it affects 'fundamental aspects of identity'. It remains unclear exactly what this will mean in terms of sexuality and asylum seeker claims. Sending someone back to a place where they could be killed for their sexuality, and advising them to 'be discreet', is hardly best practice. It also goes against a High Court decision in 2003 where a majority of judges rejected sending gay refugees back to their original country with the expectation they should 'cover up' or remain 'discreet' about their sexual orientation to avoid persecution.[27]

The new legislation seems to ignore this landmark decision.[28] Late in 2011, the RRT rejected an appeal made by two Bangladeshi asylum seekers, identified in court as SZQYU and SZQYV. These men were seeking asylum in Australia because they argued that they were gay and may have faced persecution in their home country. The RRT rejected the case because it wasn't convinced that the applicants were gay. The men lodged an appeal to the Federal Magistrate's Court, where the Federal Magistrate disputed the Tribunal's decision. Along with other

299

evidence presented to the Magistrate's Court, a CD containing photographs of the two men 'having sex with each other' had been presented to the Tribunal, which it 'failed to consider'; perhaps watching gay sex was too much for members of the Tribunal? The case was sent back to a differently constituted tribunal to review the evidence.[29]

This highlights the difficulty in verifying the 'identity' of the person applying for asylum. People of ethnic origin come from a community of others like themselves, where cultural practices and connections can be investigated and confirmed. But people of dissident sexualities are not born into their community; their sense of their 'sexual difference' is individual, often emerging around or just after puberty. And it is not something that they can flaunt in their country of birth.

Neil Grungras, founder of ORAM International, an organisation that advocates for LGBTQI refugees, has said Australia is 'well on its way to becoming impenetrable for LGBT asylum seekers'.[30] He also pointed out that many LGBTQI refugees faced bigotry from their own ethnic communities even when they reached Australia.

While the Australian population in general seem somewhat indifferent to the fate of any refugees, let alone specifically gay or lesbian refugees, other gay issues, as well as cultural and political activities, generate interest outside the gay community and wide coverage in the mainstream press. The most obvious examples are homophobia, youth suicide, same-sex marriage and inner-city politics.

The Australian obsession with sport makes it a rewarding place to start a campaign about eradicating homophobia. And the need is clear. As one commentator noted recently:

Homophobia is rife in Australian sport. Whether playing at the local park or representing their country, gay and lesbian athletes routinely hide their sexuality to avoid abuse while pursuing the sport they love.[31]

Ian Thorpe is an excellent example of someone who long hid his sexuality from the world to pursue his swimming career – and winning Olympic Gold medals for it.

Out on the Fields, a recent landmark international study of almost 10 000 people, including 3000 Australians, noted significant issues with respect to homophobia in sport across the English-speaking countries it surveyed – Australia, New Zealand, Ireland, the UK, Canada and the USA.

Their research into LGB participation in team sports showed that discrimination and homophobia is commonplace on Australian sporting fields. One in five gay men did not play team sports in their youth, with 43 per cent citing negative experiences during physical education classes as a major driver away from team activities, and a further 36 per cent citing fear of rejection for their sexuality. Forty-five per cent of all participants and 57 per cent of gay men believed LGB people are 'not accepted at all' or only 'accepted a little' in sporting culture. Seventy-two per cent of gay men thought homophobia was more commonplace in Australian sports than in society at large.[32]

According to the study, the impact of homophobia in Australian sport is clearest in male team sports. At the time of the report, there was not a single openly gay player in any of the major men's team sports in Australia at the national level. As La Trobe University sports academic David Lowden puts it:

> We have a problem, we definitely have a problem. We have
> gay soldiers, gay artists, but for some reason in sport it's one
> step too far.[33]

The casual homophobic language, including from friends and
teammates, with terms like 'faggot' and 'poof' bandied around
all the time, make many gay footballers reluctant to come out.
Brennan Bastyovanszky, who plays for gay rugby team the
Sydney Convicts, points to a recent incident at a Super Rugby
match between the Waratahs and the Brumbies at Allianz Sta-
dium in Sydney:

> You had the incident with the Waratahs where Jacques
> Potgieter called somebody a faggot a couple of times. It's
> rumoured that there are gay people on both the Waratahs
> and the Brumbies. Some of my friends have dated them
> … we know of people through rumour that play on the
> Wallabies, the Brumbies, the Waratahs and the All Blacks.[34]

Potgieter was fined $20 000 for using 'homophobic slurs', but
half the fine was 'suspended', which makes something of a
mockery of the penalty. At least he was required to undergo
'additional awareness training'.

It is hard to believe that it was 20 years ago, in 1995, when
Ian Roberts became the first high-profile Australian sports
person and first rugby footballer in the world to come out to
the public as gay. He continued playing grade football for a few
more years, until injuries ended his career. The first Australian
Rules Player to come out is Jason Ball, an amateur footballer in
country Victoria (not to be confused with the ex-Swans player
of the same name); he has become the face of a number of campaigns against homophobia in sport since 2012, including the

influential 'No To Homophobia' ads aired by the AFL during the 2012 preliminary finals. Ball pointed out that:

> It's a culture that has traditionally been very masculine and with that comes a lot of homophobia, a lot of homophobic language, and this is what needs to get challenged.[35]

He also said major sporting codes needed to be less afraid of engaging with homophobic fans, and argued players wouldn't stay in the closet if they knew they had the support of their clubs.

Out on the Fields shows a snapshot of male team sport as an arena fraught with barriers to participation by gay men, and found that homophobic discrimination is commonplace in sporting culture across the English-speaking world.[36] But there are ongoing campaigns against homophobia. The Bingham Cup competition, played in Sydney in 2012, publicly highlighted homophobia in sport. Former Australian Wallabies captain John Eales said the Bingham Cup event was more than just a rugby tournament:

> Regardless of the football code you would like to play, sexuality should be an irrelevant consideration.
>
> Unfortunately this is not a reality and there is still work to be done to eliminate negative stereotypes and homophobia in sport.[37]

It will take time, but if more and more major players come out, the stereotypes will fall away and stigma will be reduced. At the moment, homophobia remains an issue, not only in elite sport in Australia, but also at the community level.

The effects of homophobia can be far more destructive than merely discouraging participation in sport. Recently, attention has turned to suicide among young LGBTQI people so that its critical issues can be addressed.

In 2014 a university study, to determine whether or not young LGBT individuals who die by suicide constitute a unique sub-population of youth suicides, made some disturbing findings.[38] It found a greater level of emotional distress and conflict, with a significantly higher prevalence of depression (70.6 per cent and 52.4 per cent respectively) and relationship problems (65.7 per cent and 33.3 per cent respectively) in LGBT suicide cases when compared with non-LGBT suicides.

These findings suggest the need for targeted approaches in mental and general health services, schools, and public health and stigma reduction campaigns. The greater level of emotionality in LGBT suicides indicates a need for preventative activities to address interpersonal conflict and distress. Self-acceptance and stigma reduction are also important issues to target, given that LGBT individuals who died by suicide experienced greater conflict over their sexuality.[39]

Musician and radio presenter Brendan Maclean talks about growing up in Sydney's Sutherland Shire. When his homosexuality was made known at school, the windows of his house were smashed, his school bag was turned inside out, and even a guy who had said he 'liked him' hurled a fistful of cement at his head. His experience is not untypical for a young man coming to terms with a different sexuality in the suburbs. As Maclean points out:

> It's suburbs like this that can offer insight into why certain young people come to believe that the best option is to end it all; that in their moment of unliftable loneliness, a son

or daughter becomes convinced that, because of the love welling up inside them, it is better to die than to hope for a happy future.[40]

In 2013, beyondblue published *Families Like Mine*, an e-book aimed at saving the lives of young same-sex attracted, bisexual and gender diverse people. At its launch, Quentin Bryce, then Governor-General and beyondblue patron, said that the high rate of deaths of gender diverse people was 'too high a price to pay':[41]

> Fear of rejection and, particularly, fear of being rejected by a loved one is shown to increase anxiety and the risk of suicide and self-harm. But a supportive family can make all the difference.[42]

This is a far cry from 2009, when the *Herald* reported that beyondblue had knocked back repeated funding requests to support depressed young people struggling with their sexuality. They quoted Sue Hackney, of the WayOut program, who said children growing up in country areas were particularly at risk because they could feel like 'they're the proverbial only gay in the village':

> The suicide rate for this group is up to eight times higher than for their heterosexual peers, often due to homophobic bullying, abuse and anxiety about 'coming out'.[43]

In Sydney, the LGBTQI youth group Twenty10 has also addressed the issue:

Homophobia and/or transphobia has a serious impact on many young people's educational experiences, with some changing schools multiple times, and others dropping out of school altogether.[44]

Twenty10 partnered with the University of Western Sydney and the Young and Well Cooperative Research Centre and recently released *Growing Up Queer: Issues Facing Young Australians Who are Gender Variant and Sexuality Diverse.*[45]

So the issue of suicide among young people of dissident sexualities and gender diversity is at last starting to receive the attention that it requires. And increasing numbers of Australian schools are adopting the Safe Schools program, which fights homophobia and transphobia while encouraging diversity and acceptance. Yet the programs have their critics. Fred Nile, a long-time opponent of civil rights for LGBTQI people, said in an ABC *Q & A* program in June 2015, 'My observation is that teenagers are going through sexual development and it can be quite dangerous, I think, to promote homosexuality in schools to children.'[46] He didn't see that schools were promoting an acceptance of difference, surely a virtue in our multicultural society; rather, he saw them 'promoting homosexuality'.[47]

People like Nile are out of touch with contemporary Australian society, as is clear from the latest Australian Human Rights Commission report, *Resilient Individuals: Sexual Orientation, Gender Identity & Intersex Rights 2015*. But while the report shows that the world has moved beyond Nile's obsessions, it also notes issues that still need to be addressed, arguing that

public services (including education, health and welfare services) in receipt of taxpayers' funds should not enjoy

religious exemptions under anti-discrimination law for
employment or selection of clients.[48]

Australian politicians rarely lead the pack, preferring to angst
over what opinion polls tell them, especially in marginal elec-
torates which may differ from the broader community. Conservative politicians have influence here too. This caution means
that changes to the law are slow to be implemented. Nowhere is
this more obvious than in the issue of same-sex marriage, which
the electorate clearly supports. Tensions over the issue have
prompted the Human Rights Commission to point out that

> Legislating marriage for same-sex couples is necessary to
> achieve equality before the law [but] it is appropriate to
> have necessary safeguards to ensure religious groups are not
> required to marry same-sex couples if it is not consistent
> with their faith.[49]

There are now well over 20 countries around the world that
have legislated for same-sex marriage with no negative impacts
on society, including many Christian and Catholic countries:
Argentina, Spain, Portugal, Brazil, Uruguay and parts of Mexico.
In Europe, Holland (including the Caribbean Netherlands),
Belgium, Sweden, Norway, France, Luxembourg, Finland, Den-
mark, Iceland and Ireland have introduced same-sex marriage.
Commonwealth countries such as Canada, South Africa, New
Zealand and the UK have also introduced same-sex marriage.
In June 2015, the American Supreme Court ruled that same-
sex marriage was a constitutional right.

When laws allowing same-sex marriage were passed in the
UK under the leadership of Conservative Prime Minister David
Cameron, he said:

I am a strong believer in marriage. It helps people commit to
each other and I think it is right that gay people should be
able to get married too. This is, yes, about equality, but it is
also about making our society stronger.[50]

Australia is a secular state and the intellectual justification for
obstructing the push for same-sex marriage is unclear. Is it
simply a reflection of the power of the fundamentalist religious
lobby and conservative churches, and their influence on conservative politicians?

The Catholic Church responded to moves to legalise same-
sex marriage in Australia by sending a letter to its parishioners.
Tasmanian Archbishop Julian Porteous said the letter was issued
to help Catholics understand why the church was opposed to
changing the legal definition of marriage.

This Pastoral Letter is offered to parishioners in the hope
that it will deepen their appreciation of the beauty and
dignity of marriage and family life according to the plan of
God.[51]

The letter started with the statement that 'We now face a struggle for the very soul of marriage', and went on to say that 'if the
union of a man and a woman is different from other unions,
not the same as other unions, then justice demands that we
treat that union accordingly'.[52] The spokesperson for Australian
Marriage Equality Rodney Croome responded:

The Marriage Act is a civil law which does not and should
not enshrine the values of any particular religion.[53]

He pointed out that his group did not wish to force the church or any other group to do anything it did not want to do.

> The Catholic Church will not be forced to marry same-sex
> couples and in return I ask it not to force its views on the
> rest of the community through the Marriage Act.

It would appear that the majority of Australians were not attuned to the view of the Catholic Church, seeing no reason why same-sex marriage shouldn't be legalised. Opinion polls show that well over 60 per cent of Australians believe that same-sex couples should have the right to marry; even a majority of Christians (53 per cent) support marriage equality; and 75 per cent believe the reform is inevitable. Younger respondents were even more supportive with 81 per cent of people between 18 and 24 years old in favour of marriage equality.[54]

I sometimes watch the marches in support of same-sex marriage, as they wend their way from Town Hall Square to Taylor Square, and I am always impressed by the enthusiasm of those involved. There are always a few older supporters – perhaps parents of children who are denied the right to marry their loved one – but the marchers are predominantly young. Most of them look as if they have just left school, smooth-faced and eager, and respectably dressed. The demonstrations look so different from those in the early days of gay lib, when the new hippie look was much in evidence – long hair, a few beards, tie-dyed shirts, sandals, as well as some leather jackets and one or two old army greatcoats.

One young friend told me that at least half the marchers do not identify as gay or lesbian; many of them are heterosexuals, simply the friends and relatives of lesbians and gay men. They cannot understand why something that is available to them should not also be available to their 'queer' friends.

Some things don't change: now, as then, the future is made by the young.

Many Australians, particularly the young, did not understand why Australia's then Prime Minister, Tony Abbott, was so adamant in rejecting a conscience vote for his Liberal Party colleagues on same-sex marriage in Federal Parliament. Indeed, his refusal even hurt his standing; in the opinion polls, seven out of ten voters (68 per cent) disagreed with his trenchant refusal to legalise same-sex marriage.[55] A more interesting statistic perhaps is that 76 per cent of Coalition voters wanted him to allow a conscience vote.

As trends around the world have shown, the push for same-sex marriage in Australia is merely history in the making. All liberal democracies have gone down that path, and there is no conceivable reason why Australia won't follow suit at some point. But like King Canute, who was so arrogant he thought he could hold back the tide, Abbott was determined to fight this issue until the bitter end. His sister, Christine Forster, is living in a same-sex relationship and has expressed a desire to marry her female partner. She believes that public support for gay marriage has galvanised so strongly that it will be accepted in Australia 'sooner rather than later'.[56] Malcolm Turnbull replaced Abbott as Prime Minister in a coup on 14 September 2015 but, despite his own personal support for same-sex marriage, internal tensions within his party make it unlikely he will change the Coalition's stance in the immediate future.

In a liberal democracy, all people should be treated equally. The same-sex marriage battle has moved from being about gay rights to being about civil rights – equality for all citizens. And while removing inequalities is commendable, for some people the fight for same-sex marriage flies in the face of what gay lib radicals fought for in the 1970s: a state-recognised civil partnership, free of the religious connotations of 'marriage'.[57]

While many political commentators have been taken aback at the speed with which same-sex marriage burst into political importance, it ought not to have been utterly unexpected. Social change, particularly as reflected in the young who are far more open to new ideas and attitudes, has been an obvious phenomenon in Australia since the late twentieth century. As far back as the early 1970s, the way gay culture was 'infiltrating' mainstream culture provoked comments,[58] and the process has subsequently escalated. Perhaps even then, Sydney was a leader in integration of gay cultures into the mainstream.

Many issues that once might have been seen as only relevant to Sydney's LGBTQI communities have now entered the mainstream. In inner-city politics, the gay vote plays an important role.

Late in 2012, the O'Farrell Coalition government passed what had become known as the 'Get Clover' Bill, a Bill to force any member of State Parliament also a member of a local council to quit one of those offices. Clover Moore – who was both Lord Mayor of Sydney, a position she had held since 2004, and the independent member for the seat of Sydney, a seat she had held for the previous 24 years – sensibly decided to stay as Lord Mayor. A further 27 affected MPs chose to bow out of council politics when the local government elections were held in September 2012.[59]

O'Farrell claimed that he was trying to remove an obvious conflict of interest – 'The Sydney CBD is too important to be held hostage to the political constituency of Clover Moore,' he proclaimed.[60] It was not an issue that had agitated previous state governments in relation to Sir Archibald Howie, Joseph Jackson, Ernie O'Dea and Pat Hills, all of whom were Lord

Mayor while sitting in the NSW Parliament. And it seems that the voters of the Sydney LGA didn't share O'Farrell's view either; when Moore opted to run again for Lord Mayor at the election, she again increased her vote, to 51.1 per cent.[61]

Moore named the enemies of her progressive policies in her Valedictory Speech to State Parliament, after winning the Lord Mayoralty:

> I am being forced out of Parliament because of legislation
> enacted by the O'Farrell Liberal government with the
> support of the Shooters and Fishers Party and Fred Nile.[62]

After Moore was forced to vacate, she endorsed Alex Greenwich as a candidate in the ensuing by-election for the seat of Sydney. Greenwich had previously been national convenor of Australian Marriage Equality and had organised over 40 000 submissions to the 2011 Senate inquiry into same-sex marriage. He had also run successful campaigns to get the Australian Bureau of Statistics to count same-sex couples in the 2011 national census. Against Greenwich, and hoping to capture some of the gay vote, the Liberal Party put up Shayne Mallard, an openly gay former City Councillor. In a battle of the 'gay cuties', Greenwich successfully won the seat with a 47.3 per cent primary and 63.7 per cent two-candidate preferred vote.

Greenwich's high profile in the gay community and Moore's endorsement undoubtedly helped his election.

After a recent electoral redistribution, Greenwich lost much of his Surry Hills heartland. He went into the 2015 state election campaign with a margin of just 0.3 per cent. He won 42 per cent of the primary vote and, after preferences, 58 per cent on a two-party preferred basis.[63] The vote clearly showed that Sydney residents are happy to have an openly gay independent as their voice in state Parliament.

The Council of the City of Sydney is aware of the power of the gay vote and pays close attention to issues concerning the LGBTQI communities, as it does for many other communities in the city. The same is true in many other inner-city councils. For example, the City Council has a dedicated LGBTQI officer, and supports many gay happenings. It recently decided to erect a giant rainbow flag in Sydney's Taylor Square, flying six storeys above Oxford Street, to honour the importance of the area's LGBTQI's history.

'LGBTQI concerns' also emerged in the 2015 state elections, in the newly created and closely contested seat of Newtown. On one side was an open lesbian, the ALP's Penny Sharpe, a member of the Legislative Council, and a strong advocate of LGBTQI issues. Against her was Jenny Leong of the Greens Party, able to capitalise on the Greens long advocacy of LGBTQI issues. It was a tightly fought campaign, reminiscent of the campaign that Clover Moore had fought back in 1995, when Susan Harbin, an open lesbian and former President of the Mardi Gras, was recruited by the ALP to run against her. In both cases, the sexuality of the candidate was seen as being of lesser importance than the candidate's – or their party's – history of support for LGBTQI causes. This might imply that several inner-city Sydney seats, long regarded as ALP strongholds, but with a high concentration of gays and lesbians, might be vulnerable to the Greens, whose policies have long set benchmarks for equality.

Events that might have once been considered part of the city's gay cultures – like Fair Day, Mardi Gras, theatrical performances like *Holding the Man*, and the Lesbian and Gay Choir performing at Sydney's Town Hall – have now moved to the mainstream. In an article headlined 'From hostile politicians

to homosexuality, we've come a long way', the then Justice
Michael Kirby pointed to the ready acceptance afforded to his
homosexuality and the role of his partner Johan van Vloten,
who attended all High Court functions with him:

> People are getting used to it ... hiding the truth because
> some people don't want to face it, is over.[64]

Have we come to the stage where we are being seen as 'just
like everybody else'? In early 2006, Tim Dick, writing in the
Sydney Morning Herald, observed that 'The gay world is looking straighter every day', but went on to ask, 'Or is the straight
world a bit more bent?'[65]

Convergence has its rewards, but also its costs. If we are now
'just like everybody else', what does that mean for a gay identity?

An interesting sideline from late in the twentieth century
was the emergence of a new social identity, 'queer', to define
someone who feels somehow outside of the societal norms in
regards to gender or sexuality, but avoids the specificity of 'gay',
'lesbian' or 'transgender'. Its main problem for the outside world
is its lack of specificity about anything.

If, as Kinsey argued decades ago, there are no such things
as homosexuals, only 'homosexual acts', what does that mean
about 'queer'? Kinsey rejected the idea of an identity defined
by a sexuality; but the gay movement proved that such an identity could have political benefits, particularly for an oppressed
minority. As Ignatius Jones, of Jimmy and the Boys, sang back
in 1979, 'I'm Not Like Everybody Else'. If that difference has
gone, if that minority is no longer oppressed, what is the role
of that identity? Does it still have a 'shelf life'? Is it like left-
handedness, once seen as the mark of the devil, a sinister signi-
fier, but now an irrelevant fact?[66]

The issue is worth considering. It has been in the forefront of the minds of some older activists, as historian Robert Reynolds discovered when researching his book *What Happened to Gay Life?*. Many older gay activists bewail what has become of 'gay life', despairing that young gays today are materialistic, apolitical and indifferent to issues like refugees and climate change.[67] But isn't this the dilemma of ageing itself? Our youthful dreams must come to terms with the realities of life. And convergence of lifestyles, acceptance of 'almost equality' – an equality some think that same-sex marriage might deliver – isn't it a good thing? Don't we want a true multicultural society, in which all minorities, cultural, religious and ethnic – be they gays, Muslims, Christians, Indigenous peoples, vegetarians, tree-huggers, nudists – live in tolerance and peace? If this is achieved for the LGBTQI communities, isn't that the sort of future they want for themselves?

Many of the old activists are unhappy that gay life has simply been assimilated into the dullness of the mainstream; living in suburbia, getting a mortgage, raising children, walking the dog, shopping at the local supermarket, going to school soccer matches. They wonder if they have participated in a 'lost revolution'. Have the gay communities given up their 'outsiderness' – a once-critical role that gave us perceptive insights into our society – for a sense of security? But were all homosexual or camp men blessed with this ability for critical insight? Over most of the twentieth century, many – probably most – lived a suburban life, with all that this entails. Today they have a sense of security which they never had before. They are getting on with the sort of life they wish to lead, even if it offends old activists, who had envisaged a different sort of future, where perhaps the gays could still be the radical outriders. One old radical, not interviewed for Reynolds' book, has altered his website from being a gay man to being 'a Buddhist homosexual', no longer acknowledging himself as 'gay'. For him, the word 'gay' has been depoliticised and lost its meaning.

Not all of Reynolds' interviewees regretted the changes that had created this brave new world. The younger ones accept the world as it is; indeed, for them 'history' is history. As Reynolds notes:

> they live their homosexuality lightly. This liberates their
> passion for the things that are important to them: love and
> marriage, architecture and design, study, family, and, of
> course, friends.[68]

Still, there is one fundamental difference for LGBTQI people not shared by ethnic, religious or cultural minorities. For these groups, the next generations are born, supported and acculturated from within the community. But this is not true for LGBTQI identities, which emerge in individuals, generally at the onset of puberty. So we oldies will always have a place, as role models, as supporters, as defenders for the next generations, because there will always be those who dispute our legitimacy. It is certainly not necessary to have a 'contiguous' community, and the geographic dispersal of gays is occurring for a range of commendable and necessary reasons, but there are costs if something like an Oxford Street disappears as both a symbolic and real safe haven for LGBTQI people. There will always be a need for those of a dissident sexuality to find a place where there are 'others like themselves', until they determine how they want to fit into society.

It's also worth asking if gay culture can survive integration. Will equality mean that our difference, and what it gave us, is no longer relevant? A decade ago, the American political commentator Andrew Sullivan argued, in the journal the *New Republic*, that 'slowly, but unmistakably, gay culture is ending':

> In fact, it is beginning to dawn on many that the very concept of gay culture may one day disappear altogether. By that, I do not mean that homosexual men and lesbians will not exist – or that they won't create a community of sorts and a culture that sets them in some ways apart. I mean simply that what encompasses gay culture itself will expand into such a diverse set of subcultures that 'gayness' alone will cease to tell you very much about any individual. The distinction between gay and straight culture will become so blurred, so fractured, and so intermingled that it may become more helpful not to examine them separately at all.[69]

Are we moving into a 'post-gay' world? If we continue on the present path of integration into the mainstream, what will 'gay' mean in the future? After all, who can complain if we have full legal equality? There will always be prejudice in any society, and we are not alone in facing it – or even dishing it out. If what we do in bed is the only difference, and this doesn't seem to concern our fellow citizens, what's the issue? Isn't this just what we have fought for?

But there is hope for our culture. If I can amend a quote by historian Robert Reynolds here, it might be appropriate:

> In imagining new ways of becoming oneself and belonging, 'post-gay' might address that crucial tension of late modern life – how to reconcile a creative invention of self with the art of being in common.[70]

So if we are now 'just like everybody else', will there be a 'gay sensibility' in the future? Will gay, like those old euphemisms that once described our difference from the mainstream and its values – being theatrical, artistic, musical – have any meaning anymore?

There has always been a role for the outsider in society. The English writer Colin Wilson long ago argued that the 'outsider-ness' of creative people, of thinkers, writers and artists – a sense of dislocation or of being at odds with society – gave them their ability to so perceptively critique that society in thought, word or image.[71] In Australia, Patrick White put it quite bluntly: 'My homosexuality ... gives me all the insights that make me a great writer.'[72] And could such a book as Dennis Altman's *Homosexual: Oppression and Liberation* have been written by anyone other than an outsider, as he was when he wrote it?

And as for me, today, in a funny way, my life almost seems to have come full circle. I live in an apartment on Oxford Street, a street that has been so much a part of my life, right from my childhood years. The apartment building is on the site of Winn's, that old department store where, as a kid, I used to have my favourite lunch.

And some nights, up in my little eyrie, I even think I get a whiff of those long-past meals, that distinctive smell of meat pies, mashed potato, peas, gravy and tomato sauce. But it is just some aroma wafting up from the myriad of trendy restaurants that now inhabit East Sydney. And even though I know this to be true, it still conjures up a remembrance of things past.

History has told us this one story; as for what future stories will be, only time will tell.

NOTES

1 'I Thought Men Like that Shot Themselves'

1 Media coverage improved for the next Mardi Gras (1984) when a similar sized parade and an estimated audience of approximately 40 000 received slightly more attention. But much of the attention focused on a dispute over its starting point in Sydney Square between the organisers of the parade and the joint 'owners' of Sydney Square – the Sydney City Council and the Anglican Church – rather than those taking part in the parade and what they represented.

2 *Age*, 21 February 1983 p. 5. Moomba is Melbourne's major annual festival.

3 Leo Schofield's column, *SMH*, 26 February 1983, was written and published a week after the event, and as such hardly constitutes 'news' coverage.

4 See Sections 79–8lb, *NSW Crimes Act 1900* (as amended).

5 The amendment to the *Anti-Discrimination Act* went through on 20 December 1982.

6 *Gay Guide*, Gay Counselling Service of NSW, 1984.

7 Phillip to Sydney, 28 February 1787, *Historical Records of New South Wales*, vol. 1, pt 2, pp. 52–53.

8 See R French, *Camping by a Billabong*, Blackwattle Press, 1993, pp. 9–11.

9 See P de Waal, *Unfit for Publication*, at <www.unfitforpublication.org.au>.

10 See G Wotherspoon, 'A Sodom in the South Pacific: male homosexuality in Sydney 1788–1809', in G Aplin (ed), *A Difficult Infant: Sydney Before Macquarie*, New South Wales University Press, 1988, pp. 91–101.

11 C White, *Short Lived Bushrangers*, Marchant and Co, 1909, p. 14.

12 Scott to D Harbord, 19 December 1878, in Letters of Scott and Rogan, Colonial Secretary's Special Bundles 4/825.2, 1889; State Records New South Wales.

13 See G Wotherspoon, 'Moonlight and ... Romance? The Death-Cell Letters of Captain Moonlight and Some of their Implications', *Journal of the Royal Australian Historical Society*, vol. 78, pts 3–4, December 1992, for full details.

14 *Scorpion*, vol. 1, no. 1, 24 April 1895, p. 1.

15 *Scorpion*, p. 2.

16 H Ellis, *Studies in the Psychology of Sex, Volume 2: Sexual Inversion*, FA Davies, 1924, pp. 185–186.

17 See C Faro, *Street Seen: A History of Oxford Street*, Melbourne University Press, 2000, p. 104.

18 *The Model Trader*, April 1909, as quoted in Faro, p. 103.

19 *Scorpion*, p. 1.

20 See French, pp. 59–61.

21 See French, p. 60.

22 See French, pp. 59–61 for the full story.

23 T Morgan, *Somerset Maugham*, Jonathan Cape, 1980, p. 149.

24 R Murray, *The Confident Years: Australia in the Twenties,* Allen Lane, 1978, p. 11.

25 RTE Latham, 'The Law and the Commonwealth', *Survey of British Commonwealth Affairs,* vol. 1, 1937. See V Windeyer, 'A Birthright and Inheritance: The Establishment of the Rule of Law in Australia', *Tasmanian University Law Review,* vol. 1, pt 5, 1962, pp. 635–669.

26 The arrangements whereby the highest Court of Appeal for Australian law was the British House of Lords were only ended in 1975, when Australia's own High Court took on that role.

27 See W Fogarty, '"Certain Habits": The Development of a Concept of the Male Homosexual in NSW Law, 1788–1900', in R Aldrich and G Wotherspoon, eds, *Gay Perspectives, Essays in Australian Gay Culture,* University of Sydney, 1992; and M Kirby, 'The sodomy offence: England's least lovely law export?', *Association of Commonwealth Criminal Lawyers Journal of Commonwealth Criminal Law,* Inaugural Issue, 2011.

28 BA Santamaria, first editorial, quoted in M Hogan, *The Sectarian Stand: Religion in Australian History,* Penguin, 1987, p. 119.

29 JR Robertson, '1930–39', in F Crowley (ed.), *A New History of Australia,* Heinemann, 1974, p. 445.

30 Quoted in K Dunstan, *Wowsers,* Cassell, 1968, p. 148.

31 Quoted in Dunstan, p. 147.

32 P Coleman, *Obscenity, Blasphemy, Sedition: Censorship in Australia,* Angus & Robertson, 1974, p. 19.

33 Coleman, p. 19.

34 As quoted in Dunstan, p. 101.

35 E Campion, *Australian Catholics,* Viking, 1987, p. 107.

36 H McQueen, *Social Sketches of Australia,* Penguin, 1978, p. 116.

37 *DT,* 17 January 1935.

38 Murray, p. 5.

39 K Reiger, *The Disenchantment of the Home: Modernizing the Australian Family 1880–1940,* Oxford University Press, 1985, p. 196.

40 Reiger, p. 190.

41 RV Storer, *Sex in Modern Life,* James Little & Son, 1933, p. 146.

42 S Freud, 'Letters to an American Mother', *Collected Papers,* Hogarth Press, 1956–57. See also the increasingly frank discussion of sexual matters in such literature as M Piddington, *Tell Them, or the Second Stage of Mothercraft,* Beatty, Richardson & Co, 1925; Storer, *A Survey of Sexual Life in Adolescence and Marriage,* Science Publishing Co., 1932; Storer, *Sex in Modern Life;* RV Storer, *The Book of Life,* Health and Physical Culture Publishing Co., 1933. See also, for example, the article 'Sex and Immortality', *Australian Worker,* 27 January 1926, p. 13.

43 P Robinson, *The Modernization of Sex,* Harper and Row, 1972, pp. 5–6.

44 A Comfort, *The Anxiety-makers,* Nelson, 1967, pp. 13–14.

45 B Nichols, *The Sweet and Twenties,* Weidenfeld and Nicolson, 1958, p. 104.

46 *ADB,* vol. 7, (1891–1939: A-Ch), p. 136.

47 *SMH,* 11 June 1931, p. 9.

48 *SS,* 11 June 1931, p. 1.

49 *SMH,* 12 June 1937, p. 11; *DT,* 12 June 1931, p. 8.

50 *DT*, 12 June 1931.
51 *SMH*, 15 June 1931, p. 10.
52 *Smith's Weekly*, 20 June 1931, p. 31.
53 *SMH*, 2 March 1931, p. 9.
54 French, p. 63.
55 See *SS*, 2 March 1937, p. 9; *ST*, 7 March 1937, p. 13.
56 *ST*, 21 March 1937, p. 14.
57 *SMH*, 9 April, 1937, p. 12; 10 April 1937, p. 10; *ST*, 4 April 1937, p. 19; 11 April 1937, pp. 10–21; *SS*, 8 April 1937, p. 11; 9 April 1937, p. 9; *DT*, 10 April 1937, p. 4.
58 *DT*, 9 April 1937, p. 4; 10 April 1937, p. 4.
59 D King, 'Transport Commissioner Railroaded', *Campaign*, no. 42, April, 1979, p. 11.
60 *SMH*, 10 April 1937, p. 10.
61 *SMH*, 10 April 1937, p. 10.
62 See, for example, *MT*, 12 March 1938, p. 1.
63 This material on vaudeville and homosexuality has been taken from V Chance, 'Chaotic, Eclectic and Grand: The world of Australian vaudeville 1918 to the Depression', BA (Hons) thesis, Department of History, University of Sydney, 1987, p. 61.
64 M Saltmarsh, *Highly Inflammable*, Angus & Robertson, 1936. This descriptive material is spread over pp. 101–104, and p. 45.
65 Having created, through his descriptions of Kuhn, the image of a cowardly effeminate, Saltmarsh then has his villain become besotted with a white Russian adventuress who, however, is besotted with the Scottish hero who, in turn, is in love with a nice English girl.
66 C Stead, *Seven Poor Men of Sydney*, Angus & Robertson, 1934, p. 165.
67 Stead, p. 165.
68 Stead, p. 145.
69 M Clark, *A History of Australia*, vol. VI, Melbourne University Press, 1987, p. 448.
70 K Mackenzie, *The Young Desire It*, Angus & Robertson, 1937, p. 79.
71 Mackenzie, p. 114.
72 Mackenzie, p. 123.
73 Mackenzie, p. 79.
74 See, for example, three German feature films: *Different from the Others*, directed and produced by Richard Oswald, 1919; *Michael*, directed by Carl Theodor Dreyer, Universum Film, 1924; and *Sex in Chains*, directed by Wilhelm (later William) Dieterle, Essem-Film GmbH and Vereinigte Star-Film GmbH, 1928.
75 V Russo, *The Celluloid Closet: Homosexuality in the Movies*, Harper & Row, 1987, Chapter 1.
76 *Smith's Weekly*, 19 November 1938, p. 13.
77 Russo, p. 34.
78 Russo, pp. 33–34.
79 Quoted in B Nichols, *The Sweet and Twenties*, Weidenfeld and Nicolson, 1958, p. 101; see also T Morgan, *Somerset Maugham*, Jonathan Cape, 1980, p. 549.

2   … But They Didn't

1   See G Simes, 'History of Naughty Words', *OutRage*, no. 57, February 1988, p. 18; Simes, 'What's in a Word? Queens', *OutRage*, no. 55, December 1987, p. 18; Simes, 'The Words that Have Defined Us', *OutRage*, no. 46, March 1987, pp. 34–5. See also J Rose, *At the Cross*, Deutsch, 1961, for some common colloquialisms.

2   K Tennant, *Evatt: Politics and Justice*, Angus & Robertson, 1979, p. 41.

3   J Lindsay, *The Roaring Twenties*, Penguin, 1982, p. 50.

4   *NSWPD*, 29 March 1955, p. 3317.

5   Lindsay, p. 32.

6   E Salter, *Helpmann: The Authorised Biography*, Angus & Robertson, 1978, p. 35.

7   Salter, p. 40.

8   Salter, p. 40.

9   G Wotherspoon, 'History', *Campaign*, no. 53, May 1980, p. 12.

10   Interviews with Ian D, September 1977; Brian B, March 1980; copies of these interviews are held in the Mitchell Library. See also R Connell, 'The Way it Was', *OWN*, no. 25, 20 October 1983.

11   B Warren, 'The Good Old Days of Kamp', *Campaign*, no. 53, May 1980, p. 13.

12   Interview with Ian D.

13   Interview with Madam Helen Pura, July 1979; letter from Madam Pura's solicitor to author, 1 July 1979; see also R Hartley, 'Our Hearts were Young and Gay', in G Wotherspoon (ed.), *Being Different: Nine Gay Men Remember*, Hale & Iremonger, 1986, p. 33.

14   C Stead, *Seven Poor Men of Sydney*, Angus & Robertson, 1934, p. 165.

15   Interview with Madam Helen Pura.

16   Lindsay, p. 94.

17   Ray Lindsay, quoted in Lindsay, p. 16.

18   D Deamer, 'The Golden Decade', *SMH*, 5 November 1983, p. 40.

19   Interviews with Ian D; John C, March 1980.

20   Interviews with Ian D; John C.

21   S Zweig, quoted in S Everett, *Lost Berlin*, Hamlyn, 1979, p. 68.

22   M Green, *Children of the Sun: A Narrative of 'Decadence' in England after 1918*, Basic Books, 1976, p. 170.

23   Warren, *Campaign*, p. 13. For details of some American bars, see L Forrester, 'D.C. Bars in the 1930s: From Poetry to Parody', *Washington Blade*, vol. 17, no. 36, 5 September 1986; G Spague, 'Chicago Past: A Rich Gay History', *Advocate*, 18 August 1983.

24   A Bissett, *Black Roots, White Flowers: A History of Jazz in Australia*, Golden Press, 1979, p. 31.

25   See J Boswell, *Christianity, Social Tolerance and Homosexuality*, University of Chicago Press, 1980, pp. 188–193, 218–228.

26   D Hilliard, 'UnEnglish and Unmanly: Anglo-Catholicism and Homosexuality', *Victorian Studies*, Winter, 1982.

27   Interviews with Tommy G, May 1988; John C and Brian B, and Ian D.

28   Lindsay, p. 179.

29   See for example, *MT*, 27 May 1922, where the 'certain practices' are alluded to.

More details are in *MT*, 3 June 1922, 16 June 1922 and 24 August 1929. For a full discussion see G Tillet, *The Elder Brother: A Biography of Charles Webster Leadbeater*, Routledge & Kegan Paul, 1982, Chapters 9 and 17.

30 Interviews with Hal H, May 1986; John C; Peter S, August 1980; see also Hartley, p. 34.

31 The Lugar Brae Musical Society in Waverley was one of the more notorious of these.

32 Green, p. 17.

33 Barry Pearce, *Elioth Gruner 1882–1939,* Art Gallery of NSW, 1983, p. 8.

34 Lindsay, p. 10.

35 Pearce, p. 14.

36 Evidence that the Turkish Baths in Liverpool Street were an important homosexual meeting place comes from several sources, mainly taped interview: interviews with John C and Brian B. But the baths are also referred to in H Ellis's *Studies in the Psychology of Sex Volume 1,* Random House, 1936. See Case XXXII in *Sexual Inversion in Men* (pp. 185–186) which gives details of one man's experiences at the baths in Sydney.

37 See for example, 'John's Story' in Wotherspoon (ed.), *Being Different*, p. 46. Also interview with Tommy G, May 1988.

38 Interview with John C, May 1985.

39 Interviews with John C; Brian B.

40 R Connell, 'The Way it Was', *OWN*, No. 75, 20 October, 1983, p. 19.

41 Connell, p. 19.

42 See L Humphreys, *Tea Room Trade: Impersonal Sex in Public Places*, Aldine Press, 1970. Humphreys, using standard and well-defined sociological techniques, made the then amazing discovery that a majority of the practitioners of fast, anonymous public toilet sex were in fact heterosexually married men.

43 Interview with John C.

44 S Payne, *The Beat*, Gay Men's Press, 1985, p. 15.

45 See for example, *MT*, 26 January 1924, 4 October 1924, 18 October 1924, 14 April 1928, 14 September 1929. The doctor was HM Moran, whose *Viewless Winds: Being the Recollections and Digressions of an Australian Surgeon*, Peter Davies, 1939, has details on p. 132. See also V Kelly, *The Bogeymen,* Angus & Robertson, 1956, particularly Chapter 7, for details on the use of pimps and undercover men.

46 But see for example *MT*, 12 June 1920, for what was obviously a case of a gang of youths setting upon someone they thought was homosexual and extracting an 'appropriate' vengeance.

47 J Rose, *At the Cross*, Deutsch, 1961, p. 5.

48 Rose, p. 15.

49 Lindsay, p. 30. Lindsay has also mentioned the obviousness of male homosexuals in these neighbourhoods.

50 Lindsay, p. 51.

51 Lindsay, p. 53.

52 Rose, p. 5.

53 Rose, p. 10.

54 Lindsay, p. 54.
55 Lindsay, p. 44.
56 Rose, p. 17.
57 Rose, p. 182.
58 Rose, p. 183.
59 Rose, p. 185.
60 Rose, pp. 16–17.
61 Rose, pp. 17–18.
62 Rose, p. 18.
63 As quoted in P Kirkpatrick, *The Sea Coast of Bohemia: Literary Life in Sydney's Roaring Twenties*, University of Queensland Press, 1992, p. 271.
64 For a description of these balls see D Beck, 'Scandalous nights: Sydney's artists' balls', Dictionary of Sydney, 2013, viewed October 2015, <dictionaryofsydney.org/entry/scandalous_nights_-_sydneys_artists_balls>.
65 D Deamer, *The Queen of Bohemia: The Autobiography of Dulcie Deamer*, University of Queensland Press, 1998, p. 109.
66 Deamer, p. 110.
67 Lindsay, pp. 158–163, gives a long description of an Artists' Ball in the Sydney Town Hall. See also *NSWPD*, 1924, vol. XCVI, pp. 1638ff; *Evening News*, 30 August 1924; *Sunday Times*, 1 September 1924.
68 Quoted in Everett, p. 68.
69 SL Elliott, *Eden's Lost*, Michael Joseph, 1970, p. 80.
70 Elliott, p. 16.
71 Elliott, p. 52.
72 Elliott, p. 78.
73 Interviews with Nick M, April 1980; John C; Brian B.

3   An End to Unknowing
1 A Marwick, *War and Social Changes in the Twentieth Century*, Macmillan, 1974, p. 124.
2 P Fussell, *The Great War and Modern Memory*, Oxford University Press, 1975, p. 170.
3 Quoted in D Walker, 'The Getting of Manhood', in P Spearritt and D Walker (eds), *Australian Popular Culture*, Allen & Unwin, 1979, p. 137.
4 See, for example, M Hogan, *The Sectarian Strand*, Penguin, 1987, Chapter 9; see also J Costello, *Love, Sex and War 1939–1945*, Pan, 1985, Chapter 17.
5 See, for example, P Luck, *This Fabulous Century*, Circus Books, 1980, pp. 81–82; Walker, 'The Getting of Manhood', p. 137; JH Moore, *Oversexed, Over-Paid and Over Here: Americans in Australia 1941–1945*, University of Queensland Press, 1981; for some newspaper responses, see G Blaikie, *Remember Smith's Weekly*, Rigby, 1967, p. 154.
6 Fussell, p. 170.
7 Robert Graves, quoted in Fussell, p. 179.
8 Fussell, p. 172; R Aldrich, *Colonialism and Homosexuality*, Routledge, 2003, pp. 187–189. For a more general discussion of homoeroticism among 'empire adventurers' – including military figures – see R Hyam, *Britain's Imperial Century*

1815–1914: A Study of Empire and Expansion, Batsford, 1976, Chapter 5, 'The Dynamics of Empire and Expansion'; also R Hyam, 'Empire and Sexual Opportunity', *Journal of Imperial and Commonwealth History*, vol. XIV, no. 2, January 1986.

9   J Ackerley, *My Father and Myself*, Penguin, 1971, p. 100.

10 Noel Greig, quoted in *SMH*, 4 February 1987. See also H Moran, *In My Fashion*, Dymocks, 1946, pp. 116, 123–132, for details of homosexuality in the armed forces.

11 AG Butler, *The Australian Army Medical Services in the War of 1914–1918*, Australian War Memorial, 1943, p. 137. The writer, in an illuminating footnote (fn 15, p. 137) does note that 'As to this problem in other armies, the reader may be referred to the *Sexual History of the War* edited by Magnus Hirschfeld. Though it contains some gross errors, the authors of this unpleasant book seem to know what they are talking about.' Why Australia should be so different from other societies appears not to have occurred to this writer.

12 *NT*, 30 January–5 February 1983, p. 8; see also *Campaign 77*, May 1982, for another report of the same statement. Several years later, Ruxton was still asserting that 'I never saw any in my battalion, and if there had been any they would have been sorted out in 20 minutes', *SMH*, 12 January 1987.

13 Walker, 'The Getting of Manhood', p. 126.

14 J Barrett, *We Were There: Australian Soldiers of World War II*, Viking, 1987, particularly Chapter 12.

15 Walker, 'The Getting of Manhood', p. 126.

16 *MT*, 14 June 1941, p. 1.

17 A Foster, 'Getting Physical', *OutRage*, no. 65, October 1988, p. 15.

18 Foster, *OutRage*, p. 18.

19 Foster, *OutRage*, p. 17. Foster notes another paradox in the history of the repression of homosexuality: that physique photography reached its zenith in the 1950s, during the great witch-hunts of the McCarthy era.

20 See, for example, *MT*, 1 November 1941, 10 January 1942, 27 June 1942, 20 February 1943, 17 April 1943, 4 December 1943, 15 January 1944, 10 February 1945, 31 March 1945.

21 *Sunday Telegraph*, 9 August 1942. See R French, *Camping By a Billabong*, Blackwattle Press, 1993, pp. 85–88 for more details.

22 French, p. 86.

23 Barrett, pp. 165, 367. See also J Costello, *Love, Sex and War*, Pan, 1987, pp. 156–173; S Terkel, *The Good War: An Oral History of World War II*, Pantheon, 1984, pp. 178–185; interview with Jack A, August 1979. Jack had experience of homosexual love affairs in Changi Prison camp. Eventually even 'RSL leaders in NSW ... all said it was obvious that homosexuals would have been in the armed forces ...', *Campaign 77*, May 1982.

24 J O'Donnell, 'John's Story', in G Wotherspoon (ed.), *Being Different: Nine Gay Men Remember*, Hale & Iremonger, 1986, p. 49.

25 Quoted in D Altman, 'Gore Vidal in Australia', in *Coming Out in the Seventies*, Wild & Woolley, 1979, p. 198.

26 R Hartley, 'Our Hearts Were Young and Gay', in Wotherspoon (ed.), *Being*

Different, pp. 36–7.

27 L Glassop, *We Were the Rats*, Angus & Robertson, 1945, p. 71.

28 Glassop, *We Were the Rats*, p. 79.

29 L Glassop, *The Rats in New Guinea*, Horwitz, 1963, p. 21.

30 Glassop, *The Rats in New Guinea*, p. 21.

31 Barrett, p. 367.

32 Barrett, p. 165.

33 Barrett, p. 367

34 Several of the 'femmes' mentioned in Michael Pate's *An Entertaining War*,
    Dreamweaver Books, 1986, were habitués of drag parties in Sydney or
    Melbourne before and during – and after – the war: interview with Clive M,
    January 1988. See also R Hartley, 'Our Hearts were Young and Gay', in
    Wotherspoon (ed.), *Being Different*, p. 36, and interviews with John C, March
    1980; Brian B, March 1980, for some details on drag queens in the war.

35 Pate, p. 72.

36 Walker, 'The Getting of Manhood', p. 133.

37 K Tennant, *Tell Morning This*, Pacific Books, 1967, p. 18.

38 Tennant, p. 19.

39 See, for example, A Berube, 'Coming Out Under Fire', *Mother Jones*, February–
    March 1983, pp. 13–29, 45; A Berube, 'The History of the Gay Bathhouses',
    Coming Up, December 1984, p. 16; G Sprague, 'Chicago Past: A Rich Gay
    History', *Advocate*, 18 August 1983.

40 B Warren, 'The Good Old Days of Kamp', unpublished manuscript, pt II.

41 Warren, unpublished manuscript, pt II.

42 Warren, unpublished manuscript, pt II.

43 See Berube, *Coming Up*, p. 16.

44 Interview with Walter, March 1980.

45 Interviews with Jack A; Walter.

46 Interviews with Walter; Nick M, April 1980.

47 Warren, unpublished manuscript, pt II.

48 *MT*, 25 September 1943, p. 14.

49 *MT*, 25 September 1943, p. 14.

50 *MT*, 2 January 1943, p. 1.

51 Warren, unpublished manuscript, pt II; G Simes, 'History of Naughty Words',
    OutRage, no. 57, February 1988, p. 19.

52 *SMH*, 12 January 1987.

53 Interview with Clive M, January 1988.

54 J Rose, *At the Cross*, Deutsch, 1961, has these colloquialisms sprinkled through it.

55 Interviews with John C and Brian B.

56 *MT*, 2 January 1943.

57 Interviews with John C and Brian B.

58 All the previous descriptions were from Rose, pp. 98, 102–103.

59 *MT*, 20 February 1943, p. 8.

60 *MT*, 13 March 1943, p. 17.

61 WA Sinclair, *The Process of Economic Development in Australia*, Cheshire,
    Melbourne, 1976, p. 135

62 See, for example, C Allport, 'The Princess in the Castle: Women and the
    New Order Housing', and S Alomes, 'The 1930s Background to Postwar
    Reconstruction Ideas'; papers given at the Postwar Reconstruction Conference,
    Canberra, 3 September 1981. Indeed it was specifically argued at the time that
    the 'family unit' was to be the basis for all wage decisions, and that 'no man
    without wife or children should be regarded as notionally equal in value to a
    man with wife and children', *Report of the National Health and Medical Research
    Council*, Canberra, 1944, p. 12.

63 *Australian Women's Weekly*, 5 February 1944, p. 10.

64 For a fuller treatment of aspects of this in Australia see CD Faro, 'Social
    Constructions of Women and Work: Australia, 1939 to 1954', Economic History
    IV Honours Thesis, 1983, Department of Economic History, University of
    Sydney. See also J Weeks, *Sexuality and Its Discontents*, Routledge & Kegan Paul,
    1985, pp. 106–107.

65 They were indeed expressed all around the world. See, for example, J Costello,
    Love, Sex and War, Pan, 1987, pp. 356–359; M Hogan, *The Sectarian Stand:
    Religion in Australian History*, Penguin, 1987, Chapter 9.

66 *SMH*, 4 January 1946, p. 8. This was the continuation of a long-running
    campaign that had been initiated during the war. See *SMH*, 3 April 1943, p. 1

67 Hogan, Chapter 9.

68 Report of the Police Department of NSW, 1945, p. 3.

69 Walker, 'The Getting of Manhood', p. 126.

70 'Sexual Behaviour in the Human Male', *Medical Journal of Australia*, 1 October
    1948, p. 469.

71 'Sexual behaviour', *Medical Journal of Australia*, p. 469.

72 'Sexual behaviour', *Medical Journal of Australia*, p. 469 (my emphasis).

73 'Sexual behaviour', *Medical Journal of Australia*, p. 469.

74 'Sexual behaviour', *Medical Journal of Australia*, p. 469.

75 For a scathing review of *Angry Penguins* and Max Harris's obsession with Freud,
    see KS Pritchard, 'Hoax Renders Service to Literature', *Communist Review*,
    March 1945, pp. 456–457.

76 See, for example, *Adelaide Truth*, 31 January 1948. The same story was syndicated
    in both the *MT* and *ST*.

77 Report of the Police Department of NSW, p. 3.

78 Report of the Police Department of NSW, p. 4.

79 See, for example, 'Police war on sex perverts', *DT*, 15 December 1948, p. 10;
    'Police campaign to rid city of sex perverts', *SMH*, 5 January 1949, p. 1; Editorial
    on 'Prevention of Sex Crimes', *SMH*, 23 March 1949, p. 1 ; 'Sex perversion ...
    the greatest social menace in Australia', *SS*, 1 August 1951, p. 11; 'Report from
    Chief Superintendent of CIB on "steep increase in sexual perversion among
    males in Sydney"', *SMH*, 20 October 1951, p. 4.

80 See, for example, *DM*, 31 May 1948, p. 3; *SS*, 8 June 1948, p. 1; *ST*, 20 June
    1948, p. 7; *SMH*, 23 August 1948; *SS*, 18 July 1949, p. 1; *SMH*, 15 November
    1949, p. 1; *SMH*, 2 March 1950, p. 6.

81 *MT*, 13 April 1946, p. 3. This sentence was given because it involved sex with a
    minor. It was not, however, carried out.

82 See, for example, *DT*, 17 May 1948, p. 5; *DM*, 31 May 1948, p. 3;
    SMH, 23 August 1948; *SS*, 18 July 1949, p. 1; *SS*, 20 November 1949, p. 6;
    SMH, 19 December 1949, p. 3.
83 *ST*, 20 June 1948, p. 7.
84 *ST*, 11 December 1949, p. 14.
85 For other major reports, see *ST*, 20 November 1949, p. 3, and 27 November
    1949, p. 52.
86 *ST*, 11 December 1949, p. 14.
87 Geoffrey Dutton, *The Innovators: The Sydney Alternatives in the Rise of Modern
    Art, Literature and Ideas*, Macmillan, 1986, p. 80.
88 Dutton, p. 79.
89 As quoted in Dutton, p. 101.

4 The Greatest Menace Facing Australia
1 See, for example, F Crowley (ed.), *A New History of Australia*, Heinemann, 1974,
   pp. 493–502; and A Curthoys and J Merritt, *Australia's First Cold War, Volume 1:
   Society, Communism and Culture*, Allen & Unwin, 1984. However, as Curthoys
   and Merritt note, (pxiii), 'the resolutions were not always as complete as they
   appear …', indeed, 'the direction of social and economic change and the political
   struggles themselves allowed contrary developments'. This, as will be seen, was
   certainly true of state attempts to stamp out homosexuality.
2 P Spearritt, *Sydney Since the Twenties*, Hale & Iremonger, Sydney, 1978, p. 168.
3 R Boyd, *The Australian Ugliness*, Cheshire, 1960, pp. 80–1.
4 G Godfrey, *SS*, 18 January 1951.
5 E Linklater, *A Year of Space*, London, 1953, p. 187.
6 Quoted in M Hogan, *The Sectarian Stand*, Penguin, 1987, pp. 1–2.
7 See, for example, 'Police war on sex perverts', *DT*, 15 December 1948, p. 10;
   'Police campaign to rid city of sex perverts', *SMH*, 5 January 1949, p. 1; Editorial
   on 'Prevention of Sex Crimes', *SMH*, 23 March 1949, p. 1; Request to establish
   a sex offenders bureau reported in *Sunday Telegraph*, 15 January 1950, p. 12;
   Magistrate's complaints about sexual offenders from *SMH*, 2 March 1950,
   p. 6; 'Sex perversion … the greatest social menace in Australia', *SS*, 1 August
   1951, p. 11; 'Report from Chief Superintendent of CIB on "steep increase
   in sexual perversion among males in Sydney"', *SMH*, 20 October 1951, p. 4.;
   'Alarming rise in Male Sex Crimes', *SMH*, 19 April 1952, p. 5; 'Dramatic rise in
   homosexuality in Australia', *DM*, 9 November 1954, p. 3.
8 R French, *Camping By a Billabong*, Blackwattle Press, 1993, p. 90.
9 See French, pp. 89–93.
10 A Debenham, *All manner of people*, Edwards and Shaw, 1967, p. 52.
11 *SMH*, 10 September 1949, p. 5.
12 See, for example, *Sunday Telegraph*, 15 January 1950, p. 12; *SS*, 1 August 1951,
    p. 11; *DM*, 9 November 1954, p. 3.
13 *SMH*, 11 June 1958, p. 5.
14 This section had been amended in 1924 (no. 10 of 1924) to make the period a
    statutory 14 years. Prior to 1924, the period of servitude had been 'for life or any
    term not less than five years'.

15 The added wording reflected that some problems could arise from the terminology of 'assault' if both parties were consenting. See 'Where have all the Fairies Gone', *Green Park Observer*, May 1983, p. 30.

16 See HM Hyde, *The Love That Dared Not Speak Its Name*, Little Brown, 1970, p. 113.

17 Hyde, p. 114.

18 See in particular F Cain, *The Origins of Political Surveillance in Australia*, Angus & Robertson, 1983, especially Chapters 7 and 8.

19 N Mitford, *The Blessing*, Penguin, 1951, pp. 110–111.

20 Hyde, p. 114.

21 Hyde, p. 114; see also J Weeks, *Sex, Politics and Society*, Longmans, 1982, Chapter 12.

22 *NSWPD*, 23 March 1955, p. 3223.

23 This new clause was in fact almost identical with the so-called Labouchere clause introduced in England in 1885.

24 *NSWPD*, 23 November 1954, p. 1874.

25 See *SMH*, 17 November 1954, p. 1 editorial; and also the views canvassed in Parliamentary Debates: *NSWPD*, 23 March 1955, pp. 3248–3250, 3252.

26 *NSWPD*, 23 March 1955, p. 3250. This view, by R Askin, was supported by lawyers K McCaw and V Treatt.

27 *NSWPD*, 23 March 1955, p. 3252. And indeed, the publicity had been critical in a case earlier that decade. The newspaper reports of the Douglas Annand case, which is discussed later in this chapter, had brought forth a series of independent witnesses whose evidence conflicted with that of the police on what had happened outside the toilet where Annand was arrested, and then later on what had happened outside the police station where he was charged. It was perhaps this independent evidence that helped the appeals judge determine that the police were liars, and uphold Annand's appeal.

28 *NSWPD*, 24 March 1955, p. 3293.

29 BD Burton, *Teach Them No More*, Australasian Book Society, 1967, pp. 118–119.

30 *SMH*, 9 March 1957, p. 5.

31 *NSWPD*, 24 March 1955, p. 3293.

32 *NSWPD*, 24 March 1955, p. 3295.

33 The psychiatrist was the Professor of Psychiatry at Sydney University, WH Trethowan; the endocrinologist was Dr DWJ Hensley, Senior Lecturer in Bio-Chemistry at Sydney University; there were two ministers of religion (who had other useful attributes) – the Reverend RC Weir, an Anglican chaplain who was also a member of the Civil Rehabilitation Committee, and Father John Roche, a Catholic priest who was a former RAN chaplain; the social sciences were represented not by an educationist but by a senior field officer in the Prisons Department, Mr MFD Hayes, also secretary of the Post-Graduate Committee of Social Work. The final committee member was the Deputy Controller of Prisons, JA Morony. See *SMH*, 1 July 1958, p. 4.

34 See Registrar's File 16279, Norman Haire Bequest, Faculty of Medicine, University of Sydney.

35 Report to Registrar, University of Sydney: File 16279, Norman Haire Bequest,

Faculty of Medicine, University of Sydney.

36 It has been reported that the two academics on the committee became convinced that homosexuality was not necessarily a sickness, nor that it should be 'treated'. Thus the committee split with the academics questioning the whole purpose of the exercise. See L Watson, 'The Anti-Gay Laws, Irrationality and Public Policy Making', *Seminar on Victimless Crime*, NSW Department of Attorney General and Justice, 1977, p. 107.

37 See G Wotherspoon, 'The flight of the "exiles of the spirit": male homosexual artists and the onset of the Cold War', in S Fitzgerald and G Wotherspoon (eds), *Minorities: Cultural Diversity in Sydney*, State Library of NSW Press, 1995, pp. 124–139.

38 B Adams, *Portrait of an Artist: A Biography of William Dobell*, Hutchinson, 1983, pp. 7, 77, 88.

39 Editorial, *SMH*, 17 November 1954, p. 1.

40 *NSWPD*, 23 March 1954, p. 1873.

41 *SMH*, 22 March 1957, p. 4. The original story had just appeared in the *Police Association Monthly News*.

42 For example, in early 1950, cases came to light of a policeman being solicited in February in a lavatory in the middle of Centennial Park (*SMH*, 2 March 1950, p. 6); in March of a doctor being charged with soliciting a policeman in Waverley Park (*SMH*, 16 March 1950, p. 6); and in June of a man charged with soliciting a policeman in Green Park in Darlinghurst (*SS*, 18 June 1950, p. 11; *DM*, 18 March 1950, p. 1, and 25 March 1950, p. 3). These were all well-known Sydney 'beats' of the time.

43 *SMH*, 31 July 1953, p. 5.

44 *SMH*, 29 August 1957, p. 9.

45 *SMH*, 28 February 1958, p. 7.

46 Interview with Jack A, August 1979; interview with Ian D, September 1977.

47 See, for example, editorial in *SMH*, 26 August 1954, p. 1; *SMH*, 14 June 1958, p. 1 (letter); *SMH*, 18 June 1958, p. 1 (letters). For further discussion of this, see Watson, p. 106.

48 R Hauser, *The Homosexual Society*, The Bodley Head, 1962, p. 48

49 A detailed study of this aspect appears in Watson.

50 *SMH*, 23 April 1952, p. 1.

51 *SMH*, 24 June 1954, p. 1.

52 *SMH*, 23 June 1954, p. 1.

53 *SMH*, 12 March 1953, p. 1.

54 *SMH*, 16 March 1953, p. 1.

55 *SMH*, 22 April 1952, p. 1.

56 *SMH*, 28 August 1953, p. 1.

57 *SMH*, 31 August 1953, p. 3.

58 *SMH*, 27 September 1953, p. 4.

59 R Auchmuty, 'The Truth about Sex', in P Spearritt and D Walker (eds), *Australian Popular Culture*, Allen & Unwin, 1979, p. 179.

60 Auchmuty, p. 180.

61 Auchmuty, p. 182.

62 Auchmuty, p. 184.
63 Auchmuty, p. 184.
64 Letter to Lex Watson from Penguin Books Australia, 22 June 1982.
65 DJ West, *Homosexuality*, Penguin, 1960, p. 9.
66 *Time*, 17 April 1950, p. 17.
67 *Time*, 16 November 1953, p. 16.
68 See, for example, *Time*, 28 December 1953, p. 40; 26 December 1955, p. 17; 16 December 1957, pp. 12ff; 16 June 1958, p. 44.
69 *Life*, 26 June 1964, pp. 66–80; *Time*, 21 January 1966, pp. 52–53.
70 See, for example, *Time*, 11 December 1964, p. 55; 25 December 1964, p 4; 12 November 1965, pp. 51–52; 21 January 1966, pp. 52–53; 28 January 1966, pp. 3–4; 26 August 1966, p. 16; 30 December 1966, p. 15; 14 July 1967, p. 18; 8 August 1969. Many of these issues were taken up in other magazines.
71 *Time*, 24 October 1969, p. 44. This article was based on the findings of a US government-funded task force, chaired by Dr Evelyn Hooker, who prepared the report for the National Institute of Mental Health.
72 *Time*, 31 October 1969, p. 38.
73 G Hawkins, 'Homosexuality: Australia's "Greatest Menace"?', *Bulletin*, 8 May 1965, p. 12.
74 B Buckley, 'The Sexual Revolution', *Bulletin*, 14 May 1966, p. 10.
75 R Taylor, 'Night Out with "The Boys"', *Pol*, no. 3, 1969, pp. 93–95; D Altman, 'Boys in the Band', *Pol*, no. 7, 1969, pp. 85–86.
76 *Cosmopolitan*, December 1969, pp. 126–129.
77 *Cosmopolitan*, December 1969, p. 127.
78 G Vidal, *The City and the Pillar*, John Lehmann, 1948; J Baldwin, *Another Country*, Michael Joseph, 1962.
79 M Renault, *The Charioteer*, Longmans Green, 1953; R Garland, *The Heart in Exile*, Allen & Unwin, 1953; G Freeman, *The Leather Boys*, A Blond, 1961. Blond made this statement in the Introduction to the 1985 Gay Men's Press reprint of *The Leather Boys*.
80 R Heinlein, *Stranger in a Strange Land*, New English Library, 1969 edition, p. 325.
81 C MacInnes, *June in Her Spring*, MacGibbon & Kee, 1952; S Lauder, *Winger's Landfall*, Eyre & Spottiswoode, 1962; N Jackson, *No End to the Way*, Barrie & Rockliff, 1965.
82 D Maynard, 'Athlete', *Bulletin*, 26 August 1959, p. 57; 'conversations', *Westerley*, no. 3, 1959, pp. 11–14.
83 G Dutton, *The Innovators: the Sydney alternatives in the rise of modern art, literature and ideas*, Macmillan, 1986, pp. 79–80.
84 Interview with Jack A; interview with Clive M, January 1988.
85 Interviews with Jack A; Clive M.
86 Interviews with Jack A; Clive M; *ST*, 11 December 1949 has one such exposé.
87 Interviews with Jack A; Clive M.
88 Interviews with Jack A; Clive M.
89 Interview with Kandy, June 1981; interview with John C and Brian B, March 1980.

90   Interviews with Kandy; Jack A.
91   Interview with Nick M, April 1980.
92   Interviews with Nick M; Ian D.
93   '21 Years of Pollynesians', *Campaign*, no. 116, August 1985, p. 1.
94   '21 Years of Pollynesians', p. 1
95   '21 Years of Pollynesians', p. 1. See also 'Doing it with Style: The Knights of the Chameleons', *Star Observer*, 5 September 1986, p. 13.
96   Interviews with Nick M; Jack A. See also G Wotherspoon, 'No Hard Feelings Mate: Violence in the Suburbs', *Bulletin*, 5 December 1970, p. 15, for a description of a 'poofter-bashing' after one of these dances.
97   See below, Chapter 5.
98   M Foucault, *A History of Sexuality, vol. 1, An Introduction*, Vintage Books, 1980, p. 43.

5   The Personal Becomes the Political
1   WJ Hudson, '1951–72', in F Crowley (ed.), *A New History of Australia*, Heinemann, 1974, p. 546.
2   A Milner, 'Radical Intellectuals: An Unacknowledged Legislature?', in V Burgmann and J Lee (eds), *Constructing a Culture*, McPhee Gribble/Penguin, 1988.
3   Milner, p. 174.
4   Milner, pp. 175–177.
5   D Altman, 'The Counter-Culture: Nostalgia or Prophesy?' in AF Davies, S Encel and MJ Berry (eds), *Australian Society: A Sociological Introduction*, 3rd ed, Longmans Cheshire, 1977, p. 452.
6   C McGregor, 'Mass Culture, Pop Art, and the Common Man', *People, Politics and Pop: Australians in the Sixties*, Ure Smith, 1968, p. 59.
7   F Moorhouse, 'Becker and the Boys from the Band', *The Coca Cola Kid*, Angus & Robertson, 1982, p. 101
8   Hudson, p. 548.
9   H Moll, *The Faith of Australians*, Allen & Unwin, 1985, pp. 56–58; see also M Hogan, *The Sectarian Strand: Religions in Australian History*, Penguin, 1987, p. 186, where he notes that the norm has been 'a nominal adherence to one of the main denominations and a studied indifference to all but the most private aspects of religion'.
10   Hogan, p. 193.
11   See G Wotherspoon, 'The flight of the "exiles of the spirit": male homosexual artists and the onset of the Cold War', in S Fitzgerald and G Wotherspoon (eds), *Minorities: cultural diversity in Sydney*, State Library of NSW Press, 1995, pp. 124–139.
12   Hudson, p. 549.
13   R Boyd, *The Australian Ugliness*, Penguin, 1960, p. 12.
14   See P Spearritt, *Sydney Since the Twenties*, Hale & Iremonger, 1978, Chapters 5 and 6.
15   H Stretton, *Ideas for Australian Cities*, Griffin Press, 1970, p. 165.
16   Hudson, p. 551.

17 D Horne, *The Story of the Australian People*, Readers Digest, 1985, p. 165.

18 One index of personal consumption per capita in real terms indicates that, from a base of 100 in 1948/49, there was a 3 per cent increase by 1949/50, a 14 per cent increase by 1959/60, and a 36 per cent increase by 1968/69. See WA Sinclair, *The Process of Economic Development in Australia*, Cheshire, 1976, p. 148.

19 Sinclair, p. 124.

20 Sinclair, p. 124.

21 Sinclair, p. 124.

22 Horne, p. 163.

23 S Lees and J Senyard, *The 1950s*, Hyland House, 1987, Chapter 6.

24 *Year Book of Australia*, various years.

25 Spearritt, p. 170; see also S Lees and J Senyard, p. 66; Horne, p. 158.

26 *NSWYB*, various years.

27 Sinclair, p. 149.

28 *DT*, 17 January 1935.

29 M Bail, *Holden's Performance*, Penguin, 1987, p. 120.

30 See, for example, R Hartley, 'Our Hearts Were Young and Gay', in G Wotherspoon (ed.), *Being Different*, Hale & Iremonger, 1986, p. 34.

31 See Spearitt, pp. 131–135 for details of the population shift to Sydney's outer suburbs between 1945 and the early 1970s. See A Dixson, 'Adrian finds his Avalon' in G Wotherspoon, *Being Different*, p. 80, for details of travelling to suburban parties by car.

32 Horne, p. 157.

33 D Altman, 'The Personal is the Political: Social Movements and Cultural Change', in B Head and J Walter (eds), *Intellectual Movements and Australian Society*, Oxford University Press, 1988, p. 309.

34 Spearritt, p. 115.

35 *OZ*, March 1964, p. 6.

36 See, for example, 'Brownstoning', *Christopher Street*, August 1976, pp. 3–5; A Young, 'Gentrification', *Fag Rag*, no. 26, 1979; K Butler, 'Up and Coming Amid the Down and Outs', *Mother Jones*, September–October 1980; T Willenbecher, 'Gentrification: Home Sweet Homophobia', *Advocate*, 7 August 1980.

37 Interview with Clive M, January 1988.

38 Interview with Bill H, July 1981. Legend has it that the proprietor was actually an ex-carpenter from Madam Pavlova's company, who had stayed on in Sydney.

39 Dixson, p. 78.

40 Interview with Jack A, August 1979.

41 N Jackson, *No End to the Way*, Barrie & Rockliff, 1965, p. 12.

42 Jackson, p. 13.

43 L Watson, 'Development of a Gay Sub-culture and Movement in Australia', unpublished manuscript, p. 5.

44 Interview with George D, June 1980; R Connell, 'Up the Cross', *OWN*, no. 76, 27 October 1983.

45 Connell, 'Up the Cross', p. 12.

46 Interview with Kandy, June 1981.

47 See, for example, 'A Short Round of the Camps', *OZ*, March 1964, p. 7; interview with Kandy.
48 Interview with Rose Jackson, *Sydney Star*, vol. 5, no. 8, 21 October 1983, p. 19; interview with Kandy.
49 Interview with Kandy.
50 Interview with Kandy.
51 'A Short Round of the Camps', *OZ*, March 1964, p. 7.
52 K Brisbane, 'The Purple Onion', *Pol*, no. 7, 1969, p. 85.
53 Brisbane, *Pol*, p. 85. By the 1970s, drag had become quite respectable. See F Moorhouse, 'Getting up in Drag', *Bulletin*, 30 October 1971, p. 46; MD Davies, 'Dragging in the Audiences', *Theatre Australia*, vol. 1, no. 3, (Oct–Nov 1976), pp. 32–35.
54 Interview with Jack A.
55 Interview with Kandy.
56 Jackson, p. 14.
57 Watson, pp. 5–6.
58 R Connell, 'The Birth of Gay Oxford Street', *OWN*, no. 77, 10 November 1983, pp. 14–15; interview with Kandy.
59 J Edwards, 'Working Class Camp', *Nation*, 25 July 1970, p. 14.
60 Interview with Kandy; Connell, 'The Birth of Gay Oxford Street', p. 14.
61 Connell, 'The Birth of Gay Oxford Street', p. 14.
62 Edwards, *Nation*, p. 14.
63 R Maugham, *Escape from the Shadows*, Hodder and Stoughton, 1972, pp. 237–238.
64 *SMH*, 26 May 1950, p. 7.
65 R Connell, 'The Way it Was', *OWN*, 20 October 1983, pp. 18–19; C Madigan, 'Where Have all the Fairies Gone', *Green Park Observer*, May 1983, p. 30.
66 Connell, 'Up the Cross', p. 12.
67 Laud Humphreys, *Tearoom Trade: Impersonal Sex in Public Places*, Aldine, 1970, indicates that a very high proportion of men having sex in public toilets were heterosexually married, and that this was their only venue for having homosexual encounters. In Australia, research associated with HIV prevention campaigns has made similar findings.
68 K Tennant, *Tell Morning This*, Pacific Books, 1967, p. 166.
69 Tennant, p. 167.
70 D Altman, 'The Personal is the Political: Social Movements and Cultural Change', in B Head and J Walter (eds), *Intellectual Movements and Australian Society*, Oxford University Press, 1988, p. 308.
71 See in particular Frank Moorhouse's essays collected under that title, *Days of Wine and Rage*, Penguin, 1980.
72 D Altman, 'The Personal is the Political', pp. 309–310.
73 J Weeks, *Coming Out: Homosexual Politics in Britain from the Nineteenth Century to the Present*, Quartet Books, 1977, p. 171.
74 See Weeks, Parts II and IV; also J Weeks, *Sex, Politics and Society: The Regulation of Sexuality Since 1800*, Longman, 1981, Chapters 11–13.
75 J D'Emilio, *Sexual Politics, Sexual Communities*, University of Chicago Press,

1983, Chapters 1–3; B Adam, *The Rise of the Gay and Lesbian Movement*, Twayne, 1987, Chapters 2, 4 and 5, but particularly p. 76.

76 See D'Emilio, pp. 111ff.

77 A Alam, *NSWPD*, 29 March 1955, pp. 3338–3339.

78 See L Watson, 'The Anti-Gay Laws, Irrationality and Public Policy Making', *Seminar on Victimless Crime*, NSW Dept of Attorney General and Justice, 1977, p. 107. See also Chapter 4 above.

79 G Hawkins, 'Homosexuality: Australia's "Greatest Menace"?', *Bulletin*, 8 May 1965, p. 12.

80 H Mayer, 'The Wife and the Homosexual', *Australian*, 19 July 1968.

81 *Australian*, 22 June 1968, p. 3.

82 *Australian*, 22 June 1968, p. 3. This is the source for all the numbers and quotes in this paragraph.

83 R French, *Gays Between the Broadsheets: Australian Media References to Homosexuality, 1948–1980*, Gay History Project, 1986, p. 39.

84 French, p. 40.

85 *SMH*, 24 April 1967, p. 7.

86 *SMH*, 19 May 1967, p. 7.

87 *SMH*, 10 August 1967, p. 4.

88 *Australian*, 11 March 1967, p. 1.

89 P Hartigan, 'Camp Cops and Robbers', *CAMP INK*, vol. 2, no. 7, May 1972, p. 8.

90 T Mautner, 'Harming those who cause no offence', *CT*, 8 August 1969.

91 Mautner, *CT*.

92 See *CT*, 4 June 1969, p. 1 (letters); 4 July 1969, article, p. 1; 5 July 1969, p. 1 (letters); 9 July 1969, Don Aitkin's column 'Between the Lines' and letters; 11 July 1969, letters; 15 July 1969, letters; 16 July 1969, letters; 17 July 1969, letters; 18 July 1969, letters; 19 July 1969, letters; 25 July 1969, letters; 26 July 1969, letters; 28 July 1969, articles on p. 1 and p. 3; 29 July 1969, letters and major article on the draft Criminal Code for the Australian Territories; 30 July 1969, a further article on the draft Criminal Code; 1 August 1969, letters; 6 August 1969, a major article on homosexuality and the law, and letters; 7 August 1969, a major article on homosexuals in Australia; 8 August 1969, a major article on the case for law reform; 12 August 1969, letters; 13 August 1969, letters.

93 D Aitkin, 'Between the Lines', *CT*, 9 July 1969, p. 1.

94 Aitkin, *CT*, p. 1.

95 See C Johnston and R Johnston, 'The Making of Homosexual Men in Australia', in V Burgmann and J Lee (eds), *Staining the Wattle*, McPhee Gribble/Penguin, 1988.

96 See 'Gay Power on the Move', *Bulletin*, 18 March 1971, p. 38; reprinted in *OutRage*, March 1990, pp. 52–53. See also D Thompson, *Flaws in the Social Fabric: Homosexuals and Society in Sydney*, Allen & Unwin, 1985, p. 9.

97 Thompson, p. 9.

98 Thompson, p. 9.

99 Thompson, p. 9.

100 B Adam, *The Rise of a Gay and Lesbian Movement*, Twayne, 1987, p. 82.

6   The Pearl in the Oyster

1   The derivative nature of the groups formed at the universities can be seen from the name they took – CAMPus CAMP. For further detail, see D Thompson, *Flaws in the Social Fabric: Homosexuals and Society in Sydney*, Allen & Unwin, 1985, Chapter 1.

2   There were articles on CAMP Inc. and its founders in the *Australian* of 10 September and 19 September 1970, but see R French, 'Gay Issues in the Australian Press: 1953 to the Present', *Gay Information*, no. 6, Winter 1981, pp. 14–16, for a survey of reporting generally since the 1950s. But as Dennis Altman noted, the 'worst form of media coverage, however, is neither distortion nor misrepresentation, it is sheer omission'; D Altman, 'Gays Abandoned', *New Journalist*, no. 8, June 1973, p. 6.

3   Altman, *New Journalist*, pp. 6–7. Altman bemoaned the fact that so few people could understand a 'radical' perspective, 'which sees homosexuality as part of everyone's sexuality but a part which is repressed and persecuted for its threat to the "norm"'.

4   Lex Watson, 'Judge Not Though: It is part of history', *Green Park Observer*, no. 2, April 1983, p. 12.

5   It quickly showed the dramatically different perception of the world of this new wave of homosexuals. The first issue had a major article on aversion therapy: 'Rat-psychology and the Homosexual', as well as a clever cover cartoon; the second had major articles on the law and homosexuality – 'The Law-Mediaeval'; the third had a range of material from America, showing the dramatic development of gay political action there; and the fourth was concerned with homophobic attitudes in Australian society.

6   Interview with John Ware, October 1989.

7   Thus Paul Foss argues that 'CAMP gradually settled into a fairly safe reformist platform'; 'Gay Liberation in Australia', *William and John*, March 1973, p. 5; see also T Bell, 'A History of Sydney Gay Liberation Front', unpublished paper, September 1975.

8   For a clear exposition of all that went into the making of such a new identity, and beyond, see R Reynolds, *From Camp to Queer: Re-making the Australian Homosexual*, Melbourne University Press, 2002, Chapters 4–8.

9   B Adam, *The Rise of a Gay and Lesbian Movement*, Twayne, 1987, p. 73. See J Weeks, *Sex, Politics and Society, The Regulation of Sexuality Since 1800*, Longman, 1981, pp. 185–186 for a general discussion of elements of a 'gay' identity.

10   *Bulletin*, 23 October 1971. This article was published over two weeks after the event. See also *The Review*, 22 October 1971, for a more informative article which discusses the lack of newspaper reporting of this event.

11   The *Australian* was the only newspaper in Sydney to cover the story as news. *CAMP INK*, vol. 2, nos. 2/3, December 1971–January 1972, has good coverage of the event – including excellent photographs, see pp. 13–17.

12   July 1972 did see a flurry of publicity about homosexuality. In Sydney, all the newspapers gave extensive coverage to the murder of Dr George Duncan, an Adelaide academic, whose body was found in the Torrens River and in whose

death, it was implied, police were involved. This was a continuing saga. In that same month there was also a great deal of publicity about Dennis Altman's recently launched *Homosexual: Oppression and Liberation*, and the banning of two programs on homosexuality by ABC-TV management.

13 The *Australian*, 19 September 1970, p. 15.

14 *This Day Tonight*, 21 September 1970.

15 See Jill Roe and Chris Poll, 'Granny De Camps', *Nation Review*, 29 July 1972, for a discussion on the *SMH*'s failure to review the book.

16 *Nation Review*, June 1975.

17 See introduction to R Brennan, 'A Film Producer Comes Out', in F Moorhouse, *Days of Wine and Rage*, Penguin, 1980, p. 45.

18 White went public about his homosexuality with the publication of his autobiography, *Flaws in the Glass*, Jonathan Cape, 1981.

19 D Thompson, *Flaws in the Social Fabric: Homosexuals and Society in Sydney*, Allen & Unwin, 1985, p. 47.

20 The *Australian*, 13 November 1972, p. 3; *SMH*, 13 November 1972, p. 16; *Nation Review*, 18 November 1972; *Australian*, 23 November 1972 (letters); *National Times*, 27 November 1972, p. 1.

21 *CAMP INK*, vol. 1, no. 1, pp. 4–6; no. 7, pp. 4–8; no. 10, pp. 13–14. The whole issue of vol. 2, no. 11 was devoted to 'Intellectual Poofter Bashers', and much attention was paid to the rationale for aversion therapy and what it represented.

22 D Thompson, *Flaws in the Social Fabric: Homosexuals and Society in Sydney*, Allen & Unwin, 1985, p. 47.

23 Thompson, p. 47.

24 Thompson, pp. 50–51. The fact that McConaghy later 'discovered' his own homosexuality says much about repressed consciousness.

25 M MacDonald, 'A Long Cool Look at 1972', *Bulletin*, 30 December 1972, p. 13.

26 P White, *The Eye of the Storm*, Jonathan Cape, 1973, Chapter 2.

27 See V Russo, *The Celluloid Closet: Homosexuality in the Movies*, for an extended treatment of how homosexuals and homosexuality have been dealt with, mostly in American movies.

28 C Gledhill, 'Klute Part 1: A Contemporary Film Noir', quoted in D Sargent, 'Bent Angels', *Gay Information*, no. 4, October–November 1980, p. 6.

29 Russo, p. 146. See, however, R Dyer, 'Sissies, Buddies and "Gay Sensibility" in Russo's "Closet"', *Gay Information*, Nos 9–10 Autumn–Winter 1982, pp. 11–15, for some criticisms of Russo's work.

30 D Lyle, 'Sex and the Box: How the Wowsers Lost', *National Times*, 25–31 March 1983, p. 30.

31 Lyle, *National Times*, p. 30.

32 Lyle, *National Times*, p. 30.

33 C Dunne, 'Sex and Television', *Forum*, August 1981, p. 9.

34 F Wells, 'The Sale of No. 96', *Campaign*, no. 22, July 1977.

35 F Wells, *Campaign*.

36 Quoted in S McGrath, 'Hair Today, Gone Tomorrow', *Australian*, 13–14 June 1981, *Weekend Magazine*, p. 1.

37 Dennis Altman on the other hand argued that 'where gayness has been dealt

with in our theatre, it has been marginal, furtive and in need of explanation'; quoted in McGrath, *Australian*, p. 1.

38 P Blazey, 'Latest Poll in Favour of Gays', *Australian*, 7 June 1978, p. 9.

39 Blazey, *Australian*, p. 9.

40 See, for example, the *1981 Sydney Gay Guide*, CAMP Lobby, 1981. This lists 46 separate groups.

41 Most of the material for this section on the commercial subculture has been obtained from the various gay publications and from interviews.

42 S Soldatow, *Private – Do Not Open*, Penguin, 1987, pp. 6–7.

43 According to Larry Galbraith, it was in April 1976; others have suggested that it might have been earlier, in 1972, because money from Patches' and Castello's profits helped launch *Campaign*, which started in 1975.

44 Gary Dunne, *If Blood Should Stain the Lino*, in Versions, 1983, p. 19.

45 Dunne, pp. 20, 22.

46 Dunne, p. 23.

47 Interview with Rose Jackson, *Star*, vol. 5, no. 8, 21 October 1983, p. 19.

48 P McCarthy, 'Macho-chic at the Pub', *National Times*, 14–20 September 1980, p. 19.

49 McCarthy, *National Times*, p. 19.

50 See P Van Reyk, 'Confusion, Sickness, Bravery: Homosexuals in Moorhouse's Fiction', *Gay Information*, no. 7, Spring, 1982, p. 13. For homosexual characters in Moorhouse's fiction see *Futility and Other Animals* (1969), *The Americans, Baby* (1972), *Tales of Mystery and Romance* (1977), and *The Everlasting Secret Family* (1980), all published by Angus & Robertson.

51 I MacNeill, 'As the Cold War Rages Along Oxford Street', *Cargo*, no. 1, December 1987, p. 4.

52 S Payne, *The Beat*, Gay Men's Press, 1985, p. 140.

53 L Watson, 'Judge Not Though: It is part of history', *Green Park Observer*, no. 2, April 1983, p. 12. This section relies heavily on this article. See also G Tillet, 'Guide to Gay Magazines', *Forum*, August 1981.

54 A Foster, 'Getting Physical', *OutRage*, October 1988, p. 18.

55 Tillet, *Forum*, p. 82.

56 Tillet, *Forum*, p. 82.

57 N Thompson, 'Gay relationships: the myths are demolished', *SMH*, 28 September 1983.

58 S Macintyre, *Winners and Losers*, Allen & Unwin, 1985, p. 137. For some later material on the discussion in the subculture about what constituted a 'gay community' see, for example, articles by C Johnston, *Gay Information*, nos 2, 3, 4 and 5. See also L Galbraith, 'What Gay Community?' *Village Voice*, no. 74, 7 April 1988, p. 7.

59 See *CAMP INK*, vol. 2, nos 11 and 12 for details of the campaign, and the results.

60 For a detailed list of the organisations and groups that had publicly come out in support of law reform, see M Smith, 'Grim Outlook for the Gay', *Bulletin*, 7 June 1975, pp. 18–30; see also A Reid, 'Commission Recommends Legal Brothels, Abortions for Girls 14', *Bulletin*, 3 December 1977, pp. 38–39, for details on the Royal Commission on Human Relationships recommendations regarding law reform for homosexuals.

61 D McNicoll, 'Yabsley wiped out by gay backlash', *Bulletin*, 12 April 1988, p. 73.
62 See D Thompson, *Flaws in the Social Fabric: Homosexuals and Society in Sydney*, Allen & Unwin, 1985, Chapter 5, for an extended treatment of the church's attitudes to homosexuality, and the outright conflicts that have occurred in Sydney.
63 See *Campaign* and *OutRage* during 1983, for extensive reporting on both these raids and the eventual court cases. All charges were ultimately dropped, and both the NSW Anti-Discrimination Board and the Ombudsman eventually investigated the raids, with findings against the police.
64 A Wilson, 'How a Carnival turned into a vicious brawl', *Australian*, 26 June 1978, p. 1.

7 It Was the Worst of Times, Never the Best of Times
1 P Curson, *Times of Crisis: Epidemics in Sydney, 1788–1900*, Sydney University Press, Sydney, 1985.
2 See, for example, 'AIDS: A Growing Threat', *Time*, 12 August 1985, pp. 46–52; Australian Federation of AIDS Organisations, *Getting It Right: A Media Worker's Guide to AIDS*, Australian Co-operative Media Enterprises, 1987, p. 57; 'Global War on AIDS', *Time*, 25 May 1987, pp. 42–49; D. Altman, *AIDS and the New Puritanism*, Pluto Press, 1986.
3 See Sydney *DT*, 1 March 1983; the story was confirmed by Senator Don Grimes, for the Minister for Health, in May that year. See *Australian*, 5 May 1983.
4 E Whitton, 'AIDS! The Media, Paranoia, and the Wrath of God', *SMH*, 17 August 1985, p. 41.
5 R Duffin, 'Introduction' to R French, *Mossies could spread AIDS: Australia Media References to AIDS 1981–1985*, Gay History Project, 1986, p. 8. This book gives an excellent coverage of how the media dealt with AIDS.
6 See, for example, S Quest, 'In a Medical Vein', *Gay Community News*, Vol. 4, No. 3, April 1982, p. 39.
7 *DM*, 27 May 1983.
8 A Lansdown, 'The Politics of AIDS: Dennis Altman and the New Puritanism', *Quadrant*, March 1987.
9 Lansdown, *Quadrant*, p. 33.
10 L Chipman, 'The Politics of AIDS may lead to our Downfall', *Illawarra Mercury*, 17 March 1987.
11 Chipman, *Illawarra Mercury*.
12 *Financial Review*, 14 January 1993, p. 11.
13 For details see G Sheridan, 'Still Nowhere Near a Cure', *Weekend Australian*, 18–19 May 1985, p. 15; *Time*, 25 May 1987, p. 48; French, pp. 7–12; A Carr, 'Goodbye to the Politics of Self-Indulgence', *OutRage*, no. 43, December 1986, p. 19.
14 The Queensland government passed particularly draconian legislation in 1984. See D Altman, 'Legitimation Through Disaster: AIDS and the Gay Movement', in E Fee and D Fox (eds), *AIDS: The Burden of History*, University of California Press, 1988, for a coverage of many aspects of this in Australia.

15 Duffin, p. 8.
16 For Ankali see: <thealbioncentre.org.au/ankali/the-ankali-project/>; the NSW Gays Counselling Service forms AIDS Home Support, to look after home care needs of people living with AIDS, from which the Community Support Network (CSN) later emerges: see <www.acon.org.au/wp-content/uploads/2015/04/History_of_HIV_5th-Edition.pdf>, p. 12; Bobby Goldsmith Foundation: <www.bgf.org.au/about-bgf/who-was-bobby-goldsmith/>; for more details of the activities of these organisations, see J Power, *Movement, Knowledge, Emotion: Gay Activism and HIV/AIDS in Australia*, ANU E-Press, 2011.
17 See A Carr 'Goodbye to the politics of Self-Indulgence', *OutRage*, no. 43, December 1986, p. 19; Altman, 'Legitimation Through Disaster'; D Altman, 'The Emergence of Gay Identity in the USA and Australia', in C Jennett and RG Stewart (eds), *Politics of the Future: The Rise of Modern Social Movements*, Macmillan, 1988.
18 A Horin, 'Why grief is denied the lover who survives', in *SMH*, 19 July 1988, p. 17.
19 This line of argument was also taken up by homophobic critics, some of whom argued that AIDS was introduced into the wider community 'by homosexuals themselves in order to ensure their own protection against public anger and legislative censure and to ensure adequate public funds for AIDS research and treatment'. Lansdown, *Quadrant*, p. 18.
20 See, for example, J Lee, 'AIDS Politics: Triumph or Tragedy', *Sydney Star Observer*, no. 89, 30 September 1988, p. 19.
21 T Carrigan, 'Facts of Our Lives', *OutRage*, no. 59, April 1988, p. 35.
22 G Sheridan, 'AIDS: Still Nowhere Near a Cure', *Weekend Australian*, 18–19 May 1985, p. 15.
23 Carrigan, *OutRage*, p. 35.
24 Australian Federation of AIDS Organisations, 'STIs Amongst Gay Men', Discussion Paper, November 2005, viewed October 2015, <www.afao.org.au/_data/assets/pdf_file/0016/4480/DP1104_STI_Gay_Men.pdf>.
25 'The Big Finish', *Four Corners*, ABC, a program about Stuart Challender, transcript viewed October 2015, <www.abc.net.au/4corners/stories/s351714.htm>.
26 Duffin, p. 7.
27 Altman, 'Legitimation Through Disaster'.
28 Sydney's Pride History Group website, viewed October 2015, <camp.org.au/80s>.
29 Jason Bartlett, 'GLRL: 25 Years of Advocacy and Fighting for Equality', *Gay News Network*, 21 October 2013, viewed October 2015, <gaynewsnetwork.com.au/feature/ft-new-south-wales/glrl-25-years-of-advocacy-and-fighting-for-equality-12178.html>.
30 Australian Lesbian & Gay Archives: New South Wales, *Homosexual Law Reform in Australia*, Australian Lesbian & Gay Archives Inc., 1993, pp. 1–2.
31 Australian Lesbian & Gay Archives; New South Wales, p. 1.
32 Australian Lesbian & Gay Archives; New South Wales, pp. 1ff.
33 C Clews, '1983. Politics: Sydney Gay Rights Embassy', 31 March 2014, viewed

October 2015, <www.gayinthe80s.com/2014/03/1983-politics-sydney-gay-rights-embassy/>.

34 See G Wotherspoon, *Making a Difference: A History of Positive Life NSW*, Positive Life NSW, 2009.

35 G Honnor, in J Rule (ed.), *Through our eyes*, National Association of People With HIV Australia, 2014, p. 79.

36 'Global War on AIDS', *Time*, 25 May 1987, p. 42.

37 Altman, 'Legitimation Through Disaster'.

38 Altman, 'Legitimation Through Disaster'.

39 See discussion about Sydney becoming the 'City of Events' in the entry on 'Sydney' at <dictionaryofsydney.org/entry/sydney>.

40 Z Begg, 'Lesbian and gay rights: Is Mardi Gras enough?', *Green Left Weekly*, 24 February 1999, viewed October 2015, <www.greenleft.org.au/node/20215>; C Johnston, 'Think Globally, buy locally', in *A Sydney Gaze*, Shrilton Press, 1998, pp. 264–267.

41 'Our History', Sydney Gay and Lesbian Mardi Gras, viewed October 2015, <www.mardigras.org.au/history/>.

42 'Our History', Sydney Gay and Lesbian Mardi Gras.

43 Johnston, pp. 264–267.

44 D Gallagher (ed.), *Love and Death: an anthology of Poetry and Prose*, Print's Realm, 1987.

45 B Law, 'Holding the Man and AIDS in Australia', Long View Project, Wheeler Centre, viewed October 2015, <www.wheelercentre.com/projects/the-long-view/holding-the-man-and-aids-in-australia>.

46 The AIDS Memorial Quilt, About, viewed October 2015, <www.aidsquilt.org/about/the-aids-memorial-quilt>.

47 The AIDS Memorial Quilt, About.

48 M Hogan, *Cradle of Australian Political Studies: Sydney's Department of Government*, Connor Court Publishing, 2015. The author was also one of the activists in the Merewether Building.

49 Bartlett, *Gay News Network*.

50 See K Davis, 'Thin Air', *Continuum: Journal of Media & Culture Studies*, vol. 19, no. 3, September 2005, pp. 421–426.

51 Bartlett, *Gay News Network*.

52 Bartlett, *Gay News Network*.

53 Bartlett, *Gay News Network*.

54 Margaret Otlowski, *Doyle and Doyle*; Family Court Awards Custody to Homosexual Father', *University of Tasmania Law Review*, vol. 11, no. 2, 1992, viewed October 2015, <www.austlii.edu.au/au/journals/UTasLawRw/1992/21.pdf>.

55 Royal Commission into the New South Wales Police Service, Police Integrity Commission NSW, viewed October 2015, <www.pic.nsw.gov.au/ContentPage.aspx?PageId=25>.

56 See M Dodkin, *Bob Carr: The Reluctant Leader*, UNSW Press, 2003, p. 107, for an interesting account of what went on at the relevant Caucus meeting.

57 D Buchanan, 'Homosexual "Pedophilia" and the NSW Police Royal

Commission'; Australian Institute of Criminology Conference, *Paedophilia: Policy & Prevention*, University of Sydney, April 1997, viewed October 2015, <aic.gov.au/media_library/conferences/paedophilia/buchanan.pdf>.

58   Dodkin, p. 150.
59   H Evans, 'Franca Arena and Parliamentary Privilege', *Papers on Parliament number 52: Selected Writings of Harry Evans*, December 2009, viewed October 2015, <www.aph.gov.au/About_Parliament/Senate/Research_and_Education/~/~/link.aspx?_id=DE330751F1914E4BA792BE67613C6B88&_z=z>; see also M Hill, 'Satan's Excellent Adventure in the Antipodes', IPT (Institute of Psychological Therapies), vol. 10, 1998, viewed at <www.ipt-forensics.com/journal/volume10/j10_9.htm>.
60   Dodkin, p. 161.
61   A Carr, 'Questions of Consent', *OutRage*, March 1997, viewed October 2015, <www.adam-carr.net/004.html>.
62   N Rogers, 'Mad mothers, over-zealous therapists and the paedophile inquiry', *Southern Cross University Law Review*, vol. 3, 1999, p. 125.
63   The paper in question was one of 64 that had been given over the previous eight years; the topics ranged widely, from 'Afro-Brazilian Spiritualism and Homosexuality' to 'The Struggle for Homosexual Law Reform in Australia'.
64   Carr, *OutRage*.
65   Michael Brown, 'Holding judgment', *SMH*, 9 June 2007, viewed October 2015, <www.smh.com.au/news/national/holding-judgment/2007/06/08/1181089328815.html>.
66   Evans.
67   'Sydney wins gay games', Cool Running Australia website, News, 15 November 1997, viewed October 2015, <www.coolrunning.com.au/news/1997n064.shtml>.
68   'Sydney wins gay games'.
69   'Sydney wins gay games'.

8   Into the New Millennium
1   S Fitzgerald, 'Sydney', Dictionary of Sydney, 2011, viewed 5 June 2015, <dictionaryofsydney.org/entry/sydney>.
2   See 'Mob violence envelops Cronulla', *SMH*, 11 December 2005, viewed October 2015, <www.smh.com.au/news/national/mob-violence-envelops-cronulla/2005/12/11/1134235936223.html>; and *Cronulla Riots: The Day that Shocked a Nation*, SBS documentary, viewed 6 July 2013, <www.sbs.com.au/cronullariots/>.
3   Richard Florida, 'The Rise of the Creative Class', *Washington Monthly*, May 2002, viewed October 2015, <www.washingtonmonthly.com/features/2001/0205.florida.html>.
4   Fitzgerald, 'Sydney'.
5   B Hallett, 'Gay Games VI Opening Ceremony', *SMH*, 4 November 2002, viewed October 2015, <www.smh.com.au/articles/2002/11/03/1036308205226.html>.
6   Hallett, *SMH*.
7   Gay Games VI, Under New Skies 2002, Sydney, Australia, viewed October 2015, <gaygamescom.site.securepod.com/en/participants/results/gg6/>.

8   Sydney 2002 Gay Games collection 1982–2002, Manuscripts, oral history and pictures, State Library NSW, viewed October 2015, <acms.sl.nsw.gov.au/item/itemdetailpaged.aspx?itemid=430583>.

9   See *Advocate*, 13 Apr 2004, p. 46, for an analysis of why the Sydney Gay Games were a financial disaster.

10   'Robbo Heffered', *Workers Online*, no. 297, 3 March 2006, viewed October 2015, <workers.labor.net.au/297/news6_heffered.html>.

11   AJ Brown, 'Justice left hanging in the breeze', *SMH*, 2 April 2011, viewed October 2015, <www.smh.com.au/national/justice-left-hanging-in-the-breeze-20110401-1crbg.html>.

12   See 'Kirby, Michael', in R Aldrich and G Wotherspoon (eds), *Who's Who in Contemporary Gay and Lesbian History, From World War II to the Present Day*, Routledge, 2001, pp. 231–232.

13   'Bill Heffernan's disgraceful speech under parliamentary privilege', Australianpolitics.com, viewed October 2015, australianpolitics.com/2002/03/11/heffernan-disgraceful-speech-under-parliamentary-privilege.html>.

14   Brown, *SMH*.

15   Brown, *SMH*.

16   Brown, *SMH*.

17   Brown, *SMH*.

18   Brown, *SMH*.

19   For the full and intriguing story of what went on behind the scenes, see Brown, *SMH*.

20   Linda Mottram, 'Future of Heffernan's Senate seat', AM, ABC Local Radio, 20 March 2002, AM archive transcript, viewed October 2015, <www.abc.net.au/am/stories/s508611.htm>.

21   See *SMH*, 10 April 2008, for details.

22   See Chapter 7 for details of this.

23   Michael Hogan, *Cradle Of Australian Political Studies: Sydney's Department of Government*, Connor Court Publishing, 2015, p. 131.

24   R Reynolds, *What happened to gay life?*, UNSW Press, 2007, p. 1.

25   T Duggan, 'Mardi Gras gets government funding', *same same*, 1 October 2008, viewed October 2015, <www.samesame.com.au/news/3069/Mardi-Gras-Gets-Government-Funding>.

26   'Our History', Sydney Gay and Lesbian Mardi Gras, viewed October 2015, <www.mardigras.org.au/history/>.

27   R Reynolds, p. 1.

28   Quoted in Reynolds, p. 1

29   *SMH*, 3 December 2011.

30   M Akersten, 'Mardi Gras regrets name change "cheat"', *same same*, 17 December 2011, viewed October 2015, <www.samesame.com.au/news/7772/Mardi-Gras-regrets-name-change-cheat>.

31   Ken Davis, *SMH*, 3 December 2011.

32   Akersten, *same same*.

33   'Our History', Sydney Gay and Lesbian Mardi Gras.

34   S Rubinsztein-Dunlop, 'Police investigate Mardi Gras brutality claims', *ABC*

News, 6 March 2013, viewed October 2015, <www.abc.net.au/news/2013–03–06/claims-of-police-brutality-at-mardi-gras-parade/4554958>.

35   D Callander, 'Police violence against Mardi Gras revellers reminds us of an intolerant history', *The Conversation*, 28 February 2014, viewed October 2015, <www.theconversation.com/police-violence-against-mardi-gras-revellers-reminds-us-of-an-intolerant-history-23562>.

36   See C Faro, with G Wotherspoon, *Street Seen: A History of Oxford Street*, Melbourne University Press, 2000, pp. 233–271.

37   B Ruting, 'Whither gay Sydney: the decline of Oxford Street as gay space', *On Line Opinion*, 9 February 2007, viewed October 2015, <www.onlineopinion.com.au/view.asp?article=5479&page=0>.

38   B Ruting, 'The Oxford Street exodus', *Australian*, 18 October 2006, viewed October 2015, <www.news.com.au/national/the-oxford-street-exodus/story-e6frfkwi-1111112378196>.

39   A Leese, *The spatial distribution of subcultures: gay men in Sydney*, School of Town Planning, University of New South Wales, 1993.

40   See C Johnston, 'How gay is my Oxford Street?' in *A Sydney Gaze*, Schrilton Press, 1998, pp. 260–263.

41   Johnston, p. 260.

42   Johnston, p. 262.

43   See Chapter 5.

44   'The links between gays and gentrification', *Planetizen*, 2 October 2003, viewed October 2015, <www.planetizen.com/node/11290>.

45   For a discussion of the works of Gary Gates and Richard Florida, and the gay Index and creativity in cities, see D Lillington, 'Do gays influence property values?', *Urban Economics*, 4 February 2014, viewed October 2015, <sites.duke.edu/urbaneconomics/?p=1054>.

46   N Berg, 'The geography of same-sex couples', *City Lab*, 6 October 2011, viewed October 2015, <www.citylab.com/design/2011/10/geography-same-sex-households/259/>.

47   See S Farrar, 'How the Inner West Was Won', *Star Observer*, 20 April 2008.

48   See Farrar, *Star Observer*.

49   See Farrar, *Star Observer*.

50   'Oxford Street: Still the Heart of Gay Sydney?', *Sydney Star Observer*, 7 February 2008.

51   The Institute of Many website, viewed October 2015, <www.theinstituteofmany.org/>.

52   See Chapter 7, for details of the issues that the gay community faced in the early days of AIDS.

53   'Our History', ACON, <www.acon.org.au/about-acon/who-we-are/#our-history>.

54   See Chapter 6 for the early developments.

55   See Chapter 7 for details of this.

56   D Arcuri, 'Greg Fisher: The fall of Satellite Media "still breaks my heart"', *same same*, 18 September 2015, viewed October 2015, <www.samesame.com.au/news/12771/Greg-Fisher-The-fall-of-Satellite-Media-still-breaks-my-heart>.

57 D Altman, *The Homosexualization of America, The Americanization of the Homosexual*, St Martin's Press, 1982, p. 164.
58 See G Wotherspoon, 'Telling it like it is: the emergence of Australia's gay and lesbian media', in L Featherstone, R Jennings & R Reynolds (eds), *Acts of Love and Lust: Sexuality in Australia from 1945–2010*, Cambridge Scholars Publishing, 2015.
59 G Wotherspoon, *Hairy, Chunky and Gay: A History of the Harbour City Bears*, Harbour City Bears, 2012.
60 K Bashford, as quoted in G Wotherspoon, *Hairy, Chunky and gay: a history of the Harbour City Bears*, Harbour City Bears, 2012, p. 32.
61 S Hyslop, 'The Rise of the Australian Bear Community since 1995', in LK Wright (ed.), *The Bear Book II: Further Readings in the History and Evolution of a Gay Male Subculture*, Harrington Park Press, 2001, p. 173.
62 Wotherspoon, *Hairy, Chunky and Gay*, p. 32.
63 Sydney Convicts Rugby Union Club, viewed October 2015, <sydneyconvicts.org/>.
64 N Klein, 'Sydney to host gay rugby world cup', *Herald Sun*, 12 October 2012, viewed October 2015, <www.heraldsun.com.au/news/national/sydney-to-host-gay-rugby-world-cup/story-fndo317g-1226494144698>.
65 'Gay rugby world Bingham cup smashing stereotypes in Australia', *SBS News*, 27 August 2014 (updated 28 August), viewed October 2015, <www.sbs.com.au/news/article/2014/08/27/gay-rugby-world-bingham-cup-smashing-stereotypes-australia>.
66 'Gay rugby world Bingham cup smashing stereotypes in Australia', *SBS News*.
67 Klein, *Herald Sun*.
68 Klein, *Herald Sun*.
69 Sydney Rangers Football Club website, viewed October 2015, <sydneyrangersfc.com.au/2015/07/10/register-for-justin-fashanu-cup/>.
70 G Wotherspoon, 'Drag and cross dressing', *Dictionary of Sydney*, 2008, viewed October 2015, <dictionaryofsydney.org/entry/drag_and_cross_dressing>.
71 Wotherspoon, 'Drag and cross dressing'.
72 This was how 2015 Fair Day was advertised on the Mardi Gras website, but the original link is now obsolete. It is also quoted on the Australian Human Rights Commission website, viewed October 2015, <www.humanrights.gov.au/news/events/fair-day-0>.
73 Bingay, ACON website, Get involved, Events, viewed October 2015, <www.acon.org.au/get-involved/events/-bingay>.
74 Sydney Candlelight Memorial 2015, ACON website, viewed October 2015, <www.acon.org.au/sydney-candlelight-2015/>.
75 Sydney Pride Festival website, viewed October 2015, <www.sydneypride.com/>.
76 See G Wotherspoon, *City of the Plain: History of a Gay Sub-culture*, Hale & Iremonger, 1991, pp. 69, 110.
77 G Wotherspoon, 'Looking into the Precipice', *Gay News Network*, 18 February 2013, viewed October 2015, <gaynewsnetwork.com.au/feature/looking-in-the-precipice-10561.html>.
78 The following paragraphs are based on Wotherspoon, 'Looking into the

Precipice'. This material in turn was taken from a series of *SMH* articles, from 27 July to 12 August 2013.

79 E Alberici, 'Scott Johnson Inquest: Chief inspector Pamela Young removed from investigation after candid Lateline interview', *ABC News*, 22 April, 2015, viewed October 2015, <www.abc.net.au/news/2015–04–21/scott-johnson-investigation/6410320>.

80 *SMH*, 27 December 2014.

81 J Wells, 'Third trial finds man guilty of killing lover', *ABC News*, 28 March 2013, viewed October 2015, <www.abc.net.au/news/2012–11–28/leung-found-guilty-after-three-trials/4397252>.

82 *SMH*, 27 December 2014.

83 *Sunday Telegraph*, 25 March 2012.

84 *Sunday Telegraph*, 25 March 2012.

85 *Sunday Telegraph*, 25 March 2012.

86 *SMH*, 28 March 2013.

87 *SMH*, 27 December 2014.

88 *SMH*, 27 December 2014.

89 *SMH*, 27 December 2014.

90 *SMH*, 27 December 2014.

9   Just Like Everybody Else?

1 S Chalkley-Rhoden, 'One in four Australians had a negative attitude towards Muslims', *ABC News*, 29 October 2014, viewed October 2015, <www.abc.net.au/news/2014–10–29/one-in-four-australians-had-a-negative-attitude-towards-muslims/5849744>.

2 'Club Arak', *Star Observer*, viewed October 2015, <www.starobserver.com.au/tag/club-arak>.

3 NSW Attorney General's Department, *'You shouldn't have to hide to be safe', A Report on Homophobic Hostilities and Violence Against Gay Men and Lesbians in New South Wales*, NSWAGD, December 2003.

4 D Marr, 'Stonewalled', *SMH*, 13 April 2012, viewed October 2015, <www.smh.com.au/lifestyle/stonewalled-20120413-1wyec.html>.

5 Marr, *SMH*.

6 B Law, 'Kiss me, I'm Asian', *SMH Good Weekend*, March 2012, viewed October 2015, <benjamin-law.com/kiss-me-im-asian/>.

7 Tony Ayres, 'China Doll – The experience of being Gay Chinese Australian', in Peter Jackson and Gerard Sullivan (eds), *Multicultural Queer: Australian Narratives*, Harrington Park Press, 1999, pp. 87–98.

8 S Lee, 'Gay Australia's best clubs, bars, events and culture', *same same*, 11 July 2013, viewed October 2015, <www.samesame.com.au/features/6324/Gay-Australias-best-clubs-bars-events-and-culture>.

9 R Domingo, 'All about A-Men', *Gay News Network*, 20 February 2012, viewed October 2015, <gaynewsnetwork.com.au/feature/a-new-voice-4764.html>.

10 Long Yang Club Global Network, viewed October 2015, <sydney.longyangclub.org/lycnetwork.htm>.

11 As quoted in SL Ross, 'Homosexuality and Aboriginal culture: a lore

unto themselves', *Archer Magazine*, 20 October 2014, 27 August 2015,
<archermagazine.com.au/2014/10/homosexuality-and-aboriginal-culture-a-lore-
unto-themselves/>.

12   Ross, *Archer Magazine*.

13   M Chapple and S Kippax, *Gay and homosexually active Aboriginal men in
     Sydney*, Report, National Centre in HIV Social Research, HIV, AIDS and
     Society Publications 1996, viewed October 2015, <reconciliation.tripod.com/
     chreferences.htm>.

14   Ross, *Archer Magazine*.

15   Chapple and Kippax.

16   H Szoke, 'Racism exists in Australia – are we doing enough to address it?',
     Australian Human Rights Commission News, 16 February 2012, viewed
     October 2015, <www.humanrights.gov.au/news/speeches/racism-exists-
     australia-are-we-doing-enough-address-it>.

17   Human Rights and Equal Opportunity Commission, *Social Justice Report 2000*,
     HREOC, Sydney, 2000, Chapter 5.

18   Chapple and Kippax.

19   For an interesting discussion on the intricacies of this, see NA Lester,
     MD Goggin (eds), *Racialized Politics of Desire in Personal Ads*, Lexington Books,
     2008.

20   Chapple and Kippax.

21   S Raj, 'Asylum seekers either "too gay or not gay enough"', Amnesty
     International, blog article, 13 July 2012, viewed October 2015,.

22   Raj, Amnesty International.

23   Human Rights Law Centre, News, 'Australia's asylum seeker policies &
     treatment of gay refugees condemned at UN', 23 June 2014, viewed October
     2015, <hrlc.org.au/australias-asylum-seeker-policies-treatment-of-gay-refugees-
     condemned-at-un/>.

24   Refugee Action Committee, 'Australian Government ignores the horrific plight
     of gay asylum seekers held at the Manus Island Detention Centre', 18 December
     2014, viewed October 2015, <refugeeaction.org/20141218/australian-
     government-ignores-the-horrific-plight-of-gay-asylum-seekers-held-at-the-
     manus-island-detention-centre/>.

25   P Farrell, 'Australia is hostile and contemptuous to asylum seekers, says UN
     rights chief', *Guardian*, 16 June 2015, viewed October 2015, <www.theguardian.
     com/australia-news/2015/jun/16/australia-is-hostile-and-contemptuous-to-
     asylum-seekers-says-un-rights-chief?CMP=ema_632>.

26   Editorial, *New York Times*, 3 September 2015, viewed October 2015, <www.
     nytimes.com/2015/09/03/opinion/australias-brutal-treatment-of-migrants.
     html?_r=0>.

27   S Raj, '"Come out" to immigration officials or be deported? Gay asylum seekers
     will suffer under Morrison's new regime', *Guardian*, 26 September 2014, viewed
     October 2015, <www.theguardian.com/commentisfree/2014/sep/26/come-out-
     to-immigration-officials-or-be-deported-gay-asylum-seekers-will-suffer-under-
     morrisons-new-regime>.

28 See also LA Berg and J Millbank, 'Constructing the Personal Narratives of Lesbian, Gay and Bisexual Asylum Claimants' in R Robson (ed), *Sexuality and Law – Volume III: Sexual Freedom*, Ashgate, 2011, pp. 321–349.

29 R Gill, 'Sexuality of asylum seekers questioned', *Reportage*, 17 June 2013, viewed October 2015, <www.reportageonline.com/2013/06/sexuality-of-asylum-seekers-questioned/>.

30 B Brook, 'Australia "becoming impenetrable" for LGBTI asylum seekers', *Star Observer*, 17 December 2014, viewed October 2015, <www.starobserver.com.au/news/local-news/australia-becoming-impenetrable-for-lgbti-asylum-seekers/131175>.

31 S Dingle, 'Field of tainted dreams', *Background Briefing*, ABC Radio National, viewed October 2015, <www.abc.net.au/radionational/programs/backgroundbriefing/field-of-tainted-dreams/6444034>.

32 C Busby, 'Out on the fields study reveals homophobia still an issue in sports', *Gay News Network*, 11 May 2015, viewed October 2015, <gaynewsnetwork.com.au/sport/out-in-the-fields-study-reveals-homophobia-still-an-issue-in-sports-17568.html>.

33 Dingle, *Background Briefing*.

34 Dingle, *Background Briefing*.

35 B Riley, 'Gay soccer tournament to challenge homophobia in sport', *Star Observer*, 3 October 2013, viewed October 2015, <www.starobserver.com.au/news/gay-soccer-tournament-to-challenge-homophobia-in-sport/110308>

36 Busby, *Gay News Network*.

37 N Klein, 'Sydney to host gay rugby world cup', *Herald Sun*, 12 October 2012, viewed October 2015, <www.heraldsun.com.au/news/national/sydney-to-host-gay-rugby-world-cup/story-fndo317g-1226494144698>.

38 DM Skerrett, K Kolves & D De Leo, 'Suicides among lesbian, gay, bisexual, and transgender populations in Australia: An analysis of the Queensland suicide register', *Journal of Asia-Pacific Psychiatry*, published online 2 April 2014, viewed October 2015, <www.thewebconsole.com/tools/dbm/campaign/view/campaign/498742/campaign/5058f1af8388633f609cadb75a75dc9d>.

39 Skerrett et al, *Journal of Asia-Pacific Psychiatry*.

40 B Maclean, 'And why might suicide hit gay youth hardest?', *The Drum*, 7 September 2012, viewed October 2015, <www.abc.net.au/news/2012–09–07/maclean-homophobia/4248444>.

41 J Lee, 'Suicide rates of gay people too high a price to pay says Governor-General Quentin Bryce', *SMH*, 26 November 2013, viewed October 2015, <www.smh.com.au/national/suicide-rates-of-gay-people-too-high-a-price-to-pay-says-governorgeneral-quentin-bryce-20131126-2y76u.html>.

42 Lee, *SMH*.

43 J Stark, 'beyondblue "abandons gay youth"', *SMH*, 28 June 2009, viewed October 2015, <www.smh.com.au/national/beyondblue-abandons-gay-youth-20090627-d0lx.html>

44 'Research finds 42% LGBTIQ Young people think about suicide and self harm', Twenty10 website, viewed October 2015, <www.twenty10.org.au/>.

45 Twenty10 website.

46 M Akersten, 'What happened when Q&A went LGBTIQ&A', *same same*, 19 June 2015, <www.samesame.com.au/news/12436/What-happened-when-QA-went-LGBTIQA>.

47 Akersten, *same same*.

48 Australian Human Rights Commission *Resilient Individuals: Sexual Orientation Gender Identity & Intersex Rights*, National Consultation Report 2015, AHRC, 2015, viewed October 2015, <www.humanrights.gov.au/our-work/sexual-orientation-sex-gender-identity/publications/resilient-individuals-sexual>.

49 Australian Human Rights Commission *Resilient Individuals*.

50 J Macey, 'Britain approves gay marriage', *The World Today*, ABC Radio, 6 February 2013, viewed October 2015, www.abc.net.au/worldtoday/content/2013/s3684319.htm>.

51 S Ikin, 'Catholic Church issues letter explaining why it opposes same-sex marriage', *ABC News*, 18 June 2015, viewed October 2015, <www.abc.net.au/news/2015-06-17/catholic-bishops-explain-same-sex-marriage-opposition/6554500>.

52 Ikin, *ABC News*.

53 Ikin, *ABC News*.

54 Australian Marriage Equality website, Get Informed, Public Opinion, viewed October 2015, <www.australianmarriageequality.org/who-supports-equality/a-majority-of-australians-support-marriage-equality/>.

55 M Kenny, 'Voters drift away from Tony Abbott amid worsening housing affordability crisis and same-sex marriage debate', 14 June 2015, viewed October 2015, <www.smh.com.au/federal-politics/political-news/voters-drift-away-from-tony-abbott-amid-worsening-housing-affordability-crisis-and-samesex-marriage-debate-20150614-ghnofr.html>.

56 'Same-sex marriage: Tony Abbott's sister Christine Forster calls for bipartisan approach ahead of rally', *ABC News*, 1 June 2015, viewed October 2015, <www.abc.net.au/news/2015-05-31/christine-forster-calls-for-bipartisan-approach-to-gay-mar/6509748>.

57 R Reynolds, *What happened to gay life?*, UNSW Press, 2007, pp. 66–69; pp. 101–103.

58 See G Wotherspoon, 'From Subculture to Mainstream Culture: Some Impacts of Homosexual and Gay Subcultures in Australia', *Journal of Australian Studies*, no. 28, May 1991.

59 'New South Wales Election Guide', Pollbludger blog, *Crikey*, viewed October 2015, <blogs.crikey.com.au/pollbludger/nsw2015-sydney/>.

60 'What the get Clover bill got rid of', *New Matilda*, 24 September 2012, viewed October 2015, <newmatilda.com/2012/09/24/what-get-clover-bill-got-rid>.

61 'New South Wales Election Guide', *Crikey*.

62 'What the get Clover bill got rid of', *New Matilda*.

63 A Patty, 'Clover Moore delighted with Alex Greenwich's success in seat of Sydney', *Age*, 30 March 2015, viewed October 2015, <www.theage.com.au/nsw/nsw-state-election-2015/clover-moore-delighted-with--alex-greenwichs-success-in-seat-of-sydney-20150329-1ma9jz>.

64 M Pelly, 'From hostile politicians to homosexuality, we've come a long way:

Kirby', *SMH*, 19 October 2005, viewed October 2015, <www.smh.com.au/news/national/from-hostile-politicians-to-homosexuality-weve-come-a-long-way-kirby/2005/10/18/1129401256802.html>.

65   *SMH*, 11 March 2006.
66   The word 'sinister' derives from the Latin 'sinistra'; its connotations are obvious.
67   Reynolds, *What happened to gay life?*
68   Reynolds, *What happened to gay life?* p. 191.
69   Andrew Sullivan, 'The End of Gay Culture: assimilation and its meaning', at <www.newrepublic.com/article/politics/the-end-gay-culture>.
70   R Reynolds, *From Camp to Queer: Remaking the Australian Homosexual*, MUP, 2002, p. 168.
71   C Wilson, *The Outsider*, Houghton Mifflin, 1956; but see also his *The Misfits: A Study of Sexual Outsiders*, Grafton, 1988.
72   David Marr, *Patrick White: A Life*, Random House, 1992, p. 581.

INDEX

Abbott, Tony 298–299, 310
Aboud, Danny 144–145
Ackerley, JR 72
ACON (AIDS Council of NSW) 225–226, 230, 261, 271, 292–293, 295
ACT-UP 235–236
Ada 'The Parramatta Girl' 98
Adam, Barry 185
Adams, Michael 283
Adams, Mikiel 24–26
Adamson, Christine 284
AIDS *see* HIV/AIDS
air raid shelters 85
Aitken, Don 174
Al Hussein, Zeid Ra'ad 298
alcohol-fuelled violence 277
Aldrich, Robert 243, 260
Altman, Dennis 130, 143, 168, 181, 186, 243, 273
   Homosexual 186–187, 223, 259, 318
Amnesty International 261
Anderson, Peter 232
Andrew's 44
Anggerek, Peretta 254
Angry Penguins 95
Ankali 225
Annand, Douglas 121
Annexe 158, 196
Another Country (Baldwin) 130–131, 132
Aquarius Club 164–165
Arab community 290
Archibald Fountain 46–47, 51–52, 84, 165, 166
Arena, Franca 246, 247, 249
Arkell, Frank 249
Armfield, Neil 242
Armstrong, Ian 250
Armstrong, Neil 141
Arrau, Claudio 121–122
artists 48–49, 99–100, 117–118

Artists' Ball 135–136
Arts Balls 63–65
Asian Marching Boys 261
Asian men 291–293
assimilation policy 220
At the Cross (Rose) 55, 57, 58–63, 84, 88–90
Auchmuty, Rosemary 126
aunties 137
Australia Hotel 41–42, 83, 134, 155–156, 195
the *Australian* 181–182
Australian AIDS Memorial Quilt 242–243
Australian Bicentennial (1988) 240
Australian Broadcasting Commission 9, 241, 281
Australian Centre for Lesbian and Gay Research 244, 248, 258–259
Australian Gay History Project 243–244
Australian Human Rights Commission 294–295, 306–307
Australian Institute of Criminology 248
Australian Lesbian Movement 174
Australian Marriage Equality 308–309
Australian troops 73, 76–79, 93, 179
Australian War Memorial 80–81
aversion therapy 188
Ayres, Tony 291

baby boom 142, 150, 194
Bail, Murray 151
Baird, Bruce 250
Baker, Justice 246
Ball, Jason (amateur footballer) 302–303
Balmain 153, 180
Balmain Betty 86
bands 135
Bangladeshi asylum seekers 299–300
Barbara (mime) 162–163
Bartlett, Jason 233

351

Barnes, Michael 281
bars, cafés, clubs, pubs, restaurants
    41–46, 83–84, 133–138, 154–164,
    196–198, 201–203, 216–217
Bastyovansky, Brennan 302
bath-houses 6, 49–50, 84, 161, 163, 195,
    202–203
Beadle, Brent 240
bears 274–275
the Beatles 141
beats 7, 49–54, 84–85, 165–166
Beauchamp, Lord, Earl of 21–23, 36, 43
Belfields Hotel 42, 83, 156, 195
Bendigo, Bishop of 151
Beresford Hotel 201
Bergin, Paddy 247
Berlin 44–45, 66–67
beyondblue 305
Bingay 278
Bingham, Mark 275
Bingham Cup 275–276, 303
birth control 146
Black, Dr Ian 186
Black Ada's 45–46, 83–84
blackouts 82
Blazey, Peter 212
Blewett, Neil 232
Blind Society 135
Blond, Anthony 131
Blue Mountains parties 67–68, 136
Bobby Goldsmith Foundation 225
bodgies and widgies 105
Bogle–Chandler case 141
Bond, Alan 219
Bondi Beach Bathing Pavilion 50–51,
    84
Bondi Junction Steam Baths 163, 202
Bonsall-Boone, Peter 187–188
books
    banned 130–131
    censorship 16
    homophobia during war period
        78–79
    homosexuality in 27–33, 36, 203–206
    romantic love in 131, 132–133
bookshops 132–133, 200

Boomerang Street 46–47, 51–52, 136,
    165
Boswell, John 46
Boyd, Robin 104–105, 147–148
Boys in the Band (play) 130, 191, 193
Brennan, Anna 39
Brennan, Christopher 39
Brennan, Richard 187
Brereton, Laurie 222, 232, 247
Brisbane, Katharine 160
Bryce, Quentin 305
the Bulletin 129
Burgess, Guy 109–110
Burgmann, EH 14
Burgmann, Meredith 261
Burlakov's Ballet School 155
Burma railway 76
Burns, Maggie 217
Bush, Reverend Roger 146

Cahill Expressway 141
Cahill's Coffee Shop 44, 155
Caleo, John 242
Cameron, David 307–308
Cameron, Jim 185–186
CAMP (NSW) 180, 185–186
CAMP Inc. (Campaign Against Moral
    Persecution) 174–177, 178, 180–183
CAMP INK 182, 188, 206, 208
Campaign 207, 209
CAMPus CAMP 180, 183
Canberra Times 173–174
Cannell, Brian 49
Capriccio's 163–164, 198
Capsis, Paul 254
Captain Moonlight 4–5
Carlton Hotel 42, 83, 134, 155–156, 195
Carr Labor government 246, 247, 250
Cass, Michael 186
censorship 16, 34, 130–131, 187
Challender, Stuart 231
Changi 76
Chaples, Ernie 243
The Charioteer (Renault) 131–133
Cheetham, Deborah 254
Chevron Hotel, Macleay Street 158

Index

child sexual abuse 247, 248
children overboard inquiry 257–258
Chipman, Lachlan 223, 230
Chippendale 202
Christ Church St Laurence 47, 84
churches
    Anglican 146, 172, 258
    attendance 145
    Catholic 125–126, 308–309
    concern with morality 14–17,
      106–107
    as haven 46–47, 84
    influence 13, 145–146
    Methodist 171–172
    Presbyterian 172
    resistance to sex education 124–126
    in social movements 146
    support for law reform 171–172
    terminology 21
Circular Quay 102
city rail loop 101–102
civil liberties 112, 113
Clayton, Stevie 244–245
Clean Up Australia Day 220
Club 80 214
Club Arak 290
Coghlan, Reverend WG 124
Cold Chisel 161
Cold War 101, 106
Cole, Malcolm 240
Collins, Louisa 282
Collins, Peter 247
Comcar 257
Comfort, Alex 19–20
coming out 176, 184, 186–187
Commission Watch 248, 249
communism 101
Community Support Network 225
Connelli, Judi 254
conservation movement 219–220
consumer durables 150
Coogee Clive 86
Cooma Prison 115–116, 117
Cosmopolitan 130
Council of Civil Liberties 187
counter-culture 143–144

Country Women's Association 108
County of Cumberland Planning
    Scheme 104–105
crime statistics 119–120
Crimes Acts 12, 109, 112–115, 233–234,
    235
Criminal Code 173
Croft-Cooke, Rupert 112
Cronulla riots 252–253
Croome, Rodney 308–309

Dad and Dave Come to Town (film) 33,
    35
dancing bans 15–16
Darlinghurst 55–57, 148–149, 153, 201
Daughters of Bilitis 169, 174
David Jones 9
Davison, Frank Dalby 31
De Groot, Captain 9
Deamer, Dulcie 64
death penalty 12
Debenham, Arthur 108
debt reparations 13–14
Delaney, Colin 108, 112
demonstrations 141–142
department stores 6–7, 9
Deveson, Anne 186
Dick, Tim 314
DNA 273
Dobell, William 117–118
the Domain 84, 85, 165
domino theory 101
Donkin, Graeme 212
Downing, RR 116
drag balls 66–67, 88–90
drag queens 79–80, 84, 276–277
drag show clubs 158–160, 163–164
drive-in shopping centres 148
Dunne, Gary 199, 204, 205
Dutton, Geoffrey 99, 131–132
Dykes on Bikes 261

Eales, John 303
East Sydney 201
economy 13–14, 92, 149–150
education *see also* sex education

education funding 142
education levels 171
education on HIV/AIDS 228
education: state aid 146
Edwards, John 164–165
electronic media 273
Elliott, Sumner Locke 67
Ellis, Havelock 6, 18, 168
entertainment troupes 79–80
Enus, Anton 286
Enzo's 161–162, 202, 251
epidemics/pandemics 220–221
erotica 206–207
Evolution Media 272–273
Exchange Hotel 201, 216–217
exile overseas 117

Fahey, John 246
Fantasy Island 203
Fashanu, Justin 276
Father and Son Movement 124,
    126–127
feminist movement 168
films 33–36, 190–191
Fisher, Greg 272
Fitton, Doris 48
Fitzroy Gardens 165
flats and boarding houses 10, 55–57
Fleischmann, Arthur 99
Flinders Hotel 201
Florida, Richard 253, 268
Forbes, Carmel 279
Forbes, Sir Francis 4
Foreman, Prue 268
Forster, Christine 287, 310
Foucault, Michel 139
Foy, Harry 84, 87
Franklin River campaign 219
Fraser Liberal government 179
Freeman, Gillian 131, 132
Freud, Sigmund 18, 19, 95, 184
Friend, Donald 99, 117–118
friendship networks 133, 134–135,
    137–138
fuck bars 198–199
Fullerton, Justice Elizabeth 284

Fussell, Paul 72
Fyfe, Sir David Maxwell 111–112

Game, Governor Sir Philip 13–14
Gates, Gary 253
Gay 207
gay activism 168–169
Gay and Lesbian Mardi Gras
    1978 parade 207, 215–217, 278
    1981 parade 217
    1983 parade 1–2
    1988 after party 65–66
    1996 AIDS entry 237
    associated festival 261–262
    change of name 262–263
    corporate sponsorship 241
    economic benefit 260–261
    Fair Day 277
    function of 217–218
    police and 264
    as public event 218, 240–241
    telecast 241
    as tourist bait 263–264
Gay and Lesbian Rights Lobby 232–
    233, 244–246, 287–288
gay conferences 195
gay culture in early 1980s 3
Gay Embassy 234–235
Gay Games (2002) 250–251, 253–255
gay hate crimes 54, 244, 278–282
gay hate crime register 282
Gay Information 208
gay liberation 177, 183
gay Muslims 289–290
gay periodicals 272–273
Gay Perspectives 243–244
gay press 182, 198, 206–209, 222,
    271–273
gay rights 174
gay special interest groups 194–195
Gay Times 182
gay vote 213–214
gays as community 210–211 *see also*
    LGBTQI communities
gays as 'creative classes' 253
gays in post-gay world 314–318

Index

gender inversion 85–86

gentrification 153–154, 179, 267

George V 36

German homosexuals 169

Gielgud, Sir John 128

Giles Hot-Sea Baths 49–50, 84

Gillard, Julia 275–276

Glaskin, JM 131

Glassop, Lawson 78–79, 80–81

Glebe 153

Glick, Dan 279

global financial crisis (2008–09) 252, 269

Goldsmith, Bobby 225

Gorman-Murray, Andrew 260, 268

Gray, Simon 193

Great Depression (1930s) 8–9, 10, 13–15, 70

Green, Antony 243

Green Bans 179

the Greens 261, 313

Greenwich, Alex 287, 312

Greer, Germaine 186

Greig, Noel 72

Greiner, Nick 235

Grindr 291

Gruner, Elioth 48–49

Grungras, Neil 300

Grusovin, Deirdre 246–247

Guzzetti, Mario 282, 283

Hackney, Sue 305

Hair 141, 193

Haire, Norman 95, 117

Hall, Ken 33, 35

Hall, Radcliffe 21

Harbin, Susan 313

Harbour City Bears 261

Harrison, Kate 243

Harwin, Don 287

Hawkins, Gordon 129, 170

Haxton, Gerald 11

Hayden, Bill 172, 244

The Heart in Exile (Garland) 131, 133

hedonism 229–230

Heffernan, Senator Bill 255–258

Helpmann, Robert 40–41

Herbert, John 193

heterosexuality 57, 71–72, 228

Hickey, Thomas 252

High Court of Australia 256, 257, 299

Highly Inflammable 28

Hilliard, David 47

Hills, Pat 311–312

Hilton Hotel bombing 179

Hinge and Bracket 3

HIV/AIDS 220–243

    commemorations 242–243, 278, 292

    death rates 226–227, 231

    first report 222

    government financial support 228–229

    homophobia 221–224

    Indigenous Australians 295–296

    political dimension 231–232

    spread 228

    support services 225–226

Hoagland, Alice 275

Hogan, Michael 146

Holding the Man (Conigrave) 242

Holsworthy 107

Homosexual Law Reform Society 168, 173–174

homosexuality *see also* identity

    covert 39

    distinguishing 39–40

    extent 94

    gender inversion 85–86

    heterosexuality overlapping with 57

    paedophilia *versus* 247

    scientific approach to 18–19

    validity of 184

Homosexuality (West) 127

Honi Soit 259

Hooker Report (US) 129

Horin, Adele 226

Horne, Donald 149–150

Horton, Edward Everett 34

housing market 152

Howard Liberal government 255, 256–258

Howie, Sir Archibald 311–312

Hughes, Billy 8
Hughes, Tom 185–186
Humanist Societies 169, 172
Hunt, Bill 213

identity
    camp viii–ix, 103, 133, 138–139, 167,
        171
    gay 183–185, 314–318
    queer viii, 314
Independent Theatre 48
Indigenous Australians 210–211, 234,
    293–296
inner west 267–268
inner-city 55–57, 148–149, 152–154,
    200–203
inner-city politics 311–313
The Institute of Many 270
the internet 269, 271, 288, 291
Isherwood, Christopher 58
Islamic State 289
Ivy's Birdcage 163, 198

Jackson, Joseph 311–312
Jackson, Neville 131
Jackson, Rose 159, 200
Japan 85
Jenolan Caves 77–78
Jensen, Peter 258
Jewel Box 159, 196
Johnson, Mrs 159
Johnson, Scott 278–279, 281
Johnson, Steve 278–279
Johnston, Craig 213, 232–233, 241, 243,
    266
Jones, Ignatius 314
Joyce, Alan 286
Justin Fashanu Cup 276

Kandy 159, 201
Kassisieh, Ghassan 290
Keating, Paul 219
Kellaway, Alec 33
Kelly, Archbishop 17
Kelly, Laurie 234
Kemmis, Robyn 286–287

Kenna, Peter 193
Kennedy, John F 141
Ken's Baths 202–203
Kerr, Brenton Heath 240
Kerr, Sir John 179
*Khaki and Green: with the Australian
    Army* 80–81
Khan, Trevor 287
King Steam 195
Kings Cross 55–57, 148–149, 153,
    158–160, 196, 197, 277
Kinsela's Funeral Chapel 200
Kinsey, Alfred 18, 70, 314
Kinsey Report (1948) 70, 94–97, 107,
    123
Kinsey Report (1954) 123, 125
Kirby, Justice Michael 254, 255–258,
    313–314
Korean War 101
Kushner, Tony 242

Lambert, Eric 71
Lana Turner 86
Landmark 251
Lane, Reverend Richard 258
Lang, Jack 9, 13–14
lang, kd 254
Lansdown, Andrew 223
Lascaris, Manoly 72
Latin Cafe 43, 83, 155
Lauder, Stuart 131
law *see also Crimes Acts*; police
    age of consent 235, 245, 247–248
    anti-discrimination 2–3, 233, 286
    anti-vilification 244–245
    censorship cases 187
    changes in 103
    church influence on 13
    criminal 2–3
    decriminalisation 286
    derivation of Australian 11–12
    divorce 13
    double jeopardy 283
    guilty pleas 120
    inciting to commit 119–120
    indecent assault 173

Index

law courts 97
liquor 43, 133–134, 157
on male homosexuality 12
provocation 287–288
reform 169–174, 212–213, 232–235
relationship rights 245–246
soliciting 119–120
suppression of cases 114–115
vagrancy 113
Law, Benjamin 286, 291
Leadbeater, Bishop 47–48
League of Nations 8
leagues clubs 50, 141
Leahy, Gillian 186
Lecky, Jack 49
Leese, Andrew 265–266
Leong, Jenny 287, 313
Les Girls 159, 196
Lesbian and Gay Anti-Violence Project 244
lesbian separatism 183
Lester, Victoria 98
Leung, Phillip 282–285
LGBTQI communities 241, 244, 253, 270–271
libertarians 143–144
Life 128
Lindsay, Jack 39, 40, 47–48, 56, 57
Lindsay, Norman 16, 48–49
Lindsay, Percy 57
Lindsay, Ray 40
Linklater, Eric 105–106
local government elections 213
Long Bay Gaol 117
Long Yang Club 293
Lowden, David 301–302
Lyle, David 191
Lyttle, Dr JE 117

McConaghy, Dr Neil 188
McDairmid, David 240
MacDonald, Sir Hector 72
MacDonald, Marion 189, 212
McGahen, Brian 213
McGregor, Craig 143–144
MacInnes, Colin 131

Macintyre, Stuart 210–211
McKinnon, Scott 260
Maclean, Brendan 304–305
Maclean, Donald 109–110
McMahon, Billy 212
MacNeill, Ian 204, 205
McNulty, Clarence 90–91, 118
McQuade, Neville 87
Macquarie Grammar School 261
Macquarie Hotel 160
Macquarie University 230
Maddocks, Sydney Aubrey 24–26
magazines 127–128, 130
literary journals 131–132
physical culture 74–75, 206–207
Malayan Insurgency 101
Mallard, Shayne 287, 312
Mannix, Archbishop Daniel 14
Mansfield, GA 41
Manus Island 298
Marcos, Imelda 241
Marcus Clarke's 9
Marcuse, Herbert 184
Mark Foys 9
Marr, David 286
marriage 165
Marriage Guidance Council 124
Marwick, Arthur 71
Mason, Gail 260
Mathew, Sir Theobald 111–112
The Mattachine Society 168–169
Maugham, Robin 165
Maugham, William Somerset 10–11
The Mavis Bramston Show 141, 192
Mayer, Henry 170
Maynard, Don 131
medical developments 221
Medical Journal of Australia 222–223
medical profession 19–20, 94–97, 108, 123, 188
medical treatment for HIV/AIDS 235–237
Melbourne 182
Merioola, Edgecliff 99–100
Merle Oberon 98
Midnight Oil 161

The Midnight Shift 291
migration 102, 150, 153, 220, 252
Milbank, Jenni 260
Milledge, Jacqueline 280–281
Miller, Harry Tatlock 99–100, 117
Mills, Philip 144
Milner, Andrew 142
Min Fuh Teh 292
Minerva Theatre 48
Missingham, Hal 121
Mitchum, Matthew 286
Mitford, Nancy 110–111
mixed bathing 17
mobile bedrooms 151–152
Mockbell's 43–44
Montagu of Beaulieu, Lord 112, 128
Moore, Clover 213–214, 244–245, 261, 311–312, 313
Moorhouse, Frank 143–144, 167–168, 204–205
Morshead, Sir Leslie 121
Mother and Daughter Movement 124
motor cars 17, 102, 150–152
Mottram, Linda 257
Mr Leather contest 196
multiculturalism 220, 289
Muncaster, Ron 240
Mundine, Anthony 293
Murphy, Tommy 242
Murray, Alec 99–100
Music Academy, Rowe Street 155
Muslim community 289–290

Nader, JA, QC 249
Nation Review 194
national census 312
Nazi Germany 26
negative gearing 269
Nesbit, James 4–5
Neville, Richard 187
New Guard 9
new left 143, 185
New York Times 298–299
newspaper reportage see also gay press
    in 1890s 5–6
    in 1970s 181–182

Beauchamp divorce scandal 22–23
    with false information 135
    on HIV/AIDS 221–224, 239
    homosexuality in wartime 74–75
    investigative 96–97
    Kinsey Report 96
    postwar 107–108
    quality press 128–129
    sources 96–97
    suppression of cases 114–115, 118, 119
Newtown 202, 268, 313
Nichols, Beverley 21
Nile, Fred 222, 230, 241, 245, 250, 294, 306
No. 96 192–193
No End to the Way 132
Noffs, Reverend Ted 172
Norman, Charles 27
North Shore Ball Committee 136
Notley-Smith, Bruce 287
Nott-Bowes, Sir John 111–112

O'Brien, Reverend John A 126
O'Brien, Justin 99, 117
O'Dea, Ernie 311–312
O'Donnell, John 76–77
O'Farrell Coalition government 311–312
Olympic Games (Sydney 2000) 252
ORAM International 300
Oxford Street 2, 6, 161, 163, 197–200, 264–270
OZ 141, 153–154, 187

Paddington 149, 153, 202, 267
paedophilia 246–249
Page, DS Stephen 279–281
Palmer, Ros 144
pandemics/epidemics 220–221
Pangborn, Frank 33, 34
Paris 45, 67, 267
Parkhill, Nicolas 282
parks 24, 50, 52, 53, 85, 165, 197, 279 see also Archibald Fountain
Parr, Dr 116–117

Parry, Thomas 12
parties 58–63, 67–68, 88, 134–135, 136, 155
Pate, Michael 80
Patterson, Wayne 256, 257
Payne, Simon 205–206
Pearce, Max 213
Pearson, Mark 287
Pelligrini's 44
People Living With AIDS 235–236
Peters, Susanne (Michael) 98
Petersen, George 233–234
Peterson, Michael John 24–26
Peyrefitte, Roger 132
Pfahlerts Hotel 42, 83, 195
Phelps, Kerryn 272
Phillip, Governor Arthur 3–4
physical culture magazines 74–75, 206–207
pink float 272
Pink Triangle 202
Pitt-Rivers, Michael 112
Planetout 263
Plato's *Phaedrus* 132
Pol 130
police *see also Crimes Acts*; law
    as *agents provocateurs* 90–91, 118–122
    in Akubras 156
    Arts Balls 65
    cases 7–8, 24, 75–76, 107–108
    entrapment 25–26, 53–54
    Gay Mardi Gras 264
    homophobia 281–282
    influence on *Crimes Act* amendments 112
    Operation Taradale 279–281
    role in social change 118
    royal commission into corruption in 246–249
    sexual offence statistics 96–97
    Vice Squad 46, 159
Policeman's Ball 65
politics 182–183, 212–214, 311–313
Poll, Chris 176, 186
Pollynesians 136–137
poofter-bashers *see* gay hate crimes

population growth 102, 142, 150, 179
Porteous, Julian 308
Positive Life NSW 261, 270
postwar reconstruction 92–93, 104
postwar social and state harassment 102–103
Potgieter, Jacques 302
Potts Point 55–57
Powell, Reverend Gordon 125
Price, Justice 283
Pride History Group 260
Prince Edward 148
Prince Henry Hospital 227
prison, homophobic violence in 283–284
prisoner segregation 115–116
prisoner-of-war camps 76
privatisation 272
Probyn, Elspeth 260
public discourse on homosexuality 104, 123
public opinion on law reform 170–171, 194
public opinion on same-sex marriage 309
public toilets 52–54, 84
Pura, Madam Helen 43
Purple Onion 159, 160
The Push 143, 187, 204

Quadrant 223
Quatrefoil (Barr) 132, 133
Quest, Dr Simon 222

Race, Kane 260
racism 294–296
Raj, Senthorun 297
Ramsey, Jon-Benet 279
Randall, Tony 191
Randwick 202–203
Redfern 201–202
Redfern riots 252
the Reels 161
refugees 257–258, 296–300
Refugee Review Tribunal 297, 299
the Regent 148

relationship rights 245–246
Relationships Register NSW 287
Repin's Coffee Shop 44, 83, 155
Rex Hotel, Macleay Street 158
Reynolds, Robert 260, 315–316
Rhodes, Cecil 72
Rhodes, Erik 34
Rickards, Jocelyn 99–100
Ricketts, Jimmy 80
Rita Hayworth 86
Roaring Twenties 8
Roberts, Ian 302
Robinson, Shirleene 260
the Rocks 179
Rolik, Michael 263
Rose, Jon see At the Cross (Rose)
Ross, Steven Lindsay 293
Rothman, Stephen 282–283
rough trade 156, 157, 160
Rowe Street 132–133
Royal Air Force 112
Royal Commission into the New South
  Wales Police Service 246–249
Royal Commission on Human
  Relationships 214
RSL (Returned Soldiers' League) 73
Rumble, Dr Leslie 146
Russell, John 280–281
Russo, Vito 33, 34, 191
Ruxton, Bruce 73

Saddle-tramps 216–217
Safe Schools 306
safe sex 230–231
St Clement's Anglican Church, Mosman
  187–188
St James Church, Hyde Park 47, 84
St Mary's Cathedral 46–47, 52
St Paul's Anglican Church 125
St Stephen's Church, Bellevue Hill 258
St Vincent's Hospital 226–227
Sainthill, Loudon 99–100, 117
Sale, David 192–193
same-sex marriage 307–311, 312
Sant, Kathy 245–246
SAPA (Social Aspects of the Prevention

of AIDS) 230
Satellite Media 272
saunas 163, 277
Scott, Andrew George 4–5
Seven Poor Men of Sydney (Stead) 29–30,
  43
sex education 18, 123–126, 237–238
sex education manuals 125, 127
sex shops 200
Sexual Behaviour in the Human Male
  (Kinsey) 70, 94–97
Sexual Liberation Forum 186
sexuality 17–18, 20 see also
  homosexuality
sexually transmitted infections 93,
  230–231
Shalimar 43, 83, 155
Shark Arm murder 9
Sharp, Martin 147
Sharpe, Penny 287, 313
Sheahan, Billy 112, 115, 116, 119
Sisters of Perpetual Indulgence 3, 194,
  260
Skase, Christopher 219
Smart, Jeffrey 117
Smith, Martin 194, 212
social change 118, 141
Sodersteen, Emil 41
Soldatow, Sasha 197, 204
Somerville, Jimmy 254
South Sydney 'Rabbitohs' 141
Soviet Union 108
Spanish flu epidemic (1919) 8
Spearritt, Peter 153
Spears, Steve J 193
sports 300–303
Stanley, Ted 27
Star 207–208, 209
Star Observer 272
State Theatre 148
Stead, Christina 29–31, 43
steam baths 163, 195, 196, 202–203
Stevenson, Robert Louis 11
Stewart, Douglas 132
Stone, John 223–224
Stone, Louis 44

Stonewall Riots 169, 278
Storer, Robert 18
Stranger in a Strange Land (Heinlein) 131
Stretton, Hugh 148–149
suburbia 10, 53, 104–105, 209
Sullivan, Andrew 317
Surry Hills 201, 202
Sutton, Grady 34
swinging sixties 140–141, 147–148
Sydney
    CBD 147–148, 152, 195, 252, 311–312
    interwar 9–11, 37–38, 50, 68–69
    'me decade' 219
    redevelopment 105–106
    suburbs *see* inner-city; suburbia
    wartime 81–84
Sydney Convicts Rugby Union Club 275
Sydney Gay Liberation 182, 183
Sydney Harbour Bridge 9
Sydney Morning Herald 181
Sydney Opera House 147, 179
Sydney Pride Festival 278
Sydney Rangers 276
Sydney to Hobart Yacht Race 92
Sylvia and the Synthetics 144–145
Szubanski, Magda 286

Taylor, Ray 130
television 138, 191–193, 241, 277
Tell Morning This (Tennant) 82–83, 166–167
Tennant, Kylie 38, 82
terminology
    beat 51
    church 21
    clone 210
    gay enters lexicon 87–88
    gay *versus* camp 176, 199–200
    homosexual enters lexicon 20
    homosexual *versus* gay vii–viii
    lunch 200
    self-identifying viii
    tolerance *versus* acceptance 211

wartime Sydney 87
Tharunka 187
theatre 26–27, 44, 48, 148, 193, 242
Theatre Royal 44
Theban Band 72
Theosophist Society 47–48
Thomas, Josh 286
Thor 187
Thorne, Graeme 140
Thorpe, Ian 286, 301
Thorunka 187
Till Death Us Do Part (TV series) 192
Time 128–129, 237–238
Tomsen, Steve 243, 260
Tooley, Des 46
Toolshed 200
Toongabbie Tex 86
Tourism Council of Australia 250
Town Hall Hotel, Balmain 201
Traffic Lights 251
trams 140
Trethowan Committee 116–117, 123, 170
Trocadero 135–136
The Trolley Car Bar 202
Truth 97–99
Tully, Peter 240
Turkish Baths (Liverpool Street) 6, 49–50, 84, 161
Turnbull, Malcolm 310
Turner, Richard 191
Twenty10 305–306

Uluru hand-back 220
United Airlines Flight 93 275
United Kingdom 111–112, 190, 267
United Nations Human Rights Council 297–298
university academics 243–244, 260
University of New South Wales Gay Society 203
University of Sydney 243–244, 259
university social movements 142–143
Unsworth Bill 234
USA
    American War in Vietnam 142, 167,

179
  films 34, 190
  gays in 168–169, 197–198, 267
  security campaign 109–111
  sexual mores 94
  troops 76–78, 86–87, 93, 161
Ushers Hotel 42, 83, 155–156, 195

van Vloten, Johan 314
Vatican II 146
Versailles 8
Victorian attitudes 11
Vidal, Gore 77, 130–131, 132
Vietnam moratoriums 142, 167
The Viscountess 98
visiting firemen 161
Vivien (Wally) Leigh 86, 98
von Cramm, Baron Gottfried 26

Waddell, Dr Tom 253
Walker, Reverend Allan 125
Walker, David 73, 74
Walker, Frank 233
Wallis, Reverend HE 15
Ware, John 176, 182, 186
Warren, Ross 280
Warringah Expressway 141
Watson, Lex 181, 232–233, 243, 259
WayOut 305
Wayside Chapel 172
We Were There (Barrett) 73–74, 79
Weeks, Jeffrey 168
West, DJ 127
Westfield 269
White, Patrick 72, 132, 179, 187, 189,
  318
Whitlam Labor government 140,
  178–179, 189
Whitman, Walt 132
Whitton, Evan 221–222
Widdup, David 212

Wildeblood, Peter 112
William and John 182
Willis, Eric 193, 212
Wills, Sue 243
Wilson, Colin 318
Wilson, Jennifer 249
Wilson, Tim 286
Wolfenden Committee (Britain) 117,
  168, 181
women 124, 210–211
Wong, Senator Penny 286
Wood, Justice James 246, 247
Woolloomooloo 55–57
World AIDS Day 227
World Health Organization 248
World League for Sexual Reform 168
World War I 73
World War II 70–92
Wotherspoon, Garry [author] 122,
  144–145, 203, 209, 216–217, 251,
  269–270, 318
wowserism 15
Wran Labor government 2–3, 233,
  234–235

Yabsley, Michael 214
Yeldham, Justice David 249
Yellow House, Macleay Street 147
Young, DCI Pamela 281–282
The Young Desire It (Mackenzie) 31–33,
  36
youth culture 102
youth market 150
youth moving out of home 154
youth suicide 304–307
Yu, Bing 291–292

Zahra, Paul 286
Zeigfeld Club 84, 87
Zweig, Stefan 66–67